# Sunset

## WESTERN
# Garden
# Annual
### 1995 EDITION

By the Editors of *Sunset Magazine* and Sunset Books

*New eggplants for your garden (page 100)*

NORMAN A. PLATE

**Sunset Publishing Corporation** ■ **Menlo Park, California**

## SUNSET BOOKS

**President and Publisher:**
Susan J. Maruyama
**Director, Finance & Business Affairs:** Gary Loebner
**Director, Manufacturing & Sales Service:** Lorinda Reichert
**Director, Sales & Marketing:**
Richard A. Smeby
**Editorial Director:**
Kenneth Winchester
**Coordinating Editor:**
Suzanne Normand Eyre
**Contributing Editor:**
Philip Edinger

## SUNSET PUBLISHING CORPORATION

**Chairman:**
Jim Nelson
**President/Chief Executive Officer:**
Robin Wolaner
**Chief Financial Officer:**
James E. Mitchell
**Publisher:**
Stephen J. Seabolt
**Circulation Director:**
Robert I. Gursha
**Editor, Sunset Magazine:**
William R. Marken
**Managing Editor:**
Carol Hoffman
**Executive Editor:**
Melissa Houtte

**Cover:** Virginian stock combines beautifully with red and white 'New Design' tulips (see page 13). Design by Jacqueline Jones Design. Photography by Russ A. Widstrand.

**Back cover:** Mexican hat *(Ratibida columnifera),* a useful native perennial for dry climates (see pages 282, 284, and 285). Photography by Charles Mann.

First printing March 1995
Copyright © 1995 Sunset Publishing Corporation, Menlo Park, CA 94025. First edition. All rights reserved, including the right of reproduction in whole or in part in any form.

ISSN 1073-5089
Hardcover edition: ISBN 0-376-03856-X
Softcover edition: ISBN 0-376-03857-8

Printed in the United States.

All material in this book originally appeared in the 1994 issues of *Sunset Magazine.*

*Sunset Western Garden Annual* was produced by Sunset Books. If you have comments or suggestions, please let us hear from you. Write us at:
Sunset Books
Garden Book Editorial
80 Willow Road
Menlo Park, CA 94025

If you would like to order additional copies of any of our books, call us at 1-800-759-0190 or check with your local bookstore.

NORMAN A. PLATE

**BRING YOUR HARVEST INDOORS** *with this hang-up made from fresh and dried ingredients. We tell you how on page 290.*

# Gardener's Inspiration

Here's the second edition of our *Western Garden Annual,* an indispensable companion for home gardeners west of the Rockies. Offering a full year's worth of gardening inspiration, this volume collects all the gardening and outdoor living articles from *Sunset Magazine*'s 1994 regional issues into one book for handy reference.

Each chapter begins with a Garden Guide, filled with news and ideas from around the West; regional checklists highlight the important gardening jobs for the month.

Articles feature all facets of gardening, from plant selection guides and composting techniques to suggestions for simplifying your work and guidance on choosing the right tools. You'll also find reviews of useful garden books and descriptions of outstanding public and private gardens throughout the West.

We hope you enjoy this *Western Garden Annual,* and that it provides you with many hours of enjoyment and inspiration.

# CONTENTS

# Where Western Gardeners Find Information and Inspiration

The West! In few other parts of the world will you find such diversity in geography and climate in a single region. Sweeping from the Pacific Ocean to the Rocky Mountains, from the Canadian border to Mexico, the West encompasses alpine glaciers, subtropical beaches, temperate rain forest, and shimmering deserts—as well as prime agricultural land and vast timbered preserves.

Reflecting this diversity, gardening in the West is characterized by a spirit of experimentation. And for some 65 years, *Sunset Magazine* has chronicled the evolution of the Western garden, providing information on seasonal maintenance, features on environmental issues, and reports on gardening "news"—new plants, new techniques, new ideas in garden planning.

This volume, our second *Western Garden Annual*, presents a broad picture of Western gardening as well as timely information aimed at specific geographic localities.

Divided into 12 chapters (one for each month of the year), the book includes all the feature articles published in *Sunset*'s seven regional editions during 1994, along with monthly checklists of gardening tasks by region.

Each chapter starts off with a Garden Guide, combining seasonal news on garden-related topics with practical tips for particular regions.

Feature articles include discussions of plants and planting as well as advice on tools, techniques, and landscaping. Learn which bulbs are best for naturalizing; admire rosarians' favorite antique roses and find out where to buy them. Discover the charm of miniature cymbidiums and tabletop topiaries; use our extensive lists to pick native plants that will thrive in your garden. Learn how to shop for bare-root trees and bedding plants, how to create an organic garden, and how to choose garden hoses and the best knives for a variety of chores. You'll find tips on planting showy flowers in containers and growing salad greens in a wheelbarrow. Down-to-earth advice ranges from suggestions for rampant bougainvillea to the how-tos of planting on steep lots. Traveling gardeners will appreciate our updates on outstanding public and private gardens, from iris growers' fields in Oregon to stunning Lotusland in Southern California. Some articles are climate-specific, but many apply to most of the West's regions.

The climate zones we use are based on *Sunset*'s intensive study of the West's varied climates. We organize the entire territory into 24 distinct regions, each defined by its temperatures, precipitation, altitude, and/or latitude. For definitions of these zones and maps establishing their boundaries, consult the *Sunset Western Garden Book*.

**FIERY FALL COLOR** *delights these nursery shoppers (see page 268).*

JANUARY IS THE TOP MONTH *for bare-root planting in mild-winter areas of the West. For details on the bright companions pictured here— 'Ballerina' rose and beautyberry—see page 12.*

# JANUARY

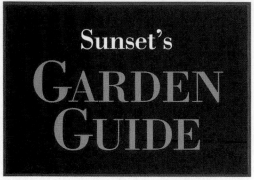

# GARDEN GUIDE

## January is for planting and planning: roses, saucer magnolias, tulips, and more

oses make their appearance in January. Just days after the calendar officially announces winter, growers announce spring by shipping out tens of thousands of bare-root plants.

In the coldest parts of the West, you won't see them for a couple of months, since nurseries schedule delivery for planting time, but you can still make selections from mail-order catalogs. In mild-winter areas, you can buy bare-root roses in nurseries now and plant them immediately for flowers in June.

'Buff Beauty', a hybrid musk rose with soft, creamy flowers, is pictured at right climbing a garden fence in Carmel, California. Whichever varieties of rose you like, order them now or head to the nursery for the best selection.—*Jim McCausland*

### All-America Selections for 1994

While you're browsing through mail-order seed catalogs this month, you might watch for the 1994 All-America Selections—three new plants that have been judged outstanding by the seed industry. They may also be available as nursery transplants later this spring.

'Lavender Lady' English lavender (*Lavandula angustifolia*) blooms its first season from seed; even though it is technically a hardy perennial, it can be used as an annual. The plants grow 12 to 18 inches tall their first year and produce fragrant, deep blue flower spikes four to six months after sowing. 'Lavender Lady' grows best in warm-summer areas, in full sun, and in well-drained soil. It is fairly drought tolerant once established.

'Big Beef' tomato is a large beefsteak-type with improved tolerance to nematodes and many diseases. The plant is indeterminate (vinelike) and probably needs staking; pinch side shoots to help increase fruit size. Harvesting usually begins within 73 days of planting.

'Fanfare', a dwarf bush cucumber, is ideal for containers or small gardens. Plants also are resistant to powdery mildew, downy mildew, scab, cucumber mosaic, and leaf spot. 'Fanfare' does not need a pollinator to produce fruit. Cucumbers should be ready to harvest in about 63 days from sowing outdoors.—*Lance Walheim*

GLENN CHRISTIANSEN

## Wooing wildlife to your garden

The National Wildlife Federation (NWF) supports gardeners who are serious about attracting wildlife to their gardens, and it recognizes home landscapes that meet certain criteria for a healthy habitat for birds, butterflies, lizards, and insects.

To assist gardeners, the NWF offers a packet that includes a pamphlet, a book called *The Backyard Naturalist,* and an application for certification.

The Backyard Habitat Packet costs $5.25; order (number H379919) from the National Wildlife Federation, 1400 16th St. N.W., Washington, D.C. 20036; (800) 822-9919.

Once your garden meets the NWF criteria for a wildlife habitat, you may choose to have it certified. Just fill out the application form detailing your efforts and submit a $15 enrollment fee to the NWF. You will receive a certificate, and the NWF will send a press release to your local newspaper. —*Lynn Ocone*

## Eureka! Gold dust grows indoors, too

Gold dust plant (*Aucuba japonica* 'Variegata') is a crossover shrub: it's sold in most of the West as a landscape plant, but it turns out to be a fine indoor plant, too. Look first for gold dust plant with nursery outdoor plants. Price will be relatively low for a large specimen.

Pot it up and put it indoors near a bright window, and it

## Mini-chili peppers spice up flower bed

Recently at *Sunset*'s headquarters in Menlo Park, California, our gardeners grew pepper plants (*Capsicum annuum* 'Chili Pepper'). The peppers' striking foliage and small, glossy fruits (pictured at right) made an impressive addition to a flower border. The purple-fruited kind has purple foliage marked with white; the green-fruited kind has green foliage marked with white.

The chili-like fruits, which are blushed with red as they age in fall, are edible as well as ornamental. Don't confuse 'Chili Pepper' with the similar looking Jerusalem cherry (*Solanum pseudocapsicum*), which is strictly an ornamental; its fruits are toxic.

Seed of the purple and green kinds are sold together as 'Variegated Mixed'. One source is J. L. Hudson, Seedsman, Box 1058, Redwood City, Calif. 94064 (catalog

$1). Seeds germinate in two to four weeks.—*Emely Lincowski*

NORMAN A. PLATE

will probably become one of your favorite foliage plants. If you grow this as an outdoor plant as well, you'll notice that indoors its foliage is cleaner (no snail or slug holes, or wind-dried leaf tips). Put the indoor and outdoor plants within sight of each other and you'll visually link indoors and outdoors.

Several forms of *A. japonica* are available. Some gardeners prefer one of the pure green versions, but they grow faster and taller (to 15 feet); consider the dwarf form (*A. j.* 'Nana') if green is your color of choice. It stays at about 3 feet. Taller forms do, however, take well to pruning.

Don't try these broadleafed evergreens outdoors where winter temperatures fall much below 10°, or remain below 20° for more than a few days.—*J. M.*

## Tips for a successful citrus harvest

January is prime time for homegrown citrus in much of California. 'Washington' navels have just the right balance of sugars and acids that translates to rich flavor when eaten fresh or juiced. Many mandarins, 'Meyer' lemons, and grapefruits are also at or nearing peak flavor.

Before you store quantities of citrus in a bowl for more than a few days, make sure the fruit is dry. Fruit that's wet from rain or fog bruises easily and can decay quickly. Pick only what you need: citrus stores best on the tree. Keep whatever fruit you do pick in the refrigerator.

January is also a time to watch the weather closely. Most citrus fruits will suffer damage if temperatures drop much lower than 27°. If such

temperature drops are forecast, protect the trees with burlap or cloth covers. The coldest temperatures are right before sunrise.

This month, you should also start working to ensure a quality citrus crop next year. Toward the end of the month, make your first application of a high-nitrogen fertilizer. Apply it again at least once in spring or early summer. Packaged citrus fertilizers will provide application rates.—*L. W.*

## The fog belt's great green buds

It is no surprise that artichokes grow better along the Northern California coast and around San Francisco Bay than anywhere else in the country. About 79 percent of the U.S. crop comes from those emerald green fields near Castroville—the "artichoke capital of the world"— where winters are mild and summers are cool.

With such an embarrassment of riches at your own back door, is it worthwhile to grow your own? The answer from many gardeners is a resounding yes. The fountain of silvery green leaves is attractive, even in the back of flower beds. A single plant can yield five or six buds in late winter or spring and again in late summer (if you cut plants back between crops). Even if you're lukewarm on the taste of these green thistle buds, the flowers can be worthwhile for big bouquets.

This month, nurseries sell bare-root divisions. Before planting, work ample amounts of compost into the top foot of soil. Space plants about 4 feet apart in an area that gets full sun (if gophers are a problem in your garden, line the planting hole with a mesh basket, or plant the artichokes in whiskey half-barrels).

Plant the woody root vertically with growth buds and any leaf shoots just above soil level. Then apply a layer of mulch. Water regularly to

keep the soil moist, not soggy. Fertilize when new growth appears in spring and lightly each month through the growing season with high-nitrogen fertilizer.

To harvest buds for cooking, pick when they are tight, round, and fleshy—their most tender stage. For bouquets, leave buds on the plant until they open enough to reveal tufted purplish blue centers. After leaves begin to yellow, cut off old stalks to about 15 inches above the ground; new shoots will soon appear.
—*Kathleen Norris Brenzel*

## Mixed borders: an American tradition?

Much of the technique and style in American gardening comes directly from Britain. The traditional herbaceous perennial border is a classic example. But the idea of creating a sweeping palette of color and texture has taken a new course in this country. To create a year-round mixed border, gardeners are using shrubs and small trees (both deciduous and evergreen), along with vines, perennials, and even ground covers.

In a new book, *The American Mixed Border: Gardens for All Seasons* (Macmillan Publishing Co., New York, 1993; $35), Northwest writer Ann Lovejoy chronicles a simple thesis: the traditional border, made up of perennials, floriferous perhaps for seven months but dormant for five, has seen its day; come winter, you shouldn't be looking at a strip of brown dirt.

This book is filled with handsome color photographs and page after page of ideas on how to build mixed borders.—*Steven R. Lorton*

## Eucalyptus leaves in mulch?

Eucalyptus trees drop leaves and other debris that contribute significantly to the region's green waste. But can you safely recycle eucalyptus

**HARVESTING THE CITRUS CROP** *is familiar and pleasant winter activity in many parts of California. This old 'Washington' navel orange tree provides recreation in the process.*

**A SPRINGLIKE FLORAL EXPLOSION** *comes from saucer magnolias (Magnolia soulangiana), available in white, pink shades, and purple. January is prime flowering time in mildest-winter areas of California.*

leaves in mulches and compost without adversely affecting plants? No, many gardeners say. The common belief is that the leaves are toxic to plants, and better candidates for the trash heap.

But research reveals that eucalyptus mulches are not toxic to plants. James Downer, environmental horticulture farm adviser for UC Cooperative Extension, tested the toxicity of both fresh and composted eucalyptus as a mulch around 48 newly planted 1-gallon sycamore trees. He discovered that eucalyptus did not inhibit growth. On the contrary, the mulched trees grew rapidly. Roots proliferated in the areas where the mulch and soil met, and mulched trees produced more feeder roots in the upper 18 inches of soil than unmulched trees.—*Lauren Bonar Swezey*

## The spectacular saucers

This month in Southern California (a bit later elsewhere in the state), elegant pastel flowers blanket leafless trees of saucer magnolias (*M. soulangiana*). These deciduous cousins of the evergreen magnolia have showier blooms that range from rosy purple to pink to pure white. Many are fragrant. The trees grow to about 25 feet tall and spread 20 to 30 feet.

Named varieties to look for in nurseries (most likely in bloom this month) include

**'Alexandrina',** 7-inch blooms in various colors, but usually white inside, purplish pink outside.

**'Coates',** 6-inch blooms with rose-red at the base gradually turning to white at petal tips.

**'Lennei',** 6-inch dark purple flowers.

**'Lennei Alba',** 6-inch white blooms with slight pink blush at base of petals.

To show off these magnificent trees, choose sites that are uncrowded with other trees and shrubs. Plant in full sun and in rich, moist, well-drained soil. Mulch after planting with compost, peat moss, or composted bark. If strong winds are likely, stake trees. Iron chlorosis (yellow leaves with green veins) may appear in alkaline soils; to correct it, apply iron chelate and an organic mulch.

A cutting-grown saucer magnolia in a 5-gallon container costs about $20. If you can't find named varieties at your nursery, check with Gossler Farms Nursery, 1200 Weaver Rd., Springfield, Ore. 97478 (catalog $2). Mail-order plants are smaller (1 to 2 feet tall) and also cost about $20.—*Michael MacCaskey*

## 'Sally Holmes', a mild-climate superstar

She flaunts her colors well, freely covering herself with single blooms that open buff pink and age to white. And in mild-winter climates, she really soars, growing taller than elsewhere (to 18 feet or more), according to Tom Carruth, research director of Weeks Roses, in Upland, California.

Without a doubt, 'Sally Holmes' gives a delightful performance. Flowers on this repeat-blooming climbing rose grow in clusters "like a grand hydrangea," says Carruth. They last 10 days or longer in the garden and can withstand both heat and cold.

They bloom on new wood, so you can expect color the first year. Blooms open about 10 days later than on a typical rose. At first the plant looks demure like a floribunda, "but then it kicks into gear, and off it goes," Carruth says.

Plant in full sun and well-drained, fertile soil. Since this climber is so vigorous, choose a structure that is large and sturdy enough to support it at maturity. Place the rose about 15 inches from its support. To promote repeat bloom, remove faded flowers.

You'll find 'Sally Holmes' in nurseries this month in 5-gallon ($15) and 7-gallon ($22) containers.—*L. O.*

## Keep your cut flowers fresher longer

Using material that you may already have in your cupboards, you can make a cut-flower preservative that keeps flowers looking fresh longer. The solution was developed by Michael Reid at UC Davis.

Mix 1 part lemon-lime soda

**BLUSHING BLOSSOMS** *of 'Sally Holmes' rose open to 3 inches across in large clusters.*

CLAIRE CURRAN

FROST-FREE COASTAL GARDENS *can enjoy winter through summer bloom on Lotus maculatus 'Gold Flash'. During flowerless period, plants present attractive filigree of gray foliage.*

(not diet) with 3 parts water. For each quart of the mixture, add ¼ teaspoon of household bleach. The sugar in the soda helps buds open and last longer, the acid improves water flow in the stems, and the bleach reduces the growth of bacteria and fungus.—*L. O.*

## A flash of gold for warm-winter gardens

It may be the dead of winter according to the calendar, but the plant sold as *Lotus maculatus* 'Gold Flash', a cool-season perennial, is now blooming in coastal Southern California. In the Newport Beach garden pictured above, 'Gold Flash' blooms repeatedly from January into spring or early summer, when night temperatures rise into the 60s.

Hanging baskets are perfect for this lotus; stems cascade over their edges, showing off silver-flushed needlelike foliage and 1-inch golden flowers. 'Gold Flash' requires consistently moist soil, which for gardeners translates into frequent watering. If you'd rather not have to water it so often, plant it in the ground or in a large planter.

In the ground, the plant spreads from a central root system to about 3 feet across and 6 to 8 inches high.

Plants thrive in full sun on the coast and light shade inland. Feed with a complete fertilizer according to package directions. As flowers fade, shake them off the stem (blasting stems with water may cause flowers to rot). Plants are hardy to around 30°. Given optimum growing conditions, they live about three years.

'Gold Flash' is available at nurseries this month. An 8- to 10-inch hanging basket costs about $16.—*L. O.*

## Coping with tumbleweed critters

Coming home from east of the Cascade or Sierra Nevada mountains, you spot a tumbleweed caught by a fence along the road. You scramble to make room for it in the car. At home, you put it on display. Suddenly spiders and other critters begin crawling around. Help!

Put the tumbleweed (or any piece of wild, dry flora or foliage) in a large plastic garbage bag. Spray the plant material thoroughly with household insecticide, close the bag and tie it shut. In two weeks, remove the dried material, air it out, and put it where you want it.—*S. R. L.*

## Some tasty fruits to grow

Looking for a flavorful stone fruit to plant bare-root this month? If so, you'll want to know the results of a taste test conducted last summer at Dave Wilson Nursery (a wholesale grower of deciduous fruit in Hickman, near Modesto, California). Twenty-six nurserymen and fruit growers taste-tested 18 varieties of early to midseason peaches, nectarines, and one pluot (plum and apricot interspecific hybrid); all were grown in California's Central Valley.

Even though nursery representatives caution that cultural practices and weather can influence fruit quality as much as the variety you choose, and that testing will continue, almost all the varieties that came out on top in the test are well known for flavor.

'Flavor Supreme' pluot, which looks like a plum with mottled green skin and sweet, deep red flesh, rated highest. For best production, it requires a pollenizer like 'Santa

Rosa' plum or another pluot.

Following 'Flavor Supreme' were 'Loring' peach, 'Double Delight' nectarine (attractive in bloom), and 'Independence' nectarine. White-fleshed 'Heavenly White' nectarine, 'Mericrest' nectarine, and 'July Elberta' peach tied for fifth place. —*L. W.*

## Bright companions: 'Ballerina' rose and beautyberry

Right now, you can put barren sticks into the ground that will be leafy wonders by spring and colorful standouts by summer. The rose 'Ballerina', a hybrid musk, and beautyberry (*Callicarpa bodinieri giraldii*) are perfect cases in point. They're pictured on page 6 in a Portland garden designed by John Nausieda. You can duplicate this striking combination, or create your own variations, by planting this and other roses from bare-root stock now, and coupling them with complementary shrubs, perennials, or vines planted from 1-gallon cans. Beautyberry bears clusters of lilac flowers followed by violet fruits that hang on into winter.

Nurseries and mail-order sources offer bare-root roses by the hundreds this month. Get your purchases into the ground as soon as possible. The longer they wait, the greater the stress on the new members of your garden. —*S. R. L.*

## Tulips and friends in San Diego County

In this mild-winter region, the ideal time to plant tulips is from after Christmas until about mid-January—after they've been chilled in the refrigerator crisper for four to six weeks. When you plant prechilled tulips (or if you've already planted them), consider teaming them with quick annuals for a two-tiered color show like the one in the Fallbrook garden pictured on this page. Virginian stock, combined with red and white 'New Design' tulips, was planted January 15 for bloom in late March, when the picture was taken.

The following four annuals grow fast from seed and combine very well with tulips.

***Chinese forget-me-not** (Cynoglossum amabile)*. Blooms in 8 to 12 weeks from seed. Plants grow 1 to 2 feet tall. 'Firmament' has rich blue flowers.

***Forget-me-not** (Myosotis sylvatica)*. Blooms eight weeks after seeding, then reseeds profusely and will persist in the garden for years. Grows 6 to 12 inches high. Improved varieties include 'Blue Ball', 'Blue Bird', 'Carmine King', and 'Ultramarine'.

***Sweet alyssum** (Lobularia maritima)*. Blooms six weeks after seeding, then reseeds with modest persistence. Grows 3 to 12 inches tall. White varieties include 'Carpet of Snow', 'Little Gem', and 'Tiny Tim'. 'Pink Heather' and 'Rosie O'Day' are lavender-pink, and 'Oriental Night' and 'Violet Queen' are purple.

***Virginian stock** (Malcolmia maritima)*. Blooms six to eight weeks after seeding, and reseeds sparsely. Grows 8 to 15 inches high. White, yellow, pink, lilac, and magenta are available.

Annuals with white flowers are the safest bet. They go well with any of the tulip colors. Blues and yellows also combine well: for example, Chinese forget-me-not and 'Mrs. John T. Scheepers' tulip. Or try combining plants with flowers in similar colors, such as pink 'Carmine King' forget-me-nots with 'Pink Diamond' tulips.

Look for seeds at a well-stocked nursery, or order them by mail from Park Seed Co., Cokesbury Rd., Greenwood, S.C. 29647, (800) 845-3369; or Thompson & Morgan, Dept. 165-4, Jackson, N.J. 08527, (800) 274-7333. —M. M.

## Lilacs that take California's valley heat

Lilacs are often overlooked as colorful flowering shrubs for California's Central Valley landscapes. And with good reason: flowers pale in the intense sun, and may not last as long as they might in cooler climates. But many varieties do thrive here. They're worth growing for their large clusters of fragrant spring flowers in shades of blue, pink, lilac, red, and purple, and for their dark green foliage, which makes a handsome backdrop or hedge.

Since lilacs will be available in nurseries bare-root this month, we asked a Visalia nurseryman who has grown more than 40 varieties to share with us his favorite selections. Most are hybrids of *Syringa vulgaris*.

**'Burgundy Queen'** produces large clusters of early, vibrant burgundy red flowers on a tall-growing shrub (to about 12 feet).

**'Esther Staley'** is an especially heavy bloomer with single, delightfully fragrant, pure pink blooms.

**'Excel',** one of the earliest varieties, produces large clusters of light lavender flowers.

**CAPTURE THE CHARM** *of a Victorian valentine in a combination of tulips with early-blooming annuals (such as this Virginian stock) in complementary colors.*

## PORTABLE POWER PRUNER

This little pruner puts the power of a ⅓-horsepower chain saw at your fingertips. It zips through branches up to 3 inches thick, and it's quieter and lighter (less than 3½ pounds) than a full-size chain saw. An extended-reach model (about 6 pounds) trims branches up to 15 feet from the ground.

NORMAN A. PLATE

Woodzig is available at hardware stores in plug-in and cordless versions ($60 for a hand-held, plug-in model to $140 for a battery-operated telescopic version). Replacement chains cost $8 to $9 for two, a cassette (with chain, bar, and sprocket) costs $10, and an extra rechargeable battery pack costs $50.— *Kimberly Chrisman*

---

*'Forrest K. Smith'* is a tall grower (to about 12 feet) with large lavender blooms.

*'Ludwig Spaeth'*, one of the most popular lilacs, bears large clusters of late, deep purple flowers.

*'Madame Lemoine'* produces immense clusters of large, double white flowers.

*'Président Grévy'* is a profuse bloomer with large clusters of lavender buds opening into double, very fragrant, blue flowers.

*Chinese lilac, S. chinensis* or *S. rothomagensis,* produces an abundance of graceful, small clusters of sweetly fragrant purple flowers in late spring to early summer. It makes a wonderful hedge.

These deciduous shrubs grow best in full sun or with late-afternoon shade, in slightly alkaline soil (add lime to acid soils), and with regular applications of nitrogen fertilizers. Water regularly. Plants are somewhat drought tolerant once established. In fact, many gardeners believe that letting plants go dry in late summer increases bloom. Prune after bloom to remove spent flowers and to shape the plants. Young plants tend to start out slowly and may not bloom the first year.—*L. W.*

### Pink-flowered strawberry

Intending to grow them for fruit, many gardeners find that strawberry plants also hold up well as ornamentals. If only the flowers came in something besides white. Well, now they do.

'Pink Panda' strawberries produce deep pink flowers with yellow centers. (The fruit that follows is acceptable, but not great.) We've seen it used effectively as both ground cover and potted plant. Flowers and fruit are most prolific in full sun, but the plant takes shade as well.

Plants cost around $3 each, depending on quantity, from Park Seed Co., Cokesbury Rd., Greenwood, S.C. 29647. For a free catalog, write or call the firm at (800) 845-3369 weekdays between 8 and 4:30 (Eastern time).—*J. M.*

### Feeding and watering the birds

After birds use up food supplied by nature, they start seeking out feeders to supplement their winter diets. Insect-eating birds go for suet and peanut butter, while seed eaters prefer sunflower seeds, millet, and mixtures of wild bird seed.

Put the food in a high place that has trees or shrubs nearby; birds will want to dive into them to escape hungry hawks. Don't put feed on the ground near shrubs, where cats can lurk and pounce on the birds.

In freezing weather, keep ice off your birdbath, which may be the only source of unfrozen fresh water around. —*J. M.*

### Moth orchid secrets

The numerous varieties of moth orchids (*Phalaenopsis*) are reliable bloomers, although they're considered a bit tricky for beginning gardeners. But Bill Calderhead of Olympia, Washington, who calls himself "just a backyard gardener," grows plants that produce such a long succession of robust blooms that even his most knowledgeable gardening friends are scratching their heads in wonder. Here are some of his secrets.

He places plants in the warmth of a south-facing window, where light is diffused by a sheer, white curtain. He maintains the nighttime temperature at 65°. The orchids grow in a standard orchid mix of coarsely ground bark, and the potting medium is kept constantly moist. To ensure good drainage, the pots rest on a saucer filled with pea gravel. In summer, Calderhead often waters every other day. With each watering, he mists the plants heavily from a plastic spray bottle.

He feeds plants prodigiously with liquid plant food. When plants are out of bloom, he fertilizes them monthly at the roots with a solution of 20-20-20 (1 tablespoon to 1 gallon of water). When plants are in bloom, Calderhead spray-feeds the leaves every two weeks with 15-30-15 (1 tablespoon to 1 gallon of water).

Flowers start appearing in mid-March and bloom well into fall. If you have a *Phalaenopsis* or buy one out of bloom (and likely at a reduced price now), begin a feeding program at once.—*S. R. L.*

### What to do with woody prunings

It's remarkable how much wood one person can prune out of the garden (or off a Christmas tree). Since it takes years to compost, some gardeners either run it through a chipper or throw it onto a shrub pile in an out-of-sight corner of the garden. But lately we've seen another worthwhile wood-disposal system.

After you prune, cut all side branches bigger than a pencil off your prunings. The largest branches—those that are too big to reduce any further with hand pruners—go in one pile, to be cut into 2-foot lengths for the fireplace.

Finger-diameter branches go into a second pile to be dried and used as plant stakes or woven into brush fences. Pencil-diameter branches are cut into 1-inch lengths and thrown under shrubs as mulch.

This sounds like a lot of cutting, but it actually goes quickly and works well. Just wear gloves to avoid blisters.—*J. M.*

## January Checklist

### PACIFIC NORTHWEST

☐ **ADD TO THE COM-POST.** Wind-downed branches, prunings, and holiday greens should all be chopped and added to the compost pile. Turn the pile if you didn't do it late last summer or fall.

☐ **BAIT FOR SLUGS.** Neither rain, nor sleet, nor snow . . . slugs are as persistent as mail carriers. They slow down in winter, but they continue to nibble. Bait in places that stay dry: along building foundations, and under rocks and big planters. Be careful not to put bait where pets can get it; it can be fatal. Under stones and pieces of garden art, you're likely to find clusters of tiny white balls—slug eggs; crush them.

☐ **BUY AND PLANT BARE-ROOT.** Shop in nurseries or mail-order catalogs for dormant roses, shrubs, fruit and shade trees, berries, and vines. Plant them as soon as you bring them home or receive them in the mail. But if you can't, heel them in by laying plants in a shallow trench and cover with moist sawdust or soil.

☐ **BUY CONTAINER PLANTS.** Nurseries often have January sales, and you can pick up some great bargains. Bring plants in containers home, water them well, and put them in a sheltered location, such as under an overhang or in a carport.

☐ **CARE FOR HOUSE PLANTS.** In most cases, slow down (or stop) feeding dormant house plants. Those producing flowers or fruit should be fed. Slow down on watering, too. Water only when soil is a bit dry on top. Groom plants by snipping off faded flowers and yellowed leaves. If plants are dusty, set them in the shower and hose them off. A hand-held shower head is perfect for this job.

☐ **CHECK STORED BULBS.** Check corms, tubers, and produce. Sprinkle water on shriveled bulbs and toss out ones that show signs of rot. Dahlias are the exception: cut out bad spots, dust with sulfur, and segregate damaged bulbs from the others.

☐ **CHECK STORED GERA-NIUMS.** Some foliage yellowing and dieback is normal during winter, but if this is extreme, give plants a brighter spot and a bit more water.

☐ **FERTILIZE PEREN-NIAL VEGETABLES.** Feed artichokes, asparagus, rhubarb, and other perennial vegetables with a good top-dressing of well-rotted manure or with a fertilizer high in nitrogen.

☐ **ORDER SEED.** Send in seed orders now. Some seed should be sown indoors in flats as early as February.

☐ **PRUNE FRUIT TREES.** When temperatures are well above freezing, remove rangy top and side growth as well as inward-pointing, dead, and damaged branches. If branches are crossed, step back, eye the plant for its form, and remove the branch that makes the least contribution.

☐ **PRUNE ROSES.** Hybrid teas should start the growing season with three to six strong canes. Find these, cut them back a third to a half, and remove the others. As you prune, try to develop a vase shape with the canes so that plants will be open, allowing air to circulate and branches to develop without growing into one another.

☐ **SHOP FOR WINTER-FLOWERING SHRUBS.** You'll be startled by the offerings. Bring home a plant in a can and enjoy it first slipped into a decorative container near an entry or on a patio. Then plant it outside. Water container plants well. If a killing freeze threatens, move them into the protection of a garage, tool shed, or basement.

☐ **SOW PERENNIALS.** Seeds of delphiniums, hellebores, veronicas, and violas can all be sown in coldframes or greenhouses. When seedlings develop and danger of frost is past, you can set them out into the garden.—*S. R. L.*

## January Checklist

### NORTHERN CALIFORNIA

**APPLY DORMANT SPRAY.** Before flower or leaf buds swell, spray fruit trees with a dormant spray such as bordeaux or lime sulfur. But hold off if temperatures are expected to drop below freezing or if rain is predicted.

**CARE FOR GIFT PLANTS.** After plants bloom, trim spent blossoms and move hardier plants such as azaleas, cinerarias, cyclamen, and cymbidiums to a protected spot outdoors. Keep tender plants such as amaryllis and kalanchoe indoors in a bright spot. Water and fertilize plants regularly.

**ORDER SEEDS.** For best selection, order seeds of warm-season flowers and vegetables as soon as catalogs arrive. Sow through early February for transplanting in the garden by March and April.

**PLANT ANNUALS.** To brighten pots or fronts of beds, choose from calendula, candytuft, cineraria, English daisy, Iceland poppy, pansy, primroses, snapdragon, stock, sweet pea, and viola.

**PLANT BARE-ROOT.** This is the prime month to buy and plant dormant roses, shrubs, fruit and shade trees, and vines. Bare-root plants cost less and adapt more quickly than ones in containers.

**PLANT BERRIES AND VEGETABLES.** Artichokes, asparagus, blackberries, grapes, raspberries, and strawberries are available bare-root this month. If soil is dry enough to be worked, set out seedlings of broccoli, brussels sprouts, cabbage, cauliflower, kale, lettuce, peas, spinach, and Swiss chard. You can also start seed potatoes and sow seeds of beets, carrots, onions, and radishes.

**PROTECT PLANTS FROM FROST.** Watch for dry, still nights when it's clear enough to see the stars. On those nights, move tender container plants beneath overhangs. Cover other frost-tender plants with burlap, cloth, or plastic; keep covering from touching the leaves.

**PRUNE.** Most dormant deciduous plants, including flowering vines, fruit and shade trees, grapes, and roses, need pruning now. Wait to prune spring-flowering plants such as lilacs and mock orange (*Philadelphus*) until after they bloom.

**WATER PLANTS.** If rainfall is light, water plants deeply this month, especially native plants and ones you set out in fall. At this time of year, natives are best able to absorb and store water, and to grow healthy root systems before the summer's dry days arrive.—*E. L.*

San Rafael

Walnut Creek

Oakland

San Francisco

San Jose

Monterey

# January Checklist

## CENTRAL VALLEY

☐ **APPLY DORMANT SPRAY.** To control fungus diseases and overwintering insects, spray deciduous plants, especially fruit trees, with a dormant spray such as horticultural oil mixed with lime sulfur or fixed copper (sold as Microcop). But hold off if temperatures are going to drop below zero or if rain is expected.

☐ **CARE FOR GIFT PLANTS.** After they finish blooming, trim spent blossoms from hardier plants like azaleas, cinerarias, cyclamen, and cymbidiums, and move them to a protected spot outdoors. Keep tender plants such as amaryllis and kalanchoe indoors in a well-lighted spot. Water regularly. If plants dry out quickly, repot with fresh soil in the next larger container. Fertilize amaryllis, azaleas, and cymbidiums after bloom finishes. Fertilize others lightly every three to four weeks. Keep plants indoors until after the last hard freeze.

☐ **CARE FOR LIVING CHRISTMAS TREES.** If you haven't done so already, move living Christmas trees outdoors. Put them in a partially shaded spot to begin with, then move into full sun after a week or two. Rinse off the foliage and thoroughly soak the soil.

☐ **CONTROL SLUGS AND SNAILS.** Reduce their numbers by reducing hiding places: clean up leaf litter and garden debris. Handpick, trap by allowing them to collect on the underside of a raised board, put up copper barriers, or use commercial bait.

☐ **ORDER SEEDS.** During rainy or cold weather is a great time to browse through catalogs and to order varieties you can't find on seed racks. Sow vegetable and flower seeds in flats indoors as soon as they arrive, so you can plant them out in February, March, and April.

☐ **PLANT ANNUALS.** For midwinter bloom, buy plants in 4-inch pots; smaller sizes will just sit until spring. Stuff plants into bigger decorative pots or set them out into flower beds. Try calendula, candytuft, cineraria, dianthus, English daisy, English and fairy primroses, Iceland poppy, pansy, stock, and viola.

☐ **PLANT BARE-ROOT.** This is a prime month to buy and plant dormant roses, shrubs, fruit and shade trees, and vines. Not only can you find the best selection of varieties bare-root, but bare-root plants cost less and adapt more quickly. Plant them right after you bring them home or receive them in the mail. If you can't, heel them in: temporarily lay them on their sides in a shallow trench and cover with moist sawdust or soil.

☐ **PLANT BERRIES AND VEGETABLES.** Artichokes, asparagus, blackberries, grapes, raspberries, and strawberries are available bare-root. You can also plant onion sets and seed potatoes. But wait until next month to plant seedlings of most other cool-season vegetables.

☐ **PROTECT PLANTS FROM FROST.** Watch for dry, still, clear nights when there's no tule fog, and watch the weather forecasts. If frost is predicted, move tender container plants beneath overhangs or into the garage. Protect other tender plants with burlap, cloth, or plastic. Keep covering from touching the leaves; prop it on stakes, and remove it first thing in the morning.

☐ **PRUNE.** Dormant deciduous plants—flowering shrubs and vines, shade trees, and roses—benefit from pruning this month. Don't jump the gun on plants that bloom in early spring, though; wait until after bloom.

☐ **WATER NATIVES.** If rainfall is light, water native trees and shrubs deeply this month. Now is the time of the year when native plants are best able to absorb and store water for summer drought.—*L. W.*

Redding

Lake Tahoe

Sacramento

Fresno

Bakersfield

**Santa Barbara**

**San Bernardino**

**Santa Monica** ● **Los Angeles**

**San Diego**

**BEGIN DORMANT-SEASON PRUNING.** Prune deciduous trees, fruit trees, grapes, roses, shrubs, and vines this month before new growth begins. Make sure saws, loppers, and shears are sharp before starting. Wait until late spring, after flowers fade, to prune trees and shrubs grown primarily for their spring flowers.

**BUY AND PLANT BULBS.** Nurseries now have good supplies of summer-blooming bulbs such as baboon flower (*Babiana*), Chinese ground orchid (*Bletilla*), calla, canna, crinum, dahlia, gladiolus, lily, montbretia (*Crocosmia*), nerine, tigridia, tuberose, and tuberous begonia. If you've refrigerated tulip bulbs for the last six weeks, now's the time to plant.

**CARE FOR BARE-ROOT PLANTS.** Keep roots moist before and after planting. If you can't plant right away, cover roots with moist soil or mulch until you set them out. Wait no longer than a week. While digging the planting hole, soak roots in a bucket of water.

**CONTROL SLUGS AND SNAILS.** Start by eliminating their hiding places, such as leaf litter, old pots, prunings, and similar debris. Handpick them at night, set out traps, or use commercial bait.

**GROOM CAMELLIAS.** If yours haven't bloomed already, they will soon. It's all right to prune now to improve the plant's appearance, but only very selectively and very lightly. If petal blight is a problem (petals turn brown and rot in the center), keep ground beneath plants clean and pick off fallen flowers promptly.

**MANAGE WEEDS.** If you haven't done so, mulch or remulch around vegetable and flower beds, shrubs, and trees. That's the best way to stay ahead of the weeds that come with winter's cool temperatures and moisture.

**ORDER SEEDS.** Place orders for warm-season flowers and vegetables. Start seeds indoors as soon as they arrive, and you'll have seedlings ready for the garden come spring. Mail-order catalogs offer a much wider choice than seed displays in grocery stores and most nurseries.

**PLANT VEGETABLE SEEDLINGS.** Buy and plant seedlings of asparagus, cabbage, chard, chives, endive, lettuce, onions, and parsley. Also try one or more of the perennial vegetables, such as artichoke, horseradish, or rhubarb (inland, give rhubarb some afternoon shade).

**PLANT WINTER COLOR.** It's not too late to plant colorful annuals and perennials to bloom now and into spring—especially in cooler coastal areas. Nurseries offer calendulas, cinerarias (these are frost-tender), dianthus, English daisies, Iceland poppies, larkspur, pansies, primroses, snapdragons, stock, sweet alyssum, sweet peas, and violas. In the low desert (Palm Springs), also plant petunias.

**SHOP FOR AND PLANT CAMELLIAS.** Since so many camellias are blooming this month, it's a good time to shop for the flower types and colors you prefer. Whether or not they're flowering, plant them right away in a location that provides good soil drainage and afternoon shade. Mulch with shredded bark. Transplant established camellias just after they finish flowering.

**SHOP FOR BARE-ROOT PLANTS.** January is bare-root month at nurseries. Most have peak supplies of healthy rose plants. You'll also find perennial vegetables such as artichokes, asparagus, horseradish, and rhubarb; fruits including cane berries, grapes, and strawberries; and ornamentals such as shade trees, hardy perennials, shrubs, and wisteria vines. In the hottest inland areas, such as Palm Springs, look for stone fruit, apple, and fig trees along with roses.

**SPRAY DORMANT PLANTS.** Inland, to prevent (or very much reduce) pest problems next winter, spray leafless and dormant fruit trees and roses. Insects such as aphids and scale and diseases such as peach leaf curl are readily controlled now with sprays of horticultural oil, or the same oil combined with either lime sulfur or fixed copper (follow label directions). All three products are stocked by most nurseries. Near the coast, if plants aren't leafless (notably 'Anna' apple), withhold water to force dormancy before spraying.

**START VEGETABLE SEEDS.** If you live near the coast, you can still start seeds of broccoli, brussels sprouts, and cabbage for planting out next month. You can also try for extra-early crops by planting a few seeds of warm-season crops such as eggplant, peppers, and tomatoes. Set seedlings out in February or March in a location protected from late frosts; until weather warms, cover them with hot caps or row covers. In the low desert, start seeds for warm-season vegetables.

**WATER NATIVE PLANTS.** Especially if rains have been light or nonexistent, water native and drought-tolerant plants. This is the season when they can best absorb and store water for summer. Plants set out in fall, native or not, also need regular, deep soaking.

**HARVEST GRAPEFRUIT:** Throughout inland areas of San Diego County, 'Star Ruby' and 'Oro Blanco' grapefruit will likely reach peak maturity this month. Navel oranges may be ripening, too.—*L. O.*

## ANYWHERE IN THE WEST, TACKLE THESE CHORES:

**CARE FOR LIVING CHRISTMAS TREES.** They need light, so you should move them outside as soon after Christmas as possible. Start them off in a place that's shaded from midday and afternoon sun (under a tree works well), moving them into full sun after a couple of weeks. You can also plant your tree out if it's among those that thrive where you live, and space allows; otherwise keep the tree in the container and baby it. Some trees can live for years as potted plants.

**CHECK STORED BULBS, PRODUCE.** Look over any tender corms, tubers, and produce you have stored away to check for shriveling and rot. You can usually reverse shriveling by sprinkling on a little water. Remove anything that shows signs of decay, except dahlia tubers: cut the bad spots out of those, dust with sulfur, and store apart from the rest.

**FERTILIZE ASPARAGUS.** Top-dress with rotted manure or organic mulch mixed with complete fertilizer.

**MAINTAIN CHRISTMAS PLANTS.** Some tabletop Christmas plants (such as poinsettias) aren't worth trying to save for another year. But others, like cyclamen, Christmas cactus, and kalanchoe, go on and on. Wash them off under a barely warm shower, feed kinds that carry fruit or flow-

ers, and put in a bright place out of drafts and away from heating and air-conditioning sources. After danger of frost is past in spring, you can move these outside for the summer.

**ORDER SEEDS AND SPRING PLANTS.** Place catalog orders for seeds and plants early for best selection, particularly if you want specialty varieties (such as Chinese vegetables, rare plants, or old roses). For seedlings, figure out when you can plant outdoors, then count backward about five weeks; that's when to sow seed indoors.

**PRUNE TREES AND SHRUBS.** Rules are the same for both: On a day when temperatures are above freezing, cut out dead,

diseased, crossing, and closely parallel branches, then prune for shape.

**SOW PERENNIALS.** Start seeds of perennials such as delphinium, hellebore, veronica, and viola in a coldframe or greenhouse for planting out when at least two sets of true leaves appear (and in coldest areas, when ground can be worked).

**WATER HOUSE PLANTS.** When it's not raining, low humidity is usually the rule in much of the West. Combine that with house heat, and—unless you have a humidifier—plants will dry out more quickly than usual. Check soil often, and water when the top ½ inch of soil has dried out.

## IN THE SOUTHWEST'S LOW DESERT, HERE ARE MORE CHORES:

**CONTROL APHIDS.** Low-desert garden areas still have aphids to deal with. Look for them on tender new growth and beneath leaves. The easiest treatment is simply to blast them off with a jet from the hose, then spray with insecticidal soap to finish off any aphids you might have missed.

**FERTILIZE CITRUS TREES.** Applied now, fertilizer will be available when bloom starts. Water trees first, then a day later, apply ammonium sulfate at the following rates for mature trees: 2½ pounds for grapefruit, 4 pounds for oranges and tangerines, and 5 pounds for lemons. Water again after application, and fertilize again in May.

**MULCH.** Winter rains bring up weeds. To keep them down, and to slow the rate at which the ground dries out, put down a thick layer of mulch around shrubs, trees, and in vegetable and flower beds.

**PLANT BARE-ROOT.** Cane fruits, fruit trees, roses, shade trees, and strawberries are all available as bare-root plants in nurseries now. Decide what you want, dig a hole, then buy your tree. Have the nursery pack roots in damp peat or sawdust and wrap them for the trip home; if unprotected roots dry between nursery and home, the plant they support will die too (but you won't know it until leaves fail to emerge in spring).

**PLANT CHILLED BULBS.** If you bought spring-flowering bulbs in November and refrigerated them to provide preplanting chill (six weeks of refrigeration is the target), now is the time to set the bulbs out. Plant in well-amended soil, water well, and shoots should emerge in a month or two.

**PLANT WINTER COLOR.** Nurseries offer plenty of choices for winter color, including calendula, cineraria, cyclamen, English daisy, pansy, primrose, sweet alyssum, and others.

**PROTECT CITRUS FRUIT.** When temperatures drop below 25° for more than 2 hours, most citrus fruits are damaged.

When temperatures below 28° are predicted, cover trees each night with a cloth (old sheets are fine), uncovering them in the morning. If fruit is damaged, pick and juice it within 24 hours.

**PRUNE ROSES.** If you're pruning hybrid tea roses, cut plants back to the three to five strongest canes. Cut top growth back by about a third.

**SOW VEGETABLES.** You can sow seeds of eggplant, melons, peppers, and tomatoes indoors now for transplanting outside when the weather warms.

**WATER PLANTS.** Deepwater trees and shrubs every two to three weeks if the rain doesn't do it.—*J. M.*

MICHAEL SKOTT

**AT HARVESTTIME,** *a gnarled old tree on Orcas Island, Washington, is laden with apples ripe for plucking by the basketful. The collection at right shows newer varieties now winning taste tests hands down.*

# Which apple for your garden?

*For cooking, for eating, or for both, here are 22 favorites to plant now*

FACED WITH CHOOSING from literally hundreds of apple varieties, you might have trouble deciding which kind to plant in your garden. Should you go with a popular new variety like 'Elstar' or 'Gala', an old favorite like 'Gravenstein' or 'Golden Delicious', or the most prevalent of all commercial apples, 'Red Delicious'?

To help you find the answer, we taste-tested apples and visited orchards. We also polled apple growers and researchers from around the West; starting on page 22, we list 22 apples recommended for their excellence in one or more of five categories. We also list wild cards: mostly new varieties that are not well known but are highly praised.

Flavors run tart to sweet. In taste tests at Oregon State University, pomologist Bob Stebbins confirmed that Westerners tend to prefer tart apples. Taste for yourself, then decide.

## APPLES FOR EATING FRESH

Nothing beats the taste of a cold, crisp, juicy apple plucked fresh from the tree, especially if it's one like 'Golden Delicious', which has delighted apple eaters for the better part of a century. Most of our raters agreed that it's underappreciated and taken for granted as a dessert apple. But good as it is, it finished behind five newer apples.

Among the up-and-comers, the tart 'Braeburn' was given a perfect score by seven apple experts.

'Jonagold' ranked second to 'Braeburn'. This offspring of 'Jonathan' and 'Golden Delicious' has great flavor. Some consider its large size a disadvantage for fresh eating but an advantage for cooking.

'Gala', a highly praised red apple with a strong following in Washington, Oregon, and California, came in third. It's gaining ground both in the garden and commercially (some roadside stands take advance orders).

The top green apple was 'Mutsu', whose virtues include great vigor, large fruit size, and sprightly flavor. It

'Gala'

'Braeburn'

'William's Pride'

PETER CHRISTIANSEN

'Pettingill'

'Anna'

'Mutsu'

'Jonagold'

'Gordon'

'Gala'

'Liberty'

'Elstar'

**MOST OF THESE** *Western winners perform well in cold-winter climates; 'Anna', 'Gordon', and 'Pettingill' are good mild-winter candidates.*

does well in cool climates if you're willing to spray for scab. 'Fuji', a sweet dessert apple, came fifth.

Two wild cards are worth considering. 'Alkmene', which matures in early September, is a fine fresh apple but doesn't keep well. 'Fiesta' compares well in flavor with 'Cox Orange Pippin' (one of its parents), has larger size and no cracking problems, and keeps well.

## APPLES FOR COOKING

Though culinary apples are easy to divide into varieties that bake well ('Rome Beauty', for example), or make good sauce ('Yellow Transparent') or pies ('Northern Spy'), you probably wouldn't put a tree in your garden for just one of those purposes. Multipurpose apples generally rated better in our survey.

Our raters chose 'Gravenstein' as the existing standard—it makes excellent sauce and pies—and voted nothing else higher. Another old one, 'Newtown Pippin', tied for first; one source said, "If I had to get down to one apple, it would be 'Newtown Pippin'."

'Melrose' rated well (third) simply because it holds shape and flavor so well when baked; it also keeps well.

Raters put 'Granny Smith',

an old Australian variety, on the list, pointing out that while you may not think much of the 'Granny Smith' apples you get in stores, tree-ripened fruits are hard to beat, and the trees do very well in warm-summer gardens. It finished fourth.

The wild cards here are 'Boskoop', a European apple that scored high in early university trials in Oregon and Washington; and 'Bramley's Seedling', a tart old English variety that delighted the raters who tried it.

## EARLY APPLES

Asked to name their favorite early apples, most of our experts said something like, "The season begins with 'Gravenstein'." But everybody we talked with has a love-hate relationship with this 300-year-old variety. The fruit is excellent both fresh and cooked, but the tree frequently drops imperfect fruit, bears fruit heavily only in alternate years, puts out rank growth, needs a pollenizer, and can't pollinate any other varieties. 'Gravenstein' comes late in the early season, bearing fruit in August or early September.

For earliest harvest, 'Discovery' is superior to 'Yellow Transparent' and 'Lodi', the previous benchmarks. This reddish English apple is good

for sauce and for earliness alone—the season's first apple always tastes pretty good, even though it may not hold up against later varieties.

'Chehalis' also made the list, but just barely (because it's late, maturing after 'Gravenstein'). The fruit is yellow-green and fairly large, is good fresh or cooked, and can be stored for up to three months. It originated in western Washington about 30 years ago and is a favorite there.

This bunch also has two wild cards. 'William's Pride', a new variety that matures in early August, is flatly described by Washington State University pomologist Robert A. Norton as "the first good early red apple." 'Ginger Gold' is later—it bears with 'Gravenstein'—and has wonderful flavor.

## ALL-PURPOSE FRUITS

'Golden Delicious' and 'Gravenstein' share a reputation as fine all-purpose fruits, tasting good fresh off the tree or cooked. But in our poll, they finished fifth and sixth, respectively.

Other fruits are making serious inroads. For a decade, 'Jonagold' has been winning taste tests and gaining a following, especially in western Washington and Oregon, where it grows best. 'Elstar',

## Your best bests

'Alkmene'. Good dessert apple but not a great keeper. Also has good disease resistance.

'Ashmead's Kernel'. Medium size; red-orange blush over rough yellow-green skin. Good mildew resistance.

'Boskoop'. Available in red or green strains. High acidity, sugar, and flavor make it great for baking, sauce, and pies.

'Braeburn'. Medium-size golden red apple with great flavor. Matures late, and does well in a wide range of climates around the West. Excellent ratio of good fruit to bad.

'Bramley's Seedling'. Unusually beautiful flowers precede red-blushed green fruit. This is the benchmark for baking, sauce, and pies in England. Resists scab and mildew.

'Chehalis'. Large yellow-green apples have juicy flesh and fine flavor. Best in cool, humid climates,

where its scab immunity is important. Can get mildew; bruises easily.

'Discovery'. Red stripes over yellow make this a handsome apple. One of the best early apples, and one of the few early ones that can be stored (it lasts a month). Best west of the Cascades. Sometimes cracks around stem end.

'Elstar'. Medium-size red-and-yellow fruit. Grows best west of the Cascades. One of the best pie and sauce apples; also bakes well. Bears in alternate years.

'Enterprise'. Dark red, late, good flavor.

'Fiesta'. Larger and better-flavored than 'Cox Orange Pippin', and doesn't crack.

'Fuji'. Grows only where seasons are long and warm; even in the Willamette Valley, it doesn't always mature.

'Gala'. Medium-size sweet, red apple that excels in most of the West. Self-pollinates, but bears better with a different pollenizer. Susceptible to scab.

**BOUNTIFUL HARVEST** *in Kathy and Bob Vieth's garden in Thousand Oaks, California, includes green 'Granny Smith' and reddish yellow 'Fuji'.*

season in your area, and the best nurseries carry only varieties that do well locally. If you wonder whether a certain variety will grow where you live, call your county cooperative extension office.

Plant bare-root trees as soon as you get them, and water thoroughly. Protect young trunks against sunburn by wrapping loosely with cloth. For help choosing bare-root trees, see page 26.

## THE FAVORITES

The rankings at left show the winners in each category. Descriptions below are arranged alphabetically. ■

*By Jim McCausland*

which is popular in Europe, has been attracting attention here as well.

While this category had many high scorers, including 'Newtown Pippin' (third), 'Gala' (fourth), and 'Melrose' (seventh), no serious wild cards were suggested.

## DISEASE RESISTANCE

In the past, orchardists who chose not to spray simply counted on throwing away a lot of fruit. There was no widely accepted benchmark apple for overall disease resistance, though 'Ashmead's Kernel' came close. Garden-

ers grew the fruit that fared best against the most serious diseases in their areas— scab in mild parts of the Northwest and Northern California, fireblight east of the Cascades, or mildew in gardens with poor air circulation and too much shade.

Recently, however, breeders have come up with apples that have strong disease resistance built in. The best is undoubtedly 'Liberty'. Two promising wild cards, 'Enterprise' and 'William's Pride', pleased raters who were familiar with them. 'Chehalis' (third) doesn't get scab, but mildew can be a problem.

## BUYING, PLANTING

Winter is the time to buy and plant apple trees bare-root. Check your nursery first: plants come in when it's planting

**OLD FAVORITES** *include (clockwise from bottom), Gravenstein', 'Granny Smith', and 'Golden Delicious'.*

PETER CHRISTIANSEN

**'Ginger Gold'.** Golden apple that matures with 'Gravenstein'. Excellent flavor.

**'Golden Delicious'.** Self-pollinates, but bears better with a different pollenizer. Susceptible to scab. Grows better in Oregon and Northern California than in western Washington; okay east of the Cascades. Tends to bear in alternate years.

**'Granny Smith'.** Easy to grow east of the Cascades and in the Willamette Valley and California. Can hold on the tree until January.

**'Gravenstein'.** Medium-size reddish apples on a vigorous tree. Bears in alternate years; needs a pollenizer (but won't pollinate anything itself). Best location is Northern California. A favorite in spite of its problems in the garden.

**'Jonagold'.** Large red-and-yellow apple does well in mild areas east of the Cascades, and west of the mountains in Washington, Oregon, and Northern California. Matures over a long season. Needs a pollenizer (but won't pollinate any-

thing else itself). Good for baking, pies, and sauce.

**'Liberty'.** Smallish red fruit, good flavor. The standard for disease resistance. This bears heavily but drops a fair amount of fruit. Can get a little mildew.

**'Melrose'.** Replaces 'Rome Beauty' as the classic baking apple. Keeps well. Susceptible to mildew.

**'Mutsu'** ('Crispin'). Large, greenish gold, and extremely tasty. This apple produces a lot of bad and

good fruit at the same time; susceptible to scab. A genetic triploid, it needs a pollenizer but won't pollinate anything else. Keeps well.

**'Newtown Pippin'.** This was the first U.S. apple good enough to ship to Europe. Grows at its prime in Hood River Valley and in central California. Takes years to come into production. Unattractive tree, blind wood (no fruit spurs).

**'William's Pride'.** Flavorful, medium-size red fruit on a moderate-size tree.

**IN ADDITION TO SEEDS,** *catalogs offer a huge assortment of tools and garden accessories, from seed flats to harvest helpers.*

# Seeds of dreams

*Along with the facts and updated choices, seed catalogs bring visions of gardens, flowers, and food*

**BEDDING PLANTS** *and seed tapes compete with seed packets for catalog space.*

NOTHING FUELS A gardener's imagination like the seed catalogs that arrive in the mail in winter. The latest, most unusual, and hardest-to-find varieties are there in blazing color, amid hopeful descriptions and enticing promises: "World's longest carrot" and "Best corn you'll ever eat."

Among the hundreds of available seed catalogs, old faithfuls like Burpee and Park Seed continue to offer flowers and vegetables from A to Z. But in the last 10 years or so, the number of specialty seed purveyors has burgeoned, with catalogs that specialize in everything from endangered plants to Asian greens. Now, you can pick and choose according to your passions.

While a typical nursery seed rack offers just 10 or so tomato varieties, mail-order catalogs like those from Tomato Growers Supply Company and Tomato Seed Company are entirely devoted to this beloved crop. Each offers hundreds of varieties.

Likewise, Horticultural Enterprises caters to pepper aficionados with dozens of varieties, and Ronniger's Seed Potatoes touts "the largest offering of organically grown seed potato varieties in the U.S. to home gardeners, small farmers, and hobbyists."

If flavor is of utmost importance, you can choose from catalogs that give the highest priority to fine-tasting vegetables. Shepherd's Garden Seeds and The Cook's Garden are two that list taste-tested varieties. As a bonus, these catalogs share recipes, such as mint-glazed carrots and celeriac rémoulade. Both sell flower seeds as well.

A number of catalogs advocate using open-pollinated

(unhybridized) and heirloom varieties. Among them are nonprofit organizations working to save varieties from extinction: KUSA champions cereal grains, Native Seeds/SEARCH specializes in traditional crops and their wild relatives of the greater Southwest, and Abundant Life Seed Foundation sells seeds for food plants and flowers that are adapted to the Pacific Northwest.

A few firms are economy-minded. They offer small seed packets for small prices. If you're gardening in a tight space or just want to test a variety, consider Pinetree Garden Seeds (edibles and ornamentals) with packets starting at 35 cents, and Le Jardin du Gourmet (mostly herbs and vegetables) with sample packets for 25 cents.

Is your garden extra-large? You'll find bulk seed available through catalogs such as Johnny's Selected Seeds and Territorial Seed Company.

## BEYOND SEEDS

Besides seeds, catalog pages brim with everything from tools and amendments to kitchen gadgets and garden art. Pinetree Garden Seeds, for example, advertises more than 100 garden books. Burpee, among others, sup-

plies garden-ready seedlings and garden designs to accompany seed packets. Before buying, peruse catalogs for the best buys.

## FREE INFORMATION

Seed catalogs, like garden primers, provide plenty of specific information. It may be as basic as the planting depth for beans, or as obscure as recommended legume inoculants. And the trivia are endless. Have you ever wondered how many pepper seeds are in an ounce? (Answer: an average of 4,000.) There's also intriguing folklore—for example, scattering caraway seed at the door to keep thieves away—and no end to curious plant names: "love-lies-bleeding," "zig-zag wattle," and "weasel's snout."

However, even the best catalogs are not necessarily written for Western gardens, so cross-check items such as hardiness zones and planting dates with regional references. For instance, Johnny's Selected Seeds and Southern Exposure Seed Exchange are exceptionally clear and helpful, as long as you're aware of regional differences.

For a synthesis of garden philosophy and plant information, Seeds of Change makes outstanding reading. And J. L.

Hudson, Seedsman, an ethno-botanical catalog, is packed with facts as well as the ornamental, medicinal, and culinary uses of plants.

## CATALOG-SPEAK

Catalog language combines plain vanilla marketing with solid information. As a result, you can expect some jargon and common euphemisms in the mix. Here is a sampling of catalog phrases and their likely meanings:

*Start seeds indoors* describes seeds that require more care than the average. They may germinate slowly or need warmer temperatures, or seedlings may demand extra time or attention prior to planting outdoors. Many perennials fall into this category.

When a vegetable is *novel* or *unusual* or has *unique* color or shape, you know flavor and texture are secondary. Similarly, *giant* is a clue to vegetables that are grand in size but perhaps better mounted above the fireplace than tossed into a winter stew.

Watch out for anything *vigorous.* It implies that the vine, shrub, or vegetable in question is ready and able to out-compete most plants in its path. If space is limited, look for *compact, bush,* or *dwarf* varieties.

Plants that *self-sow readily* are usually annuals and biennials (but could be trees or shrubs) that you plant once and have evermore. Each year a new crop of seeds germinates and grows without any help from you. Depending on the plant and your attitude, it might become a weed or a favorite companion.

*Sow in place* usually means that the plant doesn't survive transplanting well. It's wise to follow the directive when one is given. ∎

*By Lynn Ocone*

NORMAN A. PLATE

**SEEDS PLUS A GARDEN PLAN,** *packaged by Burpee, produced this back-door marigold garden.*

## •Who and where•

The following addresses are for the catalogs described in the preceding text. For a comprehensive listing, consult *Gardening by Mail*, by Barbara J. Barton (Houghton Mifflin, Boston; $19.95). The fourth edition of this volume is available this month.

*Abundant Life Seed Foundation,* Box 772, Port Townsend, Wash. 98368; (206) 385-5660 (catalog $2).

*W. Atlee Burpee & Co.,* 300 Park Ave., Warminster, Pa. 18991; (800) 888-1447 (free).

*The Cook's Garden,* Box

535, Londonderry, Vt. 05148; (802) 824-3400 ($1).

*Horticultural Enterprises,* Box 810082, Dallas, Texas 75381 (free seed list).

*J. L. Hudson, Seedsman,* Box 1058, Redwood City, Calif. 94064 ($1).

*Le Jardin du Gourmet,* Box 75, St. Johnsbury Center, Vt. 05863; (802) 748-1446 (50 cents).

*Johnny's Selected Seeds,* 310 Foss Hill Rd., Albion, Maine 04910; (207) 437-4301 (free).

*KUSA,* Box 761, Ojai, Calif. 93024 ($2).

*Native Seeds/SEARCH,* 2509 N. Campbell Ave., Box 325, Tucson, Ariz. 85719; (602) 327-9123 ($1).

*Park Seed Co.,* Cokesbury Rd., Greenwood, S.C. 29647; (800) 845-3369 (free).

*Pinetree Garden Seeds,* Box 300, New Gloucester, Maine 04260; (207) 926-4112 (free).

*Ronniger's Seed Potatoes,* Star Route 94, Moyie Springs, Idaho 83845 ($2).

*Seeds of Change,* 1364 Rufina Circle, Suite 5, Santa Fe, N.M. 87501; (505) 438-8080 (free).

*Shepherd's Garden Seeds,* 6116 Hwy. 9, Felton, Calif. 95018; (408) 335-6910 ($1).

*Southern Exposure Seed Exchange,* Box 170, Earlysville, Va. 22936; (804) 973-4703 ($2).

*Territorial Seed Company,* Box 157, Cottage Grove, Ore. 97424; (503) 942-9547 (free).

*Tomato Growers Supply Company,* Box 2237, Fort Myers, Fla. 33902; (813) 768-1119 (free).

*Tomato Seed Company,* Box 1400, Tryon, N.C. 28782 (free).

**THE GRAVENSTEIN** *apple tree on the left is a year older than the other, has a much larger root system, and will bear a crop a year earlier. Cost: $16 for the large one, $9 for the small one.*

# Savvy shopping for bare-root trees

*The best ones are a few years old with full root systems and pleasing shapes*

OLDER IS BETTER WHEN it comes to planting a bare-root tree (a dormant tree with no soil around the roots). An older tree will flower or fruit one or two seasons earlier than a smaller, less expensive one, or—if it's a shade tree—fill out faster.

Bare-root trees are 15 to 25 percent cheaper than those sold in containers, and they adapt more easily to your native garden soil. But all bare-root trees are not created equal, and finding the best deal may take some shopping around. The photograph above shows the difference in the sizes of bare-root trees found at two sources—a retail nursery and a discount department store—within a mile of each other.

## THE LOWDOWN ON FRUIT TREES

At mass merchandisers (typically 25 to 50 percent less than nurseries), we found generally small, young trees with bare roots stapled into plastic bags full of damp sawdust. If you're planting lots of fruit trees, the total cost savings might justify the extra year or two you'll have to wait for a crop. (Keep in mind that roots sometimes have to be heavily pruned to fit into those plastic bags; this might affect the health of the trees.)

At full-service nurseries, we looked at the same variety/rootstock combinations and found generally larger, older, better-branched trees with roots sunk into sawdust-filled raised beds. Nursery workers were willing to pull trees out so that we could examine the roots, and to prune the tree for shape at purchase.

These trees averaged $4 to $7 more than similar (but younger) trees sold at discount stores—a cheap price for moving the date of first harvest up a year or two.

Size alone won't tell you the age of a given fruit tree. Some varieties of apple, for example, are naturally large and vigorous, and some aren't; some come on dwarf rootstocks, some on semi-

BILL ROSS

**NURSERYMAN** *and buyers inspect a tree's roots. The healthiest ones are evenly spread and unbroken with sprouting white root hairs (the coming year's roots).*

dwarf. If in doubt, ask your nurseryman the tree's age; the best ones to start with are at least 2 years old.

## WHAT ABOUT ORNAMENTAL TREES?

Bare-root ornamentals—mostly flowering and shade trees—are virtually all less than 4 years old. One of the West's largest growers says that about half his sales are 1-year-old trees, and half 2-year-olds. There's also some demand for 3-year-olds.

One-year-olds usually have only a single central leader and a few twiggy branches. However, by pruning during the first summer, growers can force the leader to branch. A branched, 7-foot-tall, 1-year-old London plane tree might cost $18 retail.

Two-year-old trees are naturally branched and large enough to give some hint of what they will become. A London plane this age might be 10 feet tall and cost $30.

Three-year-olds are better branched, have thicker trunks, and make a more immediate impact in the landscape. But their larger size makes them more vulnerable to transplant shock: if you don't keep them well watered, they'll die or their growth will be checked. A 3-year-old London plane would be around 15 feet tall, have perhaps a 2-inch trunk, and cost around $40.

If you're prepared to give a 3-year-old tree the care it demands (plant it as soon as you get it home and keep it watered), it's a better bargain in the long run. Otherwise, choose a 2-year-old. If you need enough trees to line your driveway or property line, buy the 1-year-olds.

The bottom line: don't buy on price alone. Remember, you're buying something that will probably be on your property longer than you will. Look for a tree that is evenly branched all the way around (unless you want to espalier it to a wall). ∎

*By Jim McCausland*

BRIGHT PINK *'Carefree Wonder' borders a patio in Palos Verdes, California.*

SCOTT MILLARD

# Nonstop roses

*Here are eight that (almost) never stop blooming in mild climates*

**CLOUD OF WHITE FLOWERS** *covers 'Iceberg'. In midsummer and midwinter, flowers are fewer, but the bush is still showy.*

IS THERE SUCH A thing as an ideal landscape rose—one that blooms nonstop, resists pests and diseases, and rarely needs pruning? Perhaps not. But in mild climates, according to rose experts we interviewed, the eight roses listed here come pretty close.

Their cup-shaped flowers, borne mostly in clusters, are long-lasting and tolerant of rain and hot sun. New flowers quickly replace faded ones. Most of these roses are sterile, so faded flowers simply drop away. No developing hips remain to sap flowering vigor.

You'll find bare-root plants available this month for $7 to $10 each.

## EIGHT WINNING ROSES FOR LANDSCAPING

In the mild-winter West, these roses bear flowers every month of the year. If you live where winter temperatures drop below 27° for several days, bloom will cease—but you'll still get longer perfor-

mance with these varieties. (To avoid permanent freeze damage in cold-winter climates, choose plants growing on their own roots; check with your nurseryman.)

**'Bonica'.** Soft pink 2-inch flowers appear in heavy clusters of a dozen or more. Glossy, dark green leaves have reddish overtones. Whether grafted or on their own roots, plants grow 4 to 5 feet tall and nearly as wide.

**'Carefree Wonder'.** Bright pink flowers with white undersides are about 3 inches across, singly or in clusters of six to eight. Leaves are glossy and bright green. Plant grows 4 to 5 feet high and wide. Very easy to grow and exceptionally free flowering. Available on own roots.

**'Gourmet Popcorn'.** Fluffy white 1-inch flowers come in large clusters of 30 or more. Leaves are bright green and glossy. Plant grows to 2½ feet tall, with a slightly cascading ball shape. Excellent in containers, hanging baskets, or as a small tree. Unlike most

landscape roses, these are lightly fragrant.

**'Iceberg'.** Clear white 3- to 4-inch flowers, long-lasting when cut, are borne in dense clusters. Leaves are shiny green, and stems are almost thornless. Plant grows 4 to 5 feet tall and as wide. Perhaps the most widely grown rose in the world.

**'Pink Pollyanna'.** Coral pink 2-inch flowers come in clusters of four to eight, or sometimes singly. Leaves are dark olive green. Plant grows slightly upright to 3 feet tall and 2 feet wide.

**'Regensberg'.** Hot pink, 4- to 4½-inch flowers with white undersides. Leaves are dark green on a compact plant 3 feet high and wide.

**'Sweet Chariot'.** Sweet-scented purple-lavender 1-inch flowers in clusters of two dozen or so cover this exceptionally free-flowering small shrub. Leaves are light green. The most compact of these eight roses, it has limber stems that make it ideal as a low, mounding shrub, or spilling over a low wall.

**'The Fairy'.** Light pink many-petaled 1- to 1½-inch flowers bloom all season long in dense large, arching clusters. Leaves are small and light green. Bloom is heavy during the growing season but tapers off once the weather begins to cool. The plant reaches 2½ to 3 feet tall.

## PLANTING AND CARE

These landscape roses are vigorous, strong growers that don't require coddling. To plant them bare-root, dig a hole large enough to accommodate roots without bending or twisting them. Build a firm mound of soil in the center (high enough that the bud union will be even with or just above the soil line), position the rose on top, then spread the roots over the mound. Add some backfill soil to the hole along with some water in a gradual process until completed. ∎

*By Michael MacCaskey*

*THOUGH MANY DAFFODILS are short on fragrance, all invite close-up viewing. For more on these cheery harbingers of spring, see page 30.*

# FEBRUARY

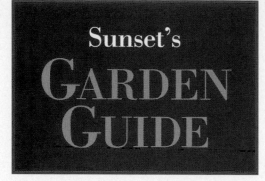

## Sunset's GARDEN GUIDE

# February daffodils forecast spring, but garden agenda features planting, pruning, and spraying

CHAD SLATTERY

Cut-and-come-again daffodils are everywhere this month. Most kinds have little or no fragrance (tazetta hybrids are a notable exception), but all make great cut flowers. Cut stems off at the base unless you have one of the multiple-flowering kinds, like paperwhites and triandrus hybrids. You can cut those as well, but you may lose less-developed flower buds. Cutting daffodils allows the plant to put more energy into regenerating its bulb, giving you more bloom next year.

Some nurseries sell daffodils in bloom this month. For instant color to brighten a porch or patio, buy several in gallon cans and plant them together in a big pot. The three daffodil varieties pictured on page 28 are 'Ceylon' (yellow-and-orange flowers), 'Ice Follies' (yellow-and-white blossoms), and 'Sweetness' (small yellow flowers).

### Oriental fountain grass blooms early and long

The wispy plumes catching light in the picture at right belong to Oriental fountain grass (*Pennisetum orientale*). In this Southern California garden, the grass flowers from May through October. The violet-pink flower tufts age to a dusky brown, eventually shattering in November. The plants are dormant in winter. Oriental fountain grass grows to 18 inches tall and equally wide. Its flower stems reach 12 to 16 inches above the light green foliage. The silky flower heads are about 4 inches long. The grass is not invasive, although seedlings might appear elsewhere in your garden.

Plant Oriental fountain grass this month. Choose a sunny spot with well-drained soil. The grass tolerates sandy soil and coastal conditions if given adequate water. A 1-gallon plant costs about $5 to $7.

If you already have this plant in your garden, watch for new growth at the base. When it appears (later this month, most likely), cut back the old growth to a couple of inches above the crown.—*Lynn Ocone*

### New cool-blue pansy

Something like a European version of All-America Selections, the Fleuroselect awards recognize world-class plants. In 1993, the Velour Blue strain of pansy won a Fleuroselect gold medal. We saw Velour Blue trial plantings in

For Montenegro, this pruning job is a month-long process.—*Michael MacCaskey*

## Success with lilies in Southern California

If you plant Oriental lilies in just the right spot—in deep, moist, well-drained soil that gets bright morning light and afternoon shade—they're surprisingly easy to grow. In Southern California, now is the time to buy and plant them.

If soil is heavy clay, amend it before planting with generous amounts of planting mix for azaleas and camellias. Set four to six bulbs 6 inches deep and 6 to 10 inches apart. Spread roots carefully, then cover bulbs with soil. Water well and cover area with a 3- to 4-inch layer of mulch.

Horticulturist Cristin Fusano's favorite is 'Casa Blanca' (3 to 4 feet, with fragrant large white flowers; florists charge $10 to $15 for a single stem). Other favorites are 'Stargazer', with fragrant scarlet-and-white flowers; 'Imperial Gold', with white-and-yellow flowers; and 'Imperial Silver', with white flowers with rusty flecks. All grow to 3 feet tall. Bulbs cost $2 to $6 each.

Plant bulbs as soon as you get them home. If gophers are a problem in your garden, plant the bulbs in a wire basket. Support the tallest lilies with thin bamboo stakes. —*M. M.*

## An apple tree for minimalists

This spring you'll see a new kind of apple tree on the market: it has a trunk, leaves, and fruit, but no major side branches. Three such apples and one crabapple have been

California last year and were impressed with this pansy's color and vigor. You should be able to find it in nurseries and garden centers this spring, and in at least a few seed catalogs.

Plant this prolific, small-flowered pansy (called a mini) in drifts for best effect. It takes frosts well, bouncing back when the weather warms up. Give it full sun in mild-summer areas, part shade in hot-summer areas.—*Jim McCausland*

## Tips for pruning wisteria

Though magnificent in bloom, wisterias are gangly vines that need annual pruning. At Southern California's Fullerton Arboretum, a vine on the arbor behind Heritage House gets pruned every February, just before buds begin to swell. We asked the pruner, assistant director Rico Montenegro, how he goes about the job.

"Pruning wisteria is similar to pruning an apple or grape," he said. "All three plants produce short, stubby buds (spurs), where the fruit or flowers originate. When you prune a wisteria, leave as many spurs as possible."

Montenegro removes most of last year's growth (the light tan wood from the leaf scars to the branch tips). Thin the vine and shorten its branches, leaving only two or three buds on each branch. "If you don't prune heavily enough, the tangle of stems may cover up many flowers."

released this spring. All grow to about 10 feet high with only a 2-foot spread.

The fruiting varieties, generically called colonnade apples, are all descended from a 'McIntosh' tree in British Columbia. After further breeding in England, they're now back in North America for release. The named varieties are 'Stark ScarletSpire' (red over green), 'Stark EmeraldSpire' (green with gold blush), and 'Stark Ultra-Spire' (dark red with yellow-green blush). All come to harvest around midseason (with 'Jonagold').

The crabapple is 'Stark Maypole'. It has pink flowers and large (1½-inch) fruit.

You'll need at least two varieties for cross-pollination (the crab can be one of them). Since these trees were bred primarily for form, none have particularly good disease re-

## Tool of the Month

PETER CHRISTIANSEN

*These 4½-inch green pins, called FabricPegs, keep black plastic sheeting in place over vegetable beds (the black plastic helps prevent weeds). The pins, made of durable plastic, have serrated tips to help them penetrate and stay put in soil. Space them evenly around edges of black plastic. Nurseries sell FabricPegs in packages of 10 ($1.99).*

sistance; you'll need to spray them regularly.

You can buy colonnade apples from Stark Brothers Nurseries and Orchards Co., Box 10, Louisiana, Mo. 63353 (800/325-4180); catalog is free.—*J. M.*

## Battle summer pests now with dormant spray

Late rains and a relatively mild summer throughout much of the West in 1993 combined to cause some unusually severe pest problems, particularly fruit tree diseases like brown rot and fireblight.

To prevent this from happening again, and to get a head start against many other summer problems, apply a dormant spray this month.

Dormant sprays have two basic components: horticultural oil to smother overwintering insects and their eggs, and a fungicide, such as lime sulfur or fixed copper (usually sold as Microcop or Mastercop), to kill disease organisms. Together they help control insects such as aphids, mites, scale, and thrips, and diseases like brown rot, fireblight, and peach leaf curl.

Where diseases are particularly troublesome, well-timed additional sprays of the same fungicide will provide further control. For example, to control brown rot or fireblight, reapply fungicide during bloom. For more information on controlling specific diseases, consult the *Sunset Western Garden Book.*

Before using a dormant spray, remove and discard any dead leaves and dried fruit remaining on the tree. Also rake up and get rid of dead leaves and prunings beneath the tree.

Follow product labels carefully (lime sulfur is very caustic; when using it, wear goggles and plastic gloves). Make sure to wet the entire tree; soaking the ground below the tree is also helpful. Repeat spray if rain comes soon after application.—*Lance Walheim*

SNOW WON'T STOP *a hardy Helleborus foetidus from flowering in February. Plants bloom well into spring.*

## New rose book for Southern California

If you are a fan of English roses, you'll be happy to know about a new book on the subject—and it's written for gardeners in this region. *English Roses in Southern California,* by Clair G. Martin III (Hortus Gardenbooks, 1993) reflects the author's 12 years of experience as curator of the rose collections at The Huntington Botanical Gardens in San Marino. Martin tends nearly 2,000 varieties and species there.

The 64-page paperback includes a short rose-growing guide and a lexicon of roses with more than 100 entries (not illustrated). The guide gives advice on all the basics, from soil preparation to pruning to cutting flowers.

The lexicon is the heart of the book. Along with descriptions of the plants and flowers, Martin shares useful anecdotes and opinions. Of the 'Ambridge Rose', Martin says, "For me, this particular cultivar is, without a doubt, the best of the newer English roses." In contrast, 'Financial Times Centenary' gets this bleak review: "At best, I get a very weak plant that throws

a flower or two and then slowly dies!"

*English Roses in Southern California* is available from the publisher. Send $11.82 (includes tax and shipping) to Hortus Gardenbooks, 284 E. Orange Grove Blvd., Pasadena, Calif. 91104. Or buy the book at Hortus, a retail nursery at the same address.—*L. O.*

## Helleborus: parrot green and penguin hardy

If you fear the killing frost, plant a *Helleborus foetidus*. This sturdy perennial blooms this month, its light green flowers standing 1½ feet above its dark green, deeply cut leathery leaves. It's a perfect complement to early daffodils like 'February Gold'.

You can buy *H. foetidus* in bloom now in 1-gallon cans, and set it out immediately. Unfussy about soil and drought tolerant, it does best in rich, quick-draining soil and part shade. Cut off bloom heads once they fade in late spring. Or, if you want the plant to multiply, allow seeds to form and scatter. It self-sows freely.—*J. M.*

## Cuttings go right into the ground

Mareen Kruckeberg, owner of MsK Rare Nursery in Seattle, has developed an easy method for adding assorted salix (willow family members) to her garden. She simply pushes cuttings directly into the ground. From the donor plant, she takes a branch about 12 inches long and as big around as a pencil, cuts it to a sharp point on the down end, then shoves the cutting 6 to 8 inches into the soil where she wants the plant to grow. Through the cool, wet spring, the salix sends out roots, leafs out, and becomes an established small plant by summer. Kruckeberg reports a 90 percent success rate using this method.

Other area gardeners have had similar success with

redtwig and yellowtwig dogwoods and members of the *Populus* genus. It's an excellent way to get a single plant or an informal hedge started.—*J. M.*

## Give dogwoods a chance to regain their health

Normally, when a native dogwood (*Cornus nuttallii*) is attacked by the anthracnose fungus, that's the end: you take the tree down in winter and burn it. Hold off this year. Due to the terribly dry, harsh summer of 1992 (which weakened dogwoods) followed by the cool, wet summer of 1993 (which caused the anthracnose to flourish), the trees have been unusually vulnerable. Give them a year or two to recover. A formerly healthy tree could well pull out of it.

Take the normal precautions: rake up any leaves under the tree and dispose of them (be sure to keep them out of the compost to avoid spreading the fungus); prune off noticeably infected branches and dispose of them.

With any luck, you'll see much less of a problem this summer and no problem by next year.—*J. M.*

## Best picks among strawberries

Southern California nurseries are well stocked this month with strawberries, sold bare-root and in cell-packs. Some varieties bear fruit the first year, and others fruit the following year.

The ones that bear fruit the first year (regardless of day length) are called day neutral or everbearing. Plants set out in February will give a small peak harvest in late spring or summer and continue setting fruit off and on through fall. 'Quinault' is an excellent everbearing strawberry with large, sweet, soft fruit. Other good varieties for Southern California are 'Fort Laramie', 'Ozark Beauty', and 'Tristar'.

MICHAEL THOMPSON

**FALLEN BLOSSOMS** *graduate from litter to decoration. Spent camellia flowers spangle wooden deck, drift on surface of garden pond.*

June-bearing strawberries (also called spring bearing) give one large crop per year in late winter, spring, or early summer. When planted in February, these types fruit the following year. 'Sequoia' is the best variety for Southern California gardens. The plants are prolific, bearing very tasty fruit for several months.—*L. O.*

## Fallen blossoms add spring accents

We often talk about the beauty of autumn leaves littering garden walkways, terraces, and beds, encouraging our readers not to be too quick about raking them up. But what about spring litter? The photograph above shows Marlene Salon grooming the terrace of her Portland garden. She left a few of the downed camellia blossoms floating in the shallow basin (and added a few more) and left other fallen flowers under the tree, away from foot traffic. It's the simplest of ideas, but timing and vigilance are everything. Start with a tidy garden—it's the difference between artful neglect and messiness. You can leave fallen blossoms in place until the oldest of them start getting soggy. Then clean up everything and allow a new batch of petal litter to accumulate.—*J. M.*

## Indoor gardening for kids

When Joel Rapp wrote *Let's Get Growing* (Crown Publishers, New York, 1993; $7), he brought to it as much parental experience as plant experience. The result is a project-oriented book for kids that really works.

Though Rapp has professionally covered all kinds of gardening, he has specialized in indoor plants, so when he gives you his top 10 hassle-free house plants, you should take notice. He also explains how to grow everything from avocados and mangoes to sweet potatoes and pineapples on your windowsill.

Other projects teach children how to raise herbs, plant a terrarium, marinate tomatoes, construct garden gifts, even graft cactus and force bulbs. By the time your kids are done with the book, there's a good chance they'll be hooked on gardening. And you might learn a thing or two as well.—*J. M.*

## Sunset's tasty trio of tomatoes

The West's favorite vegetable now comes in an incredible array of types—from yellow or orange to green-striped ones, and from large to small. Three choice varieties

**THREE TOMATOES** *to start now from seed, shown whole and sliced, are (from top to bottom) 'Better Boy', 'Yellow Stuffer', and 'Hungarian Italian'.*

we liked when we grew them last year in *Sunset*'s test garden are pictured above.

'Better Boy' is tough to beat as a tasty salad tomato. Its fruits are large, firm, and flavorful with a classic tomato taste.

'Yellow Stuffer' may look like a bell pepper, but its attractive, low-acid fruits reach 3½ to 4 inches in diameter and have great tomato taste. The flesh is firm and holds its shape nicely when cooked, making 'Yellow Stuffer' the perfect stuffing tomato for hot as well as cold recipes.

'Hungarian Italian' is a paste tomato. The meaty fruits are perfect for sauces as well as slicing fresh.

One mail-order source for seeds of 'Better Boy' and 'Yellow Stuffer' is Totally Tomatoes, Box 1626, Augusta, Ga. 30903. Seeds of 'Hungarian Italian' are available by mail from Seeds Blüm, Idaho City Stage, Boise, Idaho 83706.—*Emely Lincowski*

## Fluorescent lights for starting seeds

Fluorescent lights are perfect for starting seeds. Just suspend a fixture with four 40-watt bulbs between 8 and 12 inches over seed flats, and they'll provide inexpensive, high-quality light (and even some heat).

All fluorescents, however, are not the same: full-spectrum tubes designed for plants give better results because their light spectrum is balanced for plant growth (it's close to natural light in color and quality). They're also made with long life and stability (minimal color shift and light fall-off) in mind; some are guaranteed for as long as three years.

You can buy lights at garden centers or by mail. Output (and price) is a function of length, with tubes rated at about 10 watts per foot.

One mail-order source that specializes in fluorescents for plants is Verilux Inc.; call (800) 786-6850 for a catalog.—*J. M.*

## Tried-and-true tomato varieties for the Central Valley

Tomato plants are very sensitive to weather changes. During spring's relatively mild weather, one variety might grow better than another; but then, as the weather warms in summer, that robust spring performer might fizzle out while other varieties become more productive. Year-to-year fluctuations can make last summer's prize tomato this season's dud. Besides productivity, weather can also affect the juiciness, flavor, and size of tomatoes.

In the Central Valley, dramatic weather fluctuations are the norm. So if you're starting seeds this month for transplants in March and April, it makes sense to include one or

*GLOSSY RED PEPPERS, from big and plump to long and slender, are a few of the many kinds harvested in Southern California pepper test.*

two varieties that have a long history of dependability here. To find out what those are, we sifted through UC recommendations and surveyed Central Valley vegetable gardeners.

'Early Girl' is on almost everyone's list as the one tomato Central Valley gardeners should grow. It is a dependable producer of early, small- to medium-size tomatoes, tops in both quality and flavor. 'Ace' is another highly rated variety, with several strains. Two strains, 'Ace 55' and 'Cal Ace', feature improved disease resistance; both are recommended and produce good-size, midseason fruit.

Other highly rated varieties include 'Better Boy', 'Beefmaster', and 'Celebrity'. Among cherry tomatoes, look for 'Red Cherry' or 'Sweet 100'. 'San Marzano' is a reliable paste variety.—*Lance Walheim*

## Pepper mania

What's the best pepper for Southern California gardeners to grow? Yvonne Freeman, adult education coordinator of the Common Ground Garden Program in Los Angeles, decided to find out. Last year, she grew 35 kinds of peppers to identify those that grew best and developed the best flavor in Southern California. The picture below shows a sample of her harvest. All the hot peppers grew well, but Freeman found differences among the sweet peppers.

The most flavorful sweet pepper was 'Chocolate Beauty', though seeds were tricky to germinate. The most prolific large-fruited peppers (3 inches and up) were 'Biscayne', 'Gypsy', and 'North Star'. Smaller sweet peppers are always more prolific, but 'Cherry' exceeded expectations—supplying especially hefty crops.

Sow seeds in flats 8 to 10 weeks before planting outdoors in late March or early April. Place in a warm (70° to 80°) location; the seeds will germinate in 10 to 20 days and be ready to plant 8 to 10 weeks later.

Order seeds now. Mail-order catalogs offer the best selection. Sources for the varieties tested include Ed Hume Seeds, Box 1450, Kent, Wash. 98035 (catalog $1); Gurney's Seed & Nursery Co., 110 Capital St., Yankton, S.D. 57079, (605) 665-1930 (free); and Porter & Son Seedsmen, Box 104, Stephenville, Texas 76401 (free).—*M. M.*

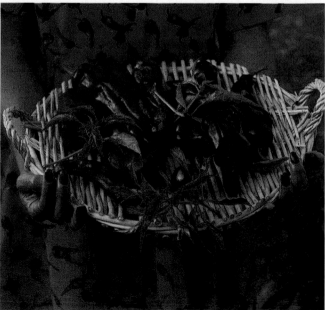

## February Checklist

### PACIFIC NORTHWEST

☐ **BAIT FOR SLUGS AND SNAILS.** They will reduce newly set-out primroses to stubs overnight with their continuous nibbling. Bait around plants you've just set out, plants that send up new shoots early in the year, and winter bloomers like hellebores. Be careful about spreading bait if you have pets: some aren't attracted to bait; others eat the toxic stuff.

☐ **BUY FLOWERING PRIMROSES.** Blooming primroses in 4-inch pots abound this month. For Valentine's Day giving, pop the red, pink, and white varieties into decorative pots or baskets. All colors, including yellows, blues, and purples, make for lively containers indoors and out. Water all plants well. As blooms fade, pick them off. Give plants a deep watering with a complete liquid plant food (12-12-12 is a good choice) diluted to half-strength to encourage a second or third crop of flowers. Exhausted plants can be planted in shady beds for bloom next year.

☐ **CHECK STORED BULBS AND PRODUCE.** Examine stored bulbs, fruits, and vegetables; discard any showing signs of rot.

☐ **FERTILIZE HOUSE PLANTS.** Start a feeding program now for house plants that are showing new growth, blooming, or fruiting. Use a half-strength solution of fertilizer until April, when days grow longer and sunlight increases.

☐ **FORCE FLOWERING SHRUBS.** Flowering apricot and plum, forsythia, and ornamental quince are among the plants that can be cut and taken inside for forced flowering. Put these branches in a vase of warm water in a bright place. Pussy willows (and almost any willow) can also be forced.

☐ **PLANT BARE-ROOT.** Some trees, shrubs, vines, and cane berries are still available bare-root. Plant immediately and water thoroughly.

☐ **PRE-SPROUT PEAS.** Soak peas overnight, then put them between several layers of wet paper towel on a cookie sheet. Set them aside in a warm place. When the peas sprout, plant them outside and they'll grow.

☐ **PRUNE AND FEED HYDRANGEAS.** If you left any blooms on for winter interest, clip them off now and prune plants lightly to shape them. Feed plants with a complete granular fertilizer food (15-15-15), scattered according to label specifications.

☐ **PRUNE ROSES.** Cut hybrid teas back by about a third. Cut out injured or dead canes. Cut out parallel or crossing branches. Prune with an eye for a handsomely shaped plant.

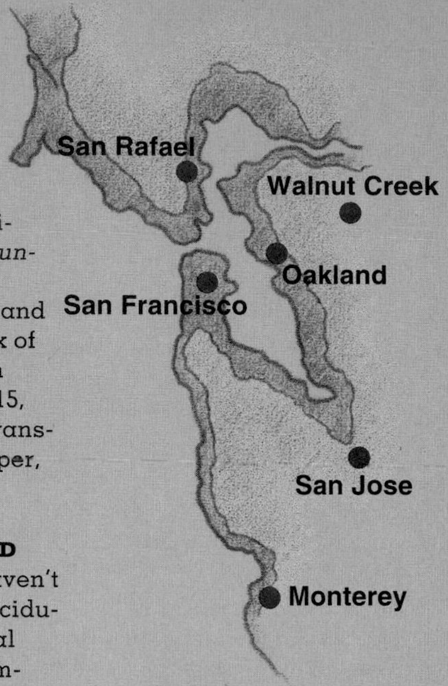

**BUY SEEDS.** It's still early enough to order seeds of less common varieties of vegetables and flowers from catalogs.

**CONTROL SNAILS AND SLUGS.** As night temperatures rise, slugs and snails are more active and can quickly devour flowers such as daffodils, Iceland poppies, and pansies. Handpick them at night, or use commercial baits (where pets can't get to them).

**DIVIDE PERENNIALS.** To increase your plantings, lift and divide perennials such as black-eyed Susan, blanket flower, catmint, coreopsis, daylily, diascia, geranium, ground morning glory, lamb's ears, penstemon, shasta daisy, society garlic, and yarrow.

**FERTILIZE PLANTS.** Fall-planted annuals and perennials as well as established trees and shrubs get a boost from fertilizing now. Wait to feed azaleas, camellias, and rhododendrons until after bloom; use an acid fertilizer.

**PLANT SPRING ANNUALS.** Choose from calendula, cineraria, English daisy, fairy primrose, Iceland poppy, pansy, snapdragon, stock, sweet William, and viola. For a longer display of flowers in the warmer inland areas, choose from the more heattolerant annuals such as *Chrysanthemum paludosum* and sweet alyssum.

**PLANT SUMMER BULBS.** In the colder areas (*Sunset* zone 14), begonias, caladium, cannas, dahlias, and tuberoses can be planted in flats for a head start. In milder zones, plant these by the end of the month directly in the ground.

**PLANT VEGETABLES.** Set out artichokes and asparagus, and seedlings of broccoli, cabbage, cauliflower, celery (only in *Sunset* zones 15, 16, and 17), green onions, kohlrabi, and lettuce. By the last week of the month, gardeners in milder climates (zones 15, 16, and 17) can set out transplants of eggplant, pepper, and tomatoes.

**PRUNE TREES AND SHRUBS.** If you haven't already pruned your deciduous fruit and ornamental trees, grapes, roses, summer-flowering shrubs, and wisteria, do so by midmonth. Wait until after bloom to prune springflowering plants such as rhododendron.

**SOW VEGETABLES.** Sow seeds of beets, carrots, chard, lettuce, peas, and spinach; they grow easily and are less expensive than transplants. Indoors, start seeds of eggplant, pepper, and tomatoes.

San Rafael

Walnut Creek

Oakland

San Francisco

San Jose

Monterey

**WATER.** If rains are light or separated by long periods, deep-water plants when soil is dry. Be sure to keep seedbeds moist for good germination, and keep seedlings watered until established.

## February Checklist

### CENTRAL VALLEY

☐ **CONTROL SLUGS AND SNAILS.** As nighttime temperatures rise above 40°, slugs and snails become more active and quickly consume flower favorites such as crocus, daffodil, pansy, and primrose, as well as vegetables. To reduce pests, handpick and destroy them at night (with flashlight in hand), when they are most active. Or use beer traps, copper barriers, or commercial baits.

☐ **FERTILIZE PLANTS.** Fall-planted annuals and perennials benefit from feeding now. Also feed established trees and shrubs—if they lack vigor or their leaves look pale—as new growth begins. Wait to feed azaleas, camellias, and rhododendrons until after bloom; use an acid fertilizer. Later this month, feed lawns. If you haven't fed citrus trees, do so now. As the new leaves expand, also apply a liquid spray of micronutrients to the foliage and the roots, following label instructions.

☐ **PLANT FOR SPRING BLOOM.** Choices include bleeding heart, calendula, campanula, candytuft, cineraria, coral bells, dianthus, English daisy, marguerite, pansy, Iceland poppy, English and fairy primroses, forget-me-not, *Primula obconica*, snapdragon, stock, sweet William, and viola.

☐ **PLANT VEGETABLES.** Set out artichokes and asparagus and seedlings of broccoli, cabbage, cauliflower, kohlrabi, lettuce, and green onions. From seeds, plant beets, carrots, chard, lettuce, peas, and spinach. Start eggplant, pepper, and tomato seedlings indoors.

☐ **PRUNE.** If you haven't pruned deciduous trees and shrubs, do so by midmonth. The time to prune spring-flowering plants is after bloom.

☐ **START SUMMER-BLOOMING BULBS.** Start tuberous begonias, calla lilies, cannas, crocosmias, dahlias, gladiolus, tigridia, and tuberoses.

☐ **WEED.** Soon after weeds germinate, hand-pull, hoe, or spray with nontoxic SharpShooter weed killer (made from fatty acids) or more toxic glyphosate. Spray on a calm, dry day; do not let spray drift onto desirable plants.

Redding

Lake Tahoe

Sacramento

Fresno

Bakersfield

☐ **CARE FOR CITRUS.** In the low desert (Sunset climate zone 13), treat mature trees with a complete citrus food according to package directions. Prune lightly to remove dead twigs and to lighten lowest branches. Mulch with ground bark, compost, or similar organic matter.

☐ **FERTILIZE PLANTS.** In coastal (zones 22–24), inland (zones 18–21), and low-desert gardens, feed deciduous fruit trees with a complete fertilizer two to three weeks before they bloom. Feed spring-blooming flowers with a complete fertilizer now.

☐ **PLANT VEGETABLES OUTDOORS.** In coastal, inland, and high-desert (zone 11) gardens, plant seedlings of broccoli, cabbage, chard, chives, endive, lettuce, onions, and parsley. If soil isn't soggy, sow seeds of cool-season plants, including beets, broccoli, carrots, chard, chives, kohlrabi, onion (bulb or green types),

and radishes. In the low desert, many warm-season vegetables, including tomatoes and peppers, can go into the ground after mid-month. Also, consider trying one or more of the perennial vegetables such as artichoke, horseradish, or rhubarb.

☐ **PLANT WINTER COLOR.** In coastal gardens, it's not too late to plant colorful annuals and perennials to bloom now and into the spring. Nurseries offer calendulas, cinerarias, dianthus, English daisies, Iceland poppies, larkspur, pansies, primroses, snapdragons, stock, sweet alyssum, sweet peas, and violas.

☐ **PLANT CAMELLIAS.** There's still time to choose and plant blooming camellias. Before planting, scrape off and dispose of the top inch of soil to eliminate dormant spores of petal blight.

☐ **FINISH SHOPPING FOR BARE-ROOT PLANTS.** Some bare-root plants are still available at nurseries. In addition to roses, you'll find perennial vegetables such as artichokes, asparagus, horseradish, and rhubarb; fruits including cane berries, grapes, and strawberries; and ornamentals such as hardy perennials, shade trees, shrubs, and wisteria vines.

☐ **ORDER SEEDS.** You can still place orders for warm-season flowers and vegetables from mail-order catalogs. Start seeds indoors as soon as they arrive so seedlings will be ready for the garden in six to eight weeks.

☐ **START BULBS.** In coastal and inland areas, you still have time to buy and plant caladium, calla lily, canna, montbretia (Crocosmia), dahlia, gloxinia, Oriental lilies, tigridia, tuberose, and tuberous begonias. Nurseries also still have good supplies of other summer-blooming bulbs such as baboon flower (Babiana), Chinese ground orchid (Bletilla), crinum, gladiolus, and nerine.

☐ **COMPLETE DORMANT-SEASON PRUNING.** Before growth begins this month (depending upon weather), finish pruning deciduous trees, fruit trees, berries, grapes, roses, shrubs, and vines. In late spring, after flowers fade, prune trees and shrubs grown for their spring flowers.

☐ **SPRAY DORMANT PLANTS.** To reduce pest problems from insects such as aphids and scale, and to prevent diseases such as peach leaf curl, spray leafless and dormant fruit trees, roses, and shrubs. Use horticultural oil, or horticultural oil combined with lime sulfur or fixed copper; follow label directions.

☐ **CONTROL SLUGS AND SNAILS.** Control, as described in the January checklist, is an ongoing process. If you use poison bait, place it underneath slightly raised boards so it is inaccessible to birds and pets.

☐ **WATER NATIVE PLANTS.** Unless rains have been heavy, continue watering native and drought-tolerant plants and young plants set out in fall.

Santa Barbara
Pasadena
San Bernardino
Santa Monica
Los Angeles
San Diego

## February Checklist

**HERE IS WHAT NEEDS DOING**

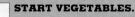

## ANYWHERE IN THE WEST, TACKLE THESE CHORES:

☐ **CLEAN UP HOUSE PLANTS.** Spray off small ones with lukewarm shower water, covering soil in the pot with plastic wrap. Then prune off yellowing and dead leaves, check for insect infestations, and treat if necessary. If you have to spray, first cover the plant with a plastic garment cover—the kind you get from the dry cleaner—to confine the spray to the plant.

☐ **FERTILIZE WINTER RYE LAWNS.** Apply 2½ pounds of ammonium sulfate per 1,000 square feet of lawn. Water afterward.

☐ **ORDER SEED FOR SUMMER.** If you plan to use mail-order seed, order this month, before suppliers start running out of popular and unusual varieties.

☐ **PREPARE SOIL.** To get vegetable and flower beds ready for spring planting, dig in compost or other organic matter when soil can be worked. Add 2 pounds ammonium phosphate and 3 pounds soil sulfur per 100 square feet to increase fertility and adjust pH.

☐ **START VEGETABLES.** You can start seeds of cool-season vegetables indoors late in the month. Try broccoli, cabbage, cauliflower, and Chinese vegetables. Set the vegetables out when they have two sets of true leaves.

## IN THE SOUTHWEST'S LOW DESERT, HERE ARE MORE CHORES:

☐ **CONTROL APHIDS.** Check tender new growth for aphids. When you see them, blast them off with a jet of water and follow up with a spray of insecticidal soap.

☐ **FERTILIZE BEARDED IRIS.** Late in the month, sprinkle complete fertilizer in the soil over the iris rhizomes. Water in well.

☐ **FERTILIZE CITRUS.** If you didn't do it last month, scatter complete fertilizer over the entire root area (everything under the tree's canopy) and water thoroughly.

☐ **FERTILIZE ROSES.** Pick a day late in February when nighttime temperatures are expected to remain above freezing. Water established roses, let the soil drain, apply complete fertilizer, and water again.

☐ **MAINTAIN DRIP SYSTEMS.** Now, before you need them, clean or replace your drip system's filters. Then turn on the system and check each emitter. When you find one that can't be unclogged, install a new emitter next to it.

☐ **PLANT GROUND COVERS, VINES.** Set out Hall's honeysuckle, perennial verbena, star jasmine, trailing indigo bush, and *Vinca major* or *V. minor*.

☐ **PLANT PERENNIAL WILDFLOWERS.** For bloom this spring, set out desert marigold, evening primrose, penstemon, and salvia.

*Luscious pink blooms of 'Fantin-Latour' unfurl as cups of folded petals, typical of centifolia roses.*

# Antique *Roses*

## *for today's gardens. Grow them for their beauty, fragrance, and history*

### *By Kathleen Norris Brenzel*

RENEE LYNN

NORMAN A. PLATE

*Creamy white blooms come in clusters on 'Nastarana' (1879), a musk hybrid.*

O n a warm spring day, delicious fragrances float in the air above a sunny clearing in a valley near the California coast. It's bloom time in this 1-acre display garden at the Wiley family's Roses of Yesterday and Today, and roses are unfurling with perfumed madness, attracting visitors from around the world. They come to amble among the blossoms, to sniff, and to take photographs.

"I had no trouble finding the garden," says one visitor as she steps out of a sports car. "I just rolled down the windows and followed my nose."

Much of this heady fragrance comes from the Wileys' collection of antique roses (also called old garden roses)— ones belonging to classes that were developed before 1867, the year that 'La France', the first hybrid tea, ushered in the era of modern roses. As with other commercial growers of old roses, the Wileys' love of these historic beauties grew into a business.

*As they age, the flaming orange petals of Austrian Copper rose (R. foetida 'Bicolor') drop, leaving behind starbursts of yellow stamens.*

As Pat Wiley leads this visitor through the forest of shrubs, ramblers, and climbers, each cloaked with sumptuous blossoms, she introduces her favorite roses as though they are old friends: 'Baronne Prévost' is "perfection itself," 'Petite de Hollande' has "buds that hold their shape beautifully when dried in potpourri," and 'Salet' is "my favorite old moss." In the garden's center, white-flowered *Rosa moschata* scrambles up a tall, rusted windmill "in memory of a cow named Rosey who used to live here." Just down the hill, 'Maréchal Niel' drapes its long canes over an old apple tree and dangles its yellow blossoms above eye level ("the flowers seem to follow you, like they're watching you," Wiley says).

*Heavily perfumed blooms make 'La Reine' (hybrid perpetual) a choice rose for potpourri.*

As bustling as their garden is on this bright spring day, for the Wileys, winters are the busiest time of year. That's when they ship some 95,000 bare-root plants, grown in fields near Wasco, California, to gardeners around the country. (February is not too late to order old roses for blooms in your own garden by late spring.)

The Wileys and other growers report rising demand

for old roses. What accounts for their renewed popularity? "There's such an interest in old things now—art, furniture, family heirlooms. I get calls from couples who are restoring Victorian houses in San Francisco. They want roses that are in keeping with the period architecture, the gingerbread trim, and the lace curtains."

Indeed there's magic to growing roses so steeped in history: the musk rose immortalized by Shakespeare in *A Midsummer Night's Dream,* for example, or the Rose of Castile brought to California by Spanish missionaries in the 1700s ("hardly a mission garden was without one," Wiley notes), or the Harison's Yellow rose pioneers brought West in their covered wagons.

The names of many old roses suggest regal elegance and romance: 'Prince Camille de Rohan', 'Empress Josephine', 'Belle Amour'. But their names don't begin to describe the delicious fragrances of many of these old charmers—the fruitiness of ripe apples, the spiciness of cloves, or the heady sweetness of the most floral perfume. Neither do they evoke the beauty of their blooms—big, loose cabbages, short-petaled powder puffs, or single-petaled starbursts—nor their range of colors, from creamy white to bright orange to pink striped with cherry red, like ribbon candy.

There's a stately grace to the plants themselves, and many kinds possess the toughness and disease resistance that have made them survivors.

How do you choose from so many kinds now available? We asked Wiley and other growers around the West to name some of their favorites ("about as easy as singling out your favorite child," one commented). The box on the opposite page lists 18 kinds; use it as a guide to get started. Order plants now (sources are listed at top right) and plant as soon as you get them.

## Choosing the best types for your garden

Old roses range widely in habit. There are compact, 4-foot shrubs with wide clusters of small flowers (China roses). And then there are taller, 5- to 8-foot shrubs with big, opulent, often very fragrant flowers (hybrid perpetuals). You'll also find vigorous, somewhat gangly shrubs with cup-shaped blooms (Bourbons).

Some old roses (albas, damasks, gallicas, centifolias, and most moss roses) bloom only once a year. Others, including most Bourbons, Chinas, hybrid perpetuals, hybrid musks, rugosas, and teas, are repeat bloomers; choose these for prominent spots in the garden.

Choose roses that are most suited to your climate. China, Noisette, and tea roses, for example, are somewhat

*A bucket of blooms shows just a few of Pat Wiley's treasured old roses from her display garden near Watsonville, California.*

*Climbing 'New Dawn' scrambles over a weathered split-rail fence.*

NORMAN A. PLATE

RENEE LYNN

tender and thrive only in mild-winter climates, or in greenhouses. Bourbons, hybrid perpetuals, and Portlands are somewhat hardier but still need protection in cold-winter areas. The hardiest ones for the West's coldest climates (Alaska, Colorado) include autumn damasks, gallicas, centifolias, and species roses such as *Rosa rugosa* and its hybrids.

## Where to buy old roses

Well-stocked nurseries are beginning to sell some old roses. But for the best selection, order bare-root plants by mail. The following five suppliers offer good selections. Expect to pay $9 to $10 per plant, plus shipping.

**Greenmantle Nursery,** 3010 Ettersburg Rd., Garberville, Calif. 95542; (707) 986-7504. About 275 kinds; ships from January into early April. For a list, send a self-addressed, stamped envelope.

**Heritage Rose Gardens,** 16831 Mitchell Creek Dr., Fort Bragg, Calif. 95437. Lists more than 200 old roses. Catalog $1.50.

**High Country Rosarium,** 1717 Downing St., Denver, Colo. 80218; (303) 832-4026. Mostly wholesale, but will fill individual orders of 10 or more roses. Free catalog lists about 120 kinds. Ships year-round.

**Roses of Yesterday and Today,** 802 Brown's Valley Rd., Watsonville, Calif. 95076; (408) 724-3537. More than 250 kinds of old, rare, and fragrant roses; ships January through May. It also sells some plants in containers through September; it's open from 9 to 3 weekdays, and during the first three weekends in May (call to check hours). Catalog $3 shipped book rate, $5 first class.

**Vintage Gardens,** 3003 Pleasant Hill Rd., Sebastopol, Calif. 95472; (707) 829-5342. About 900 roses (most, but not all, are antique; some are in limited supply); ships January and February. Free list; catalog $4. ■

# Best of the old roses? Here are rosarians' favorites

## Best for beginners

**'Alfred de Dalmas'** (hybrid moss, 1855). "A charming rose with fragrant blush pink to white blooms. It's compact—great for small gardens—and tough."—*Pat Wiley, Watsonville, California*

**'Jacques Cartier'** (also called 'Marquise Boccella', 1842). "Cup-shaped pink flowers are packed with petals, all folded inside. Plant is a repeat bloomer."—*Joyce Demits, Fort Bragg, California*

**'Souvenir de la Malmaison'** (Bourbon, 1843). "It's easy, even in containers. I've grown it in a big pot for 25 years, and it blooms twice a year."—*J. D.*

**'Reine des Violettes'** (hybrid perpetual, 1860). "Thornless, easy to grow, always in bloom. The most blue of all roses."—*P. W.*

## Unforgettable fragrance

**'Baronne Prévost'** (hybrid perpetual, 1842). "Big, open flowers with many small, tightly packed rose-pink petals that are very perfumy."—*P. W.*

**'Boule de Neige'** (Bourbon, 1867). "Everybody's favorite. Snowy white, camellia-like blooms smell like cold cream."—*P. W.*

**R. eglanteria** (sweet briar, before 1551). "Should be in every big garden against a back fence where its marvelous, fruity, ripe-apple fragrance can waft across to patios and into open windows."—*P. W.*

**'La Reine'** (hybrid perpetual, 1842). "Heavy damask fragrance is very pleasing to the nose."—*P. W.*

**'Sombreuil'** (climbing tea, 1850). "The most fragrant of all teas. One bloom will fragrance a room."—*P. W.*

**Musk rose** (*R. moschata*, ancient). "Pungently fragrant, single white blossoms smell spicy—like allspice or cloves; the scent lingers with you long after you've left the flowers."—*J. D.*

**'Charles de Mills'** (gallica, early 1800s). "Deep rose pink blooms have a heavy, fruity scent."—*William Campbell, Denver*

## Standouts in desert heat

**'La Reine Victoria'** (Bourbon, 1872). "Stands regal and unwilted in spite of high temperatures and little rain."—*P. W.*

**'Madame Hardy'** (damask, 1832). "Big bush is very hardy; its gorgeous, soft white blooms have green button eyes."—*Peggy Jones, Glendale, Arizona*

**Lady Banks' rose** (*R. banksiae*, 1824). Vigorous climber with clusters of small yellowish blooms. "Well known in the desert; will take off and cover a fence in no time."—*P. J.*

## Cold-hardy favorites

**Austrian Copper** (*R. foetida* 'Bicolor', before 1590). "Huge old plants have been known to overwinter without protection."—*P. W.*

**'Banshee'** (damask, 1928). Not technically an antique, but it's great for the intermountain West. "It's tough and can survive without much water. You can smell its blooms a mile away. And it's especially forgiving in gardens above 6,000 feet."—*W. C.*

**Harison's Yellow** (*R. foetida* hybrid, 1830). "Vigorous bush with cheerful yellow blooms. It's one of the first to bloom in Colorado."—*W. C.*

**R. glauca** (species, before 1830). "The coloring of the bush makes this a stunner; small, pink, star-shaped blooms are followed by hips that start orange, then turn bright red. Beautiful plum-tinged leaves turn orange in fall."—*Brenda Mowery, Denver*

*A garland of dried roses adds a touch of spring to a straw garden hat. Wiley is in the process of experimenting with freeze-drying roses to keep their colors intact.*

# 43 yards of compost and 3 weekends

*Started from bare ground, this Santa Barbara, California garden yields vegetables year-round*

A FRENCH POTAGER (kitchen garden) inspired the design of this Santa Barbara vegetable garden. In wedge-shaped beds, owners Peggy and Bryan Rishe grow vegetables year-round. Since the garden is all organic, it's also a haven for birds, butterflies, and beneficial insects. "We've managed to create a little slice of nature in suburbia," says Peggy Rishe.

Creating the garden was a challenge for the Rishes, both first-time gardeners and recent transplants from the Midwest. "We had a clear idea of what we wanted, but we literally didn't know the difference between a seed and a bulb," Peggy Rishe says.

Before they started the project, she read every garden book and catalog she could get her hands on and took adult education classes in gardening. Soon she was hooked. "I was raised in a farming town; I guess learning about gardening brought out the dormant farmer in me."

At first, the Rishes were going to put in a lawn, but once the project was under way, they decided that grass would demand too much water and maintenance without giving anything in return ("You can't eat grass clippings," Bryan Rishe observes). That's when the vegetable garden idea took shape.

**FIRST HARVEST** *of ripe, red 'Celebrity', 'Lorissa', and 'Marmande' tomatoes will be a taste treat.*

**TO BLANCH STALKS,** *trench-planted leeks are covered with mulch (to a 6-inch depth) as they grow.*

## IMPROVING THE SOIL TOOK THREE WEEKENDS

The first step was to improve their adobe soil. During construction of their house, the topsoil had been scraped off and the remaining soil was compacted. For three weekends, the Rishes shoveled in 33 yards of mushroom compost and manure, 14 yards of sand, and 10 yards of redwood compost.

To counteract the garden's rectangular shape, the Rishes formed wedge-shaped beds bordered by crisscrossing, wood-chip-covered paths.

Then the planting began. To get the greatest selection, Peggy Rishe started plants from seed, and she's always trying new kinds.

For summer harvest, she grows five successive plantings of yellow, white, and bi-color sugar-enhanced corn ('Miracle' is her favorite); six kinds of basil; high-yield

**BOUNTIFUL VEGETABLE GARDEN** *has narrow rows for easy tending. Flowers around the perimeter add color and attract beneficial insects.*

and rely very little on commercial fertilizers.

***Rotate crops.*** To discourage crop disease, the Rishes rotate beds so no vegetable is planted in the same site longer than three years in a row.

***Choose flowering plants that attract beneficial insects.*** Encircling the vegetables are flowers to attract and maintain the beneficial insects that Peggy Rishe introduces in spring, as well as ones that arrive on their own. She also grows the flowers for drying.

She finds that perennials such as asters, tansy (if you have room), and yarrow are more effective than annuals like marigolds. She also allows some of the carrots, Chinese chives, cilantro, dill, and parsnips to flower; these also attract beneficial insects.

***Use least-toxic pest controls.*** To control aphids, mites, thrips, and whiteflies, she released green lacewing eggs and trichogramma wasps (1,000 of each every other week for six weeks). She already had ladybugs from previous introductions. She handpicks beetles and caterpillars and sets out sticky traps for whiteflies and thrips, and beer traps for snails.

She doesn't try to completely eradicate insect pests, so that beneficial insects will have a continual food source. She doesn't use toxic chemicals. For serious outbreaks, she spot-sprays as needed with *Bacillus thuringiensis*, insecticidal soap (mixed with rubbing alcohol for whiteflies), and pyrethrum.

***Drip irrigate.*** The entire garden is watered with ooze tubing. Each bed is on a separate line and turned on manually, so plants get just the amount of water they need when they need it, not according to a schedule. ■

*By Lauren Bonar Swezey*

'Early Pride' cucumber; 'Celebrity', 'Lorissa', and 'Marmande' tomatoes ('Lorissa' and 'Marmande' are high producers, but not as flavorful as 'Celebrity') and 'Macero II' paste tomatoes; 'Ambrosia' melons; 'Sunburst' squash; and a rainbow of sweet peppers.

She is always plugging in new plants. She grows lettuce in the shade of corn, and successive plantings of carrots as a border around several beds.

## STRATEGY FOR AN ORGANIC GARDEN

"People think that growing everything organically is difficult, but we found it cheaper, easier, and more healthful than traditional methods. Lots of products and tricks can help," explains Peggy Rishe. Here are some of the most successful.

***Enhance the soil regularly with compost.*** Before planting, the Rishes mix in compost, which they make in their barrel composter with garden waste and manure from their two rabbits. After planting, they add a 3-inch layer of mulch. To further increase nitrogen and organic matter in the soil, they plant a different bed each fall with a cover crop of clover, hairy vetch, and buckwheat, which they turn under in spring.

Building up the soil has paid off. They now have an active earthworm population

**MADAME GANNA WALSKA** *posed beside spined agave in 1957, on her 70th birthday.*

# Lotusland

*Once a private estate, this piece of historic Santa Barbara is a one-stop botanical tour of the world—now open for viewing*

F EW OTHER GARDENS ON EARTH CAN MATCH the artful eccentricity of Lotusland, a 37-acre estate garden in Montecito, near Santa Barbara, California. Here, extraordinary plants from around the world are displayed with unconventional grandeur among such novel garden ornaments as large hunks of uncut amethyst. It's a garden that could happen only in Southern California: heavenly climate made it possible for the late Madame Ganna Walska, an eccentric Polish opera diva with seemingly unlimited resources and an unleashed passion for plants, to create this horticultural treasure.

When Walska settled into her estate in 1941, she veered to horticulture from a colorful past as an international socialite with a persistent though lackluster opera career. She spent the last four decades of her life amassing plants and orchestrating her garden creations with the help of several talented landscape architects.

After Walska died in 1984 at the age of 97, Lotusland was entrusted to the nonprofit foundation that manages it today. It opens to the

**LOTUS** *flower in summer.*

WATER GARDEN *teeming with lilies and lotus reflects a backdrop of towering trees and the 1920s bathhouse; part of the water garden originally was a swimming pool.*

public this month for its first full season of tours.

## A PLANT FANTASYLAND

Tours start at a new visitor center fashioned after the estate's 1920s Spanish colonial revival bathhouse, designed by George Washington Smith. The newly planted Australian garden that surrounds the center contrasts dramatically with the long-established plantings beyond the entrance.

Manicured paths weave through 13 distinctive gardens. Two of the more fanciful are the theater garden, a tiered performance area where a troupe of 17th-century stone figures resides on the lawn against a backdrop of fern pines, and the nearby topiary garden, where large evergreen animals graze around a giant in-ground clock.

The luminescent blue garden is home to some of the oldest trees on the grounds. Magnificent Chilean wine palms tower alongside blue Atlas cedars. The palms were planted 100 years ago by R. Kinton Stevens, a pioneer nurseryman and the estate's first owner. Walska added a dense ground cover of ornamental blue fescue and the blue-gray succulent *Senecio mandraliscae*. Like rough-cut chunks off an iceberg, large pieces

WILLIAM B. DEWEY

**FLAILING ARMS** *of thriving Euphorbia ingens greet visitors near entrance to Lotusland's villa.*

of blue-green glass from a bottling company edge the path and mirror the plantings.

Other gardens are strictly Madame Walska, with crafty disregard for conventional taste. In the aloe garden, for example, Walska grouped more than 100 kinds of aloes, both tree and ground-hugging types, with spiny, fleshy sword-shaped leaves and flower spikes of vermilion, coral, and yellow. At the heart of this alluring, almost eerie garden lies a shallow concrete pond filled with milky blue water. Two giant clamshell fountains spill water into the pond, and lustrous abalone shells fringe its edges.

Lotusland's pink stucco villa, first designed in 1919, serves as a colorful foil to one of the most bizarre yet regal plantings. An army of spiny golden barrel cactus marches down the drive and through the courtyard to the villa's entranceway, where it is halted by towering *Euphorbia ingens* plants. Their long, undulating arms reach rooftop height only to twist and plunge earthward, finally snaking along the ground. The villa is now the foundation office, not open for touring.

Horticulturists consider Walska's cycad garden, developed in the late 1970s, the crème de la crème of the landscape. More than 370 specimens rise from grassy hummocks. With their stiff, green featherlike fronds topping coarse, stout trunks, they look at first glance like chubby palms, but these are primitive cone-bearing plants more closely related to conifers. This collection is one of the finest in the world and home to the rarest of cycads, including *Encephalartos woodii*, which is now extinct in the wild.

And the garden's namesake lotuses? They were introduced to California by Kinton Stevens in 1893. At one time, Walska had an acre or so in bloom, with their huge round leaves waving on slender stalks above the water. Today, they grow in fewer numbers in the Japanese garden pond and in the lavish water garden near the bathhouse. Also growing in the water garden are water lilies, including the giant Amazon water lily, which has leaves 5 feet across; reeds; and an island of papyrus.

## ARRANGING YOUR VISIT

Garden tours are by reservation only. A restricted number of visitors are allowed to visit Lotusland each year, so plan well ahead and be patient—a visit is worth the wait.

The garden is open from February 15 through November 15. Tours, at 10 and 1:30 Wednesdays through Saturdays, last $1\frac{1}{2}$ to 2 hours and are led by trained docents. Saturdays are booked through midsummer, although an occasional cancellation may open up a space.

Admission ranges from $6 (with three or more people per car) to $10 (with one person per car). Children under 12 are not allowed. To reserve a tour, call (805) 969-9990 weekdays between 9 and noon, or write to Tour Reservations, Ganna Walska Lotusland, 695 Ashley Rd., Santa Barbara, Calif. 93108. Once you reserve a space, the foundation will send directions. ■

*By Lynn Ocone*

**FANTASTIC ALOE FOREST** *encloses a shallow pool ringed with pearlescent abalone shells. Water spills from a giant clamshell fountain and laps at the feet of tufa rocks.*

# Nothing's subtle about statice

*Showy blooms in vibrant colors are long-lasting in bouquets and in the garden*

K. BRYAN SWEZEY

**IN A PATIO POCKET**, *Limonium perezii sends up airy clusters of papery purple blooms. The plants tolerate some drought.*

**BASKET** *holds Limonium sinuatum flowers in mixed colors, and purple and white L. perezii. The long, lavender-rose spikes to the right of the basket are L. suworowii.*
DARROW M. WATT

IN GARDENS AND IN florists' bouquets, statice (*Limonium*) is no shrinking violet. Its vibrant blooms announce their presence in shades of bright white to deep purple. Drifts of naturalized purple *L. perezii* thrive in wind and salt spray along the California coast from Monterey to San Diego, and flowers of the annual *L. sinuatum* are staples of florists for their long-lasting beauty in bouquets. These and the statice listed here are good for cutting, are mostly easy to grow, and air-dry well.

Appearance varies by species, but most have basal rosette-forming leaves and clusters of small papery flowers on nearly leafless stems.

Plants require excellent drainage and full sun (light afternoon shade in hot inland climates). They tolerate heat; once established, the perennials withstand some drought.

Nurseries sell a few types of statice. Seed catalogs offer the best selection; now is the time to order. Since seeds are slow to germinate (two to three weeks), it's best to start them indoors about eight weeks before planting outdoors. Transplant them in April in mildest climates, May elsewhere.

## ANNUALS FOR QUICK COLOR

**L. sinuatum** (also sold as *L. sinuata*) has deeply lobed leaves. Flowers open in flat clusters atop rigid, branching stems; they come in white, yellow, pink, apricot, blue, and lavender, and seeds are available in mixed or individual colors. Most of these plants reach 24 to 30 inches tall; dwarf strains are 10 to 12 inches. Cut flowers often to encourage more blooms.

**L. suworowii** (also called *Psylliostachys suworowii* and Russian statice) has slender 1½-foot spikes of tiny lavender-pink or bright rose flowers. Stems may be single or branched, gracefully twisting and curving as they grow.

## PERENNIALS FOR REPEAT PERFORMANCE

With the exception of *L. sinense* (also sold as *L. sinensis*), which blooms the first year from seed, these statices bloom in their second year.

**L. latifolium** develops an airy 3-foot-wide cloud of flowers over a base of 10-inch oblong leaves; flowers may be bluish or shades of pink. The plant grows to 2½ feet high. It is not suitable in *Sunset* climate zones 11, 12, and 13.

**L. perezii,** shown above, is a dependable plant for mild-climate California (it is damaged by temperatures below 25°). Deep green leaves grow to 1 foot long. Purple flowers with tiny white throats bloom over a long season in clusters on stems up to 3 feet tall; flower mass can measure 3 feet across. Nursery-grown plants are readily available and fast-growing.

**L. sinense** grows to 1½ feet with multiple branches bearing clusters of white flowers with yellow throats.

**L. tataricum** (also called German statice) is similar to *L. latifolium,* but the plant (10 to 18 inches tall) and flowers (whitish to light blue) are smaller and stems are stiffer.

## CATALOG SEED SOURCES

**Park Seed Co.** Cokesbury Rd., Greenwood, S.C. 29647; (800) 845-3369 (free catalog).
**Shepherd's Garden Seeds.** 6116 Highway 9, Felton, Calif. 95018; (408) 335-6910 (catalog $1).
**Thompson & Morgan.** Dept. 164-4, Jackson, N.J. 08527; (800) 274-7333 (free catalog). ■

*By Lynn Ocone*

AT ELK ROCK, *giant trunks cast long shadows across a lightly frosted lawn, and crocus and winter aconite (Eranthis hyemalis, inset) create little pockets of bright color.*

# Winter magic in Portland's great public gardens

*Visit them now and you'll come home with ideas for winter-blooming bulbs and shrubs to brighten your own garden*

IN FEBRUARY, Portland's public gardens take on a special beauty. On some days, the low winter sun casts long shadows across lawn that is greener than green or, perhaps, blanketed with snow. Dark branches make a filigree against a regularly brooding sky. Evergreens glisten with rain or sparkle with tiny frost crystals. Here and there, spots of color catch your eye, and traces of fragrance delight your nose. Witch hazels, early camellias, and viburnums vie for the pollinating attention of the few insects hardy and brave enough to fly through the chilly breezes.

Gone are the hordes of picture-snapping visitors who tour the gardens when spring brings on the greatest color show. Silence prevails, and the void is gently filled with sounds of birds, squir-rels, water, and wind.

And, with annuals gone, perennials down, and deciduous leaves fallen and raked, you see the workings of a garden and its structure.

Here we note the season's highlights at five great gardens. Wear warm clothes, take a notebook and camera to record ideas, and bring a winter picnic if you like. Area code is 503.

At *Washington Park International Rose Test Garden,* you'll see how hybrid teas are pruned and climbers trellised and tied. And you'll see how large geometric evergreens, such as chamaecparis, cryptomeria, incense cedar, and even holly, can anchor a garden through the winter— giving form to the scramble of naked branches and the long beds of brown earth.

Washington Park, at 400 S.W. Kingston Avenue (823-3636), is open 7 A.M. to 9 P.M.

MICHAEL THOMPSON

**FLOWERS OF FEBRUARY** *include giant snowdrop (Galanthus elwesii), above, and an old cherry red Camellia japonica.*

daily. Admission is free.

*Berry Botanic Garden* offers similar lessons in its trough garden. Here you'll see how large, uniform stones add form to the winter garden, and how alpines shine and color up in winter cold. And you'll see the plump buds of the garden's more than 20 varieties of magnolias, firm and ready to pop, standing like candles on elaborate candelabra.

The garden is at 11505 S.W. Summerville Avenue; call 636-4112 for an appointment and directions (the garden is a bit hard to find). It's open Mondays through Saturdays during daylight hours. Admission costs $2.

*Bishop's Close at Elk Rock,* a 13-acre estate started in the early 20th century, contains trees that are now among the oldest and handsomest specimens in the Northwest. Beds that are brimful with perennials in warm months now host sweeps of crocus, galanthus, hellebores, and winter-blooming iris.

Elk Rock, at 11800 S.W. Military Lane (636-5613), is open daily during daylight hours. Admission is free, though contributions are welcome.

At *Leach Botanical Gar-*

*den,* February fragrance hovers in the morning fog. The first plants to flaunt their perfume are viburnums—*V. grandiflorum* and *V. farreri.* Then come *Chimonanthus praecox, Sarcococca confusa,* and a huddle of witch hazels. The unexpected scents are accompanied by vivid colors in the twigs and bark.

The garden, at 6704 S.E. 122nd Avenue (761-9503), is open 9 to 4 Tuesdays through Saturdays, 1 to 4 Sundays. Admission is free.

*Hoyt Arboretum* is filled with evergreens from around the world, including Northwest natives such as Brewer's weeping spruce and Sitka spruce. They darken the sky, grow frighteningly active in a strong wind, and fill the air with their woodsy odors. From U.S. Highway 26, take the Washington Park/Knight Boulevard exit north. The arboretum is open 6 A.M. to 10 P.M. daily. Admission is free. For details, call 823-3654. ∎

*By Steven R. Lorton*

**IN WASHINGTON PARK** *rose test garden, snow dusts upright sticks of pruned hybrid tea roses. Conifers border the garden.*

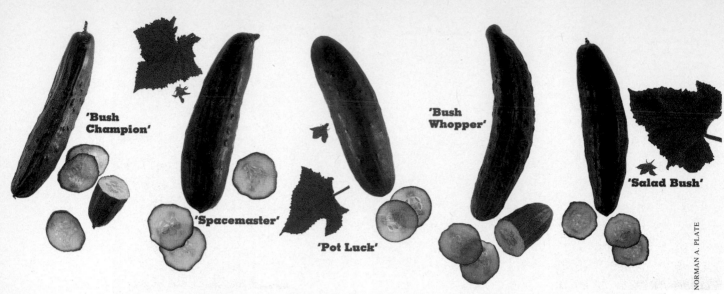

'Bush Champion'

'Spacemaster'

'Pot Luck'

'Bush Whopper'

'Salad Bush'

NORMAN A. PLATE

SLICING CUCUMBERS *from bush plants are ready to harvest when 7 inches long.*

# Cucumbers under control

*These bush varieties fit small spaces. Now's the time to order seeds*

I F YOUR GARDEN IS small, and thoughts of sprawling vines deter you from growing cucumbers, consider a bush variety. A compact plant thrives in a container or in the ground and yields about two dozen or more sweet, juicy fruits per season.

To find how bush cucumbers compared for plant size, vigor, disease resistance, productivity, and flavor, we planted seeds of seven varieties—including two pickling types. We sowed seeds last spring, after danger of frost had passed, in *Sunset*'s Menlo Park, California, test garden. Here's what we learned.

Plants ranged from 24 to 88 inches across. Generally, the larger the plant, the more cu-cumbers it produced. 'Bush Baby', a pickler, was the most vigorous, longest-lived, and largest—not compact by our measurements. We harvested 99 cucumbers from the 88-inch plant. 'Bush Pickle' produced 34 cucumbers and measured 48 inches.

Among the slicing cucumbers, 'Bush Champion' topped the list at 43 cucumbers and 64 inches. Runners-up for fruit count were 'Salad Bush' (35 cucumbers, 44 inches), 'Bush Whopper' (28 cucumbers, 46 inches), 'Spacemaster' (20 cucumbers, 36 inches), and 'Pot Luck' (18 cucumbers, 24 inches).

'Bush Champion' and 'Salad Bush' ranked tops for sweet flavor in our tastings. Generally, flavor differences among slicers were subtle.

Plants are most productive when young. As they age, pests and disease diminish plant vigor, and fruit flavor and texture decline. Even varieties labeled disease resistant eventually succumb. For maximum production through the summer, plant in succession two to three weeks apart; pull out older plants as they become tired or diseased.

## CUCUMBER CULTURE

Now is the time to order seeds. To get a jump on spring, start some indoors three to four weeks before the date of last frost in your area. Plant two seeds in a 4-inch container; when plants show their first true leaves, thin to one strong seedling. For later plantings, sow in the garden.

Cucumbers require full sun, fertile soil, and a steady supply of water. Fruits from water-stressed plants taste bland or bitter. Avoid overhead irrigation—it encourages disease. Mulch to conserve water. The mulch also keeps fruit off the ground; contact with soil turns it yellow.

Pick every other day during the harvest season. If cucumbers are left on the vine, production drops dramatically. Slicers are best when about 7 inches long and no more than 2 inches in diameter. Harvest picklers at 4 inches long.

## SEED SOURCES

Varieties described here are found among these mail-order catalogs. Catalogs are free unless noted.

*Henry Field's Seed & Nursery Co.,* 415 N. Burnett St., Shenandoah, Iowa 51602; (605) 665-9391. *Ornamental Edibles,* 3622 Weedin Court, San Jose, Calif. 95132 (catalog $2). *Park Seed Co.,* Cokesbury Rd., Greenwood, S.C. 29647; (800) 845-3369. *W. Atlee Burpee & Co.,* 300 Park Ave., Warminster, Pa. 18991; (800) 888-1447. ∎

*By Lynn Ocone*

'Bush Baby'

'Bush Pickle'

SIMILAR IN NAME *but not in plant size: 'Bush Baby' grows 7 feet across, 'Bush Pickle' just 4 feet. Harvest pickling cucumbers when 4 inches long.*

AGRICULTURAL RESEARCH SERVICE/USDA

**AFRICANIZED HONEYBEE,** *enlarged above, looks the same as its familiar European cousin.*

# Here come the dreaded "killer" bees

*Experts offer help in understanding the habits of these Africanized honeybees*

THE 35-YEAR migration started in Brazil, hit Texas in 1990, then spread to Arizona last summer and New Mexico last fall. Now, the much-feared Africanized honeybees—called killer bees—are moving into Southern California. At press time, these bees were ¼ mile from the Imperial County line, and were predicted to arrive this spring. The bees are expected to expand their range by 100 to 300 miles a year, spreading throughout the mild-winter West and beyond.

Here is advice from experts with UC Cooperative Extension and the California Department of Food and Agriculture to help you coexist safely with these bees.

### WHO ARE THESE BEES?

Africanized honeybees look like the European honeybees now commonly found in our gardens, and like their relatives, they make honey. They are fairly docile when they are foraging, but they defend their nests ferociously. And though their "killer" reputation has been exaggerated, people who work or play outdoors risk being stung.

Like ordinary honeybees, Africanized bees sting only once, and their venom is no more toxic than that of ordinary honeybees. But Africanized bees are more sensitive to disturbance and react defensively when people or animals get too close to their nests. They sense activity, like children running, 50 feet or more from the nest, and vibrations from power equipment 100 feet or more away. Once disturbed, they may pursue a victim—by the hundreds—for ¼ mile or more.

The bees pose the greatest threat to those unable to flee an attack, particularly children, the elderly, and confined pets. In severe encounters, the number of stings received usually ranges between 200 and 300 (although incidents of 1,000 and more stings have been reported). Individuals not allergic to bees have survived more than 500 stings with prompt medical care.

### WHERE THEY HIDE

Africanized bees are less discriminating about nesting sites than European honeybees are. They make nests in containers and in walls or trees with entranceways ¼ inch or larger. They swarm to form new colonies more frequently, resulting in more nests in a given area.

To eliminate potential nesting sites around your house and garden, seal openings in walls, vents, and tree cavities with ⅛-inch hardware cloth. Or use wood or caulking to plug holes in areas that don't require ventilation. Remove all empty containers and debris piles.

From spring to fall, when bees are more likely to swarm, check your garden weekly. Bees repeatedly entering or leaving an area can indicate an active nest. If you see a nest or swarm, call a structural pest control company or your county agricultural commissioner's office.

Use caution when working outdoors or when entering outbuildings where bees may nest. Listen for the sound of buzzing, and look around the whole property for bees before turning on power equipment. Keep an escape route and shelter in mind.

### BEE STINGS

If you know you are allergic to bee stings, consult your doctor about bee sting kits.

Whether you're allergic or not, if bees attack, run for cover. Protect your face with clothing, and seek shelter quickly in a building or car.

Don't swat at bees or try to pull a victim to safety in the midst of an attack, or you will be stung, too. If you have quick access to a blanket, throw it over the victim to prevent further stings. Call 911 or emergency services if the victim needs help.

As soon as the victim is sheltered from the bees, remove the stingers. Use your fingernail, the edge of a credit card, or a knife blade to scrape the stingers from the skin. Squeezing or pulling a stinger releases more venom.

Once stingers are removed, wash the wounds with soap and water. Apply an ice pack to diminish pain and swelling. For 15 or more stings, or if breathing is difficult, seek immediate medical care. ∎

*By Lynn Ocone*

ALTERNATING ROWS *of lettuces and other greens create a striking edible tapestry. For details on this colorful salad garden, see page 60.*

# MARCH

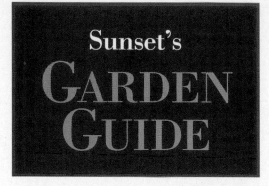

# Sunset's
# GARDEN GUIDE

# Planting, planting, planting: March provides weather and incentive

RUSS A. WIDSTRAND

**M**arch is a month of contrasts in the West. In the mountains it may feature snow, while wildflowers bloom in the desert. Northwesterners enjoy the first crocuses; daffodils and late camellias are at peak in northern California; while in the southern part of the state winter-flowering annuals have reached a colorful crescendo. There's no shortage of things to do in the March garden—from late pruning, bare-root planting, and dividing to planting of warm-season annuals and summer vegetables. It all depends on where you live.

### Celebrating the blues

In garden beds, some plant partners play off each other to create splendid overall effects. The planting pictured above marries two handsome performers, both with lavender-blue flowers: pride of Madeira and sea lavender. You can start both in your garden this month.

Pride of Madeira (*Echium fastuosum*), a shrubby perennial, is excellent in coastal gardens. Several heavy branches grow from the base to 3 to 6 feet tall. Leaves—hairy, gray-green, and narrow—combine to form roundish, irregular mounds at branch tips. The magnificent flower spikes appear in midspring and continue to bloom as late as June. Each spike carries hundreds of ½-inch-long flowers. After the last flowers fade away, cut off the entire spike.

Sea lavender (*Limonium perezii*) grows about a foot tall.

Its bloom begins slightly later and lasts much longer than pride of Madeira, sometimes well into summer and again in fall. Flower stalks are some 3 feet tall, topped with clouds of tiny lavender-blue and white flowers. The long-lasting flowers retain their color after drying.

Pride of Madeira and sea lavender tolerate heat, sun, and drought once established. Both plants do well on slopes. Pride of Madeira costs $11

to $15 for a 5-gallon plant; gallon-size pots of sea lavenders cost $4 to $6.—*Michael MacCaskey*

### A profusion of picklers

"Cornichons are incredibly vigorous plants," says gardener Bud Stuckey, who grew these baby cucumbers last summer in the garden he tends at *Sunset*'s headquarters in Menlo Park, California.

*LAVENDER-BLUE SPIRES of pride of Madeira tower over a bed of sea lavender, a rich springtime accent for this coastal Southern California home.*

## Orchids outdoors in winter? Try cymbidiums

They look like hothouse lovelies, with waxy flowers clustered like so many butterflies atop gracefully arching stems. But cymbidiums are surprisingly tough. In mild-winter coastal belts, you can grow these orchids outdoors all winter (they thrive in cool temperatures—60° to 85° during the day, 40° to 60° at night).

From January into mid-March, the bloom season of the earliest foot-tall miniatures overlaps with that of the 4-foot standards. Both present their full range of flower colors—from soft pastel pinks to bright yellow, lime green, and deep burgundy or rust. This month, while most varieties are blooming, is a good time to add a plant to your garden. Nurseries sell miniatures in 8-inch pots or gallon cans ($15 to $25), standards in 1- or 2-gallon cans ($25 to $30).

*PRIME FOR PICKLING, these tiny cornichons measure just about an inch long.*

"They produced, and produced, and produced."

If you're a fan of these dense-fleshed mini-picklers, now is the time to order seeds. Plant cornichons after the soil warms and danger of frost has passed.

If slugs and snails are not a problem in your garden, you can sow directly in the soil. If they are troublesome, give plants a head start by planting them indoors about three weeks before transplanting them into the garden. They require full sun, fertile soil, and consistent moisture. Mulch around plants to conserve moisture.

It's best to grow these sprawlers in a cage or on a trellis where you can harvest the fruits easily (Stuckey planted two seedlings inside a cage). The plants cling and climb on their own.

As plants mature, check them daily for fruit. For pickling, pick fruits when they are an inch or so long. Larger, 2- to 2½-inch fruits are best for eating fresh. Although our plants produced nonstop, cornichons often come in flushes. In some gardens, the plants remain vigorous through the summer. In others, they weaken after the first major fruit set.

One mail-order seed source is Shepherd's Garden Seeds, 6116 Highway 9, Felton, Calif. 95018, (408) 335-6910; catalog $1.—*Lynn Ocone*

Give plants as much light as they can take without burning the foliage (full sun on the coast). Leaves should be pale green; if they're dark green, they are most likely not receiving enough light to produce flowers. Or you may be giving the plants too much nitrogen fertilizer. Water and feed them until summer's end with high-nitrogen fertilizer, then switch to a low-nitrogen one. Avoid wetting flowers since moisture can spot them. To protect flowers and flower spikes from heavy rain and cold, move the plants under a patio roof or wide overhang.

Once bulbs fill their pot, either repot the clump into a larger pot or divide it. To divide the clump, carefully separate bulbs by shaking and picking soil mix off roots; keep three to five green bulbs for each division. Cut roots or rhizome between bulbs if necessary, and pull out or prune away old, dead roots.

Cymbidium orchids need loose, well-drained soil that also retains moisture. A good mix is 3 parts ⅛- to ¼-inch seedling bark, 2 parts perlite, and 1 part horticultural charcoal. Moisten soil before using. Lightly mist the leaves (but don't drench the soil) for about three weeks after repotting.—*M. M.*

## Grow asparagus the European way

If you've been lucky enough to travel in Europe during asparagus season, you may have sampled the tender, delicate-tasting white asparagus that is commonly available there (don't try to compare the fresh kind with the tasteless, overcooked, canned type). White asparagus isn't a different variety; it comes from the same type of plant as the green asparagus we grow here, but it's been blanched.

Blanching asparagus is easy for home gardeners (it's not done commercially in the United States because it's too labor intensive). In early spring before spears emerge, mound soil 8 inches high over your row of asparagus (if some spears have already begun to emerge, they won't be completely white). When the tips emerge from the top of the soil, cut the spears off with a knife at the base of the mound. The blanched spears are usually fatter than normal and have less-developed tips.

Level mounds after the harvest season, or whenever you want to stop the blanching process.—*Lauren Bonar Swezey*

## Plant a bleeding heart for perennial spring beauty

Delicate wands of dangling pink and cream blossoms make common bleeding heart (*Dicentra spectabilis*) one of the perennial hallmarks of the early spring Pacific Northwest garden. Now the white form 'Alba' (also known as 'Pantaloons') is becoming almost as common. Blooming plants of both kinds will be for sale this month in nurseries in 1-gallon cans. Act fast and you can still order by mail for immediate delivery (but you probably won't get flowers this year).

This perennial flourishes in the coastal Northwest's acid soil and cool, moist weather.

MICHAEL THOMPSON

Give it a spot in shade or filtered sun. It goes well with ferns and other shade-loving foliage plants. The flowers are so delicate that they are best seen alone, rather than in combination with other spring flowers.

When leafy stems yellow in late spring, cut them back to the ground. Sprinkle a bit of rhododendron food around the crown of the plant when you fertilize other spring bloomers and top-dress with compost in winter to ensure vigorous plants with plenty of flowers—*Steven R. Lorton.*

## A new book of plant lists for Southern California gardenrs

Every gardener seems to have at least one hard-to-plant spot in the garden. No matter what you try, the plant is just not quite right—it struggles or dies. A new book, *Reference Lists of Ornamental Plants for Southern California Gardens,* by Philip E. Chandler (Southern California Horticultural Society, 1993), suggests plants for just about every situation—for soil with poor drainage, for steep hillsides, or for deep shade.

The book contains more than 60 plant lists to help you design your garden. It lists plants by their attributes—fragrant flowers, good cutting flowers, plants for noise or dust control. It lists conspicuous flowering trees and includes their bloom times.

Best of all, this book is written for Southern California gardeners by a Southern Californian with more than 50 years of gardening experience in this region. Chandler, now in his 80s, is a nurseryman, landscape designer, and teacher who over the years developed these indispensable lists for his classes.

**LIKE JEWELS IN A NECKLACE,** *delicate blossoms of common bleeding heart hang suspended over a collage of its finely divided leaves.*

**DOUBLE WHITE LADY BANKS' ROSE** *gives a solid month of floral exuberance during March in this Pasadena, California garden.*

The book is quite personal and almost quirky, filled with little gems of information. It's not intended to be encyclopedic or all-inclusive. Some plant entries include a brief descriptive text; others do not.

You can buy the book at bookstores in botanical gardens for $19.95, or order it from the publisher by sending $25.60 (includes tax and shipping) to Southern California Horticultural Society, Box 41080, Los Angeles, Calif. 90041.—*L. O.*

## Bright, new Chinese redbud

The sight of your first redbud can be a shock. One fine spring day you glimpse a small tree literally covered with bright, magenta-purple flowers. You look more closely and find that the color is really from buds, not flowers—thus "redbud." Now a new redbud is on the market, and it may just be the best yet.

The newcomer was discovered as a chance garden seedling in Avondale, New Zealand. Now *Cercis chinensis* 'Avondale' is doing extremely well in American redbud trials, well enough to warrant a place in the garden.

Like many other redbuds, this one grows about 10 feet tall in 10 years. Its flowers run more to purple than the magenta you may have seen in other redbuds. The plant puts so much energy into flowers and seedpods that it doesn't have much left for plant growth, so it tends to remain relatively small.

'Avondale' should thrive in all but desert areas. To plant this spring, order it by mail from Wayside Gardens, Hodges, S.C. 29695; call (800) 845-1124 or write for a free catalog.—*Jim McCausland*

## Sea Shells for the garden

Cosmos (*C. bipinnatus*) is an easy-to-grow, familiar annual that has changed relatively little since our grandparents' day. Breeders have developed dwarf and semidouble strains and varieties with stripes or eyes (central zones of deeper color), but the flat-flowered form is much as it has always been. The Sea Shells strain, with quilled, rolled, or fluted petals, represents a departure from the common form.

The rolling gives Sea Shells' flower heads greater depth and substance than in the older flat cosmos strains, and in many plants a subtle difference in color intensity between the outer and inner surfaces of the petals lends a two-tone effect. The color range, like that of other *C. bipinnatus* strains, runs from white through pink to red. Plants grow 3 to 4 feet tall and nearly as wide, with finely divided see-through foliage.

Cosmos make first-rate cut flowers, nicely set off by the lacy foliage; they last well in water. Cut as soon as flowers open and place in water at once. Frequent cutting encourages more bloom, and plants can flower until frost. They have many garden uses; try them as summer fillers in perennial or shrub borders, in the cutting garden, or in large pots or tubs of mixed flowering plants. Quick to grow and not at all fussy about soil, they are especially useful for background planting in new gardens.

Where spring comes early and summers are warm, sow seed directly where plants are to grow. Where soils are slow to warm up and summers are cool, start indoors in peat pots or flats. They thrive in full sun, need little or no feeding, and require little water once deeply rooted.

Seeds are available from Park Seed Co., Cokesbury Road, Greenwood, S.C. 29647, (800) 845-3369; and Thompson & Morgan, Dept. 175-4, Jackson, N.J. 08527, (800) 274-7333. Catalogs are free.—*Richard Dunmire*

## Springtime sensation in Pasadena

In Southern California, Lady Banks' rose (*Rosa banksiae*) displays billowing clouds of blooms this month. This harbinger of spring usually flowers just once each year, although it sometimes gives a second, smaller bloom in fall. The older the plant, the longer it flowers (up to six weeks).

Now, while the rose is in bloom, is the best time to shop for Lady Banks'. Two types are available in nurseries: double-flowered white ('Alba Plena'), like the one pictured at left, and double-flowered yellow ('Lutea'). The white is mildly fragrant, reminiscent of violets.

Both types are evergreen, with slender, green, thornless stems and glossy green leaves. Make sure you get a thornless plant; *Rosa fortuneana* sometimes is sold as a double white Lady Banks' but it bears larger leaves on thorny canes. Lady Banks' is resistant to aphids and usually disease-free.

Give it plenty of room to grow; it needs a minimum of

**ROLLED AND FLUTED** *petals give this new strain of cosmos its name—Sea Shells.*

**POPPING OUT** *from a carpet of spring-green leaves, flowers of creeping anemone may be blue, shades of pink and purplish red, or white, depending on the variety.*

12 feet to spread and may grow as wide as 20 feet. The rampant sprawler will cover slopes, arbors, fences—even trees. It also makes a lovely freestanding shrub, reaching to 6 feet tall. Prune only when absolutely necessary or to remove dead wood; flowers bloom on year-old wood and are diminished by pruning.

Plants are usually sold in 1-gallon containers for $6 to $8 and in 5-gallon containers for $18 to $22.—*L. O.*

## This anemone likes to creep

Creeping anemone (*A. blanda*) from southeastern Europe and Asia Minor is well known to woodland gardeners throughout the West, not hard to find, and not hard to grow. Recently, this little plant has been turning up in 4- and 6-inch pots at nurseries and even on supermarket plant racks.

Planted in shade under rhododendrons, azaleas, Japanese maples, or other small trees and shrubs, creeping anemone will form a carpet of bloom and leaf in spring that vanishes in summer. These plants also go well with small spring-flowering bulbs—miniature daffodils, tulips, and scilla.

Flowers 1 to 2 inches across come one blossom to a stem, in shades of blue, purplish blue, pink, rose, and near red. Named varieties include 'Blue Star', 'Pink Star', and 'White Splendor'. Spot plants from 4-inch pots about a foot apart. In three years, they will form an underground network of fibrous roots that will spread and become more floriferous with each year of soft light, regular water, and fertilizer gleaned from neighboring shrubs. —*S. R. L*

## Sow some leeks

Gourmet cooks find leeks to be an indispensable ingredient in many dishes. Milder and sweeter than most onions, leeks are especially easy to grow in the rich soil and gentle climate of the Pacific Northwest.

There are lots of new, and formerly hard to find, leeks available from mail-order suppliers. Look for 'Otina' and 'St. Victor' from France (both are sold by Shepherd's Garden Seeds, 6116 Highway 9, Felton, Calif. 95018; 408/335-6910). Other good choices include 'Splendid', for long, slim stems; 'Unique', for long, thick stems; 'Arcona', for a longer life in storage; and 'Titan', which has a two- to four-week shorter growing season (all four kinds are sold by Stokes Seeds, Box 548, Buffalo, N.Y. 14240; 716/695-6980).

Plant seeds early. They take a long time to germinate, and when they emerge, they look spindly, but then take off. To plant seeds, dig furrows 5 inches deep in rows 18 inches apart in full sun. Sow two seeds per inch (as plants mature, thin to 6 inches apart). As plants grow, fill in furrows gradually with soil. Keep soil around plants constantly moist and weed-free.

Apply a good mulch to help control weeds and retain soil moisture.

When plants have put on considerable top growth, mound soil up around the fat base so that the edible part is white and mild. Pencil-size young leeks are delicious and can be harvested through the summer. Mature leeks will be ready to harvest in the fall. —*S. R. L*

## Tapestry of salad greens

Vegetable gardens aren't normally the highlight of the landscape. But that's not the case with the California garden pictured on page 54. Designer Joan Marie Hedberg of Boynton Beach, Florida, and a team of 15 Master Gardeners created the 24- by 48-foot Salad Green Tapestry Garden with 1,000 seedlings of specialty greens and lettuces in a variety of colors. The geometric patterns of greens grew into a textural delight.

Home gardeners can adapt the idea on a smaller scale. Depending on where you live, you can sow seeds now or buy seedlings at the nursery to go straight into the ground. Use gypsum and string to mark out the design.

This planting included eight different kinds of lettuce (three are 'Lollo Rosso', 'Royal Oak Leaf', and 'Sangria'), as well as 'Fordhook Giant' and 'Ruby Red' chard, baby bok choy and 'Tah Tsai' Chinese cabbage, 'Green Ruffles' and 'Purple Ruffles' basil, endive, fennel, mustard, nasturtiums, parsley, radicchio, red orach, salad burnet, spinach, and violas. —*L. B. S.*

## California garden catalog with a bonus

Gardeners interested in indigenous plants will find Las Pilitas Nursery's *A Manual of California Native Plants* (Las Pilitas Rd., Santa Margarita, Calif. 93453; 805/438-5992; $6) one of the most informative garden catalogs available. The 100-page manual doesn't look like a typical catalog; it has no pictures or drawings (although the separate price list has handsome line drawings of a number of plants and lists availability), and graphics are not one of its strong points. But it contains an amazing amount of information about more than 900 plants, as well as about plant ecology and landscape guidelines. Climate zones listed for each plant come from the *Sunset Western Garden Book*, the U.S. Department of Agriculture, and Las Pilitas.

Gallon-size plants such as ceanothus and manzanitas are sold by mail and shipped in bags or bare-root. Most plants cost $4.50 each, plus a $10 handling fee (for an unlimited number of plants); shipping is extra.—*L. B. S.*

## Saving leftover seeds

*If you have seeds left over after sowing a row or two, don't put them on a shelf and forget them. Mark the date on the seed packet with an indelible marking pen and put the packet in a glass jar that's clear (so you can see into it easily) and airtight (to keep seeds dry). Store the jar in a cool, dark place. Most seeds are viable for a year. Seeds that don't keep well include lettuce, parsley, and onions.*

## March Checklist

### PACIFIC NORTHWEST

☐ **DIVIDE PERENNIALS.** Asters, chrysanthemums, coral bells, and other summer- and fall-flowering perennials can be divided now. Wait until autumn to divide spring bloomers. Use a spade or a large knife to cut clumps apart. Generally a clump the size of a dinner plate will divide into two pieces, four if you want more plants and can wait a year or two for a big bloom show.

☐ **FEED BERRY PRODUCERS.** Blackberries, blueberries, currants, gooseberries, and raspberries all benefit from complete dry fertilizer sprinkled over their root zones. Before planting strawberries this month, enrich the soil with organic matter such as compost or well-rotted manure. Wait until after harvest in June to feed strawberries.

☐ **FEED EVERGREENS.** Broad-leafed and needled evergreens will benefit from a scattering of high-nitrogen fertilizer around the base of the plants atop lightly cultivated ground. Before you fertilize, rake up and dispose of any debris.

☐ **FEED ROSES AND EARLY-FLOWERING SHRUBS.** Give fertilizer high in nitrogen to roses now and to early-blooming shrubs as soon as they have finished flowering. Scatter fertilizer onto groomed beds.

☐ **FERTILIZE LAWNS.** Grass growth starts this month. The plants will be hungry. Apply ½ pound actual nitrogen per 1,000 square feet of lawn in a mix with a nitrogen-phosphorus-potassium ratio of 3-1-2.

☐ **HOE SPRING WEEDS.** Eliminate weeds while they're still small.

☐ **OVERSEED LAWNS.** Rake bald spots in lawns, vigorously. Use a thatching rake if you have one, then seed. Sprinkle a bit of well-sifted soil or compost over the seed to keep it moist and so that wind won't blow it away and birds won't eat seeds.

☐ **PLANT BARE-ROOT.** This month ends bare-root planting. Shop immediately for fruit trees and other bare-root plants.

☐ **PLANT BULBS AND CORMS.** At midmonth, plant calla lilies, crocosmia, gladiolus, ranunculus, and tigridia for summer bloom.

☐ **PLANT COOL-SEASON VEGETABLES.** Beet, carrot, lettuce, pea, radish, and spinach can all be sown this month, as can most cabbage family members. A cloche helps warm the soil and gives seedlings an early start. Bare-root artichokes, asparagus, horseradish, and rhubarb are available.

☐ **REVIVE FUCHSIAS AND GERANIUMS.** Bring overwintered plants out of storage and into light and warmth. Water them well. When new growth appears, feed them with a half-strength solution of liquid plant food. Feed them again in mid-April, then step up to a full-force summer feeding program.

☐ **SOW ANNUALS.** Seeds of bachelor's buttons, calendula, clarkia, cosmos, godetia, larkspur, Shirley poppy, snapdragon, and sweet alyssum can all be sown directly onto the ground this month. Cover seeds with a thin layer of compost or sifted loam. Keep plantings consistently moist.

☐ **SOW PERENNIALS.** They take time from seed, but for out-of-the-way places, seed-sowing is a good way to enlarge your collection inexpensively. Direct-sow hardy arabis, columbine, coral bells, delphinium, and veronica.

☐ **TRANSPLANT EVERGREENS.** Plants are still dormant or just waking up. Transplant now and you can be fairly sure plants won't suffer setback. Before you dig, get the planting hole ready so the move is quick and roots don't dry out. Don't feed newly transplanted plants. Keep them well watered through the summer.

**AMEND SOIL.** Before planting in fast-draining or heavy clay soils, amend with compost, ground bark, or other organic material to help improve soil texture and water retention. If you use ground bark or another wood product, make sure it has been nitrogen stabilized (read the label or ask the supplier). If not, add a high-nitrogen fertilizer or plant growth will be retarded. Use 2½ to 5 pounds of 20-10-10 or 16-9-12 per 500 square feet.

**CARE FOR HERBS.** To rejuvenate perennial herbs like mint and sage, cut back old or dead growth on established plants, then fertilize and water them to stimulate new growth. Plant new herbs such as mint, parsley, rosemary, sage, and thyme in loose, well-drained soil.

**CHECK FOR INSECTS.** Check plants for early signs of insect pests, such as aphids (look for distorted new growth and tiny, often green or black insects) and spittlebugs (look for white foam on the stems). Blast them off with spray from the hose; or use insecticidal soap to control aphids.

**CLEAN, REPAIR DRIP SYSTEM.** Flush out sediment from filters and check screens for algae. Clean with a toothbrush, if necessary. Turn on water and check to make sure all emitters are dripping water; clean or replace clogged ones (if you can't get an emitter out, install a new one next to it). Check for and repair leaks in lines.

**COMPOST.** Save garden refuse for the compost pile. To help branches break down faster, chop or shred them into smaller pieces. Alternate layers of high-carbon material (leaves, straw, tree prunings) with layers of high-nitrogen material (green grass clippings, succulent weeds, and manure). Turn pile frequently; keep it damp.

**FERTILIZE TREES AND SHRUBS.** Apply a high-nitrogen fertilizer such as 20-10-10. If you use a granular or timed-release fertilizer on plants watered by drip, apply it in holes drilled into the soil around the plant so it will contact water. Otherwise the fertilizer won't dissolve enough for plants to benefit from it.

**MONITOR SPRING RAINS.** Weather can be variable this month, and rains may not supply enough moisture to water plants. Check soil moisture by digging near the plant with a trowel.

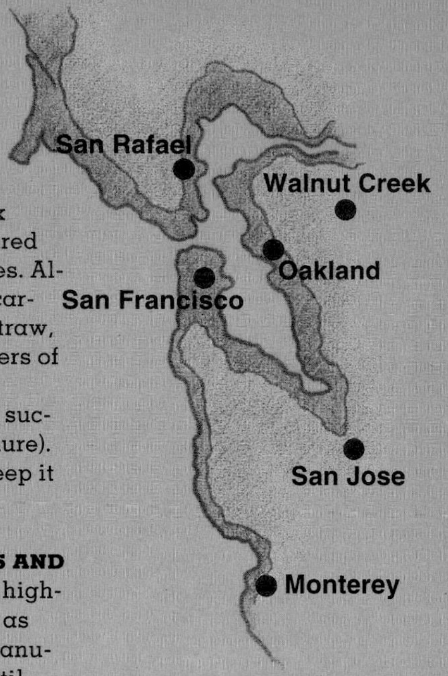

**PLANT CITRUS.** For fast establishment, buy young trees in 5-gallon cans. Try 'Washington' orange, 'Eureka' or 'Meyer' lemon, 'Oroblanco' grapefruit-pummelo hybrid, or 'Moro' blood orange. In cool coastal areas, try 'Trovita' orange.

San Rafael

Walnut Creek

Oakland

San Francisco

San Jose

Monterey

# March Checklist

## CENTRAL VALLEY

☐ **CHECK FOR PESTS.** Succulent new growth and tender seedlings attract many kinds of raiders this month. Check plants for early signs of insect pests such as aphids, and control them while their numbers are still low. Dispatch them with a blast from a hose, or apply insecticidal soap. Handpick, bait, or trap earwigs, slugs, and snails.

☐ **CONTROL WEEDS.** Hand-pull large weeds where possible and lightly cultivate around plants. Mulch beds with 1 to 2 inches of organic matter.

☐ **DIVIDE PERENNIALS.** Summer- and fall-blooming perennials such as agapanthus, chrysanthemums, coreopsis, daylilies, and Shasta daisies can be divided now while they are still semidormant. Do this if plants are crowded or last season's bloom was sparse. Lift clumps with a spading fork, and make a clean cut with a spade. Replant the outer portions of the clumps; discard old center growth.

☐ **FEED LAWNS.** Bent, bluegrass, fescue, and rye grass begin their spring growth spurts now. Feed them soon, while the cooler weather holds out, with a complete fertilizer such as 16-8-4 at a rate of 1 pound of actual nitrogen per 1,000 square feet. If necessary, select a product with preemergence crabgrass control.

☐ **PLANT FLOWERS.** Shop for drought-tolerant perennials such as coreopsis, gaillardia, penstemons, and salvias. Many Central Valley nurseries now tag drought-tolerant plants or have special codes to make it easy to identify them. Also plant summer bulbs like calla, canna, dahlia, gladiolus, and tigridia. You can also find summer bedding plants such as impatiens and petunias. Sow cosmos and marigold seeds directly in the ground.

☐ **PLANT VEGETABLES, HERBS.** Continue to sow these winter-spring vegetable seeds in the ground: beets, carrots, lettuce, peas, radishes, Swiss chard, turnips. Set out broccoli, cauliflower, cabbage seedlings. Plant potato and Jerusalem artichoke tubers. Also plant young herbs, including chives, parsley, and rosemary. Late in the month, start peppers, squash, and tomatoes under floating row covers.

☐ **PLANT WOODY PLANTS.** Set out hardy plants first; later in the month, plant frost-tender avocado, citrus, and vines like bougainvillea.

☐ **PRUNE.** Remove storm-damaged branches. Prune frost-damaged wood when you see new growth. Cut branches of spring-flowering trees and shrubs to enjoy indoors.

Redding

Lake Tahoe

Sacramento

Fresno

Bakersfield

□ **CARE FOR HERBS.** To rejuvenate established perennial herbs such as mint and sage, cut back old or dead growth, then feed with a complete fertilizer and water them. Also set out young plants of chives, mint, oregano, parsley, rosemary, sage, and thyme.

□ **DIVIDE PERENNIALS.** If summer- and fall-blooming perennials (agapanthus, asters, bellflowers, callas, daisies, daylilies, rudbeckia, yarrow) are weak and crowded and last year's blooms were sparse, it's time to divide. Do it this month, just as growth begins. Dig each clump so the rootball comes up intact. Wash or shake off excess soil so you can cut sections with a sharp knife. Each division should have some leaves and plenty of roots. Plant immediately.

□ **FERTILIZE PLANTS.** In coastal, inland, and low desert zones (*Sunset* zones 22–24, 18–21, and 13, respectively), most bedding plants, citrus, ground covers, shrubs, trees, tropicals, and vines benefit from feeding this month. Use a complete fertilizer according to package directions. If plants were damaged by frost, hold off until new growth shows.

□ **PLANT ANNUALS.** As weather warms in coastal, inland, and low-desert areas, replace fading winter-spring annuals with summer flowers such as ageratum, marigolds, petunias, and scarlet sage. Late this month in medium- to high-desert areas (zone 11), set out marigolds, petunias, and zinnias. Nurseries have an abundance of flowers in cell-packs and 4-inch pots. To plant, remove rootball carefully and gently loosen roots at bottom; transplant immediately into moistened and prepared soil.

□ **PLANT BULBS, CORMS, TUBERS.** In coastal and inland areas, continue planting summer bulbs such as caladium, calla, canna, dahlia, gladiolus, gloxinia, nerine, tigridia, tuberose, and tuberous begonia.

□ **THIN FRUIT.** Apricot and peach trees routinely set more fruit than the tree can ripen. Remove extras when they are pea- or marble-size. Leave two of the largest and healthiest young fruits on each 12 inches of stem.

□ **PRUNE TREES AND SHRUBS.** Wait until flowers fade to prune spring-flowering trees and shrubs such as cherry, crabapple, peach, plum, and quince. Wait until new growth appears to prune frost-damaged plants such as bougainvillea, calliandra, citrus, and Natal plum. Prune evergreen hedges, such as boxwood, before the spring growth surge.

□ **MAKE COMPOST.** Add prunings, leaves, grass clippings, and kitchen waste to compost pile. Chop or shred branches into small pieces, and add a layer of garden soil every foot or two. Turn and mix pile frequently; keep moist.

□ **MULCH PLANTS.** Early this month, before spring weeds germinate, renew mulch around trees, shrubs, and ground covers. Use a 3-inch-thick layer of bark chips or compost. Keep mulch away from the base of the plant.

□ **FEED LAWNS.** Cool-season grasses such as bluegrass, rye grass, and tall fescue (which includes 'Marathon') are growing very fast right now and need some fertilizer. But not too much: apply the equivalent of 1 pound of actual nitrogen per 1,000 square feet, or 5 pounds of a fertilizer that contains 20 percent nitrogen as in 20-10-15.

□ **SOW FLOWER SEED.** You can start many flowers from seed either in flats or directly into the garden where you want them to grow. Try aster, bachelor's button, marigold, nasturtium, and zinnia. As a rule, plant seeds twice as deep as their thickness. Then press soil firmly against them and keep moist.

Santa Barbara

Pasadena

San Bernardino

Santa Monica

Los Angeles

San Diego

## ANYWHERE IN THE WEST, TACKLE THESE CHORES:

☐ **FERTILIZE EVER-GREENS.** Sprinkle high-nitrogen fertilizer over the root zone and water it in well.

☐ **FERTILIZE SHRUBS.** Apply high-nitrogen fertilizer to early-flowering shrubs as soon as they've finished blooming. Do this on a mild day when temperatures are well above freezing. Feed roses right away.

☐ **FERTILIZE SMALL FRUITS.** Blackberries, blueberries, raspberries, and strawberries can all use a feeding this month. Apply high-nitrogen fertilizer or composted manure.

☐ **HOE SPRING WEEDS.** If you hoe weeds now, while they're young and shallow-rooted, they'll die outright, but if you wait until they form deep taproots, they'll rise again (and you'll weed again).

☐ **INSTALL IRRIGATION.** It's easier to put in drip- or ooze-irrigation systems now, before root and top growth makes installation more complicated. It will save you time—and help conserve water—all summer long.

☐ **MAKE COMPOST.** As you get the garden in shape for spring and summer planting, use the weeds to start a compost heap. If you layer green weeds with dry leaves, straw, or sawdust, then turn the pile weekly with a pitchfork and keep it damp, you'll have finished compost in a few weeks.

☐ **PLANT BARE-ROOT.** Early this month, set out everything from strawberries and horseradish to fruit and shade trees. Bare-root plants will cost you less than those sold in containers, and they adapt to native garden soil more quickly.

☐ **PLANT LAWN GRASS.** You can overseed an old lawn or plant a new one this month. By summer, it will be lush and ready for roughhousing.

☐ **PREPARE PLANTING BEDS.** Dig composted manure (or garden compost) into planting beds to get them ready for spring planting. For bad soil, till 4 to 6 inches of organic matter into the top foot of soil. Rake amended beds, water them, and let them settle in for a week before planting.

## IN THE SOUTHWEST'S LOW DESERT, HERE ARE MORE CHORES:

☐ **BUY SUMMER BULBS.** Shop for caladium, canna, and crinum this month, but wait until soil warms to 65° before planting. Set out dahlia, gladiolus, and iris now.

☐ **MAINTAIN DRIP SYSTEM.** Clean out sediment and algae (a solution of bleach and water helps), replace clogged emitters you can't clear, and clean filters.

☐ **MULCH PLANTS.** Late in the month, after soil has warmed, spread 3 to 4 inches of organic mulch around roses, shrubs, trees, and in rows between flowers and cool-season vegetables. The mulch will help hold in moisture and minimize soil temperature fluctuations around roots. Wait another month to mulch between warm-season vegetables.

☐ **PLANT ANNUALS.** Set out warm-season flowers, such as blackfoot daisy (*Melampodium*), celosia, globe amaranth, lisianthus, Madagascar periwinkle, marigold, portulaca, and salvia. When you take plants out of containers for planting, rough up the sides of the rootball and score the bottom deeply.

☐ **PLANT CITRUS.** This month is a good time to plant Algerian tangerine, Arizona Sweets orange, 'Kinnow' mandarin, or 'Marsh' grapefruit.

☐ **PLANT GROUND COVERS.** Among those to set out this month are aptenia, calylophus, dwarf rosemary, Mexican evening primrose, verbena, vinca, and white lantana.

☐ **PLANT PERENNIALS.** Aster, autumn sage (*Salvia greggii*), chrysanthemum, coreopsis, feverfew, gerbera, helianthus, hollyhock, penstemon, Shasta daisy, and statice can all go in now.

☐ **PLANT VINES.** Good choices include Boston ivy, Carolina jessamine, Japanese honeysuckle, Lady Banks' rose, silver lace vine, trumpet creeper (*Campsis radicans*), Virginia creeper, and wisteria. If you want to plant tender vines such as bougainvillea, mandevilla 'Alice du Pont', pink trumpet vine, and queen's wreath, wait another month.

☐ **PRUNE FROST-DAMAGED PLANTS.** Once new growth begins, you'll clearly see which twigs and branches didn't survive winter frosts. Then you can cut them away. Wait another month before you prune bougainvillea, since its new growth appears first at the base of the plant, then moves out the stems.

☐ **START VEGETABLES.** Sow seeds of asparagus (yard-long) beans, black-eyed peas, bush string beans and limas, cucumbers, melons, soybeans, summer squash, and sweet corn. You can also set out plants of peppers and tomatoes now, but be ready to cover young plants with cloth or even plastic if frost threatens. You can also start sweet potato shoots now for planting next month: just lay a whole sweet potato in a loaf pan and half cover with water; shoots will develop along the waterline.

☐ **TRIM BACK ORNAMENTAL GRASSES.** When new growth appears at the base of the plant, cut back the old grass.

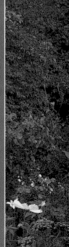

Elizabeth Murray (right) lives and works near Carmel, California, but revisits Giverny yearly. Her book, *Monet's Passion: Ideas, Inspiration and Insights from the Painter's Gardens* (Pomegranate Artbooks, San Francisco, 1989; $26.95), came from her first experiences at Giverny. Painter Claude Monet considered his garden to be his greatest work of art.

# Monet comes West

*By Elizabeth Murray*

*A California designer tended plants at the artist's garden in Giverny and brought home some ideas*

For artist Claude Monet, gardening and painting were inextricably linked. "I owe having become a painter to flowers," he confessed. "More than anything, I must have flowers always, always." He considered his garden at Giverny, northwest of Paris, to be his greatest work of art as it evolved over 46 years.

When I first saw Monet's garden, I was struck by the beauty and abundance of the flower beds. I wanted to know the garden more intimately, to know all the flowers in each season, to be there from spring through autumn, digging, pruning, planting, feeding, rejoicing. In short, I had fallen in love. So I left my garden design position in Carmel and arranged to work at the garden in exchange for lodging.

During my stay at Giverny, I learned much about color and composition in the garden and about the play of light through flowers—elements that were important to the French artist. And I gathered many ideas to bring home to California; some of them are pictured on these pages.

## LIVING TAPESTRY OF COLOR AND LIGHT

Monet organized his garden into different color zones. Some played off two complementary colors—rich pinks and purples, for example, or fiery tones of yellow and red. Others featured large blocks of one color. To unify the whole garden, each season he chose a dominant color—such as lavender—to weave throughout.

Trellises of different sizes and shapes, which supported vines and

Autumn crocus (*Colchicum autumnale*) adds dashes of lavender-pink to the lawn above. In summer, peel back small pieces of sod, plant corms in soil beneath, then lay the sod back down and water well.

Mounding purple solanum at left adds height to a raised bed; it's surrounded by lower-growing annuals and perennials.

Oriental poppies contrast with deep blue *Anchusa azurea* at far left. Monet preferred single flowers, like poppies, because they allow light to play through their petals.

Bicolor flowers like the picotee cosmos at top left add subtle nuances of color to otherwise monochromatic beds.

Blooming umbrella—a blush pink rose trained on an umbrella-shaped support—reigns above purple sweet rocket (*Hesperis matronalis*), above.

Trio of yellows consists of calendula, bronze-tinged rudbeckia, and tiny *Zinnia haageana* (often sold as *Z. angustifolia* or *Z. linearis*), right.

Trellises of vines frame pathway at left. Climbing roses display a variety of colors from spring into autumn; white-flowered scrambling vine is spring-blooming anemone clematis *(Clematis montana)*. English lavender (not yet in flower) provides a uniform pathway border.

roses, added height and structure to the garden. In beds mounded 6 inches high, the largest plants filled the center and the smallest plants—nasturtium, for example—softened the edges.

Like an exquisite flower arrangement, the beds blended flowers and foliage in a variety of shapes and textures. Monet incorporated wild native plants and annuals that reseed themselves into the garden. He interplanted bulbs, annuals, perennials, roses, vines, and fruit trees into one harmonious, ever-evolving whole. He avoided plants with variegated foliage—too spotty for his taste.

In his garden as in his paintings, Monet was especially conscious of patterns of light, which change throughout the day and from season to season. He preferred single flowers because they allow light to play through their petals, giving them the rich look of stained glass windows.

### THE GARDEN TODAY

To plan these magnificent flower beds in the spirit of Monet, who died in 1926, gardeners keep a drawing of the garden and its permanent plants on hand. On separate overlays (one for bulbs, another for annuals), they play with colored pencils until they find color combinations that work.

They plant summer annuals in May. To prolong bloom, they snip spent flowers almost daily. Plants get a light feeding with every watering.

Around October 30, gardeners pull out the annuals, then loosely aerate beds with a pitchfork and dig in compost (rich soil is one secret to keeping the flowers thriving while so tightly packed in garden beds). All kinds of garden debris go into the compost, even algae skimmed from the famous water lily pond. ■

Michaelmas daisy forms a floral fountain of rosy lavender during late-summer and early autumn. To create the effect of a living bouquet, the tall stems need support: this clump's base is staked with iron rebar.

DRYING RACKS *hold crops for seed saving, including 'Purple Queen' garlic, lemon basil, Tohono O'odham dipper gourds, June corn, and Chimayo chilies.*

CHARLES MANN

# Saving native crops

*Native Seeds/SEARCH collects and distributes seeds of endangered Southwest crops*

GARDENER CHECKS *ripening broom corn seed in Native Seeds/SEARCH garden in Tucson.*

**S**WEET, ORANGE-fleshed Chimayo melons and nutritious, nutty-tasting amaranth seeds concealed in silken burgundy plumes are among the gems of traditional Southwest crops. For many centuries, Southwest native peoples grew crops that shaped their farming methods and cultural traditions. From these crops, they selected and saved seeds, ensuring the crops' continuation from generation to generation.

"As lifeways are changing, fewer people are farming and seeds are in danger of being lost," says gardener Linda MacElwee of Native Seeds/SEARCH. This nonprofit organization works to preserve these ancient crops and their wild relatives in the Southwest and northern Mexico, and to support traditional farming methods. Since its start in 1983, the organization has become involved in everything from seed saving to land preservation, nutrition research to garden education.

You can grow some of the traditional crops from seed in your garden and share your experience growing them with Native Seeds/SEARCH. Order seeds now for your summer garden from *Seedlisting* (address below).

## SAVING SEEDS

Native Seeds/SEARCH manages a seed bank in Tucson. The bank offers seeds of more than 1,250 kinds of plants, including multicolored corn, drought-tolerant beans, wild chilies, and blue indigo dye plants.

The group collects seeds in the wild and from Native American farmers, including the Hopi of Arizona, who grow red corn, orange lima beans, and blue-black sunflowers. To maintain and increase a healthy seed stock, staffers grow the rare varieties in gardens in Tucson and Patagonia, Arizona, and in Albuquerque, New Mexico. They give seeds to Native Americans, and sell seeds to other gardeners and to farmers. And they encourage recipients to give extra seeds from new crops to tribal gardens or back to Native Seeds/SEARCH for redistribution.

The seed bank is an important source of plants that are integral to native dry-land farming—ones that farmers have selected for their toughness in extreme desert conditions (some crops depend only on rainwater and diverted floodwater for irrigation).

Some ancient crops can help improve modern hybrids. The Havasupai sunflower, for example, is resistant to rust that plagues commercial varieties; plant breeders are using it to introduce disease-resistance into commercial varieties.

Gary Nabhan, Native Seeds/SEARCH cofounder and researcher, discovered that many traditional Southwest foods—such as tepary beans and cholla cactus buds—help prevent and control diabetes among Native Americans in the region.

And the organization has established a wild chili preserve on U.S. Forest Service land near Tumacacori, Arizona, to protect chilies and other wild crops in their northernmost range.

## TO FURTHER THE CAUSE

A membership in Native Seeds/SEARCH can help support the group's conservation and education programs. Dues start at $18 a year and include a quarterly newsletter.

The semiannual *Seedlisting* ($1) offers seeds of Southwestern plants; for a copy, write 2509 N. Campbell Ave., Box 325, Tucson, Ariz. 85719, or call (602) 327-9123.

Native Seeds/SEARCH has a demonstration garden on the grounds of the Tucson Botanical Gardens, 2150 N. Alvernon Way. Hours are 9 to 4 daily. Crops are maturing from late spring into fall. ■

*By Lynn Ocone*

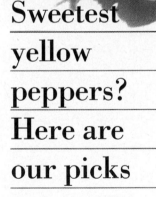

'Golden Cal Wonder'  'Yellow Cheese Pimento'  'Quadrato d'Oro'  'Gold Crest'

'Corno di Toro'  'Golden Bell'  'Yellow Cheese'  'Carsissimo di Cuneo'

NORMAN A. PLATE

**FRESHLY PICKED** *sunny yellow peppers have a variety of shapes, sizes, and flavors. We show 9 of the 10 tested.*

# Sweetest yellow peppers? Here are our picks

*We grew and taste-tested 10 varieties*

THOSE LUMINESCENT sweet yellow peppers you see in the store for as much as $4.50 a pound always look enticing, but instead of having the sweet, peppery flavor you expect, they're often watery and bland. Industrious gardeners don't have to put up with poor flavor or inflated prices. There are plenty of delicious yellow pepper varieties you can grow from seed, and now's the time to order.

## NOT ALL PEPPERS ARE CREATED EQUAL

To help you make a selection, we grew and evaluated 10 varieties. (Peppers had to turn bright yellow—not orange or red—at maturity to qualify for the test.) We planted seedlings in spring, then harvested when peppers turned from green to yellow.

For sweetness, juiciness, and pepper flavor, our taste panel judged 'Carsissimo di Cuneo', yellow 'Corno di Toro', and 'Golden Cal Wonder' best. 'Ori' (not shown)

and 'Orobelle' were close behind. Both produce well in cool climates. 'Gold Crest' and 'Golden Bell' (also good in cool climates) were crunchy and juicy but not quite as sweet. 'Yellow Cheese' and 'Yellow Cheese Pimento' lacked sweetness in our taste test, and 'Quadrato d'Oro' wasn't particularly sweet or juicy.

Climate and nutrients can alter flavors, so your results may differ from ours. In most cases, peppers need warm temperatures, a relatively long growing season, a consistent supply of nitrogen over the season, and a good supply of potassium at fruiting time.

## SEEDS NEED WARMTH TO GERMINATE

Sow seeds in flats or containers; if possible, keep soil temperature above 80° (use a heating cable or set flats on a water heater). Once seeds germinate, move seedlings into bright light for about eight weeks. Don't rush transplanting; wait until soil has

warmed. In cool climates, plant through black plastic and cover with row covers. Keep soil evenly moist through the growing season.

## WHERE TO GET SEEDS

These catalogs are free unless noted.

*Johnny's Selected Seeds,* 310 Foss Hill Rd., Albion, Maine 04910; (207) 437-4301. 'Gold Crest', 'Orobelle'.

*Ornamental Edibles,* 3622 Weedin Court, San Jose, Calif. 95132. Catalog $2. 'Carsissimo di Cuneo', yellow 'Corno di Toro', 'Golden Cal Wonder', 'Ori', 'Orobelle', 'Yellow Cheese Pimento'.

*Seeds Blüm,* Idaho City Stage, Boise, Idaho 83706. Catalog $3. 'Yellow Cheese'.

*Shepherd's Garden Seeds,* 6116 Highway 9, Felton, Calif. 95018; (408) 335-6910. Catalog $1. Yellow 'Corno di Toro', 'Quadrato d'Oro'.

*Territorial Seed Company,* Box 157, Cottage Grove, Ore. 97424; (503) 942-9547. 'Golden Bell'. ■

*By Lauren Bonar Swezey*

# Salad bowl flower beds

*In these two California gardens, herbs, vegetables, and flowers mix and match handsomely*

PETER CHRISTIANSEN

**SYMPHONY OF GREENS** *near Hopland includes garden sage, straplike Egyptian onion, and feathery, bronze-colored fennel (above). Blooming chives edge a walkway (below), and a gray-green artichoke plant adds a bold accent.*

NORMAN A. PLATE

**T**UCK A FEW CABBAGE plants among a sea of purple sweet alyssum and voilà! You have a surprisingly workable marriage of practicality and beauty. In the flower bed, these plants make handsome companions. And once the cabbage is harvested, the alyssum scrambles to fill the bare spot.

While serious vegetable aficionados may prefer to confine vegetables to an out-of-the-way patch, cottage gardeners favor the mix-and-match look that comes from growing vegetables and herbs among flowers. Using vegetables as ornamentals in the landscape allows you to enjoy small amounts of home-grown produce without a big commitment of time and garden space. And there's a bonus: some vegetable plants, such as artichokes and lettuce, add rich color and texture to a flower bed.

The backyard border pictured at right belongs to garden designer Marsha Heron of Point Reyes. Heron mixed vegetables into the border but confined them to distinct zones to make maintenance, digging, and replanting easier. To keep the border looking attractive, she combined vegetables that leave holes

## FOUR VEGETABLE-FLOWER MARRIAGES

These plants combine well for color and cultural needs.
• Surround peppers and tomatoes with marigolds, red or yellow zinnias, bedding dahlias, and feverfew. Edge with nasturtiums.
• Grow purple eggplant with pink cosmos behind and blue ageratum in front.
• Plant a border with pansies in front, drifts of lettuce and parsley in the center, and Persian buttercups behind.
• Use artichokes as accents in a bed of Peruvian lilies.

**MIXED BORDER** *in Point Reyes combines vegetables and flowers in three zones: Lower-growing perennials and herbs (coreopsis, creeping thyme, catmint, and blue fescue) in front, taller vegetables and flowers in the center, tallest perennials and shrubs (daylilies, lavatera, linaria, penstemon, verbena, and yarrow) at the back. Cabbages accent foreground plantings.*

when harvested (carrots, head lettuce, cabbages, and cauliflower, for example) with flowers that spread to fill in the spaces left behind (sweet alyssum, violas, and nasturtiums).

The handsome plant combinations pictured on the opposite page were photographed at Fetzer Vineyard's Valley Oaks Food & Wine Center in Hopland. Because the vineyard's gardens were designed with fresh produce in mind, vegetables and herbs are used extensively—as edgings, as foils for colorful flowers, and to add foliage texture, shapes, and color.

### DESIGN GUIDELINES

The box at left suggests additional combinations to try. For best effects when mixing vegetables into flower beds, cluster plants in groups of three or more. Vary plant heights, and add accents (artichokes, fennel, dill). To avoid a busy look, repeat the same plants throughout the bed or border.

Combine plants with similar cultural needs and watering requirements. Avoid growing thirsty vegetables—lettuce, for example—next to established drought-tolerant plants that need water only once or twice a month; instead substitute drought-tolerant herbs such as borage, rosemary, and thyme.

Choose vegetable varieties suited for small spaces. Use bush kinds of beans, cucumbers, squash, and melons, or train sprawling types against a fence or trellis.

Avoid incorporating disease-susceptible plants—which require spraying—into the mix. ∎

*By Emely Lincowski*

# Fast-growing, colorful annual vines

*They grow and bloom in one season*

WINING AND climbing annual vines present a swift reward to even beginning gardeners. Easy to grow, the vines provide a quick cover of lush, green growth over arbors, fences, and trellises, as well as a long season of bloom. When started from seed in early spring, they're in full glory by early to midsummer.

Although usually referred to as annual vines, many are half-hardy perennials grown as annuals. In mild climates where temperatures don't

**BELL-SHAPED** *flowers dangle spring to fall from rambunctious cathedral bells vine.*

NORMAN A. PLATE

drop below 27° to 32°, cathedral bells, chickabiddy, and moonflower (see page 75) usually live over.

### START SEEDS IN WARM SOIL

To get a jump on the season and ensure a long period of bloom, it's best to start most of these vines indoors six to eight weeks before the last frost (or as soon as possible). The exceptions are morning glory, nasturtium, and scarlet runner bean, which can be sown in the ground after the last frost.

Plant seeds in containers and keep the soil warm; use a heating cable if possible or set containers in a warm place such as on a hot water heater.

PETER CHRISTIANSEN

**FRILLED YELLOW** *flowers appear in abundance on canary creeper through spring and summer. Right, the fast-growing vine covers a trellis within a couple of months.*

**LANTERNLIKE SEED PODS** *decorate love-in-a-puff.*

**SHOWY RED BLOSSOMS** *of scarlet runner bean vine are followed by tasty beans.*

Once seeds germinate, provide plenty of light. When seedlings are ready to transplant, slowly acclimate them to outdoors by gradually exposing them to stronger light over a period of about a week.

Plant vines in full sun unless otherwise noted; transplant carefully to avoid disturbing the roots. Provide support for vines. Large vines, such as cathedral bells and hyacinth bean vine, need sturdy supports.

## SHORT OR TALL:
## CHOOSE A VINE THAT'S
## RIGHT FOR THE LOCATION

*Canary creeper (Tropaeolum peregrinum).* This twining vine grows to a height of 10 feet or more and is blan-

keted by 1- to 1½-inch-long bright yellow frilled flowers. Give vine light shade.

*Cathedral bells (Cobaea scandens).* This fast grower, also known as cup-and-saucer vine, reaches 10 to 20 feet tall and produces an abundance of 2-inch-wide, bell-shaped flowers that turn from pale green to rose violet. Climbs by tendrils.

*Chickabiddy (Asarina).* Colorful trumpet-shaped flowers on vigorous or delicate vines (also called twining snapdragon). *A. barclaiana* 'Angels Trumpet' has 3½- to 4-inch-long leaves, pink flowers, and grows up to 12 feet tall. *A. scandens* 'Jewel Mixed' is much more delicate, with ¾- to 1-inch-long leaves; indigo, violet blue, pink, or white flowers; and a height of about 4 feet. Treat it like clematis: full sun on top, shade on the roots. Support both with wire or string.

*Exotic love (Ipomoea lobata,* sold as *Mina lobata).* This twining vine from Mexico, also called Spanish flag, has three-lobed leaves and grows about 6 feet tall. It produces unusual flower sprays

**CLIMBING NASTURTIUM** *is blanketed with intensely colored edible flowers.*

of 1-inch-wide blossoms that change from scarlet orange to creamy yellow. Soak seed overnight in cold water.

*Hyacinth bean (Dolichos lablab).* Fast-growing vine to 10 feet, with 3- to 6-inch-long bean-shaped leaves. Purple (sometimes white) flowers like sweet peas stand out from the vine on long stems. Purple beanlike pods 2½ inches long follow the flowers. Needs poles or string for support.

*Love-in-a-puff (Cardiospermum halicacabum).* A vigorous vine at least 10 feet tall. Also called balloon vine, it's grown for its unusual seed pods that cover the vines and look like inch-wide green paper lanterns. The tiny white flowers are not dramatic. Vine needs wire or string for support.

*Moonflower (Ipomoea alba)* has 6-inch-wide white flowers on 20- to 30-foot twining vines. Flowers open in the evening and close by midday (unless sky is overcast). For faster sprouting, soak seeds for several hours.

*Morning glory (Ipomoea tricolor).* 'Heavenly Blue' is a vigorous vine to 15 feet tall with 4- to 5-inch-wide blue flowers that open in the morning and fade by afternoon. 'Mini Sky-Blue' is a new miniature morning glory with

1½- to 2-inch-wide flowers on 6- to 8-foot-tall vines. Flowers open in the evening. Soak seeds for several hours before planting. (All parts of morning glories are poisonous.)

*Nasturtium (Tropaeolum).* Old-fashioned climber grows 4 feet tall or more and produces an abundance of brilliant orange, yellow, and red flowers; leaves and flowers are edible. Plant in well-drained soil, and support on poles or string.

*Scarlet runner bean (Phaseolus coccineus).* Bright flowers cover this 10-foot-tall twining vine, which is grown both for its looks and for its edible beans. Pick pods when young and tender ('Red Knight' produces tender, stringless pods), or wait until beans mature and use like green limas.

## WHERE TO BUY SEEDS

You won't find most of these seeds in nurseries. Here are two mail-order sources.

*Shepherd's Garden Seeds,* 6116 Highway 9, Felton, Calif. 95018; (408) 335-6910. Catalog $1.

*Thompson & Morgan,* Dept. 177-4, Jackson, N.J. 08527; (800) 274-7333. Catalog free. ∎

*By Lauren Bonar Swezey*

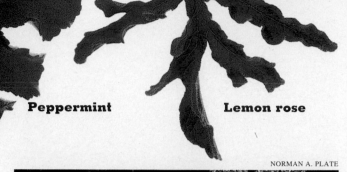

**Peppermint**

**Lemon rose**

**Lime**

**Apple**

**Lemon**

LOW GREEN MOUNDS, *interspersed with purple sweet alyssum, yield plenty of fragrant geranium leaves in Sunset's test garden. These five were among the favorites.*

# Smell-good geraniums

*Leaves are scented like lemons, apples, peppermint. Grow them for their fragrance or to flavor foods*

**B**RUSH YOUR HAND across a scented geranium's leaves and the plant will release a delightful fragrance. Depending on the variety, a potent lemon scent might greet you, or peppermint, or subtle hints of spice, or the clean, fruity scent of ripe apples. You can use these leaves to flavor oils or salads, or to make teas. In the garden, plant them where you can most enjoy their fragrance—by a path, for example.

Of the hundreds of varieties now available, some are more fragrant than others and can impart rich flavors to foods. To find out which ones those were, we staged an informal test at *Sunset* and tasted dishes and drinks flavored with various kinds. The five pictured above—each with a refreshing taste and unmistakable fragrance—rated highest.

PALE, FRAGRANT *peppermint geranium tea tastes good hot or cold.*

Scented geraniums (species of *Pelargonium*) reach 1 to 3 feet tall, with an equal spread. In summer, they bear clusters of small white to pink blooms.

Give them full sun in cool-summer areas, some shade in hottest climates. Provide fast-draining soil. In all but the hottest climates, established plants can get by with just a monthly watering.

Plants are typically sold in the herb section of nurseries in 2-inch pots. But for the best selection, order small plants by mail. Two sources with good selections are Mountain Valley Growers, Inc., 38325 Pepperweed Rd., Squaw Valley, Calif. 93675, (209) 338-2775 (free catalog); and Shepherd's Garden Seeds, 6116 Highway 9, Felton, Calif. 95018, (408) 335-6910 (catalog $1).

---

**SCENTED GERANIUMS AS FLAVORINGS**

Here are three ways to enjoy scented geraniums' intoxicating bouquet with foods.

*Flavored oil.* In a jar, cover ¾ cup clean, dry, coarsely chopped **scented geranium leaves** with 1 cup **salad oil.** Let stand for 2 hours; use, or chill airtight up to 2 days. Use at room temperature. Try oil with crusty bread, pasta, fish, or cooked vegetables.

*Fruit salad.* Add 1 to 2 teaspoons chopped, clean **scented geranium leaves** to each cup chopped **fruit** such as apples, bananas, and oranges.

*Geranium tea.* In a 2- to 3-quart pan, combine 1 quart **water,** ½ cup chopped, rinsed **scented geranium leaves,** and ¼ cup **sugar.** Bring to a boil over high heat; simmer, covered, for 5 minutes. Taste; add more sugar if desired.

Serve tea hot or cold; if making ahead, chill mixture airtight up to 2 days. Strain to serve. Makes 4 cups.

*Per cup: 51 cal. (0 percent from fat); 0 g protein; 0 g fat; 13 g carbo; 7.2 mg sodium; 0 mg chol.* ■

*By Elaine Johnson, Bud Stuckey*

NORMAN A. PLATE

**WHITE ALYSSUM** *carpets the ground around 'Chicago Peace'.*

# Floral companions to plant under roses

*Good choices to cover bare soil*

**G**ARDENERS DELIGHT in growing roses. But all too often the plants are displayed in bare patches of soil without any attention to what grows beneath or between them. A good way to dress up the legs of gawky hybrid teas or add a carpet of color beneath the greenery of shrub roses is to cover the ground with flowering annuals or perennials.

A good companion plant must be colorful, form a bushy carpet, and grow no more than about 1½ feet tall. The best plants generally have a long bloom season—preferably midspring through summer—that is compatible with the bloom season of the roses. In some cases, you may decide to sacrifice length of

DARROW M. WATT

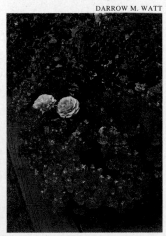

**LONG-BLOOMING** *purple catmint dresses up the feet of 'Iceberg' (left). Above, colorful nemesia adds a cheerful note to 'Amber Queen'.*

RENEE LYNN

bloom for a particularly showy plant, such as the nemesia shown below.

## COLORFUL CARPETS TO PLANT UNDER ROSES

Landscape designer Elaine Schlegel, whose Carmel Valley, California, garden is pictured at left, completely covers the soil under her roses with flowering plants.

"My three favorites—catmint, Santa Barbara daisy, and sweet alyssum—have staying power in the heat. They look good at least nine months of the year and are very easy to grow," she explains.

For added impact, Schlegel intersperses Antique Shades pansies with catmint (pansies "look outstanding planted under apricot roses") and interplants freesias through Santa Barbara daisy and sweet alyssum; the thick ground covers help keep the freesias from falling over in rain and wind. Alyssum can be used in a variety of shades, from white to apricot to purple.

Other good choices to consider (including some with shorter bloom times) are twinspur (*Diascia rigescens*); forget-me-not; Johnny-jump-up; blue, purplish, or white lobelia; nemesia; and ground cover verbenas (*V. peruviana, V. pulchella gracilior*).

Alyssum, forget-me-not, Johnny-jump-up, lobelia, and nemesia can be planted from seeds or seedlings (when starting from seed, all but the lobelia are best planted in fall). If sowing seeds directly, broadcast them evenly so they form a carpet under the roses.

Plant *Diascia*, Santa Barbara daisy, and verbena from sixpacks, 4-inch pots, or 1-gallon cans. Set plants close enough so that they grow together (to determine spacing, check plant tags or the *Sunset Western Garden Book*).

Water plants often enough to keep the soil moist. (You'll still need to deep-water the roses periodically.) ■

*By Lauren Bonar Swezey*

**LIKE A PAINTER'S PALETTE,** *this rock garden is daubed and dotted with soft spring colors from flowers and foliage. For details, see page 84.*

# APRIL

CHAD SLATTERY

# Annuals, perennials, vegetables...April brings last best chance to assure summer bounty

pril may be the garden's busiest and most important month. In the desert, the planting train pulls out now: if you miss it, you'll have to wait until cool weather returns in fall to plant. In areas where short seasons limit what you can grow, you have to get started now or wait a year for your next chance. If you get a late start on sowing seeds, stop by your nursery for ready-to-plant seedlings. And in all other climates, the accent this month is on planting for summer.

## Plant—or paint—for a lush forest look

Whether you have a real forest in your backyard or just the illusion of one painted on a wall, you'll find that nurseries sell plenty of plants especially suited to the shady conditions of a forest understory. Many are woodland natives, and some, such as columbine and coral bells, even bloom in shade.

The planting bed pictured at right combines forest plants with a realistic-looking 12- by 24-foot forest mural to add depth to a tiny back garden. Landscape architect Jana Ruzicka chose plants native to the kind of forest depicted in the mural: a grove of coast redwoods. California gray rush (*Juncus patens*), giant chain fern (*Woodwardia fimbriata*), leathery polypody (*Polypodium scouleri*), and meadow rue (*Thalictrum*) give varied texture and multiple shades of green. Color accents include coral bells (*Heuchera*), monkey flower (*Mimulus*), redwood sorrel (*Oxalis oregana*), and Western columbine (*Aquilegia formosa*).

To soften the wall and give a sensation of depth as the plants mature, Ruzicka staggered and layered them in an irregular fashion.

The mural is by artist Leah Vasquez. Of the mural, Ruzicka says, "A garden is an illusion anyway. Painting on walls is just part of the illusion."—*Lynn Ocone*

## A sweet new carrot from Idaho

After Nicholas Molenaar, an Idaho vegetable breeder, decided to focus his carrot-breeding efforts on flavor, he came up with a variety called 'Artist'. Early testers agree that this carrot does indeed have outstanding sweet flavor. It also freezes well, stays firm, and retains flavor in long-term cool storage (like a root cellar).

A Nantes type, with tapered form and a blunt end, 'Artist' grows to about 6 inches. This carrot's color is deep orange, and its vitamin A content is high.

'Artist' is new this year. You can order seed from

TOWERING TREES *painted on backyard wall create an illusion of space and give context to woodland planting below.*

vate enough for one to shuffle about scandalously . . . in one's nightclothes on a fine morning, and while there to say hello to a sufficient number of resident plant friends."

And of himself: "I myself may be about due for at least honorable mention as a garden relic, a desiccated rhizome of some sort, nevertheless with a burning, scheming spark of life safe within."

That spark comes through with every word he writes; better reading you will not find.—*J. M.*

## Video guide to composting

Compost you make yourself is better and cheaper than anything you can buy, quickly transforming the worst soil into good garden loam. *The Complete Home Composting Video Guide,* by Howard Stenn (Vernal Productions, Bellevue, Wash., 1993; $19.95), shows how you can make compost, using everything from grass clippings and woody branches to food waste.

The video gives you plenty of choices. If you're not one to build a bin, and turn and water your compost every week, just follow Stenn's instructions for making a no-turn, freestanding pile that gives good compost in 6 to 12 months. But if you're set on making the fastest-working pile in the West, he shows how to do that, too, taking you from leaves and grass to finished compost in less than a month.

You can order a VHS copy by mail from Flying Dog Enterprises, Box 118, Vashon, Wash. 98070. Add $2 for postage and handling; Washington residents add $1.65 sales tax.—*J. M*

Johnny's Selected Seeds, 310 Foss Hill Rd., Albion, Me. 04910.—*Jim McCausland*

## Gardening through a master's eyes

It's wonderful to be able to look at the world of horticulture through the eyes of a certifiable genius. You can do just that by reading *Gardening with Friends,* by George Schenk (Houghton Mifflin, New York, 1992; $19.95).

Few people have given themselves over to gardening as completely as Schenk has. Not content with just one growing season each year, he takes his spade from the Pacific Northwest to the Philippines, where he cultivates the pleasures of the tropics, then to New Zealand each fall, where he enjoys a second spring. Along the way he designs gardens for rich and poor alike, experimenting with plants, learning much,

and teaching more.

In *Gardening with Friends,* Schenk writes about everything from garden design to the sweat-drenching task of turning lawn into garden.

Of deck-rail gardening: "With a line of container plants upon it, a railing becomes the Orient Express of gardening adventures, a train of enchantments."

Of outdoor rooms: "The true garden must contain at least one outdoor room pri-

## Waldsteinia, a star Northwest ground cover

Right now, one of the best things about *Waldsteinia fragarioides,* or barren strawberry, is that not very many gardeners know about it. But it's such a good ground cover, and grows so well in the Pacific Northwest, that in time nurseries will stock a hefty supply, and the plant will pass from emerging star to old standby. If you walk through Seattle's Freeway Park, you'll see this ground cover in beds under 'Bradford' ornamental pears at the northwest edge of the park.

Waldsteinia performs well in the Northwest's typically rich, loose, acid soil. It takes full sun but seems happiest in gently filtered light or partial sun. And it stands up to dry summers with a minimum of water, except in really scorching dry spells. In winter, the leaves take on a bronzy tint. If a harsh winter batters the foliage badly, cut plants back in mid-February and foliage will sprout anew in spring. The yellow spring flowers appear over several weeks. When you feed other flowering shrubs and trees, scatter complete granular fertilizer over the planting; a winter top dressing of compost helps encourage new growth and a strong root run.—*Steven R. Lorton*

## Encore for 'Roly Poly' zucchini

Normally when we discuss a plant in the Garden Guide, we try not to come back to it again for a few years, but there are exceptions. The zucchini 'Roly Poly' is one.

After giving it a try, we touted it last spring in the Garden Guide. Readers responded by planting seeds, and our mail and phone messages told us you loved it as much as we did. Prolific producers (even in a chilly, overcast summer), the compact plants manufacture perfectly round zukes (a bit bigger than a softball) about 50 days after sowing. They have a creamy texture and nutty flavor. Eat them raw, shred them for bread or casseroles, slice and sauté them, or hollow them out, stuff them, bake them, and eat them in the shell.

Order seed now from W. Atlee Burpee & Co., 300 Park Ave., Warminster, Pa. 98119; (800) 888-1447. Where growing season is short, start seeds indoors as soon as you receive them; then set out plants when the weather warms. In other regions, sow seeds directly into the ground when warm weather arrives.—*S. R. L.*

## Pamper citrus at planting time

A healthy, well-established citrus tree is usually quite resilient. If you miss an irrigation, or if nutrients are lacking, the established tree rebounds with the return of care. In contrast, young, newly planted citrus can be fussy, and when damaged, they don't recover easily. It pays to coddle trees when they are young.

Spring is prime planting time. Trees have a few months to adjust before peak summer heat adds stress.

Choose a warm, sunny spot. Don't plant close to the house where the tree may be shaded in winter.

Citrus can't tolerate standing water, so plant in fast-draining soil. Or, if soil drains poorly, plant above the soil level in a raised bed. Average soil can be improved with amendments.

At planting time, carefully remove the tree from its container. The fragile root system on young citrus can break if you pull the tree by the trunk.

After planting, feed with a complete, high-nitrogen fertilizer.

Water consistently and deeply. A newly planted tree may require water twice a week. As the tree becomes established, a weekly irrigation to a depth of 2 feet is usually adequate in average circumstances. If the soil surface remains damp between waterings, hold off for a few days.

To help conserve moisture, spread a 2- to 3-inch-deep layer of mulch such as clean straw or compost over the soil surface; keep mulch away from the tree trunk.

If your newly planted tree starts to show signs of stress like curling or yellowing leaves, seek the advice of a nurseryman before it's too late to correct the problem.—*L. O.*

MICHAEL THOMPSON

## Extending the vase life of tulips

As cut flowers, tulips aren't particularly long-lasting. But if they're prepared correctly before arranging, they'll stay fresh a week or more.

First, handle the flowers gently and keep them cool during transport from the garden or florist. Trim the bottom end off each stem with a clean, sharp knife or shears. This allows the stem to continue absorbing water.

Wrap the bunch snugly in newspaper, leaving the lower few inches of stems exposed. Place the flowers in a con-

**GROUND-HUGGING**
*Waldsteinia fragarioides produces tiny yellow flowers above green leaf clusters on long, wispy stems.*

tainer of cool to lukewarm water just deep enough to cover the exposed stem bases, but not touching the paper. Place the container in a cool location for an hour or two. The tulips' stems will take up water and stiffen.

When arranging the flowers, use only clean, cool water and fill the vase only about a third full. Add a cut-flower preservative, or for each quart of solution, use 3 cups water, 1 cup lemon-lime soda, and ¼ teaspoon household bleach. Keep the water fresh, refilling the vase when necessary. Place the arrangements away from heat and direct sunlight.

If after several days the tulips droop, repeat the stem-cutting process.—*Loren Bonar Swezey*

## Who beat tomato blight?

Last summer had Pacific Northwest tomato growers in a stew. The cold, wet weather gave plants a slow start and set up ideal conditions for fungal tomato blight. Many gardeners saw their plants blacken and wither almost overnight.

In Washington's rainy upper Skagit Valley, gardeners Gerhard Meyer and Anna Lou Turner saw the disaster coming and challenged each other to see who could beat the blight.

Both moved their tomato plants out of their main gardens and into isolated beds.

Turner picked a south-facing slope with full sun dawn to dusk. She dug a bed 25 feet long and 4 feet wide, enriching the soil with well-rotted sheep manure. Then she laid down black plastic sheeting. She cut a row of holes (using a 1-gallon can as a pattern), 30 inches apart, down the middle of the plastic. She put 'Early Girl' seedlings in the holes and allowed them to grow unstaked, leaving all the suckers on plants.

Meyer chose a south-facing wall that also had full, day-long sunshine, and enriched

PETER CHRISTIANSEN

**DELIGHTFUL** *little salmon pink blossoms cover Silene pendula 'Peach Blossom' in spring and summer.*

the bed with sheep manure. He staked and suckered the tomatoes but left the ground uncovered. A second-story eave kept most overhead water off the plants.

Both plots were in locations that got plenty of east-west air movement. Both gardeners watered at the base of plants (not overhead) and fed twice a month with a thorough soaking of 15-30-15 liquid fertilizer.

Both Turner and Meyer harvested tomatoes well into the season, while other gardeners lost everything. But Meyer finally won. In September, Turner's plants began to show some signs of blight, so she pulled them and burned them, but Meyer's tomatoes stayed free of blight until frost.—*S. R. L.*

## A peachy silene for borders and pots

*Silene pendula* 'Peach Blossom' isn't a new plant. It was introduced in 1936, but it soon disappeared from the market and reappeared only last year.

This delicate annual grows 4 to 6 inches tall and 12 inches wide. Masses of ¾-inch-wide double blooms (shown above) start out as deep pink buds that open to salmon pink, then fade to white.

Since 'Peach Blossom' forms a small carpet, it's best used as an edging in front of the border or combined with taller plants in a container. Sow seeds in flats and then transplant the seedlings into the garden.

Seed of 'Peach Blossom' is available from Thompson & Morgan Inc., Dept. 178-4, Jackson, N.J. 08527; (800) 274-7333. The catalog is free. A packet of 100 seeds costs $1.95 plus $1.95 for shipping and handling (for up to $15 worth of any kind of seeds). —*L.B.S.*

## Want to grow something different? Try macadamias

If you're looking for something out of the ordinary to try in your home orchard, consider macadamias. Normally thought of as tropical nuts restricted to mild climates of Southern California, macadamias are actually about as hardy as lemon trees, and Central Valley nurseries are selling the trees more regularly. Some gardeners in milder parts of the Central Valley are successfully harvesting nuts.

Macadamia trees are good-looking evergreens with glossy green leaves and bronzy red new foliage. They grow slowly, eventually

reaching 20 to 25 feet tall. Long clusters of pink flowers in spring are followed by hard-shelled nuts that mature from fall to spring. When mature, the nuts fall to the ground. Eat them fresh or roasted.

The best areas in the Central Valley for macadamia trees are warm thermal belts that surround the valley floor (*Sunset Western Garden Book* zone 9). On the valley floor, plant them where they'll be protected from winter cold, such as next to a warm south-facing wall. Plant in well-drained soil, water regularly, and apply a controlled-release fertilizer in spring.

If your nursery doesn't sell macadamia trees, order through the mail from Pacific Tree Farms, 4301 Lynwood Dr., Chula Vista, Calif. 91910; (619) 422-2400 (catalog $2). 'Dr. Beaumont' is the most reliable variety.—*Lance Walheim*

## Greening up chlorotic plants

When plants show yellowing leaves with green veins, chlorosis, the result of iron deficiency, is usually the problem. Chlorosis appears most often in bottle-brush, boxwood, camellia, citrus, cotoneaster, crape myrtle, eucalyptus, gardenia, grape, nectarine, peach, and pyracantha.

The best quick treatment is to spray the foliage of affected plants with liquid fertilizer containing iron and zinc. For longer-term treatment, apply chelated iron by itself or in acid-forming fertilizer.

Chlorosis is commonest in waterlogged, alkaline soil. To really beat it, or to prevent it before you plant, improve soil aeration and drainage, and acidify soil by digging in peat moss or products containing sulfur. —*J. M.*

## Start a rock garden

Color starts to burst this month from Marietta and Ernie O'Byrne's rock garden in Eugene, Oregon. This is a good month to get started on your own rock garden. It need not be as grand as the O'Byrnes', pictured on page 78. You can start out with a mound of crushed rock as small as a yard wide and 5 feet long.

To create their garden, the O'Byrnes first laid out the pattern on flat ground with garden hose. Then they put in large rocks and filled in around them with loads of crushed rock, compost, and washed sand 6 inches deep in some places, mounded up to 3 feet in others, and 3 inches deep around steppingstones. They topped the gravel with a combination of equal parts of decomposed granite and humus. The result was a perfectly drained growing medium for a diverse collection of rock plants—conifers, sedums, lewisia, alpine wildflowers, and grasses all find a home here.

Each morning through the growing season, the O'Byrnes tour their garden admiring plants, pulling weeds and unwanted seedlings, and handpicking any slug tough enough to brave the sharp rock.—*S. R. L.*

## Passion in a pot

An exotic beauty of rich sentimental value, common passion vine *(Passiflora alatocaerulea)* is a star performer in Southern California gardens. This vigorous grower climbs by tendrils to 30 feet or more and produces spectacular flowers most of the year.

Gardeners usually curb the plant's rampant tendencies by training it against a trellis or arbor. But in Corona del Mar a common passion vine has grown successfully in an 18-inch pot for more than a year; it frames the entire porch with sprays of waxy white flowers shaded with pink and purple. After being planted in April from a 5-gallon can, the vine had grown 12 feet by September and was still blooming at Christmas.

To keep the plant happy, water it three times a week and fertilize it monthly with a water-soluble fertilizer.

*Passiflora alatocaerulea* (also sold as *P. pfordtii*) is the most commonly grown passion vine and the least susceptible to caterpillars. Two other handsome species to look for this month are *P. jamesonii* 'Coral Seas' (coral blooms) and *P. vitifolia* (deep red).—*Kathleen Sommer*

## Favorite 'Iceberg' rose is also a climber

The super-popular white 'Iceberg' rose that's both disease resistant and floriferous is a mainstay in many rose gardens. This floribunda is most commonly grown as a bush, but a climbing form is also available. Some nurseries offer it in limited quantities, but it's generally difficult to find, even by mail.

Now, a rose grower in Oregon offers ungrafted plants of 'Cl. Iceberg' by mail in 3-inch-wide by 6-inch-deep containers for $9.95 each (plus $1.50 shipping and $3.95 handling per plant). For a descriptive catalog of nearly 600 roses, send $5 to Heirloom Old Garden Roses, 24062 Riverside Dr. N.E., St. Paul, Ore. 97137; (503) 538-1576.—*L. B. S.*

## Sensational sizzler for slopes

'Rosenka' bougainvillea is becoming a common sight in coastal-influenced Southern Califronia gardens. And with good reason; it makes a handsome, informal flowering shrub in unthirsty gardens. But as a ground cover on gentle slopes, it really dazzles—blanketing the soil with golden flowers that age to pink. In a generally frost-free climate, it can bloom all year.

To grow 'Rosenka' as a ground cover, set out plants this month; place 1-gallon plants 2 to 3 feet apart, 5-gallon plants about 4 feet apart. (When planting, take care not to disturb the fragile root systems.) For added interest, some gardeners plant 'Rosenka' in swaths around clusters of spiky-leafed bronze New Zealand flax.

Bougainvillea blooms best in warm, sunny locations. For best bloom production close to the beach where cool morning fog occasionally settles in, plant bougainvillea in a spot that gets extra sun or reflected heat—on a south-facing slope or against a white wall. Feed plants in spring and summer with a complete fertilizer.

Plants set out this month should fill in completely by next winter.—*K. S.*

## Best peaches and nectarines east of the Sierras

Blessed with fewer disease problems than the area west of the Sierra and Cascades, parts of the desert and the intermountain West excel at producing peaches and nectarines. The main limitation is frost, which can kill buds before they flower, and (in worst cases) kill the trees.

But which peach and nectarine varieties should you plant? Larry Sagers, a Utah State University extension agent, recently compiled a list that can help. Most of his choices are freestone (easier for home gardeners to handle than clingstone kinds); the list gives pollinating requirements for most.

*Peaches.* Sagers's favorites include 'Cresthaven' and 'Early Elberta' for canning, 'Halehaven' for eating fresh, 'Redskin' and 'Suncrest' for all-purpose use, and 'Reliance' for coldest areas.

*Nectarines.* 'Flavortop' rises to the top, with 'Gold Mine' and 'Independence' rating well in areas that don't have enough winter chill for standard varieties.

For the complete list (free), write to USU Salt Lake County Cooperative Extension, 2001 S. State St., Room S-1200, Salt Lake City, Utah 84190.—*J. M.*

## Which geraniums to buy?

The difference in price among geraniums *(Pelargonium)* can be shocking: one garden center sells them for $2.50 a pot, while another sells them for 50 cents. Container sizes might vary slightly, but not enough, you think, to account for such a wide price spread. You're perfectly right.

The inexpensive geraniums are usually grown from seed, while the more expensive ones are grown from cuttings. You'll see the difference plainly in your garden.

Seedling geraniums usually have single flowers and lots of variability in size, flowering times, and abundance. Labels on them usually say simply "red" or "white."

Cutting-grown plants are floriferous, free blooming, and consistent in color and size. These traits are especially important if you're planting a bed or pot in which you want all flowers to bloom at the same time, in the same size and color. Most are labeled with a variety name.

If you still have your doubts, buy a few of each and see how they do; you'll probably never go back to seedlings.—*J. M.*

## Ojai demonstration garden

Ojai Valley Community Demonstration Garden is a new resource for Southern California gardeners who want to learn how to compost and conserve water. The approximately 1-acre site, landscaped with water-thrifty plants, features 14 home com-

*BLUE STAR CREEPER* *with spring flowers is a lavish filling between sandstone pavers.*

She filled the spaces with amended topsoil to ½ inch below the top of the stones. Rooted plants were spaced 4 to 6 inches on center. The blue star creeper filled in within the year.

Blue star creeper grows 2 to 3 inches tall, with a generous bloom of dainty flowers mostly in spring and summer. For best appearance give it regular water, but don't let the soil become soggy. This planting is irrigated with sprinklers. Plants look best when given a light feeding monthly from spring to fall. They accept moderate foot traffic.

Nurseries often sell blue star creeper as *Isotoma fluviatilis.* A flat costs from $15 to $20.—*L. O.*

## Mr. Rogers's seed tapes

If you've ever sown carrots or radishes, you know what a frustration it can be trying to distribute those tiny seeds evenly down a furrow. Eugene, Oregon, gardener Jim Rogers chuckles with self-satisfaction when he puts out his carrots and radishes.

Rogers makes seed tapes out of the strips of perforated paper that pull off the edges of his computer printouts. Between each hole, he puts a tiny dot of water-soluble glue; then into that dot he places one seed, alternating carrots and radishes.

When the glue is dry, he puts the tape into his planting furrows and covers it. By the time the carrots are big enough to be crowded by the radishes, the radishes are ready to pull out and eat. Thin carrots when they get to fingerling size in midsummer, and allow others to grow to full size for fall harvest.—*S. R. L.*

posting systems ranging from simple wire mesh bins to boxes that contain garbage-eating worms. Signs explain how each composter works, and brochures give construction tips.

The garden demonstrates both technical and creative components of landscaping. Whimsical sculptures and benches made from cast-off materials ornament planting beds. Many plants are labeled, and signs illustrate and describe the drip-irrigation system. An organic vegetable garden has information posted at its entrance on how to grow food without using petrochemical products.

The garden, sponsored by the city of Ojai and Ventura County Solid Waste Management Department, is at 415 S. Ventura Street. It's open daily during daylight hours. Admission is free.—*L. O.*

## Looking for seeds of rare fruits?

If so, consider joining California Rare Fruit Growers. This nonprofit group pub-

lishes a membership magazine, *Fruit Gardener,* six times a year; it's packed with growing information, recipes, and sources for plants and seeds. Tucked into each issue is the Seed Bank, a listing of edibles—mostly fruit and often rare. Members order from the list and receive inexpensive seed ($1 per packet), usually donated by other members.

"If it's really rare, I'll be deluged with orders," says Jan Davis, the volunteer who administers the bank. A rare offering, like the tasty mangosteen (*Garcinia mangostana*)— a 2- to 3-inch reddish purple tropical fruit with perfumed white flesh around large seeds—may bring in 300 or so requests. Davis fills each order on a first-come, first-served basis. The quantity per order depends on the supply. She parcels out seed, labels each packet, and encloses cultural information when provided by the donor.

"I get my jollies from being the first to try new seeds," says Davis. She's experimented with such oddities as

*Rollinia dulcis,* a tropical tree with cherimoya-like fruit.

To join the group and be eligible for seed, send $16 annual membership dues to California Rare Fruit Growers, Inc., Fullerton Arboretum, California State University, Fullerton, California 92634. —*L. O.*

## Paving pockets planted with flowers

Flowers and flagstones mingle in the showy walkway pictured above. To fill little pockets between pavers, landscape architect Carmen Allison chose blue star creeper (*Laurentia fluviatilis*) for a sunny location and baby's tears (*Soleirolia soleiroleii*) for an adjacent shady area; the two plants are visually compatible, though their light requirements differ (the blue star creeper takes full sun, or light shade where summers are hot).

Allison set each piece of flagstone on a 2-inch bed of sand. She left 4 to 6 inches between stones for planting.

## Tip of the Month

RENEE LYNN

*No fuss, no muss describes these coco fiber basket liners. Long-lasting and stiff, they're particularly useful in hanging baskets that have widely spaced bars like the one shown above. Slip the liner in a basket and cut it to fit. To insert plants, cut slots in the bottom and sides. Liners are available for hanging baskets, wall (half) baskets, and window planters from Kinsman Garden Company, Inc., River Rd., Point Pleasant, Pa. 18950. Depending on size, liners cost from $1.75 to $12.95 plus $3 shipping (for up to $14.99 worth of merchandise).—L. B. S.*

## Russian sage well suited for the West

From Afghanistan and Pakistan through Tibet, south-central Asia contains vast reaches of semiarid terrain that get very cold in winter. Sound familiar? It should be no surprise, then, that some of the plants that do well there also do well in the West. One of the best is Russian sage (*Perovskia*).

Lavender-blue, mintlike flowers rise above this plant's gray-green leaves in summer, giving it a definite look of sage. Bloom can be extended through most of the summer if you pinch off faded flowers. While perovskia has woody stems and grows waist-high, it does better when it's cut to the ground every winter. You can, however, let it stand like a shrub if you wish.

Though you won't find Russian sage everywhere, it's becoming more widely available. 'Blue Spire' is a good variety to start with. Plant it in full sun and give it regular watering for the first year. Then you can cut watering way back.—*J. M.*

## To pinch or not to pinch?

About the time potatoes begin to flower, the theories on what to do with them start flying. Some gardeners say that, to increase tuber production, you should pinch off the flower buds before they open. Others say you shouldn't. Potatoes like it dry, some gardeners say; potatoes like it wet, say others. Who's correct?

Pinching off flowers can help potato production, but it's not practical on a large scale. If you grow a small patch, go ahead and try it.

Potatoes need water, particularly right after flowering, when the tubers are setting. But they don't do well in soggy, poorly drained soil. Just after flowering and while tubers are gaining size, give them a consistent supply of moisture. Too much water at irregular intervals can result in hollow heart; too little water will produce a poor crop. —*L. B. S.*

## Five annuals that love the Central Valley's summer heat

As you shop for plants this month, don't forget the tried-and-true annuals that have a long history of standing up to California's hot Central Valley summers. Here are five troupers that rarely disappoint. Use them where you need a long-lasting show of color, such as near an entry, around decks and patios, or in containers.

**Cosmos** comes in shades of yellow, orange, white, pink, and red, the flowers borne on airy plants that range from 2 to 6 feet high. Plant seeds or transplants.

**Madagascar periwinkle** or annual vinca (*Catharanthus roseus*) produces bright white, pink, or reddish rose flowers that often have contrasting eyes. Bushy, dark green plants reach 1 to 2 feet high. Avoid overwatering. Start with transplants.

**Marigolds** bear flowers in shades of yellow, orange, bronze-red, and white. They grow 6 inches to 4 feet high and are easy to start from seed or transplants.

**Mealy-cup sage** (*Salvia farinacea*) is a perennial grown as an annual. It yields spikes of blue, silver, or white flowers on 1- to 2-foot plants. Start from transplants.

**Zinnias** come in almost every shade but blue and range in size from 6 inches to 5 feet. They make great cut flowers. You can start from seed or set out transplants.—*L.W.*

## Group vegetables by water needs

When planning and planting a vegetable garden, pay attention to each kind of plant's water requirements. Otherwise, you might plant high-water-use vegetables beside ones that need less water; this can waste water and harm plants.

According to extension vegetable specialist Dr. Tim Hartz of UC Davis, a good guideline is to group plants by how big they get and how fast they grow (the bigger and faster-growing they are, the more water they'll use). Shallow-rooted beets, bush beans, carrots, lettuce, spinach and other greens, and radishes grow at about the same rate and use similar amounts of water.

Corn, cucumber, melons, tomatoes, and squash combine well, too, since all grow rapidly and need lots of water. Don't mix new (successive) plantings of carrots, lettuce, and other crops with existing ones; water use changes as plants mature. —*L. B. S.*

## Butterfly a rootball

When you buy a potted plant (especially if it hasn't been repotted in a while), you'll probably find a thin fabric of roots sheathing the rootball. Yes, you have to score and tease them into strands that will grow easily into surrounding soil, but there's another simple trick you can do as well: butterfly the rootball before you plant.

Start by cutting into the rootball from the bottom with a sharp knife, pulling the rootball's sides apart as you go, until they spread like an upside-down butterfly. Your slice shouldn't come more than halfway up the rootball.

The process exposes more root surface, so the plant grows into planting soil faster. Butterflying works best with plants that have fibrous root systems, like perennials, vegetables, and flowers.—*J. M.*

# April Checklist

## PACIFIC NORTHWEST

**ADD TO COMPOST.** Lawn clippings, prunings, and spent flowers all go onto the pile. Keep the pile moist (you may want to cover it); a sheet of black plastic works well.

**BUY BEDDING PLANTS.** Nurseries will bulge with bedding plants this month. Shop early for the best selection. Geraniums, impatiens, lobelia, marigolds, and other summer favorites can go in by midmonth.

**CHECK OUT DAHLIA TUBERS.** If you didn't let dahlias stay in the ground through the winter, you can take them out of storage now and plant them.

**CONTROL SLUGS AND SNAILS.** As the weather warms and the food supply increases, slug and snail activity increases, too. Bait liberally now and you'll lessen your problems later on. Take care with bait. Pets can eat it and ingest a lethal dose.

**CONTROL TENT CATERPILLARS.** Break up their tents with a strong jet of water from your hose, then spray with *Bacillus thuringiensis*. Or cut off entire branches—tents intact—and burn them, or close them up in plastic bags that you've sprayed inside with household insecticide.

**DEADHEAD FLOWERS.** As azaleas, rhododendrons, and other blossoms bloom, the plants look and perform better if you remove faded flowers. With blossom heads gone, the plants channel energy into the production of new growth rather than seed.

**DIVIDE PERENNIALS.** Daylilies, hostas, phlox, Shasta daisies, and other summer-flowering perennials can still be divided. Dig now, and divide with a spade or sharp knife. A clump the size of a dinner plate can be quartered. Do the same for early-flowering perennials as soon as blooms fade.

**FEED AND WATER ASPARAGUS AND RHUBARB.** As new growth emerges, the plants get thirsty and hungry. Give them lots of water and feed them with finished compost or well-rotted manure, or scatter high-nitrogen fertilizer around the bases of the plants.

**FEED CONIFERS.** Scratch the soil under plants, being careful not to damage tender surface roots. Following manufacturer's instructions, broadcast a complete granular fertilizer around the base of each plant (12-12-12 works well). Water plants well if nature doesn't.

**FEED FLOWERING SHRUBS.** Give them a nitrogen-rich fertilizer so that new growth after bloom is strong and the plants are healthy and ready to roar when it's time for next year's bud set.

**MOVE OVERWINTERING PLANTS OUTDOORS.** Cymbidiums can go out early this month. Put begonias, fuchsias, and geraniums outside about midmonth.

**MOW LAWNS.** When a dry day appears, race out and mow the lawn. In cool, rainy weather, grass grows faster than ever, but mowers get clogged.

**PLANT BARE-ROOT.** This month ends bare-root planting season. Get plants into the ground as soon as possible. Between nursery and planting hole, keep roots moist. If they dry out, the plants are likely to die.

**PLANT SUMMER BULBS, CORMS, AND TUBERS.** Acidanthera, calla, crocosmia, dahlia, gladiolus, montbretia, ranunculus, and tigridia will all be for sale, ready to plant this month.

**PLANT VEGETABLES.** Immediately set out all cool-season crops: cabbage, carrots, lettuce, parsnips, peas, potatoes, radishes, spinach, and Swiss chard. It's not too late to sow seed for crops of arugula.

**PROPAGATE CHRYSANTHEMUMS.** New shoots will emerge around the bases of established plants this month. Take them as cuttings. Grasp and gently pull these shoots from the parent plant, getting a bit of root with each shoot. Put these rooted cuttings in pots of sterile soil (you may want to dip the bottom end of the cutting in rooting hormone). These potted cuttings will do fine outdoors, but you'll find they'll grow faster in the warmth of a windowsill, coldframe, or greenhouse.

**WEED.** Hoe or pull weeds before they set seed that scatters all over the garden. Established perennial weeds like thistles and dandelions must be pulled. For dandelions, use a large, dull kitchen knife. Slip it into the ground along the taproot. Wiggle the knife handle and pull on the plant with a strong, steady pressure. Big thistles will require a shovel and gloves.

**CONTROL MILDEW ON GRAPES.** Powdery mildew infects leaves, shoots, stems, and berries with a white fungal growth. Apply sulfur dust when shoots are 6, 12, and 18 inches long and then every two weeks through spring (do not apply when temperatures are above 95°).

**CORRECT CHLOROSIS.** If plants such as camellias, citrus, grapes, and gardenias are chlorotic (yellow mottling between leaf veins), spray leaves with a foliar fertilizer containing iron and zinc. For longer-lasting results, apply chelated iron or an acid-forming fertilizer containing chelated iron.

**DIG OR HOE WEEDS.** Dig out deep-rooted weeds such as dandelions with a hand weeder or trowel (water first to loosen soil). To make sure you get the entire root, slip the tool into the soil and pry up the taproot. You can remove all types of weeds when they're small by cutting just below the soil surface with a sharp hoe or push-pull cultivator.

**FEED AND MOW LAWNS.** To promote deeper rooting and, eventually, a less-thirsty turf, mow cool-season grasses such as tall fescue and bluegrass to 2 to 2½ inches tall. Feed lawns with a lawn fertilizer; water well afterward.

**GROOM AND FEED SPRING BULBS.** Remove spent flowers where the stems arise from the base. Leave foliage to manufacture nutrients for next year's show, and feed with a fertilizer formulated for bulbs. When leaves start to yellow, cut back on water.

**MULCH THE SOIL.** To save water, smother weeds, and keep soil cooler, spread 1 to 3 inches of bark chips, compost, wood shavings, or other organic material under shrubs and trees, around flowers and vegetables, and in pots. To prevent crown rot, keep mulch away from trunks and stems.

**PLANT FOR PERMANENCE.** Container-grown trees, shrubs, and ground covers, as well as sod lawns, can be planted now. If you live in a windy area, stake young trees; use ties that won't strangle trunks, and remove them after one growing season. In areas where wind isn't a problem, leave trees unstaked; they'll develop stronger trunks.

**PLANT PERENNIALS.** When plants are blooming, they're easier to combine effectively. Relatively unthirsty, easy-care choices include bearded iris, coreopsis, dianthus, echinops, gaillardia, Mexican evening primrose, penstemon, yarrow, and gray foliage plants such as lamb's ears.

**PLANT VEGETABLES AND HERBS.** Sow seeds of beans, corn, cucumbers, squash, most root crops (beets, carrots, radishes, turnips), greens (chard, lettuce, mustard, spinach). Leave space for another planting—two to three weeks later—of bush beans and root crops. Set out seedlings of eggplant, peppers, and tomatoes. This month, nurseries will have sixpacks of many herbs, including basil, mint, oregano, and parsley.

**PRUNE.** After new growth appears, prune freeze-damaged wood on tender plants such as bougainvillea and citrus. Also, prune to shape spring-flowering shrubs (after bloom) and overgrown hedges.

**ROTATE VEGETABLE BEDS.** If you have room in your garden, rotate planting sites to avoid a buildup of diseases and insects that can survive in the soil or on plant residue. Don't plant the same or closely related plants where they grew in the last two to three years.

**SHOP FOR TENDER PLANTS.** Set them out now so they'll get established long before winter comes. Try bougainvillea, hibiscus, jacaranda, Mexican lime, mandevilla, pandorea, plumeria, and podranea. There's no guarantee plants will live through next winter, particularly if a severe freeze comes. The best way to protect them is to plant them in containers, then move the containers to a protected area in winter.

**THIN VEGETABLE SEEDLINGS.** Use scissors to snip out extra seedlings of basil, beets, carrots, green onions, turnips, and other vegetables that were sown too thickly.

San Rafael
Walnut Creek
Oakland
San Francisco
San Jose
Monterey

Coastal (zone 17)
Inland (zones 14–16)

☐ **CARE FOR RHODODEN- DRONS.** Gently snap off blooms as they fade. Be sure not to damage tiny leaf buds below the flower clusters; these represent upcoming summer growth.

☐ **COMPOST.** To make your own rich soil amendment, build a pile of garden debris such as lawn clippings and leaves. Keep the pile moist (not wet), and add a handful or two of high-nitrogen fertilizer for every 18 to 24 inches of depth. To speed up the composting process, turn the pile with a pitchfork every week or two.

☐ **FERTILIZE.** Feed lawns, citrus, roses, and fall-planted shrubs and ground covers. Bedding plants benefit from monthly feedings—if you don't use controlled-release fertilizer at planting time. To keep citrus leaves deep green, spray them with liquid fertilizer containing the chelated micronutrients iron, zinc, and manganese.

☐ **FOIL PLANT DAMAGERS.** Snails and slugs come out in force now that the weather is milder and there's a lot of tender foliage to eat. Control them by handpicking or putting out bait or copper barriers. Hose off aphids before populations get out of control, and cover seedlings with netting or row covers to protect them from birds. To control worms on maturing cole crops, use the least toxic spray—*Bacillus thuringiensis.*

☐ **PLANT CITRUS AND OTHER TENDER PLANTS.** Now that the danger of frost has passed in all but the highest elevations, you can start planting tender plants such as citrus, bougainvilleas, and hibiscus.

☐ **PLANT PERENNIALS.** Blooming plants are easier to combine effectively. Relatively unthirsty, easy-care choices include coreopsis, dianthus, echinops, gaillardia, bearded iris, Mexican evening primrose, penstemon, salvia, and yarrow. Don't forget gray foliage plants for accent.

☐ **PLANT FOR SUMMER COLOR.** Nurseries should have great supplies of summer bedding plants to choose from this month. These include spring or cool-season annuals such as dianthus, nemesia, pansy, and viola, as well as summer favorites such as cosmos, marigolds, and zinnias, which can also be planted from seed. Also consider heat lovers such as annual salvia, asters, celosia, dwarf dahlias, Madagascar periwinkle, petunias, and portulaca. Impatiens and bedding begonias do well in shady gardens.

☐ **PLANT SUMMER BULBS, CORMS, AND TUBERS.** For planting beds or containers, try caladium, calla (consider yellows, pinks, and other shades as well as white), canna, crocosmia, dahlia, gladiolus, montbretia, tuberose, tuberous begonia, and watsonia.

☐ **PLANT VEGETABLES AND HERBS.** Now is a good time to put out seedlings of eggplant, pepper, and tomatoes. Sow seeds of beans, carrots, corn, cucumbers, and radish. You also have a good choice of herbs to plant this month, including basil, oregano, rosemary, tarragon, and thyme.

☐ **THIN FRUIT.** Pinch off pea-size excess fruit from apples, apricots, peaches, plums, and nectarines. Remove injured or weak-looking fruit first, then thin out all but one or two in each cluster. Make sure to space clusters at least 4 to 6 inches apart.

Redding
Lake Tahoe
Sacramento
Fresno
Bakersfield

▨ Valley (zones 7–9, 14)
▧ Mountain (zones 1, 2)

☐ **TRIM HEDGES.** Shear soon after the big flush of spring growth, cutting the top a little narrower than the base to compensate for faster growth there and to let light reach the lower limbs.

☐ **WATER AS NEEDED.** Watch seedlings and transplants carefully. If the weather warms, water when the top few inches of soil dries.

☐ **WEED.** Pull or hoe out weeds soon, before they scatter seeds. Or spray or sponge stubborn types with glyphosate.

**BUY AND PLANT BULBS.** In coastal (*Sunset* climate zones 22–24), inland (zones 18–21), and low-desert (zone 13) areas, cannas and dahlias are available now, and both grow fast and provide a long season of bloom. Tuberoses can also be planted this month. In low-desert areas, buy gladiolus corms, but store in the refrigerator crisper until planting time in August. For continuous summer bloom in the high desert (zone 11), plant gladiolus at two- to three-week intervals.

**CARE FOR GRAPES.** In both low- and high-desert areas, once new shoots are 5 to 8 inches long, control mildew with sulfur dust or lime sulfur spray. Repeat applications if needed. Water deeply while plants are growing actively.

**CHOOSE ANNUALS CAREFULLY.** To conserve water, use annuals sparingly and cluster them for impact. Choose less-thirsty kinds such as celosia, cosmos, portulaca, sanvitalia, and sweet alyssum. Select healthy plants that are not root-bound; plants in cell-packs generally adjust with less stress than overgrown plants in 4-inch containers.

**COMPOST.** Put prunings, leaves, grass clippings (except grasses that reproduce by runners), and kitchen vegetable waste on the compost pile. For fastest breakdown, chop or shred branches; add a layer of garden soil and a handful of fertilizer every foot or two. Turn and mix pile weekly, and keep it as moist as a damp sponge.

**CULTIVATE TO CONTROL WEEDS.** Dig out deep-rooted weeds such as dandelion with a hand weeder (water first to loosen soil). Slip weeder into soil and pry against taproot to make sure you get its entire length. Use a sharp hoe to scrape out other kinds of weeds when they're small; cut them just below the soil surface.

**DIVIDE CYMBIDIUMS.** In coastal and inland areas, it's time to refresh plants if pots are packed with bulbs, some brown and leafless. Knock the root mass out of the pot and separate as many clumps as you can by hand, or use pruning shears. Keep at least three healthy bulbs, with foliage, in each division. To discourage rot, dust cuts with sulfur.

**FERTILIZE PLANTS.** Most plants benefit from a feeding of all-purpose fertilizer (such as 10-10-10). Apply with a light touch; overfeeding now will result in softer, thirstier growth. Conversely, plants struggling for nutrients also use water less efficiently.

**PLANT ANNUALS.** Start summer flowers such as ageratum, coleus, dahlias, dianthus, impatiens, lobelia, marigolds, nicotiana, petunias, silene (for a new one, see page 83), and zinnias. In the high desert, there's still time to plant pansies, snapdragons, stock, sweet alyssum, and violas. To save water, minimize the size of planting beds, and mulch them.

**PLANT SUMMER VEGETABLES.** If you live within sight of the ocean, you can continue planting cool-season crops like broccoli, cabbage, cauliflower, leaf lettuce, and spinach. Inland, shift attention to warm-season crops—beans, corn, cucumbers, eggplant, pumpkins, squash, tomatoes. High-desert gardeners should delay planting for two to four weeks; until mid-month, frost is still a possibility.

**PREPARE GARDEN BEDS.** Add organic matter to the soil before planting your summer flowers, herbs, and vegetables. Spread compost 2 to 3 inches deep over planting area, then sprinkle a regular or controlled-release fertilizer at label rates. Deeply cultivate the mixture into the soil.

**TREAT PLANTS FOR IRON DEFICIENCY.** In coastal, inland, and low-desert areas, if bottlebrush, camellias, citrus, eucalyptus, gardenias, geranium (*Pelargonium*), hibiscus, pyracantha, and roses have yellowing leaves with green veins, feed them with a fertilizer containing chelated iron.

**SHOP FOR UNUSUAL PLANTS.** Plant societies and garden organizations offer plants for sale this month that may be difficult to find in nurseries; native and drought-tolerant plants are good examples.

Santa Barbara
Pasadena
San Bernardino
Santa Monica
Los Angeles
San Diego

☐ Zones 18–21
☐ Zones 22–24

## ANYWHERE IN THE WEST, TACKLE THESE CHORES:

☐ **DIG OR HOE WEEDS.** When weeds are small, wait until soil is dry, then hoe early in the day. Sun and dryness will kill tiny roots by day's end. For larger weeds, water thoroughly, then pop weeds out, roots and all, with a hand weeder. Let whole weeds dry in the sun before you compost them; otherwise they'll retain enough life to flower and disperse seeds.

☐ **MULCH SOIL.** A 2- to 3-inch layer of organic mulch suppresses weeds, holds in moisture, and (when the weather heats up) keeps roots cool. Mulch around annuals, perennials, trees, and shrubs, especially if summers are hot and dry where you live. Until the weather gets warm, keep mulch a few inches back from warm-season vegetables—their roots can use the heat. If you sift compost before applying it, you can use the coarse leftovers as mulch.

☐ **ROTATE VEGETABLE BEDS.** It's a good idea to rotate vegetable beds to prevent disease buildup in the soil. Where you had corn last year, plant beans this year; where you had cucumber, melons, and squash last year, put lettuce; and where you had eggplant, peppers, potatoes, and tomatoes, put carrots and peas.

## IN THE INTERMOUNTAIN WEST, DO THESE CHORES:

☐ **APPLY DORMANT SPRAY.** After pruning, spray fruit trees with a mixture of oil and lime sulfur or oil and copper. If rain washes it off, reapply. If you use oil and copper, keep spray off walls, fences, and walks that might be stained.

☐ **FERTILIZE LAWNS.** Apply 1 to 2 pounds high-nitrogen fertilizer per 1,000 square feet (more on heavily used lawns and those growing in poor soil). Water it in well.

☐ **PLANT BARE-ROOT.** Set out berries, grapes, and other small fruits, fruit and ornamental trees, asparagus, and rhubarb.

☐ **PRUNE.** Early in the month, before new growth emerges, finish pruning deciduous fruit and ornamental trees, vines, grapes, and roses. You can wait until after flowering to prune shrubs such as forsythia and spiraea that bloom in early spring. Or prune them lightly after buds swell, and put the cuttings in vases indoors; they'll flower there.

☐ **SOW HARDY VEGETABLES.** As soon as you can work the soil, sow seeds of beet, carrot, endive, kohlrabi, lettuce, onion, parsley, parsnip, pea, radish, spinach, Swiss chard, and turnip. Set out transplants of broccoli, brussels sprouts, cabbage, cauliflower, and onion; plant seed potatoes. Floating row covers (sold at garden centers) will protect seedlings, take the edge off cold nights, and get plants off to a fast start.

## IN THE SOUTHWEST'S LOW AND INTERMEDIATE DESERTS, THERE'S MUCH TO DO:

☐ **FEED PLANTS.** Almost everything in the garden can use a dose of complete fertilizer. Apply about 1 pound 10-10-10 per 100 square feet. Water the day before you spread the fertilizer, and immediately afterward.

☐ **FERTILIZE LAWNS.** To give Bermuda grass a push for the summer, apply 3 to 4 pounds high-nitrogen fertilizer per 1,000 square feet about two weeks after the grass greens up. Water the lawn thoroughly to wash nutrients down to turf roots.

☐ **FINISH POST-FREEZE PRUNING.** Check plants damaged by frost. New growth makes damaged older growth apparent, giving you easy targets as you move in and prune out dead and damaged wood.

☐ **PLANT ANNUALS.** You have lots of choices this month. Among them: ageratum, calliopsis (*Coreopsis tinctoria*), celosia, cosmos, four o'clock, globe amaranth, gloriosa daisy (*Rudbeckia*), kochia, lisianthus (*Eustoma grandiflorum*), marigold, Mexican sunflower (*Tithonia*), portulaca, strawflower, Madagascar periwinkle (*Catharanthus roseus*), and zinnia. Before you plant, amend soil well with organic matter (such as compost).

☐ **PLANT CITRUS.** This is the best month to plant all kinds of citrus from 5- or 7-gallon containers. Plant in full sun, putting the citrus tree in a hole that's the same depth as the rootball, but two to three times as wide. After planting, build a low berm around the drip line to make a watering basin. You'll need to water two or three times a week at first, but by summer's end you'll be watering only once every five to seven days—more in sandy soil, less in clay soil. To protect trees from sunburn, wrap trunks in white cloth, or slap on a coat of white latex paint.

☐ **PLANT LAWNS.** As soon as average nighttime temperatures rise above 70°, plant hybrid Bermuda grass. In higher-elevation parts of the desert, choose a cold-hardy kind, such as buffalo grass or blue grama. Wait until fall to plant tall fescue.

☐ **PLANT PERENNIALS.** Start chrysanthemum, columbine, coreopsis, gaillardia, gerbera, hollyhock, Michaelmas daisy, salvia, or Shasta daisy from plants or seed; gazania and geranium are usually available only as plants.

☐ **PLANT SUMMER BULBS.** After danger of frost is past, plant caladium, canna, crinum, dahlia, daylily, gladiolus, iris, or montbretia. You can also buy container-grown agapanthus, society garlic (*Tulbaghia*), and zephyranthes.

☐ **PLANT VEGETABLES.** In low-desert areas, sow beans and cucumbers by mid-April; set out eggplant, okra, peanut, squash, and sweet potato any time this month. Gardeners at intermediate elevations can sow cucumber, melon, okra, pumpkin, soybean, squash, and watermelon, as well as plant seedlings of eggplant, pepper, sweet potato, and tomato.

SHOPPER'S DILEMMA: *Which plant to buy? The best value and longest performance come from the 4-inch foxglove (left); the bloom on the 1-gallon plant will fade soon.*

# How to be a really smart nursery shopper this spring

"WHEN I GO NURSERY SHOPPING, I'M LIKE A KID IN A candy store. Everything's so beautiful that I want to buy one of each!" says one eager spring shopper.

The colorful promise of a nursery in April is irresistible, with literally thousands of annuals and perennials to choose from. But impulse buying is a sure way to run up a major tab, and it all but guarantees a mishmash in the landscape.

Our advice for great performance and the most value for your dollar? Be a smart shopper.

Before you leave home, have an idea of your needs based on space, sun exposure, and soil conditions. And think about potential plant combinations with an eye toward compatible bloom times, colors, heights, and frequency of watering and fertilizing. Also, estimate how many plants you'll need, allowing for growth. (Whether you plant a coreopsis from a jumbo pack or a 1-gallon container, the ultimate size is the same.)

These details, plus the four smart-shopping guidelines on these pages, will help you navigate nursery aisles with ease.

## 1. LET THE SEASON BE YOUR GUIDE

How do you choose from among so many plant possibilities? It depends upon whether you're searching for summer-long bloom, a splash of instant color, or both. The following tips will help you choose the right annuals and perennials for what you wish to accomplish.

*Annuals* (plants that complete the life cycle in one growing season). Some annuals grow during the warm season, while others are cool-season plants. In March and April, you'll find a relatively small selection of cool-season annuals but an abundance of warm-season annuals.

Cool-season annuals (listed below left) look good now in nurseries, and are great when you want a burst of color for a party or special occasion. But in inland areas, they'll bloom themselves out as summer sets in, and plants will die. (In mild coastal areas, they may flower into summer.) These annuals are better planted in the fall in mild-winter regions.

Warm-season annuals (listed below right) are a better buy at this time of year. You can expect a full summer of bloom from young, healthy seedlings. Plants will fade at summer's end.

*Perennials* (these grow and bloom each year, usually for at least three years). Longevity distinguishes perennials from annuals. Each perennial variety has its own bloom season.

Spring bloomers (which include columbine, coral bells, foxglove, and rockcress) are often near peak bloom in nurseries in March and April, but once you transplant them in the garden they may be on their way out of flower. It's best to plant these perennials in fall for bloom from early spring into summer.

Perennials that bloom through the summer (coreopsis, gaillardia, penstemon, rudbeckia, salvia, Shasta daisy, verbena, and yarrow) are a better bet. Although fall is the best time to plant most of these perennials, if you buy and plant these soon, you can expect excellent results.

---

### COOL-SEASON ANNUALS   OR   WARM-SEASON ANNUALS

*The following plants grow in the cool season. You'll find some or all of these in nurseries now, with a bigger selection in the Northwest and mountain regions. Though they provide instant color, they'll bloom out by summer. You'll get the longest bloom if they're planted earlier (in fall in mild-winter climates, in early spring in colder regions).*

- Annual phlox (Southern California and desert only)
- Bachelor's button
- Chrysanthemum multicaule
- C. paludosum
- Dianthus (Southern California and desert only)
- Forget-me-not
- Nemesia
- Pansy
- Poppy
- Sweet alyssum

*These annuals grow during the warm season and provide summer bloom. Depending on where you live, they start appearing in nurseries in February (Southern California, desert areas), March (Northern California), April (the Northwest and warmer parts of the mountain region), or May (mountain region).*

- Ageratum
- Annual phlox
- Celosia
- Cosmos
- Dianthus
- Impatiens
- Lobelia
- Marigold
- Nasturtium
- Nicotiana
- Petunia
- Portulaca
- Salvia
- Sunflower
- Sweet alyssum
- Verbena
- Zinnia

NORMAN A. PLATE

NORMAN A. PLATE

*DIANTHUS (usually grown as an annual) comes in a variety of container sizes. Not shown: jumbo pack, with six 2½-inch cells; $2.30 to $4.*

8-inch pulp pot
$6 to $7

1 gallon
$3.50 to $7

4-inch pot
$1.10 to $1.80

Sixpack with
1-inch cells
$1.75 to $2.70

# 2. PLANTS COME IN ALL SIZES, BUT SMALL IS USUALLY BEST

Nurseries now carry plants in different sizes of containers. Choices can be overwhelming.

Annuals are readily available in sixpacks (also called pony packs and cell-packs), with six 1-inch-wide cells; jumbo packs (or color packs), with six 2½-inch-wide cells; 4-inch pots; 1-gallon containers; and 8-inch-wide pulp pots. And in Southern California, annuals are sometimes sold in undivided flats, as shown at right.

In the past, perennials were sold primarily in 1-gallon containers. Then a few years ago, nurseries started carrying plants in 4-inch pots. Over the past couple of years in California, more and more perennials have become available in sixpacks or jumbo packs.

Which should you buy?

If cost is a concern, small plants are a better value (see

**IN SOUTHERN CALIFORNIA,** *you'll find a flat of 64 or 81 annuals for $15 to $20; sometimes quarter- or half-flats are sold.*

"Know how to get the best value," on page 96). But even if cost isn't a consideration, healthy plants in small containers, if not rootbound, generally go through less transplant shock and get established faster than larger plants. In most cases, they catch up to their larger counterparts within a few weeks and bloom longer (see *Sunset's* test on the facing page).

Also, most horticulturists agree that for a long season of bloom it's best to buy plants before they flower. (In some areas, it may be difficult to find even the smallest plants without bloom.) That doesn't mean you never should buy blooming plants in 4-inch or 1-gallon containers. If you're having a party and want instant color, go ahead and splurge. Or, if it's late in the season and you don't want to wait the few extra weeks for flowers, indulge yourself.

*(Continued on page 96)*

**PERENNIALS LIKE THIS** *coreopsis often come in three sizes: sixpacks ($1.95 to $3.50), 4-inch pots ($1.50 to $3.50), and 1-gallon containers ($4.50 to $7).*

## Sunset tested the effects of container size on growth. Here are our results

Last spring, we bought three kinds of perennials—perennial statice (*Limonium perezii*), delphinium (not shown below), and erodium—in sixpacks, 4-inch pots, and 1-gallon containers. We planted them in our Menlo Park, California, test garden to compare performance of the small and large sizes. The test was replicated five times. We monitored their growth.

Within six weeks, growth of the 4-inch statice, delphinium, and erodium caught up to the 1-gallon plants. There were more blooms on the 4-inch statice and erodium (although the statice flowers weren't open completely). About three weeks after our photograph, the sixpack sizes of statice and delphinium caught up. Only the sixpack of the slower-growing erodium remained smaller the first season of growth than the plants from 4-inch and 1-gallon containers. For slower-growing perennials such as armeria, coral bells, and erodium, you may want to buy plants in 4-inch containers so they fill in faster. Otherwise, sixpacks are your best buy and give the best performance for the money, though many perennials are still available only in gallons.

**BEFORE PLANTING:** *Sixpack, 4-inch, and 1-gallon sizes of statice, delphinium, and erodium line up.*

*ERODIUM SIX WEEKS AFTER PLANTING*

1-gallon    4-inch    Sixpack

*STATICE SIX WEEKS AFTER PLANTING*

1-gallon    4-inch    Sixpack

PETER CHRISTIANSEN

# 3. KNOW HOW TO GET THE BEST VALUE

In flowering plants, you'll obviously get better value from a plant that blooms all summer long (or that has a long bloom season) than from one with a brilliant but temporary display.

Smaller plants are also a better value. You can often buy a sixpack—which contains six plants—for the same price as a 4-inch plant. And you can get at least two 4-inch pots for the price of a 1-gallon plant.

A 1-gallon annual can cost more than $5, which could buy you at least two sixpacks (up to $2.50 each)—a whopping 12 plants for the price of 1.

.(Note that there is a substantial decrease in cost if you plant the perennial garden shown in the illustration below from jumbo packs and 4-inch containers rather than from 1-gallon containers.)

## SMALL PLANTS BRING BIG SAVINGS

*This 6- by 9-foot perennial garden can cost you as little as $17 or as much as $72.*

The size of containers purchased accounts for the difference in cost. Prices and plant availability vary from region to region and nursery to nursery, but many perennials are found in jumbo packs of six plants (about 46 cents per plant), 4-inch containers (average cost about $2.34 per plant), and 1-gallon cans (average cost about $5.15 per plant). If you plant the penstemon, daisies, and coreopsis from jumbo packs and the brachycome and catmint from 4-inch containers (they're generally not available in jumbo packs), the cost is about $17. But if all are planted from 1-gallon containers, the cost comes to about $72.

It pays to compare prices and to shop around for small containers. From one nursery to the next, the cost of a perennial in a 4-inch container ranges from as little as $1.50 to as much as $3.30—a big difference when you're using dozens of plants.

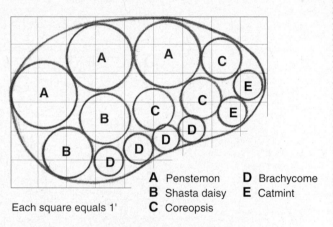

Each square equals 1'

**A** Penstemon    **D** Brachycome
**B** Shasta daisy    **E** Catmint
**C** Coreopsis

**THE GARDEN CONTAINS** *14 perennial plants: 3 hybrid penstemons, 2 dwarf Shasta daisies, 3 coreopsis, 4 brachycome, and 2 catmint.*

LUCY I. SARGEANT

# 4. KNOW HOW TO CHOOSE HEALTHY PLANTS

Annuals and perennials planted now for summer bloom need to grow vigorously. By choosing healthy seedlings and caring for them properly, you won't be disappointed. As a general rule, nurseries tend to take better care of plants than discount stores that sell everything from clothing to plumbing supplies.

No matter where you shop, look for compact plants with good leaf color. Leaves should be perky, not limp or wilted. Straggly or stretching seedlings may indicate crowding or insufficient light. If plants are rootbound, pass them by.

Occasionally you'll find seedlings that were recently planted into their cell-pack or 4-inch containers and aren't yet ready for the garden. If the leaves of the plant extend to the edge of the container, then the root system is probably developed enough for transplanting into your garden. ■

*By Lynn Ocone, Lauren Bonar Swezey*

**BUYER BEWARE!** *When you shop for plants, knowing what not to buy is as important as what to buy. Snapdragon at left is pale and wilty because of dry soil; delphinium (center) is too wet, and plants are rotting; and campanula is young and too small for the pot. Dusty miller in shopper's hand is overgrown and rootbound.*

## IF YOU CAN'T FIND SMALL PERENNIALS AT THE NURSERY

No matter where you live, your nursery probably carries a wide variety of annuals in all sizes of containers. But in some areas, perennials in six-packs or 4-inch containers may be difficult to find. If you can't locate plants in these containers, you can order by mail from one of the following sources. Depending on the source, plants are grown in 2- to 4-inch pots. Catalogs are free unless noted.

**Bluestone Perennials,** 7411 Middle Ridge Rd., Madison, Ohio 44057; (800) 852-5243. Wide assortment of perennials.

**Canyon Creek Nursery,** 3527 Dry Creek Rd., Oroville, Calif. 95965. Catalog $2. Uncommon perennials.

**Daisy Fields,** 12635 S.W. Brighton Lane, Hillsboro, Ore. 97123; (503) 628-0315. Catalog $1. Old-fashioned perennials.

**Digging Dog Nursery,** Box 471, Albion, Calif. 95410; (707) 937-1130. Catalog $2. Tried-and-true perennials, along with grasses, shrubs, and trees.

**Forestfarm,** 990 Tetherow Rd., Williams, Ore. 97544; (503) 846-7269. Catalog $3. Native plants, common and uncommon perennials, shrubs and trees.

**Heronswood Nursery Ltd.,** 7530 288th St. N.E., Kingston, Wash. 98346. Catalog $3. Common and uncommon perennials, as well as shrubs and trees.

**Joyce's Garden,** 64640 Old Bend Redmond Highway, Bend, Ore. 97701 (503) 388-4680. Ultrahardy perennials, ground covers, and herbs.

**Lamb Nurseries,** 101 E. Sharp Ave., Spokane, Wash. 99202; (509) 328-7956 (no telephone orders). Catalog $1. Hardy perennials and rock garden plants, as well as some vines and shrubs.

**Milaeger's Gardens,** 4838 Douglas Ave., Racine, Wis. 53402; (800) 669-9956. Catalog $1. Sells more than 900 garden perennials.

**Mountain Valley Growers,** 38325 Pepperweed Rd., Squaw Valley, Calif. 93675; (209) 338-2775. Fragrant and ornamental perennials, culinary herbs, and everlastings.

MICHAEL THOMPSON

**'OREGON PRIDE'** *paste tomato produces fruits that can weigh up to 2 pounds apiece.*

# Best short-season crops

*Here are proven performers among melons, peppers, tomatoes, and other favorites*

O VER MUCH OF THE West, a short growing season demands vegetables that go from seed to harvest relatively quickly. With that in mind, we visited Tim Peters, who breeds vegetables and flowers in the mountains of southern Oregon, to find out which vegetables he thinks are best for short-season growing areas of the West.

He showed—and let us taste—his favorites in several categories. They include one of his introductions, but most are the creations of other breeders. You can plant most of these vegetables this month or next.

**'FRECKLES'** *Crenshaw melon is named for its skin. It's smaller than later Crenshaws, but still big enough to serve two.*

**Melons.** Among cantaloupes, 'Earligold' comes out on top, producing large, sweet, orange-fleshed fruits (shown on facing page) in about three months from planting. Peters says that great muskmelon flavor depends heavily on soil fertility. He beefs his up by digging plenty of composted chicken and steer manure into melon hills before planting.

'Freckles' Crenshaw melon was bred for earliness: it matures a couple of days ahead of 'Early Crenshaw' and two weeks earlier than regular Crenshaw. 'Freckles' produces smaller, harder-shelled fruits with comparable flavor and texture to 'Early Crenshaw'. 'Freckles', which Peters bred, is also beautiful (see the photographs below).

**Peppers.** Among bell peppers, 'Jingle Bells' colors up in early August, far ahead of most others. Fruits are small and red.

For better flavor, try 'Gypsy'. It's also larger and matures a bit later.

'Purple Flame' also ripens later than 'Jingle Bells', producing a remarkable color show in the process. Color starts out grass green, then shifts to purple over green flesh before it settles back into a kind of camouflage green. Then, just when you think the show's over, fruits turn flame red. Flavor is excellent.

'Lilac', another favorite of Peters's, is similar to 'Purple Flame', but its purple color floats over yellow flesh.

The finest hot chili pepper in Peters's test garden is 'Riot', which does double duty as an ornamental and in salads; it is a graduate of horticulturist Jim Baggett's breeding program at Oregon State University.

**Tomatoes.** For salads, Peters likes the cherry tomato 'Sweet Million', which he describes as "sweet, refreshing." It grows in racemes (close rows down each side of a stem) and doesn't have the splitting problems of the similar 'Sweet 100' and 'Gardeners Delight'.

For paste tomatoes, 'Oregon Pride', developed by OSU, rates best. It can weigh up to 2 pounds. Like seedless watermelons and other paste tomatoes, 'Oregon Pride' is mostly, but not completely, free of viable seeds.

## COOL-SEASON FAVORITES

**Asparagus.** Among the 14 varieties of asparagus in Peters's trials, 'Larac' hybrid came out on top, with double the production of its nearest competitor. The runner-up, 'UC 157' $F_2$ (not to be confused with 'UC 157' $F_1$), was twice again as productive as the rest of the pack.

**Carrots.** 'Mokum' and 'Estelle' came out on top. Both look like 6- to 8-inch tapered orange candles.

'Mokum' is sweet and crisp without being hard.

'Estelle' grows very flavorful roots in the right soil: it demands even soil moisture and only modest amounts of manure (too much ruins the carrots). This one is also susceptible to boron deficiency, which can cause carrots to fork and split.

**Celery.** A few tricks will help you grow great celery. First, choose a fast-growing variety like 'Ventura'. Grow plants close together (thin to about 1 foot apart) to force stalks to stretch out, reaching for the light. Finally, add a thick layer of manure to push growth. Peters surrounds plants with a ½-inch layer of composted chicken manure or a 2-inch layer of horse manure. He keeps plants well watered.

## SEED SOURCES

A number of mail-order suppliers sell these seeds; you'll find some on seed racks, too. Peters also sells seeds; for a catalog, send $2 to Peters Seeds, 407 Maranatha Lane, Myrtle Creek, Ore. 97457. ∎

*By Jim McCausland*

MICHAEL THOMPSON

**'EARLIGOLD' CANTALOUPES** *grow large and abundantly—rare traits for early melons. When you pick one up and the stem slips free, it's ready to eat.*

**COLORFUL ENOUGH** *to delight any artist, 'Riot' hot peppers (above) and 'Purple Flame' bell peppers (left) go through a range of color phases as they ripen. At maturity, both kinds are fire-engine red.*

NORMAN A. PLATE

YOU CAN GROW *eggplants in a variety of shapes and colors. Choices include*
**1** *'Debarbentane',* **2** *'Casper',* **3** *'Vernal',* **4** *'Black Beauty',* **5** *'Italian Pink Bicolor',*
**6** *'Blacknite',* **7** *'Pallida Romanesca',* **8** *'Osterei',* **9** *another 'Casper',* **10** *'White Egg',*
**11** *'Bride',* **12** *'Garden Huckleberry' (not a true eggplant, but closely related),*
**13** *'Imperial Black Beauty',* **14** *'Florida Market', and* **15** *'Violetta Lunga'.*

# Glossy new eggplants for the garden

*Stunning to look at, delicious to eat*

WHEN YOU GROW YOUR own eggplants, glistening globes dangling from lush plants are a visual reward. An even better payoff is edible: fruits harvested at their peak, when skins are tender, seeds are small, and flavors are rich and mellow. The ideal time to pick eggplants is when the fruits are two-thirds their full size; as the fruits mature, they lose their sheen, grow soft and bitter, and their seeds become large and coarse.

## CHOOSE FOR TASTE AND BEAUTY

Eggplant varieties vary enough in taste, texture, and color to offer a number of tempting choices; above is a selection we grew in *Sunset*'s test garden. Fruits range from deep purple to lavender, red, green, white, and subtle combinations of these hues.

Asian types such as 'Bride', 'Little Fingers', and 'Thai Green' are vigorous, highly productive, very tender, and mild-tasting. Some, such as 'Bride', 'Italian Pink Bicolor', 'Osterei', 'Pallida Romanesca', 'Rosa Bianca', 'Violetta Lunga', and 'White Egg', are particularly eye-catching, and in most cases, plants are compact. Most of these varieties do exceedingly well in small gardens and containers. Smaller-size selections include 'Baby Bell', 'Osterei', and 'Slim Jim'.

For the traditional round or oval eggplant, choose from among 'Blacknite', 'Imperial Black Beauty', 'Rosa Bianca', and 'Violetta Lunga'.

In cool- or short-summer areas, 'Dusky' and 'Mini Finger' do well because they mature almost two weeks earlier than other varieties.

## PLANTING AND CARE

About 10 weeks before the last frost date in your area, sow seeds in flats or containers. In a warm location, seeds sprout in 5 to 10 days (Asian types we tested took much longer). Keep seedlings in bright light. About 10 days before planting out, harden seedlings by placing them outdoors in a protected spot away from hot sun and drying winds. Set out in the garden when all danger of frost has passed. They also flourish in raised beds and containers.

Eggplants like even warmer growing conditions than peppers do, so be sure to plant them in your garden's warmest, sunniest spot. The soil should be rich and drain well. If it is heavy or sandy, work in organic material such as compost. To hasten growth in cool-summer areas, mulch at planting time with black plastic. For heaviest fruit production, use a balanced fertilizer such as 10-10-10 once a month. Water regularly.

## WHERE TO BUY SEEDS

*The Cook's Garden,* Box 535, Londonderry, Vt. 05148. Offers 'Bride' and 'Violetta Lunga'.

*Ornamental Edibles,* 3622 Weedin Court, San Jose, Calif. 95132. Offers 'Little Fingers', 'Rosa Bianca', and others.

*Seeds Blüm,* Idaho City Stage, Boise, Idaho 83706. Offers 10 varieties, including 'Black Beauty', 'Casper', 'Debarbentane', 'Garden Huckleberry', 'Rosa Bianca', and 'White Egg'.

*Stokes Seeds Inc.,* Box 548, Buffalo, N.Y. 14240. Offers 12 varieties, including 'Blacknite', 'Mini Finger', and 'Vernal'. ∎

*By Emely Lincowski*

RAMBUNCTIOUS *'San Diego Red' bougainvillea climbs up between garage doors, then spreads out along a trellis.*

DARROW M. WATT

NORMAN A. PLATE

COLORFUL, FAN-SHAPED *bougainvillea brightens up a plain stucco wall; stems twist around plastic-coated wire.*

# Harnessing bougainvillea

*Three ways to control these vigorous vines*

RAMPANT GROWTH IS both the blessing and the curse of tall-growing types of bougainvillea. On the plus side, the tropical vine dresses up bare walls within only a season or two in mild climates. (In cool climates, it usually takes an extra season for it to become established.) And bougainvillea's colorful, flowerlike bracts appear in great profusion from spring throughout the fall.

And the minus side? Unless you control it, bougainvillea becomes wild and unruly.

Fortunately, you can train bougainvillea in a variety of handsome ways, making it suitable for even the manicured garden. Here we show three ways inventive gardeners harnessed their plants.

## UP A GARAGE OR ALONG GARDEN WALLS

*Garage climber.* Adorning the face of Lisa and Joel Knight's house in Monterey, this 'San Diego Red' bougainvillea climbs up a narrow space between garage doors, then grows largely unchecked above; annual maintenance keeps the vine in bounds.

The base of the bougainvillea is sheared like a hedge, which prevents it from flowering and gives it a lush, green look. Landscape architect Tom Deyerle designed a trellis to cover the second story of the house using redwood 2-by-2s; a lag bolt screwed into an expansion shield attaches the trellis to the stucco wall.

*Wall sculpture.* Fanning out along a stucco wall, this colorful vine is trained to create a sculptural look. Long vine stems wrap around plastic-coated wire, and eye screws hold the wire in place. Additional lengths of wire can be attached to the wall as the stems grow.

*Trellis cover-up for a block wall.* Designed to hide an unattractive block wall, this espaliered bougainvillea climbs along a wood trellis in Van Wright's Costa Mesa garden. The 2-by-3s for the frame were salvaged from an old garage door and joined with simple glued-and-nailed lap joints. Wright secured the trellis to the block wall with nuts and washers on ¼-inch threaded rods screwed into lead anchors. The vine winds around aluminum wire that is attached to the trellis with eye screws. ∎

*By Lauren Bonar Swezey*

MARTHA WOODWARD

TRAINED ALONG *a wooden trellis, Bougainvillea spectabilis hides a plain block wall. Above, stems wind around aluminum wire that attaches to eye screws.*

# False fronts
# for flower
# holders

*Cut them from
screening or tin
to dress up the
humblest jelly jar*

PETER CHRISTIANSEN

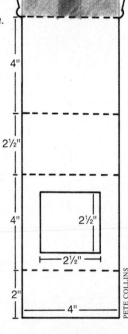

NORMAN A. PLATE

**CHEERFUL HOUSE,** *made of paper-coated hardware cloth, and a shiny aluminum basket were shaped from the pattern at right. Basket details were added with a hammer and nail. Bottom drawing shows how to fold the cut metal (lightly score it first). Designer: Françoise Kirkman.*

D ECORATIVE FAÇADES, like the aluminum basket and the sprightly yellow house pictured here, dress up small summer bouquets. When viewed from the front, they conceal glass containers (either square votive candle holders or jelly jars) that hold the flowers.

For either holder, make a pattern following the drawing.

## ALUMINUM BASKET

Trace the pattern onto a 6-by 20-inch piece of aluminum roof flashing. Mark the fold lines and jar opening. Cut the outside lines with tin snips; use a chisel and hammer to cut the jar opening. Lightly score and fold as shown in drawing. Use metal glue to attach the end piece to the back of the basket. Secure with clothespins until glue sets.

## HARDWARE CLOTH HOUSE

Trace the pattern onto a 12-by 27-inch piece of 27-gauge-wire hardware cloth with ⅛-inch grid. Use pointed tin snips to cut a hole for the jar. Layer two or three pieces of tissue paper over the front and back of the house façade (brush white glue between layers); fold paper over edges of the house as you glue. Fold the hardware cloth as shown for aluminum basket, and glue the end piece to the back of the façade. Glue a few more layers of paper over the inside seam (where folded end pieces attach to the back of the house). When glue dries, spray paint the entire piece yellow. Use a brush, sponge, or stamps to apply orange doors and windows. When the paint dries, coat the house with mat varnish. ■

*By Lynn Ocone*

4"

2½"

4"  2½" 2½"

2"  4"

PETE COLLINS

NETTING *mature trees (like this persimmon) rewards your time and effort with undamaged crop.*

# Ways to dissuade birds

*Humane methods for conserving crops*

 ARDENERS WHO LOVE birds face a dilemma. On the one hand, birds enrich our lives with song and beauty. On the other hand, our feathered friends know no limits. Cultivated strawberries and tender pea seedlings are as much a part of their dinner smorgasbord as weed seeds that fall on the path.

The strategies for coexisting with birds vary. Some gardeners plant more than they need and plan to sacrifice a percentage of their crops. Others have little space and count on every last strawberry for their pancakes and ice cream. They can't afford to let birds sample their figs and nectarines, leaving the pecked fruit to rot. For them, conserving crops can mean the difference between a good harvest and slim pickings.

Most methods for dissuading birds fall into two categories: barriers and scare devices. Here are your options.

## CROP COVERS

The surest way to protect vegetable seedlings and fruit is to cover them with flexible plastic bird netting, or aviary wire attached to a frame.

To use plastic netting, simply drape it over plants. Thorough coverage is essential, though, and the netting must be secured to the ground or gathered around the trunk of the tree so birds can't find an opening. When it's practical, suspend netting 2 to 3 inches away from the fruit. Fruit that comes in contact with the netting is vulnerable because birds will perch on the netting and peck away. Remove the netting promptly after harvest or branches might grow through it, making it harder to remove later.

Draped netting is easiest to use on cane berries, blueberries, and small bushes. It's a real project to cover a tree. Getting beneath the netting to harvest is also a challenge.

Plastic netting is sold in rolls or large pieces; a 14- by 50-foot roll, for example, costs about $19. With proper handling, the netting lasts for several years.

For row crops such as strawberries, lettuce, and peas, consider making a wooden or plastic pipe frame with aviary wire or plastic netting attached over the top and on all sides. Frames are mobile and reusable, and they can be designed to make harvesting easy.

## SCARE TACTICS

Scare devices range from inflatable great horned owls to reflective tape. Homemade solutions include scarecrows, streamers of shiny tin can tops, and sewing thread strung at 10-inch intervals over the tops of small trees. Success with these devices varies, but most experts we talked to agree that birds quickly learn to identify scare tactics. For best results, use a variety of methods and change the devices every few days while crops are ripening.

One popular tactic is flash tape. Washington apple grower John Kaye, who distributes Birdscare Flash Tape in the United States, says he gets the best results by suspending the tape loosely between stakes 6 to 8 inches above row crops. The second most effective method is wrapping the tape around the tree, and the least effective is making streamers from the tape. All of these methods tend to deter flocking birds like starlings and finches, but not solitary birds like robins and jays. A 290-foot roll of Birdscare costs about $3; the tape retains its color for six to eight weeks.

Researcher Leonard Askham of Washington State University Cooperative Extension reports success using flash tape to protect strawberry beds from flocking birds. He stretches, then twists, the tape between two stakes alongside newly planted strawberry rows (we followed his technique in the pea planting shown below). As the tape vibrates in the wind, it gives a frightening strobe effect.

The extension service has published a bulletin on Askham's results, *Protecting Strawberries from Birds* (number EB1641), which gives installation instructions. For a copy, send $1 to Bulletin Office, Cooperative Extension, Cooper Publications Building, Washington State University, Pullman, Wash. 99164.

## SOURCES FOR BIRD CONTROLS

Bird netting and scare devices are available at larger nurseries and many agricultural supply stores. A good mail-order source for netting, scare tape, and inflatable scare devices is Peaceful Valley Farm Supply, Box 2209, Grass Valley, Calif. 95945. The catalog is free. ∎

*By Lynn Ocone*

PETER CHRISTIANSEN

**BICOLORED FLASH TAPE,** *stretched and twisted, frightens birds as it rotates in the wind.*

**CONE-SHAPED** *pale green hops are ready to harvest and dry for beermaking when slightly papery to the touch.*

# Growing hops for beer or bouquets

*Hop vines are easy, quick, and useful*

**AS AN ACCENT** *in a flower arrangement, hops are attractive, unusual, and long-lasting.*

F AST-GROWING, LUSH hop vines (*Humulus lupulus*) provide a dense cover over an arbor, on a fence, or up the side of a house from summer through fall. Started from rhizomes in spring, they send up dozens of shoots that twist up posts, trellises, heavy twine, or any other strong support.

Although hop vines are often grown just for their handsome foliage and the temporary summer shade they provide, their other parts can also be put to use. Most notably, home brewers grow hops for their female flowers, which give a distinctive flavor to beers and ales.

When mature, the cone-shaped flowers are also quite decorative. Harvested green, they hold their color for weeks and make attractive accents in flower arrangements.

## WHICH VARIETY?

If you're growing hops for their ornamental value, any variety will do. 'Nugget' is a good choice for arbors; it's vigorous, it has nice foliage, and it produces many hops.

In beermaking, each variety imparts a flavor best suited for a particular type of beer. 'Cascade' lends a fruity, floral taste to light American-style beers. 'Hallertauer', 'Mt. Hood', and 'Tettnanger' provide the herbal flavor characteristic of German lager. 'Nugget' gives a bite to steam beers and bitter lagers. And 'Willamette' spices up full-bodied English-style ale.

## CHOOSE A SITE IN FULL SUN

Hop vines are vigorous, so make sure you give them plenty of space to grow. (Established vines can reach 25 feet in one season.) Vines die to the ground in winter, then resprout in spring.

Plants can be trained over an 8- to 12-foot arbor or even a 6-foot fence. If you want to train the vines horizontally on strings or wire across the top of a fence, they must be wound by hand.

To promote vigorous growth, choose a site in full sun. Vines planted in a spot with partial shade won't grow as quickly or as tall.

Provide light, well-drained soil. If your soil is clayey and poorly drained, plant in raised beds or mounds. Work in plenty of organic matter and a controlled-release fertilizer.

After the last frost, plant rhizomes vertically, with the buds pointing up, about 2 inches below the soil surface (in heavy clay soil, plant horizontally). Hops of the same variety can be planted 3 feet apart, but set different kinds at least 5 feet apart to keep them from becoming entangled. Mulch the soil and keep it moist.

To promote hops production, select the three strongest vines when they're about a foot long and wrap them clockwise around the support

**AFTER ONE SEASON,** *pull up clusters of roots and divide for replanting.*

(in future years, prune off the earliest shoots; later growth is sturdier). To control growth, prune off additional sprouts.

## HARVESTING THE HOPS FOR BEER

If you're growing flowers for beermaking, they'll be ready to harvest between July and September when the cones turn pale green and the yellow lupulin glands (pollen-like grains) are readily apparent underneath the scales. When squeezed, the flower cones should feel slightly papery and have a pronounced odor. If cones have brown spots, they're overmature.

To dry hops, spread them in a shallow layer on a screen and set them in a dark, well-ventilated area. Fluff the pile daily, so the cones dry evenly. In humid climates, it's best to use a food dehydrator (do not exceed 140°).

The hops are dry when the cones' inner stems break rather than bend, usually in three days or so. If you're not going to use them immediately, pack into heavy plastic bags and refrigerate or freeze.

## WHERE TO GET HOP ROOTS

You can order rhizomes from these mail-order sources. (The last three also sell beer-making supplies.) Shipping is mostly in March and April. Catalogs are free.

**Freshops,** 36180 Kings Valley Hwy., Philomath, Ore. 97370; (503) 929-2736.

**The Herbfarm,** 32804 Issaquah-Fall City Rd., Fall City, Wash. 98024; (206) 784-2222.

**Beer Makers of America,** 15 S. Main St., Colfax, Calif. 95713; (800) 655-5682.

**The Beverage People,** 840 Piner Rd., Suite 14, Santa Rosa, Calif. 95403; (800) 544-1867.

**Nichols Garden Nursery,** 1190 N. Pacific Hwy., Albany, Ore. 97321; (503) 928-9280. ■

*By Lauren Bonar Swezey*

MICHAEL THOMPSON

**POTTED PLANTS** *and a hose hang from ceiling. Foam lining gives raised beds extra insulation. A fan pushes rising heat back down around plants.*

# A spacious "room" for plants

*It's a plant gallery, nursery, and salad factory*

TO EXTEND THEIR GROWING season, gardeners Elva and Doug Watson of Bend, Oregon, built a structure framed more like a conventional room than a standard greenhouse. The 20- by 20-foot greenhouse provides lots of room for plants, and its wood frame is handy for hanging everything from shadecloth to vegetable support nets.

Besides being used to start seedlings, the greenhouse supplies the family with salad greens well before outdoor crops are ready to harvest, and long after autumn's first killing frost.

The greenhouse was built with standard construction materials, from insulation and plywood to 2- by 8-foot fiberglass glazing panels.

Details are adaptable for almost any greenhouse. To level soil-temperature swings in seedling beds, the Watsons lined each bed with 1-inch blue polystyrene foam insulation. For irrigation, they buried timer-controlled soaker hoses in each bed. A pumice mulch around permanent plants such as strawberries minimizes evaporation. A garden hose suspended from the ceiling provides extra overhead watering and doesn't kink when stretched.

Hanging plants are suspended from dowels attached to the rafters. At floor level, beds are spaced far enough apart to allow room for a wheelbarrow. ■

*By Jim McCausland*

**GARAGE-SIZE** *wood-frame greenhouse has corrugated fiberglass skin.*

**PAIR OF BRIGHT PERFORMERS,** *rockrose (foreground) and red-hot poker team up for a lively combination of flower colors, and foliage forms and textures.*

# MAY

# Last-chance planting and a start on summer maintenance

CHAD SLATTERY

**A**s May begins, nurseries everywhere have a huge selection of bedding plants and ornamentals. In cool-summer/mild-winter areas, you can take your time in choosing and planting. But in most other regions, the operative word is "hurry." If you garden in a short-summer climate, now is both your first and last chance to plant nearly all the year's warm-season vegetables and annual flowers. In the mountains and much of the Great Basin, if you don't plant now, you'll simply run out of time, and frost will cut off the harvest before it ever reaches its peak. In the desert, on the other hand, heat will call a halt to most garden planting by month's end.

May is also an excellent month to plant ornamental grasses and many perennials. And, as you can see in the photo at right, the rich colors and varied textures of ornamental grasses and strap-leafed plants give a wild, luxuriant look. They're growing in nurseryman Randy Baldwin's garden in Santa Barbara, California. Virtually all these plants are for mild climates.

A silver-green *Astelia chathamica* 'Silver Spear', at center, is one of Baldwin's top performers. Its bold 3- to 4-foot-long leaves form an attractive rosette that holds its shape and color year-round. 'Silver Spear' thrives in well-drained soil and full sun. It also performs well and looks great in decorative pots. This newly available plant is usually sold in 3-gallon containers for about $25. Look for it at nurseries with a good selection of Mediterranean plants.

Other prominent plants include New Zealand flax (*Phormium*), with maroon and pink leaves, and light gray dusty miller (*Centaurea gymnocarpa*), with its purple flowers in spring. Brown-tufted clumps of dark green Cape reed (*Chondropetalum tectorum*) weave through the garden. Violet pink flowers of Oriental fountain grass (*Pennisetum orientale*) add a splash of color near the path's edge.
—*Lynn Ocone*

## New short-season corn varieties

Because short growing seasons limit what you can plant in much of the West, breeders work hard to produce plants that go from seed to harvest quickly. Lately, some of their most important success has been with sugar-enhanced sweet corn. (Sugar-enhanced varieties, often labeled SE, are sweeter than normal corn, but not as extreme as the supersweets.)

Among white corn, 'Silver Choice' is the one to try. It comes to harvest in about 75 days—about two weeks ahead of 'Silver Queen', the benchmark white corn. 'Silver Choice' is 20 percent sweeter than 'Silver Queen'.

Among yellows is 'Grant', a 53-day variety that produces longer ears than 'Polar Vee'.

If you like bicolors, try 'Aladdin', a 56-day variety bred for the European market.

SPIKES, SPEARS, AND SWORDS *of foliage contrast strikingly with a varied assortment of low water-use perennials in a coastal Southern California garden.*

such shrubs, perennials, and bulbs as spiraea, Queen Anne's lace, anemone, and calla lilies. Deep within the White Garden is the Children's Secret Garden, where miniature roses, perennials, and benches reign. And in the California Mission Garden, modern and historic roses, such as the rose of Castile (*Rosa damascena semperflorens*), are combined with citrus, California pepper trees, and bougainvillea.

For more information, call (818) 952-4401.—*L. O.*

## Recycling grass by leaving clippings on the lawn

Grasscycling—recycling mowed clippings by leaving them on the lawn—is an easy way to add nutrients to the soil and help reduce the several million tons of grass clippings tossed into California landfills every year. Left on the lawn, the clippings decompose quickly and return nitrogen to the soil, which can reduce the amount of fertilizer needed by 15 to 20 percent.

Grasscycling, though, is only successful when done in concert with proper mowing, watering, and fertilizing. The goal is to produce a lawn whose growth is moderate as opposed to lush. Excessive growth wastes water and requires too much mowing.

The California Integrated Waste Management Board (CIWMB) offers a free brochure on grasscycling that covers the basics of lawn care and mowing, including proper mowing heights for various types of grasses.

To order a copy of the brochure, call the CIWMB's recycling hotline at (800) 553-2962.—*L. O.*

You can order 'Silver Choice' from W. Atlee Burpee & Co. by calling (800) 888-1447. For 'Grant' or 'Aladdin', call Stokes Seeds Inc. at (716) 695-6980.—*Jim McCausland*

## Whip weeds, not trees

Nothing knocks down weeds around saplings as well as a string trimmer, but nothing is more likely to girdle the tree and eventually kill it— young, thin-barked trees just can't take much abuse.

You can protect them by cutting a short section of large-diameter plastic pipe vertically, then cutting it lengthwise and slipping it over the trunk. As the trunk expands with age, so will the plastic sleeve.

With time, the tree will fill out and start casting enough shade to reduce the weeds around its base. Then you can take the sleeve off and dispose of it.—*J. M.*

## New rosarium at Descanso Gardens

Descanso Gardens in La Cañada Flintridge has opened its new 5-acre International Rosarium. More than 5,000 rose species and varieties were planted over the 1993–1994 winter in 18 theme gardens and other areas of the 5-acre site. Two thousand more international roses will eventually be added to the display.

The rosarium is a living history of roses, from their range to their breeding, as well as a demonstration of their uses in the landscape as shrubs, climbers, and ground covers. Theme gardens include an all-white planting of white Lady Banks' roses amid

## Brilliant Northwest combo

West Seattle gardener Betty Wood has solved the problem of a dry, west-facing bank with a dense planting for foliage texture and color as well as a burst of bloom. The two prime players, pictured on page 106, are red-hot poker (*Kniphofia uvaria*) and rockrose (*Cistus incanus*). Both plants, once established, will flourish in the coastal Northwest's hottest and driest summers without attention from the hose. (Elsewhere, they're fairly drought-tolerant but are likely to need occasional watering.)

You can set out both kinds of plants from 1-gallon cans all year except in freezing weather. Expect both to be in bloom by late this month. If the summer is an unusual scorcher, give newly set-out plants enough water to keep them from being stunted. Next year, they'll do fine on just the water nature provides. Cut back red-hot poker after hard frost brings down the foliage. Every few years, when rockrose gets leggy, cut it back in the autumn.—*Steven R. Lorton*

## Cinerarias that reseed

Shade-loving cinerarias (*Senecio hybridus*) are the kind of flowers that laid-back gardeners in coastal California love to grow. Set out a few plants, and several years down the road you'll have an incredible spring display. That's because cinerarias self-sow readily.

The plants shown below—in a Pebble Beach, California, garden designed by Michelle Comeau—are the tall types (2½ to 3 feet tall) sometimes sold as *C. stellata*. Every year in late spring and early summer, they're allowed to set seed (the flowers dry on the plant). Mature seeds drop off the plant, but you can also pick the flower heads and scatter the seeds yourself.

If the soil is kept damp, the seeds germinate without any fuss. They can be left to grow where they are or can be transplanted elsewhere in the garden when plants have several sets of leaves. By the following spring, plants should be large enough to bloom.

Some nurseries, especially in cool coastal areas, still

**VIBRANT CINERARIAS** *are Western favorites for lighting up shaded gardens. In mild coastal regions, they'll reseed to provide ongoing supply of new plants.*

K. BRYAN SWEZEY

carry cinerarias in late spring; in warmer areas, it's too late to plant. If you can't find plants now, you can start them from seed in late summer for fall planting (protect from frost), or wait to start seeds until early spring. Two mail-order sources for the shorter types are Park Seed Co., Cokesbury Rd., Greenwood, S.C. 29647, (800) 845-3369; and Thompson & Morgan, Dept. 191-4, Jackson, N.J. 08527, (800) 274-7333 (catalogs free).
—*Lauren Bonar Swezey*

## Sawdust for weed-free garden paths

We recommend only well-rotted sawdust as a mulch, since fresh sawdust robs the soil of nitrogen as it decomposes. But the fresh stuff has a good use—to cover garden paths, especially between rows of vegetables. That's where you don't want anything growing anyway, and if your soil is enriched as it should be and you fertilize vegetables as they grow, the soil around the vegetable roots won't suffer any loss of nutrients.

To establish weed-free paths between rows, one gardener we know puts down a four-sheet layer of newspaper, then covers it with a thick layer of fresh sawdust. After the harvest, you can either till between the rows, adding more sawdust to the top of the paths, or you can till the sawdust and newspaper into the soil. The sawdust will decompose by next spring and become good organic amendment for your soil.

A 2- to 3-foot-wide band of fresh sawdust around the garden perimeter will keep most slugs out. The coarser the sawdust, the less they like to crawl over it.—*S. R. L.*

## Don't let the lady get seedy

Lady's-mantle (*Alchemilla mollis*) swept into the nursery trade like Scarlett O'Hara at a plantation ball. All eyes were riveted on her, and no wonder: she's a shameless show-off. The roundish, crinkly, blue-green leaves hug the ground in lush clumps, and when dew beads up on them, they look like dazzling jewels. Then come the blooms—clouds of tiny chartreuse flowers on 12- to 18-inch stems.

What most gardeners don't know is that as the flowers darken, they are quickly forming seeds that must be cut off and composted before they ripen and scatter. If the flowers stay too long, seedlings will pop up like crazy all over the garden next spring.

The trick to living happily with lady's-mantle is to cut it back to the ground as soon as the flowers change from soft spring green to a hard summer green. Scatter around a bit of complete granular fertilizer. The plants will quickly send up new leaves, and in a couple of weeks you'll have lush flowerless growth again.

You can grow this beautiful plant in almost any soil except a bog, and in all but the heaviest shade. It's especially effective in the spaces between paving stones. It's a great complement to flowers and foliage of almost any other color.—*S. R. L.*

## Akebia quinata as a vining ground cover

As daring gardeners have used vining plants—clematis, climbing roses, Virginia creeper—as ground covers, we've reported their successes. Now, add *Akebia quinata* to the list. Well known for its handsome leaves divided into five deep green leaflets, akebia sports clusters of purple blooms in spring and, in a mild winter, stays evergreen.

Akebia will take sun or shade. To establish it as a ground cover, set 1-gallon plants out this month. Let the vine scramble through the summer. If shoots go out of

**BELL-SHAPED BLOSSOMS** *of Enkianthus campanulatus dangle from delicate stems.*

MICHAEL THOMPSON

bounds, just push them where you want them, perhaps pinning them in place with twigs. In November, shovel a 1- to 2-inch layer of compost or topsoil over the vines to encourage rooting. The plants will push up and scramble again. Add a layer of soil or compost each fall.

In three years, you'll be able to shear back in late fall. And rooted plants will pop up all over the following spring. From then on, keep the akebia lush and full by shearing it back annually in early February, and broadcasting a balanced (20-20-20) granular fertilizer around the bed early in the month.—*S. R. L.*

## Think of enkianthus as an old friend

In the flurry of exciting new plant introductions, it's easy to overlook trusted old friends. One such plant is *Enkianthus campanulatus,* often referred to as a four-season plant. It sports the spring bloom you see pictured at right. The handsome foliage stays dark green through summer. Autumn coloring can vary from vibrant yellow through orange to deep red, depending on the variety of the plant and the amount of sun it gets. In winter, enkianthus, which can reach 12 feet (occasionally more), displays its delicate form: strong upright branches are capped with clusters of branchlets carrying buds for next spring's bloom.

Give this plant a location where it will get light shade and can grow in loose, rich, acid soil that stays moist but well drained. For strong growth and heavy bloom set, feed these plants just as you do rhododendrons.

For a plant with deep red flowers, look for *E. c.* 'Red Bells', available by mail-order from Greer Gardens, in Eugene; call (800) 548-0111.—*S. R. L.*

## New red-leafed myoporum

*Myoporum parvifolium* is typically a low-growing (to about a foot tall), moderately drought-tolerant ground cover with shiny bright green leaves. Now a new form of the plant is just appearing on the market, and despite the rather inelegant name of "red leaf form," it features a handsome reddish tinge over 60 percent of the leaf surface (the center of the leaf is green). This plant is even lower-growing, staying around 4 to 5 inches tall.

To get the best color, plant this one in full sun. Set plants 3 to 4 feet apart. Water regularly to get plants established and then cut back to once every week or two.

If you can't find this new plant at a nursery, ask it to order for you from Suncrest Nurseries, Inc., Watsonville, Calif. (wholesale only). A gallon-size plant costs $4 to $6.—*L. B. S.*

## Here come the super petunias

A new spreading petunia (shown at right) is making a splash in nurseries this spring. Some are selling them as Supertunias, others as Cascadias.

Individual flowers resemble a typical bedding petunia, but the plants are truly perennial and everblooming in some mild-winter areas (possibly from coastal Northern California to San Diego). During the peak bloom months of spring and summer, flowers open in great profusion, blanketing the 3-foot-wide plants in colors ranging from white to pink to purple.

Their dense, cascading habit makes these petunias ideal for hanging baskets or window boxes. They grow quickly, and are showy in garden beds, too.

These petunias perform well in coastal and inland areas. Plant in full sun and well-drained soil. They require regular water, though it's best to let they dry slightly between

STEPHEN SIMPSON

**WITH LOTS OF SUN** *and frequent feeding, Supertunias will reward you with blooms all summer long.*

irrigations. Plants are heavy feeders; apply controlled-release granules to the soil and fertilize with a half-strength solution of liquid fertilizer every time you water (or use a full dilution twice a month). In alkaline soils, Supertunias may need regular applications of chelated iron to keep leaves green.

Tobacco budworms, which feed on petunia buds, can be a problem. If you see a hole in a bud, destroy the bud—it may conceal the worm. Control by spraying with *Bacillus thuringiensis.*—*L. O.*

## Gardens are growing at Coyote Point Museum

The gardens at this environmental education museum in San Mateo, California, have been undergoing major changes since 1993. The mu-

seum has been busy planning and planting close to 2 acres of its grounds with two new exhibits, with a third one due in fall of 1994. Landscape designer Suzanne Tognazzini and museum gardener Pierre Vendroux designed the gardens.

*Butterfly Garden.* The garden was planted to attract about a dozen types of butterflies—including fiery skipper, anise swallowtail, and California tortoiseshell. Larval food plants (for the caterpillar stage) include canyon oak, cherry, crabapple, and madrone. Nectar-producing plants for adult butterflies include butterfly bush, sweet fennel, and purple coneflower.

*Hummingbird Garden.* This garden is a habitat and nesting place for native species of hummingbirds—Anna's, Allen's, and rufous—

and other wildlife. Perennials, shrubs, trees, and vines were chosen for their attractive flowers and to provide protection. Hillsborough Garden Club developed the concept and sponsored a brochure listing plants.

*Early Use Garden.* Planned for completion in fall of 1994, this garden will feature dye and medicinal plants used by early Californians.

The museum is just off U.S. Highway 101 (Bayshore Freeway) in San Mateo. Southbound on U.S. 101, take the Poplar Avenue exit, make the first right on N. Humboldt Street, and turn right onto Peninsula Avenue. Head over the freeway, circle around onto Coyote Point Drive (left), and drive about ½ mile through Coyote Point Park to the museum. Northbound on U.S. 101, take the Dore Avenue exit onto the frontage road (N. Bayshore Boulevard) and turn right onto Coyote Point Drive. Hours are 10 to 5 Tuesdays through Saturdays, noon to 5 Sundays.—*L. B. S.*

## Act now to prevent blossom-end rot on tomatoes

It's one of summer's more frustrating disappointments: you pick what looks to be a perfectly ripe tomato off the vine, only to turn it over and see that the bottom end has turned a disgusting brown. That's tomato blossom-end rot, and it's very common in hot summer areas like California's Central Valley. However, there are things you can do this month to help prevent it later.

This disease is usually caused by moisture stress combined with high temperatures. It is also linked to the inability of the plant to absorb calcium from the soil, caused by the stress or a soil problem. The best prevention is to make sure tomato transplants develop a deep root system: wet the entire root zone with each irrigation, and water regularly throughout summer.

If you are setting out seedlings this month, start by digging a planting hole at least 2 feet deep. Mix some controlled-release fertilizer in the backfill soil and refill the hole. Plant the seedling deeply in the loose ground, leaving just the top 4 leaves above the soil line.

Next, build a watering basin at least 6 inches high around the plant. (You can do this for transplants already in the ground, too.) Each time you water, fill the basin, allow it to drain, and refill at least twice more. When the top 3 to 4 inches of soil are dry, it's time to water again. If you water with a drip system, make sure you leave it on long enough for the water to penetrate deeply. Put down a thick mulch, at least 3 inches deep, around plants.

To determine if a lack of calcium is causing blossom-end rot, have the soil tested. Then add gypsum, ground limestone, or a liquid calcium product, depending on what the test reveals. Your cooperative extension office can recommend a soil lab and give advice on correcting the problem.—*Lance Walheim*

## A ghost of a pumpkin

Although the goblins won't be flying for a few more months, now is the time to plant your pumpkin patch so the jack-o'-lanterns are ready in time for the big day.

New this past year is a ghostly-looking variety called 'Lumina', with glistening white skin. Each 8- to 10-inch diameter fruit weighs 10 to 12 pounds, which is just right for carving. The thick, bright orange flesh is tasty for baking, too.

Sow seeds directly in the ground. Plant four to six seeds in hills 6 to 8 feet apart; when plants are about 4 inches tall, snip out all but the strongest two or three vines per hill. Or sow seeds in rows 2 feet apart with about 60 inches of space between rows. Water regu-

larly. When pumpkins are tennis-ball size, remove all but three or four fruits on each vine (remove ones from the outer ends).

Seeds are available from W. Atlee Burpee & Co., 300 Park Ave., Warminster, Pa. 18991, (800) 888-1447; and Park Seed Co., Cokesbury Rd., Greenwood, S.C. 29647, (800) 845-3369.—*L. B. S.*

## Hybrid tea roses for fragrant bouquets

There's nothing quite like a bouquet of fresh-cut, fragrant roses. Their beauty and aroma can bring a whole room to life. With roses in full bloom this month, it's a good time to shop for additions to your cutting garden. Here are some varieties to look for.

The American Rose Society's James Alexander Gamble Fragrance Medal for fragrant roses has been awarded to several hybrid teas. They are red-flowering 'Chrysler Imperial' and 'Fragrant Cloud'; red-and-white 'Double Delight'; blended red, pink, and yellow 'Granada'; crimson 'Papa Meilland'; yellow 'Sutter's Gold'; and

pink-and-yellow 'Tiffany'.

However, for bouquets, a rose must have more than fragrance; its flower form and color must also be exquisite. During hot weather, bicolored roses like 'Granada' and 'Tiffany' often lose their distinction, and the colors wash together (they perform more consistently in cooler climates). On the other hand, heavy-petaled red roses reach perfection in the heat. Solid yellow and pink varieties are also good.

Other fragrant hybrid teas to consider include pink 'Glory Days' and 'Fragrant Memory'; yellow 'Midas Touch'; and deep red 'Mister Lincoln'.—*L. W.*

## Prune rhodies now for bouquets, plant form

With rhododendrons in full bloom this month, it's an excellent time to prune them. You can cut the big trusses for bouquets. Always take off flowers in a way that will enhance the plant's ultimate form. Remove large branches by taking them off flush with the next largest branch; don't

leave ugly stubs. Take what you want for arrangements from the cut branch, then compost the rest. If you are pruning to make a shapely broad-leafed evergreen tree, prune from the bottom of the plant up and from the inside out.

If you want just flower clusters, snip them off where the stem is not much bigger than a thick pencil. Two, perhaps even three, leaf buds will set near the end of each cut branch and, a year hence, you won't even notice the stubs. This is a good way to make spindly plants denser.

Immediately after pruning, scatter a complete granular rhododendron food around the base of the plant following manufacturer's instructions. This helps ensure a surge of healthy new growth. If summer is dry, irrigate plants in keeping with local water-use guidelines.—*S. R. L.*

## Specialty tomato seedlings by mail

Nurseries usually offer an abundance of tomato seedlings, but not usually specialty tomatoes that are grown organically. If you can't find what you would like locally, here's a source that sells organic tomato seedlings by mail.

The Natural Gardening Company (217 San Anselmo Ave., San Anselmo, Calif. 94960; 707/766-9303; catalog free) offers 17 varieties in 2¾-inch pots. Among the choices are heirlooms 'Brandywine' and 'Old Flame', golden 'Caro Rich' and 'Golden Mandarin Cross', paste types 'Milano' and 'San Marzano', and cherry tomatoes 'Principe Borghese' (used in Italy for sun-dried tomatoes) and 'Ruby Pearl'.

Shipments are made in multiples of six plants ($1.95 each, plus $3.75 for shipping), but you can mix and match your order with any of the several dozen vegetable, herb, and perennial seedlings also offered by mail.—*L. B. S.*

**SPOOKY PUMPKINS** *feature ghostly white skin surrounding traditional pumpkin-orange flesh.*  NORMAN A. PLATE

## Mulch vs. soil amendment: almost a tie

Last summer, Seattle Water Department and Solid Waste Utility set up growing trials with basil, lettuce, and marigolds. They wanted to learn how compost applied as mulch and soil amendment affects plant growth and water use.

We were surprised at how well marigolds, basil, and lettuce grew in beds of native soil (a sandy loam) topped only by a 2-inch compost mulch. Their performance almost equaled that of beds where the same amount of compost was dug into unamended native soil.

The success of both was partly tied to water-holding capacity: both soil-compost combinations held almost twice as much water as native soil alone. In all cases, beds were watered by drip irrigation.

Before you decide on a mulch-only approach to gardening—it's certainly easier than digging in all that compost—you should know how water moves through soil. Where two different kinds of soil meet, water has trouble crossing into the second soil until the first is saturated. But once the soil under the mulch is damp, it's easy to keep that way.

When you irrigate, make sure water reaches the roots (well-placed drip-irrigation tubes help), and the mulch-only system should work well for you.—*J. M.*

## A rich compost of essays

"Since compost is like confidence—you can never have too much—I'm always plotting ways to increase the bulk of my pile." So goes an essay on compost, one of many thoughtful pieces in *A Full Life in a Small Place,* by Janice Emily Bowers (The University of Arizona Press, Tucson, 1993; $13.95).

"No plant in my own gar-

NORMAN A. PLATE

### Tip of the Month

*When cutting fresh herbs for the kitchen, we often snip more than we can use immediately. Put the extra herbs in a vase of water and use them to decorate the table. To prolong their life, pop them into the refrigerator overnight. They'll be useful as long as they stay perky (often a week or more). Basil, marjoram, mint, oregano, rosemary, sage, and thyme are all good candidates for edible herb bouquets.*

den is safe. At the first signs of weakness, I start to eye it covetously. The gardener in me, solicitous for its ultimate health and productivity, struggles against the composter, whose fingers itch to yank it out. My compost heap is the ultimate consolation prize…. 'The grim reaper,' my husband called me when he saw the wheelbarrow piled high with the springy pile of peavines. He said he was afraid to nap on the couch in the evenings lest I haul him away, too."

Although the book is grounded in a small Arizona garden, it is not limited by property lines; Bowers bounces from tomatoes to cats to philosophy with all the alacrity of Annie Dillard. This is a great garden book, and well worth reading, wherever you live.—*J. M.*

## Hummingbird feeders, take care

Everyone who hangs a hummingbird feeder under an eave or in a tree does so with the best of intentions. But if the feeder is not kept clean, it can give its visitors a deadly infection.

Some licensed hummingbird rehabilitators estimate that at least 10 percent of the birds they see are ones with fungus infections from dirty feeders. The infection, called *candidiasis,* eventually causes the bird's tongue to swell, making it impossible for the bird to eat. What's worse, the

disease is passed from mother to offspring.

To prevent this from happening, follow these safety tips when feeding hummingbirds. Wash the feeder with hot water every two to three days. Make sure all inside surfaces are clean.

Use a solution of 1 part white sugar to 4 parts water in the feeder. Bring the sugar-and-water solution to a boil, then cool it before filling the feeder. Store extra sugar water in the refrigerator, and use it up or toss it out the next time you clean the feeder. Hang the feeder in a shady place where the birds are safe from cats. If ants are a problem, apply petroleum jelly to the hook attachment.—*L. O.*

## Registry of big trees

For gardeners, the *1994 National Register of Big Trees* (American Forests, Washington, D.C., 1994; $7.95) is a small book but a difficult one to put down. In just 48 pages, it lists the biggest of each of 799 kinds of trees growing in the United States. Of these, about 250 are in the West.

You can follow either of two lists through the book: one that organizes trees by species, and another that organizes them by geographic region and state. So if you want to learn about the biggest trees in Idaho, you can go to the state reference and see Idaho's list of champions. Or if you just want to know where the biggest Arizona sycamore can be found (in New Mexico, as it happens), thumb through to "sycamore."

Further, you can nominate a tree to challenge a champion, or one whose current champion is unknown. In all, 156 trees are without champions.

To get a copy of the *1994 National Register of Big Trees*, send $7.95 (postage is included) to American Forests, Box 2000, Washington, D.C. 20013.—*J. M.*

## May Checklist

### PACIFIC NORTHWEST

☐ **ADD TO COMPOST.** Prunings, spent flowers, and grass clippings pile up quickly. Turn existing compost, and keep the pile moist. To speed up decomposition of the new stuff, add old compost.

☐ **BAIT FOR SLUGS.** Get the little ones, and you'll save your plants plenty of grief later in the summer. Bait liberally through ground covers, under pots, and around rocks and garden ornaments. To get the most out of the bait, try to put it out when the forecast promises a stretch of dry days. Be very careful using bait if you have pets. A dog may show no interest in bait, then to your horror, gobble up a fatal dose.

☐ **CONTROL WEEDS.** As with slugs, get them while they're little. Hand-pick, hoe, or spot-spray them with glyphosate. If you weed on a warm, sunny day, the sun will help you destroy weed roots by drying them out once exposed.

☐ **DEADHEAD FLOWERS.** As spring flowers (especially rhododendron blossoms) fade, snip or pinch them off. This allows the plant to channel its energy into new growth.

☐ **DIVIDE PERENNIALS.** Act fast and you can still divide late-summer bloomers and not lose this year's flower show.

☐ **FEED INDOOR PLANTS.** House plants are out of winter dormancy now and ready to grow. They need food. Fertilize them monthly now through October.

☐ **FERTILIZE FLOWERING SHRUBS.** A scattering of high-nitrogen fertilizer will help them put out strong new growth and ensure strong flower bud set in late summer.

☐ **FERTILIZE LAWNS.** To keep lawns green and vigorous, apply ½ to 1 pound actual nitrogen per 1,000 square feet of turf. Use the lesser amount to maintain a healthy lawn; use the higher amount if the lawn looks tired. Apply the fertilizer at midmonth.

☐ **GROOM BULBS.** Remove faded blooms unless you want bulbs to cast their seed and form naturalized clumps. Leave green foliage on bulbs. When leaves yellow, push them over so that they won't be as visible in the garden. When you can grasp leaves and pull them off with a gentle tug, they are ready for removal.

☐ **MOVE HOUSE PLANTS OUTDOORS.** Many house plants like to vacation outdoors in warmer months. To prevent sunburn, move them first to a shaded spot for two weeks, then into morning light for two weeks, then into stronger light if they can take it. Water them well.

☐ **MOW LAWNS.** You don't want to take off more than a third of the top growth at once. At this time of year, that may mean you have to mow every five days.

☐ **PLANT ANNUALS.** Direct-sow seeds of bachelor's button, calendula, clarkia, cosmos, impatiens, marigold, nasturtium, nicotiana, pansy, salvia, and sunflower. Unless this is an exceptionally warm and dry May, wait a month to sow zinnias. Nurseries will offer bedding plants in abundance; you can set out any of these this month.

☐ **PLANT FUCHSIAS.** When you see one you like, buy it and plant it. The minute flowers fade, deadhead them, and feed plants lightly with a high-nitrogen food to stimulate new growth that will support the next round of flower buds.

☐ **PLANT GERANIUMS.** Geraniums in 4-inch pots are usually further along than similarly sized fuchsias. Put them in pots or beds, then feed them with liquid plant food diluted according to label instructions.

☐ **PLANT SUMMER BULBS.** It's the last month to plant summer-flowering bulbs such as acidanthera, begonias, dahlias, and gladiolus. When you plant, put stakes into the ground to mark bulbs so you won't risk spearing them when they grow tall enough to need staking.

☐ **PROTECT EMERGING PLANTS.** Use straight branches you remove in pruning as stakes to encircle emerging perennials, vulnerable bedding plants, and other plants that need some protection. This is especially important if a dog has the run of the garden.

☐ **PRUNE LILACS.** Prune for indoor flowers and with an eye for the plant's form. See the item "Prune rhodies now," on page 113, and apply the same techniques to lilacs.

☐ **SET OUT HERBS.** Set out plants from six-packs and gallon cans. Most herbs like full sun, good drainage, and coarse soil.

☐ **SOW VEGETABLE SEEDS.** To guarantee a crop by season's end, beans, corn, cucumbers, eggplants, melons, peppers, and tomatoes must be sown this month.

## May Checklist

### NORTHERN CALIFORNIA

**AERATE LAWNS.** To help improve air and water movement around roots, aerate the lawn. You can rent an aerator from an equipment supply store (look in the yellow pages under Rental Service Stores & Yards). Rake up the cores and top-dress with mulch. If you haven't fertilized recently, apply a lawn fertilizer and water in well.

**CHECK DRIP SYSTEMS.** Before the weather turns hot, clean filters, check emitters and sprays to see that they're working (replace ones that aren't), inspect lines for leaks, and adjust the timer for warmer weather, if necessary. After making any repairs, open end caps and flush lines before running the system.

**COMBAT PESTS.** Knock aphids off plants with a strong stream of water from the hose, or spray aphids with insecticidal soap. Trap, handpick, or bait for snails, slugs, and earwigs. Spittle bugs (look for foam in crotches of plants) are harmless in small numbers; knock them off with a blast of water. For large numbers, spray with insecticidal soap; add cooking oil or a lightweight summer oil as a spreader-sticker. Set out traps for gophers and moles or protect beds by burying wire mesh.

**CONTROL WEEDS.** Pull or hoe whenever possible, or spray with an herbicide formulated with fatty acids (such as Superfast Weed and Grass Killer) that won't harm humans or animals. Use more toxic glyphosate only as a last resort.

**DEADHEAD SPENT FLOWERS.** Snap off spent flowers on rhododendrons just above new growth buds (be careful not to break off new growth). Cut off faded roses just above a leaf with five or more leaflets. Remove flower heads from annuals and perennials as they fade.

**FERTILIZE.** It's time to feed many plants, from summer-blooming perennials to roses. For continued flowering and fruiting, feed annuals and vegetables regularly with a complete fertilizer.

**PLANT FOR PERMANENCE.** Now is a good time to plant almost any perennial, shrub, tree, or vine. When shopping at the nursery, look for plants that have good leaf color (green leaves should be a deep green) and attractive form. Check the bottom of containers to make sure roots aren't growing out the bottom (a sign they may be rootbound). Plants should also be well-watered.

**PLANT SUMMER FLOWERS.** Buy sixpacks or 4-inch-pot plants of ageratum, coreopsis, dahlia, gaillardia, globe amaranth, impatiens, lobelia, Madagascar periwinkle, marigold, penstemon, perennial statice, petunia, phlox, portulaca, salvia, sanvitalia, sunflower, sweet alyssum, verbena, and zinnia.

**PLANT VEGETABLES.** May is prime time to plant heat-loving vegetables, such as beans, corn, eggplant, melons, okra, peppers, pumpkins, squash, and tomatoes. In cool-summer areas, use short-season varieties and plant through black plastic.

Coastal (zone 17)

Inland (zones 14–16)

**WATER.** Water trees and shrubs deeply with drip irrigation, soaker hoses, or a deep-root irrigator. To avoid overwatering, check soil moisture first by digging down with a trowel or using a soil probe. As a guideline, water small to medium shrubs when the top 3 to 6 inches is dry, large shrubs and trees when the top 6 to 12 inches is dry.

# May Checklist

## ■ CENTRAL VALLEY

**CARE FOR ROSES.** To keep blossoms coming, cut plenty of long-stemmed flowers and remove all spent blooms. After their May show, give plants a dose of fertilizer to get them back into gear for another period of bloom.

**CHECK DRIP SYSTEMS.** Before the weather gets hot, check your drip-irrigation system to make sure it's operating properly. Clean filters, check emitters and sprays to make sure they're working (replace ones that aren't), inspect lines for leaks, and (if necessary) adjust the timer for warmer weather. After making repairs, open end caps and flush lines before running the system.

**COMBAT PESTS.** Knock aphids off plants with a strong stream of water from the hose, or spray with insecticidal soap. Trap, hand-pick, or bait for snails, slugs, and earwigs. Set out traps for gophers and moles, or protect beds by burying sturdy wire mesh before planting.

**COMPOST.** Add weeds that have not gone to seed, grass clippings, and prunings to the compost pile. Keep the pile evenly moist and occasionally add a handful of nitrogen fertilizer. Turn frequently with a pitchfork. When the compost turns deep brown in color and has a texture like soil, it's ready to use. Mix it with garden soil as an amendment or use it as a mulch.

**FERTILIZE.** Plants will grow best with regular feeding now. If you haven't already done so, apply an acid fertilizer to azaleas, camellias, and rhododendrons. Feed any trees and shrubs that have yellowing foliage (apply micronutrients if necessary). For continued flowering and fruiting, fertilize vegetables and flowering annuals regularly.

**MULCH.** To conserve water and control weeds, spread a 2- to 3-inch layer of organic matter around plants, but be sure to keep mulch away from the base of plant stems. Use bark chips, compost, straw, or other material that won't blow away.

**PLANT AND CARE FOR LAWNS.** This is a good time to plant hybrid Bermuda lawns since they thrive in warm weather. Water newly planted lawns thoroughly to encourage deep roots. If you already have a Bermuda lawn, mow the grass ¾ inch high and apply a high-nitrogen fertilizer to encourage new growth.

**PLANT AND SOW ANNUALS.** You can still sow seeds of heat lovers such as cosmos, marigold, portulaca, sunflower, and zinnia. Many nurseries will still have an abundant supply of these and other bedding plants: annual phlox, cockscomb, Dahlberg daisy, dwarf dahlias, impatiens, nicotiana, and petunias.

**PLANT VEGETABLES.** Set out seedlings of eggplant, peppers, and tomatoes. Sow seeds of beans, cantaloupe, corn, cucumbers, melons, pumpkins, squash, and watermelons.

**WATER.** Reinforce basins for larger plants not irrigated by drip systems. Watch annual and vegetable seedlings carefully; don't let them dry out now or it will hurt production of flowers and fruit later. When you irrigate, make sure you soak the entire root zone.

Redding

Lake Tahoe

Sacramento

Fresno

Bakersfield

▨ Valley (zones 7–9, 14)
▧ Mountain (zones 1, 2)

**FEED AZALEAS AND CAMELLIAS.** In coastal and inland gardens (*Sunset Western Garden Book* climate zones 22–24 and 18–21, respectively), feed monthly to support strong growth and heavy set of flower buds for next year. Use an acid-forming fertilizer intended for these plants, but don't overfeed. Or, make your own fertilizer using 4 parts cottonseed meal and 1 part chelated iron; a 5-gallon camellia that is 3 feet tall requires 2 tablespoons of this mixture.

**FERTILIZE SUBTROPICALS.** In coastal and inland gardens, the first flush of new growth on banana, bougainvillea, citrus, gardenia, hibiscus, lantana, and Natal plum tells you that this is the right time to give plants a dose of high-nitrogen food. Feed regularly through the active growing season.

**HARDEN OFF SEEDLINGS.** A week or two before planting out seedlings that you've started in a greenhouse or other sheltered place, stop fertilizing them and stretch periods between waterings. Gradually increase time exposed to outdoor light; protect from afternoon sun.

**MAKE WATERING COUNT.** To prevent seedlings and young plants from drying out, water them frequently for short durations. Irrigate just-planted trees and shrubs to soak rootballs. Water lawns in early morning, when evaporation and wind are minimal, and long enough for water to penetrate 4 inches.

**MANAGE PESTS.** Spray or dust plants that have pest caterpillars (such as cabbage worms, geranium budworm, and oak moth) with *Bacillus thuringiensis*. Spray aphids, mites, and whiteflies with insecticidal soap or horticultural oil. Green lacewings can also help control them. Trap, handpick, or bait for snails and slugs.

**PLANT BULBS.** In coastal and inland areas, acidanthera, caladium, calla, canna, dahlia, gladiolus, gloxinia, tigridia, and tuberose are still available, but selection is dwindling. Plant now for summer bloom.

**PLANT FRUIT TREES.** For best production, fruit and nut trees need regular water. But once established in coastal and inland gardens, the following can tolerate drought in water-lean years: fig, jujube, loquat, macadamia, persimmon, sapote, and strawberry and pineapple guavas. This month in coastal, inland, and low desert (zone 13) areas , you can also plant these trees with higher water needs: avocado, banana, cherimoya, citrus, and mango.

**PLANT SUMMER COLOR.** As soon as possible in coastal, inland, and low-desert gardens, set out seedlings of celosia, coreopsis, cosmos, creeping zinnia, four o'clock, gaillardia, globe amaranth, kochia, Madagascar periwinkle, marigold, portulaca, salvia, sunflower, tithonia, and zinnia. In high-desert (zone 11) gardens, plant seedlings or seeds, including ageratum, annual coreopsis, aster, begonia, celosia, cosmos, creeping zinnia, four o'clock, gaillardia, globe amaranth, gloriosa daisy, marigold, mignonette, nasturtium, periwinkle, phlox, portulaca, scarlet flax, strawflower, sunflower, sweet sultan, tithonia, and zinnia. In coastal-influenced gardens, you can try sowing seeds of celosia, globe amaranth, nasturtium, portulaca, sunflower, and tithonia

**PLANT VEGETABLES.** In coastal, inland, and high-desert gardens, sow seeds of beans, corn, cucumbers, melons, peppers, squash, sweet basil, and tomatoes. In low-desert gardens, plant Jerusalem artichokes, okra, peppers, and sweet potatoes.

**TEND ROSES.** Roses are in full bloom this month. Feed and water regularly to keep plants growing fast. Spread a 3- to 6-inch layer of mulch around plants to reduce water needs. For best flowering, remove faded blooms promptly, cutting stems just above a leaf with five or more leaflets. Also remove suckers—new shoots from the rootstock that come from below the graft.

**SMOTHER WEEDS.** Spread a 3- to 6-inch layer of mulch around trees, shrubs, perennials, and annuals. Leave a clear area around the base of trunks and stems to prevent diseases. Around newly planted trees, maintain mulch for at least three years. Mulch also serves to conserve water.

Santa Barbara

Pasadena   San Bernardino

Santa Monica

Los Angeles

San Diego

Zones 18–21

Zones 22–24

## ANYWHERE IN THE WEST, TACKLE THESE CHORES:

☐ **CARE FOR TOMATOES.** Indeterminate kinds (they keep growing all season) need to be staked or caged early to keep them from flopping. To minimize blossom-end rot, keep soil evenly moist; mulch and drip irrigation help. In hottest areas, use row covers to minimize sunburn on leaves and fruit.

☐ **FERTILIZE.** Before planting vegetables or flowers, amend soil by digging in 1 to 2 pounds of complete fertilizer per 100 square feet. Feed flowering shrubs after they bloom, and start a monthly fertilizing program for long-blooming annuals, perennials, and all container plants.

☐ **MAINTAIN INDOOR PLANTS.** After danger of last frost, you can take house plants to a shady place outside for the summer. Prune them for shape, fertilize, and water well. The extra light will help them fill out and grow strong before you bring them back indoors in fall.

☐ **MULCH PLANTS.** A layer of organic mulch can work wonders for almost everything in the garden. It improves soil, cools roots, keeps weeds down, and holds in soil moisture. Apply a 3- to 4-inch layer around trees, shrubs, and large perennials (don't let it touch the trunks), and a 1-inch layer around annuals and bedding plants. You can use ground bark, compost, rotted leaves, even sawdust as mulch.

☐ **REMOVE SUCKERS.** These are fast-growing vertical shoots that sprout from the roots of roses, fruit trees, and grafted ornamentals. Cut suckers off flush with the root system. Also cut out vertical water-sprouts along horizontal fruit tree limbs.

☐ **WEED.** Hoe small weed seedlings on a warm morning, and the afternoon sun will finish them off.

## IN THE INTERMOUNTAIN WEST, DO THESE CHORES:

☐ **CHECK DRIP SYSTEMS.** Clean and flush your drip system, checking emitters and filters to make sure that everything is working before plants grow and make the system difficult to maintain. Restart the timer for warmer weather and test the system.

☐ **FEED HYACINTHS.** If you live where hyacinths can rebloom next year, fertilize them this month with superphosphate. It fortifies bulbs for next season's bloom.

☐ **HARDEN OFF TRANSPLANTS.** Take seedlings to a lath house, patio, or partly shaded coldframe, exposing them gradually to more sun and nighttime cold. After 7 to 10 days, they'll be tough enough to transplant into the garden.

☐ **PINCH BACK FLOWERING PLANTS.** You can encourage branching and compact growth by pinching or tip-pruning plants such as azaleas, fuchsias, geraniums, marigolds, rhododendrons, verbena, and zinnias.

☐ **PLANT FOR PERMANENCE.** After danger of frost is past, set out perennials, shrubs, and trees.

☐ **PROTECT COOL-SEASON CROPS.** Suspend laths or row covers above vegetables such as broccoli, cauliflower, lettuce, and spinach to keep them from bolting (going to seed) when the weather warms up.

☐ **PRUNE FLOWERING ORNAMENTALS.** Wait until bloom ends before pruning spring-flowering plants such as lilac, mock orange, and spiraea.

☐ **START OR OVERSEED LAWNS.** Sow bluegrass, fescue, rye, or a combination of the three. New plantings should go into tilled, raked, fertilized, and relatively rock-free soil. If you're over-seeding worn or bare spots in an old lawn, rough up the soil surface with a steel bow rake, scatter seed, cover with compost or peat, and don't let the soil surface dry out until the grass is up far enough to mow.

## IN THE SOUTHWEST'S LOW AND INTERMEDIATE DESERTS, THERE'S MUCH TO DO:

☐ **CARE FOR CITRUS.** Fertilize trees whose leaves aren't dark green, spreading 1 cup ammonium sulfate per inch of trunk diameter. Water it in well. Give mature trees a 2- to 3-hour sprinkler soaking every two to three weeks (more often in sandy soil, less in clay). Soak young trees 1 to 2 hours every 5 to 10 days.

☐ **COMBAT INSECTS.** Blast aphids and whiteflies off plants with a jet of water from the hose, then spray affected plants with insecticidal soap.

☐ **INCREASE WATERING.** When the first 100° days come, check plants (especially new growth) at least twice a day for wilting. Everything needs extra water, even cactus and succulents.

☐ **NURTURE ROSES.** When heat starts to take its toll on May's flush of rose bloom, water plants deeply, mulch, and fertilize. In the Phoenix area, give plants afternoon shade.

☐ **PLANT FLOWERS FOR SUN.** As early in the month as possible, set out ageratum, celosia, coreopsis, cosmos, firebush (*Hamelia patens*), four o'clock, gaillardia, globe amaranth, gloriosa daisy, kochia, lantana, lisianthus, Madagascar periwinkle, nicotiana, portulaca, salvia, strawflower, tithonia, and zinnia.

☐ **PLANT SHADE LOVERS.** Some good choices include begonia, caladium, chocolate plant (*Pseuderanthemum alatum*), coleus, gerbera, impatiens, lobelia, oxalis, spider plant, and star clusters (*Pentas lanceolata*).

☐ **PLANT VEGETABLES.** Heat-loving crops—eggplant, okra, peanuts, peppers, soybeans, summer squash, and sweet potatoes—go in this month.

☐ **PROTECT CROPS FROM BIRDS.** Garden centers have bird netting that can protect small fruits from hungry birds. Fasten the netting's edges shut (clothespins work well).

☐ **START OR OVERSEED LAWNS.** Plant Bermuda or improved buffalo grass when nighttime temperatures rise above 70°.

**LEAFY GREEN** *perpetual spinach produces all summer when picked regularly. Swiss chard grows behind it. Below, lettuce varieties supposedly good for growing in summer turned bitter when allowed to mature.*

# Salads from your summer garden

*These are greens that thrive in hot weather*

**S**UCCULENT LEAFY greens needn't vanish from the vegetable garden with the onset of warm summer weather. Many thrive in heat.

When picked young, all of the greens shown on these pages make delicious additions to summer salads. Mature leaves of amaranth, orach, perpetual spinach, and chard taste best when cooked. (Avoid old leaves on any of the greens; they're usually tough, and sometimes bitter.) Unless you garden in a fog belt, harvest summer lettuce as described on page 122.

Flavors and textures of the different greens vary substantially, and not all of them appeal to every taste. Certain greens (particularly Malabar climbing spinach) win rave reviews from some cooks, thumbs-down from others. Experiment using different greens—in different ways—until you find the ones that you like.

Look for seeds at nurseries or order by mail as soon as possible, so you can plant early this month.

## SPINACH SUBSTITUTES THAT TAKE THE HEAT

The toughest, most heat-tolerant of the group are amaranth, Malabar climbing spinach, and New Zealand spinach. Often sold in catalogs as warm-season substitutes for spinach, they can be used as wilted greens, to replace other greens in recipes, in stir-fries, or fresh in salads.

Orach is grown in spring and fall in France and Asia, but in the West you can harvest all summer if you keep the seed heads pinched off.

*Amaranth* may be familiar to some gardeners as a 3-foot-tall ornamental plant, but it is also a tasty green. Leaves may be brilliant scarlet, plain green, or mottled red, green, and yellow. Choose leaf varieties, not grain-producing types. Harvest leaves before plants flower.

Cooked amaranth is less watery and more flavorful than spinach, although not as smooth. Its tender, young leaves add a colorful touch to salads.

*Malabar climbing spinach* is a fast-growing vine that can be trained on a trellis or fence. When eaten fresh, leaves are succulent and mild. As wilted greens, they are somewhat slippery like okra,

GLENN CHRISTIANSEN

but they'll give good flavor and body to soups.

*New Zealand spinach* is a spreading plant that grows 6 to 8 inches high. In mild-winter climates, it's perennial. Pluck off the top 3 inches of tender stems and leaves. Served raw, leaves are mild, slightly salty, succulent, and fleshy. Cooked, they taste like spinach.

*Orach* (also sold as mountain spinach; often mistaken

**DRESS A SALAD** *of tender New Zealand spinach (right) or of mixed summer greens with a mustard-tarragon vinaigrette or oil and vinegar to taste. Sprinkle nasturtium flowers over the mixed greens as a colorful, flavorful accent.*

PETER CHRISTIANSEN

DARROW M. WATT

**BRIGHT PURPLE STEMS** of Malabar climbing spinach (right) contrast handsomely with its flavorful, dark green leaves. Left, lettuce seedlings are thinned out for use in salad.

for lamb's quarters) grows 3 feet tall if leaves are pinched off regularly; otherwise, it can reach up to 9 feet. Red- or green-leaf types are available. Leaves are smaller when orach is grown in summer rather than in spring and fall. The young, tender leaves can be eaten raw in salads. Cooked orach tastes like spinach.

## GREENS YOU CAN GROW ALMOST ALL YEAR LONG

*Chard and perpetual spinach* are commonly thought of as cool-season greens, but they thrive during the summer in most areas (except the desert). Because they're biennial, they are less likely than regular spinach to bolt and go to seed. Harvest outer leaves; new leaves grow from the center. 'Rhubarb' ('Ruby Red') chard is red stemmed; perpetual spinach, a type of chard, has smaller ribs than other types of chard. Use in soups, stir-fries, lasagna, or as bundle wrappers (see recipe on facing page).

*Mâche* is a small-leafed green that's popular in France for its mild nutty flavor in salads. It's often grown in the cool season but does well in summer if seeds are sown before soil temperatures go above 65°. Choose either 'À Grosse Graine' or 'Piedmont', large-seeded types that tolerate heat better than the small-seeded kinds. Harvest individual leaves or cut the head 1 inch above ground (it will resprout).

*Nasturtium* is often grown just for its flowers, but both the leaves and flowers can be used in flavorful appetizers, as shown at left, and make tasty additions to summer salads. (Mix the peppery leaves and flowers with mild greens for interesting flavor con-

trasts.) You can buy seeds of mixed flower colors, of individual colors (apricot, cherry, mahogany, gold, yellow, and red), and of one with variegated leaves ('Alaska').

*Summer lettuce* is best grown by broadcasting seeds and then harvesting at the baby stage (see far left photo), unless you live on the coast or cover plants with shadecloth. When kept evenly moist and harvested very early, lettuce won't turn bitter—as it is likely to do if left to mature. Mix seed with sand so you can broadcast it evenly and not too thickly.

As plants grow, thin some seedlings and use them in salads. Harvest when leaves are 3 to 4 inches long.

## PLANT IN WELL-AMENDED SOIL AND KEEP MOIST

Start seeds of all but the lettuce and nasturtiums in containers, or sow all seeds directly in the ground. Once they're planted in the ground and at the seedling stage, mulch the soil to conserve water. Water regularly to keep the soil moist, and fertilize once every week or so with fish emulsion (if you use another fertilizer, follow package directions).

Train Malabar climbing spinach on a trellis.

Begin harvesting summer greens when plants can yield enough for a meal. Pick amaranth and orach regularly to control growth. Mix all types together or use individually.

## WHERE TO ORDER SEEDS

*The Cook's Garden,* Box 535, Londonderry, Vt. 05148; (802) 824-3400. Catalog $1. Sells all but Malabar climbing and New Zealand spinach.

*Ornamental Edibles,* 3622 Weedin Court, San Jose, Calif. 95132. Catalog free. Sells most types.

*Seeds Blüm,* Idaho City Stage, Boise, Idaho 83706; fax (208) 338-5658. Catalog $3. Sells every type listed.

*By Lauren Bonar Swezey*

PETER CHRISTIANSEN

**NASTURTIUM LEAVES HOLD** tiny shrimp and dollops of sour cream for a quick fresh appetizer.

AFTER BLANCHING, *fill chard leaves with chopped stems and fold into bundles. Drizzle with a piquant caper dressing before serving.*

DARROW M. WATT

PETER CHRISTIANSEN

## GREAT WAYS WITH SUMMER GREENS

Young summer greens make delicious salads; mix several varieties for interesting flavor and texture. Dress lightly with olive oil and vinegar (or lemon juice) to taste or with your favorite dressing. Some mature greens taste best cooked. To wilt lightly, cook in oil and garlic.

### Summer Greens Salad

3  quarts (¾ to 1 lb.) bite-size pieces baby leaf lettuce, New Zealand spinach, Malabar climbing spinach, nasturtium leaves, small tender orach, perpetual spinach, or 'Rhubarb' chard leaves (use 1 kind or a mixture), rinsed and crisped

Mustard-tarragon vinaigrette (recipe follows)

Salt and pepper

Nasturtium flowers (optional)

In a large bowl, combine greens and vinaigrette; mix and add salt and pepper to taste. Garnish with flowers. Makes 6 to 8 servings.

*Per serving: 73 cal. (88 percent from fat); 0.6 g protein; 7.1 g fat (0.9 g sat.); 2.3 g carbo.; 88 mg sodium; 0 mg chol.*

**Mustard-tarragon vinaigrette.** Mix ¼ cup **olive oil,** ¼ cup **white wine vinegar,** 1½ tablespoons **Dijon mustard,** 1 teaspoon **dried tarragon leaves,** and 1 clove **garlic,** pressed or minced.

### Nasturtium Leaf and Shrimp Appetizers

12  nasturtium leaves (each 2 to 2½ in. wide), stems trimmed, rinsed and patted dry

2  tablespoons sour cream

12  to 24 (½ to 1 oz.) shelled cooked tiny shrimp

Nasturtium flowers (optional)

Place leaves in a single layer on a serving platter. Spoon about ½ teaspoon sour cream in center of each leaf; top with 1 or 2 shrimp. Garnish platter with flowers, if desired. To eat, pick up and roll leaf around shrimp. Makes 12 appetizers.

*Per serving: 7.7 cal. (58 percent from fat); 0.4 g protein; 0.5 g fat (0.3 g sat.); 0.4 g carbo.; 4.6 mg sodium; 3.4 mg chol.*

### Chard Packets with Caper Vinaigrette

1½  pounds chard or perpetual spinach with leaves at least 6 by 8 inches

Caper vinaigrette (recipe follows)

Salt and pepper

Wash chard well; discard bruised leaves. Trim off discolored stem ends; discard. Cut stems off leaves; keep leaves and stems separate.

In a 5- to 6-quart pan, bring about 3 quarts water to a boil over high heat. Push chard stems into water. Cook, uncovered, until stems are limp, 6 to 12 minutes. Lift out; drain well.

Push leaves gently down into boiling water; cook until limp, 1 to 2 minutes. Lift out carefully; immerse in ice water. When cool, drain well.

Select 6 of the largest, prettiest leaves; if leaves are longer than 8 inches, trim to this length. Set leaves aside. Chop remaining leaves, trimmings, and stems together; drain well.

Lay reserved leaves flat in a single layer; mound onto each an equal portion of chopped chard about 3 inches from base of leaf. Fold sides and ends of leaf over filling to enclose; lay seam down on a serving dish. If making ahead, cover and chill up until next day. Bring to room temperature to serve. Offer caper vinaigrette to pour over bundles; add salt and pepper to taste. Makes 6 bundles, 3 to 6 servings.

*Per serving with 1 tablespoon vinaigrette: 63 cal. (69 percent from fat); 1.9 g protein; 4.8 g fat (0.6 g sat.); 4.5 g carbo.; 284 mg sodium; 0 mg chol.*

**Caper vinaigrette.** Mix ¼ cup **olive oil,** ¼ cup **white wine vinegar,** 2 teaspoons **Dijon mustard,** 2 tablespoons minced **shallots,** and 2 tablespoons drained **capers.** If making ahead, cover and chill up until the next day. Makes ¾ cup. ■

*By Linda Lau Anusasananan*

CHAD SLATTERY

**Heart** *Spring-blooming jasmine (Jasminum poly-anthum) covers frame and base. Gently wind one runner around the base and up one side of the frame. Guide the second runner around base and up the opposite side of the frame. Repeat the process, winding each runner in the opposite direction to the one under it; two or three runners per side cover the frame. Clip off unused runners near the plant's base.*

## Tabletop topiaries... almost instantly

*You just wrap a frame with a vine in a pot*

PORTABLE TOPIARIES like the ones pictured here are surprisingly quick and easy to make and maintain. They're made by guiding trailing plants up and around wire frames. Their handsome leaves and pleasing shapes make them elegant patio accents or table centerpieces.

Topiary artist Pat Hammer, owner of Samia Rose Topiary in Encinitas, California, shares her expertise in creating these trained-up topiaries.

### TOPIARY TOOLS

For each topiary, you'll need a wire frame, a heavy container, fast-draining potting soil, and cotton string or plastic ties to hold plants to the frame (if stems are too stiff to weave easily).

Painted or coated frames are best, since they are less apt to rust. Buy them at florists, garden centers, or by mail. One mail-order source is Cliff Finch's Zoo, 16923 N. Friant Rd., Box 54, Friant, Calif. 93626; (209) 822-2315 (free brochure).

After you choose a frame, find a pot to fit it. As a general guideline, when the exposed frame is inserted into the container, the frame should be at least twice as tall as the container.

### PLANTS TO USE

Although many vining plants will work for topiary (see suggestions below and on the next page), the smaller the frame, the smaller the leaf size should be. (If the leaves are too large, the shape of the frame can get lost.)

For small topiary, ivies with leaves about an inch across look best. Small-leafed varieties of English ivy (*Hedera helix*) are easy to find and use. Among the many choices offering a range of colors, leaf forms, and textures are the nine excellent varieties shown in the photos on the facing page.

Buy young trailing ivy with pliable stems. A 6-inch hanging pot with plenty of runners is enough to start any of the topiaries shown here; cost is about $8.

As an alternative, try other vining or trailing plants such

CHAD SLATTERY

as hoya, jasmine (shown on the previous page), mandevilla, and rosemary.

## TRAINING THE TOPIARY

There are two ways to make topiaries. If the vine you're using is in a hanging pot, remove the hangers and insert the pronged topiary frame into the container. Transplant from its original pot into a decorative container, then guide the runners around the frame's wires as explained below.

Or place the frame into a pot and secure it in place with soil; plant vines from plugs or 2-inch pots at the base of the frame.

To cover the wire frames, wrap one runner at a time around a wire; never force the stems or they may snap. Wrap a second runner around the same wire, in the opposite direction. If desired, wrap a third runner around the same wire, in the direction of the first. Repeat the process for each wire; don't jump from one wire to the next with the same runner, or you will lose the topiary form.

If plant stems are stiff, guide them up the wires and temporarily tie them to the frame; loosen and eventually remove the ties as the runners grow into place.

 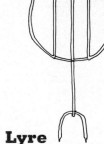 

## Tree
Rippled dark green leaves of 'Ivalace' mask the four wires of three-dimensional frame that rises about 20 inches above the container. Pinch runners to make them branch.

## Lyre
Silhouette fashioned from nonbranching 'Walthamensis' rises 30 inches above container. Wind all runners around frame base and then fan them out to cover exposed wires.

## Cone
Variegated 'Gold Heart' decorates 3½-foot frame. Guide this stiff-stemmed ivy up vertical wires and hold in place with twist-ties. Leaves disguise unwrapped horizontal wires.

## Teardrop
'Ivalace' covers 26-inch teardrop frame and cascades over container's edge. Extra runners were clipped near base of frame; too many loose runners would compete with teardrop form.

## TOPIARY MAINTENANCE

Clip or pinch new growth regularly, following the shape of the frame. The type of plant used dictates the topiary's cultural needs. If it's an outdoor plant, keep the topiary outdoors in appropriate light; bring it indoors only for brief periods. ■

*By Lynn Ocone*

## Seven ivies to train on topiaries
*From left to right: 'Walthamensis', 'Wichtel', 'Shamrock', 'Midget', 'Lady Frances', 'Deltoidea', 'Rittenkreuz'.*

NORMAN A. PLATE

**COLORFUL GARDEN** *of long-blooming lavender, yellow coreopsis, pink Mexican evening primrose, and purple Verbena bonariensis (above) is a cheerful contrast to the old lawn (left).*

# Perennial gardens that make every inch count

*Less is definitely more in these two small plots*

DESIGNING A SMALL garden is usually as much or more of a challenge than planning a large one. It's difficult being creative when space is limited. And because there are so few inches to begin with, you need to make every one count. Then there's the natural temptation to go overboard and put in too much.

The Northern California gardens shown here and on the facing page—a front-yard makeover that substituted wall-to-wall flowers for overgrown shrubs and crabgrass, and a backyard transformation from lawn to perennials—met these challenges head-on with outstanding results.

## BUNGALOW GARDEN BLOOMS IN BERKELEY

When homeowner Jane Gross spoke with landscape designer Abbey Kletz about redoing the garden, she envisioned a meadow of flowers blooming throughout the year. "I wanted it to look wild and wonderful, but I had no clear idea how to get it," says Gross. Kletz seemed to know just what she wanted.

Kletz describes it as a cottage garden with California-adapted plants. "I tried to think of everything that would bloom for as long as possible," she says. Billowing perennials and brightly colored flowers dominate the

landscape; a small gravel path adds definition and provides access for maintenance.

The garden used to be flat, but before planting Kletz brought in topsoil and organic amendments to raise the elevation under the front window. She started most plants from 1-gallon containers, set them out with controlled-release fertilizer, and later added a 2-inch layer of mulch. A drip-irrigation system waters the plants.

At first, it was too much of a good thing. "The plants went nuts and grew too fast," says Kletz. "The soil was so rich, we should have left out the fertilizer."

Gross doesn't consider the garden low maintenance. The plants need weekly deadheading and periodic pruning during the growing season. In late winter, plants get a severe pruning to encourage fresh new growth. But even so, she finds it's a lot more fun to cut flowers than a lawn.

## BACKYARD SANCTUARY GREW FROM COMBINED TALENTS

Suzanne Dupree describes her small Palo Alto backyard retreat as a "reachable garden," because everything is within easy reach for picking and fussing.

The transformation from lawn to colorful perennials was a combined effort by Dupree, landscape designer Maile Arnold, and landscaper Mike Hadi, who brought in yards of amendments to create the raised beds, laid the flagstone path, and installed the irrigation system.

Under Arnold's guidance, Dupree helped shape the garden. "I asked Maile what the flower beds should look like, and she told me, 'It's your garden. You should think about how you want them.' I really appreciated that advice once the garden was finished, because now it feels like my garden."

Dupree—who had had no prior gardening experience—sketched out the shape of the mounds and path ("it was a crude drawing") and helped direct their installation. "The guys just shoveled around the dirt and laid out the paths until it looked right to me," she says.

To decide on the plants, Dupree visited Arnold's Sebastopol property (which resembles a small botanical garden) to look for attractive textures and colors. The designer gave her advice on what would and wouldn't work. Arnold—who grows many plants to set out in her clients' gardens—then brought down small seedlings to plant in the mounds.

"The plants were so small, I thought they would take years to grow in," says Dupree. "But Maile taught me patience. She said small plants establish better than large plants, and she was right. By the following spring, the garden was beautiful."

The garden requires only periodic maintenance—trimming back ground-hugging perennials, such as catmint and diascia, and deadheading salvia, yarrow, roses, and other flowering plants. But that doesn't stop Dupree from wandering through the garden daily to fuss with her flowers and cut them for the house. ■

*By Lauren Bonar Swezey*

K. BRYAN SWEZEY

**GROUND-HUGGING** *purple catmint, silene, Santa Barbara daisy, diascia, and Origanum laevigatum 'Hopleys Purple' (at center) cascade over the flagstone path. Upright Russian sage and lavender punctuate the mound.*

**ISLAND IN THE SKY.**
*Dalmen Mayer's pocket
deck stays handsome
year-round with a mix of
deciduous, evergreen, and
perennial plants.*

DON NORMARK

# Rooftop gardens reach new heights in Seattle

*These elevated landscapes provide lessons for down-to-earth gardens as well*

REX RYSTEDT

**GLOWING IN THE MOONLIGHT.** *The nocturnal mood on the rooftop garden of Chris Opel and Parker Geissler is enhanced by white flowers (mostly geraniums and New Guinea impatiens) and glowing luminarias.*

LOOK UP, WAY UP, along Seattle's skyline. You'll see tufts of green and tiny spots of color. People are gardening up there. People like Chris Opel and Parker Geissler, who turned a barren rooftop into a verdant garden (shown at right) with richly textured evergreens, deciduous trees and vines, and white flowers.

While these high-rise gardens are as varied as most earthbound plots, they all have one thing in common: the plants must grow in some kind of container. Recently, we climbed up to a number of rooftop gardens. We discovered good ideas that can benefit any gardener who grows plants in pots.

## GARDEN SHOW ABOVE PIKE PLACE MARKET

On his deck overlooking Pike Place Market, John Fikkan created an ever-changing show of blossom and foliage, color and texture. The garden's skeleton is, basically, evergreen. A big New Zealand flax (*Phormium tenax*) and a large lavender (*Lavandula latifolia*), which was chosen for its broad leaves and big bloom spikes, anchor the garden. Assorted ivies spill out of containers.

Two deciduous vines that twine along the deck rails give the small space a gentle sense of enclosure. Perennial hops (*Humulus lupulus*) burst out of a container and scramble along one rail each spring. On another rail, Virginia creeper (*Parthenocissus quinquefolia*) climbs along, producing soft spring foliage, lush summer leaves, and brilliant autumn color.

Fikkan chooses seasonal fillers for their ease of care and long bloom periods. He moves pots around and stages them for maximum effect.

In spring, cyclamen, primroses, and bulbs take center stage, accented by forsythia, or other spring-blooming shrubs, in 1-gallon cans.

In summer, annual standbys come out in full force: geraniums, impatiens, lobelia, Marguerite daisies, marigolds, petunias, zinnias, even a few pots of dwarf sunflowers.

In fall and winter, Fikkan uses flowering cabbage and kale, winter-blooming pansies, and sometimes small conifers, dressed up at holiday time.

Though his garden has been going strong for six years, it is not without its share of problems. As Fikkan says, "Little did I dream that aphids, ants, scale, and all the garden pests could find their way up here." Even slugs ride up with nursery plants, so he sets bait for them.

## TINY BUT JAM-PACKED DECK GARDEN

Dalmen Mayer turned a horticultural whim into gardening magic—on an 81-

**A PLACE IN THE SUN.** *Daisies, geraniums, marigolds, and dwarf sunflowers brighten John Fikkan's garden from mid-April until the first hard frost in October or November.*

129

UP ON THE ROOF *of their garage, Sheila and Morley Horder harvest fresh vegetables from planting boxes.*

DON NORMARK

square-foot deck outside a fourth-floor condominium.

At one corner, he first laid down a ⅛-inch base of rigid aluminum 30 inches square over the deck surface. Atop this he mounded pea gravel to a height of about 5 inches in the center. He set some lava rock into the gravel, which he then covered with potting soil. In this loose medium, he planted assorted succulents, including sedums and sempervivums; they grew like crazy.

Mayer then planted tiny clumps of black mondo grass (*Ophiopogon planiscapus* 'Nigrescens') from 2-inch pots. Next he added three little shore pines (*Pinus contorta*); he dips their tops back in bonsai style. When he found a moss he liked, he tucked it along the shady side of the garden. On the sunny side, he planted jewel mint of Corsica (*Mentha requienii*); it grew in around the stones and up between the sedums.

In hot summer weather, Mayer waters. He mists the plants with a liquid solution of 15-30-15 fertilizer monthly April through October.

## VEGETABLES OVER THE GARAGE

Sheila and Morley Horder wanted to grow vegetables, but not in the limited space around their townhouse. So they went up to the garage roof. They installed a spiral staircase from ground level to reach the roof. Once off the ground, they got several bonuses, including full, unobstructed sunshine.

The Horders used 2- by 12-inch planks to build nine bottomless boxes, each 2½ feet wide, 8 feet long, and four more, each 3 feet square. The sides and bottoms of the boxes are lined with black polyethylene, slit to allow for slow drainage.

To fill the boxes, the Horders concocted a soil medium that was light enough not to tax the roof joists. Here's their formula: To 2

bales (12 cubic feet) of dampened peat moss, they added 3 bales (12 cubic feet) of vermiculite. Next, they mixed in 6 pounds of 5-10-10 dry fertilizer, 2 pounds of superphosphate, and 5 pounds of agricultural lime. They mixed the soil thoroughly on the ground, then hoisted it up and filled the boxes.

The Horders' garagetop crops include artichokes, arugula, beets, broccoli, cabbage, carrots, chard, corn, leeks, lettuce, onions, parsley, parsnips, peas, peppers, rhubarb, rosemary, sage, squash, and tomatoes.

The Horders garden all year, starting their annual cycle in March when they replenish the soil and put in the early pea crop. In July, they put in the last broccoli, chard, spinach, and root crops that are harvested through winter.

## LESSONS FROM ROOFTOP GARDENS

*Consider the microclimate.* North- or east-facing decks favor shade plants; south- and west-facing sites favor sun-loving plants, unless some shade is manufactured by a trellis, arbor, or awning. Temperatures normally drop faster the farther from the ground you are. Frosts come earlier, so marginally hardy plants are more vulnerable. High above the city, winds can be brisk. Tulips and long-stemmed daffodils can be reduced to a pile of petals with a couple of strong gusts. But one of our native sword ferns, zinnias in a pot, or a stocky form of Shasta daisy will stand up to a gale.

Exposed to full sun and drying winds, pots quickly lose moisture. Keep pots well watered—and never let them dry out.

*Consider the weight.* If you are planning to use a lot of pots, or several big ones, weight might be a consideration. If you're in doubt about the strength of a roof or deck, consult a structural engineer. The best light soil mix we

found is the one the Horders use for their vegetables.

*Check out the rules.* If you live in an apartment or condominium, consult with the manager or condominium association. Rules vary: Some buildings have no restrictions; others do not allow overhanging plants or water features; a few do not allow gardening at all.

*Choose the right plants.* Many perennials do well in pots and will take the extremes of high-rise living. Choose plants for their sturdy, handsome foliage and consider the bloom a bonus. The blue green leaves of *Sedum* 'Autumn Joy' or *S. spectabile* appear early in the year, stay upright and lush through the summer, then finish off the season with a large pink to coral burst. Siberian and spuria irises will be filled with handsome flowers in late spring. Hostas are another good perennial for pots, especially for a shady spot.

Vines do well in big containers. Climbing a wall or trellis or running along a rail, they can add color, provide shade, and create a privacy screen. Akebia (*A. quinata*), clematis, climbing roses, grapes, and wisteria can all be grown successfully in generous containers.

*Container plant care.* Repot perennials every couple of years. Refresh soil in annual pots yearly. If the soil has not compacted, you can reuse it; just add organic matter and mix in some granular plant food, well-rotted manure, or controlled-release fertilizer.

The trick to keeping a small tree happy in a container is root pruning. Every three years, pull trees out of their pots between late November and early March. Pull the big roots away from the rootball and cut them back. Then replant the tree, adding new soil. Scatter some controlled-release fertilizer on top of the soil and water well. In the spring, new feeder roots will shoot out to support the tree. ∎

*By Steven R. Lorton*

NORMAN A. PLATE

*AN ASSORTMENT of zinnias was planted in Sunset's test garden to determine resistance to powdery mildew. At center of left photo are white, rose, and salmon Pinwheel that grew into fall without disease. Right, 'Cherry Ruffles' is covered with mildew; 'Old Mexico' is disease-free.*

# Mildew-resistant zinnias

*Of nine kinds tested, four came out winners*

HERALDED IN catalogs as an annual that provides continuous bloom until first frost, the flamboyant zinnia sounds like a gardener's best friend. It also is heat tolerant, provides lots of colorful blooms, and needs less water than many other flowering annuals.

But if you've grown zinnias, you may have noticed one of the major drawbacks of its long performance—powdery mildew. Mildew, a white fungus that infects susceptible plants when days are warm and nights are cool, usually shows up in late summer. It's particularly severe in coastal climates, but it also infects zinnias in inland areas.

Most of the large-leafed, large-flowered types are susceptible to mildew. Infected leaves eventually shrivel and die, and the fungus may also cover the flowers, shortening bloom life and making them unsuitable for cutting.

But zinnia lovers needn't forgo the cheerful blooms.

You can expect great performance from several types—even in powdery mildew country.

## THE NINE-ZINNIA TEST

We grew and monitored nine types of zinnias. Dreamland, Peter Pan, Rainbow, Ruffles, and Sunshine have 2- to 3-inch-wide leaves and large (3- to 3½-inch-wide) double flowers.

The Pinwheel series—claimed to be a breeding breakthrough for its mildew resistance—has 3-inch-wide single daisylike flowers.

*Zinnia angustifolia* 'Orange Star' (sold as *Z. linearis*) and 'Star White', and *Z. haageana* 'Old Mexico' have narrow (½- to 1-inch-wide) leaves with 1½- to 2½-inch-wide daisylike flowers. These sprawling plants are much less formal-looking than the other zinnias. Catalogs list 'Star White' as mildew resistant, but all of these narrow-leafed kinds are considered disease resistant.

We sowed seed in mid-May and planted out seedlings four weeks later. Plants were watered with soaker hoses and fertilized with fish emulsion. Last summer was much warmer than normal, which may have delayed disease symptoms on susceptible plants.

'Old Mexico', 'Orange Star', Pinwheel, and 'Star White' bloomed all summer and fall without a trace of mildew.

Mildew appeared on Rainbow by late summer. A few weeks later, Dreamland, Peter Pan, Ruffles, and Sunshine were infected. Ruffles (in right photo) was completely covered with mildew by late September.

Our test indicated that disease development is a certainty on the large, double-flowered zinnias. On the other hand, they'll probably bloom for several months before they succumb to disease (they're not worth spraying with chemicals; it's best to rip out infected plants).

If you're looking for a brightly colored, mildew-resistant zinnia with classic upright growth (but only single flowers), Pinwheel is the best choice. Although the narrow-leafed zinnias look very different from typical zinnias, they are extremely colorful and bloom over a long period.

## WHERE TO GET SEEDS

Order by mail for widest selection. Catalogs are free.

***W. Atlee Burpee & Co.,*** 300 Park Ave., Warminster, Pa. 18991; (800) 888-1447. Sells Pinwheel series (mixed colors or single colors of cherry, orange, rose, salmon, and white), 'Star White', and *Z. a.* 'Starbright Mixed' (a mix of white, orange, and gold; new for 1994).

***Thompson & Morgan,*** Dept. 186-4, Jackson, N.J. 08527; (800) 274-7333. Sells 'Old Mexico' and 'Orange Star'. ■

*By Lauren Bonar Swezey*

**PLANTS FOR SUN CONTAINERS**

Aster
Baby snapdragon
Dianthus
Dusty miller
English ivy (several)
Felicia
French lavender
Ivy geranium
Lemon thyme
Nierembergia
Pansy
Petunia
Snapdragon
Speedwell
Verbena
Zinnia

Some are planted for full sun, and some for shade. We show one for each exposure.

The containers pictured here and on the facing page are big (26-inch diameter) and heavy. Before planting, Don built a round, wheeled trivet for each from ½-inch plywood and heavy-duty wheels from a hardware store. The trivets keep pots from staining the decks and make them easy to rotate.

Then the Cannons filled each container about two-thirds full of styrene plastic packing chips (they don't settle). Potting soil—in this case, Seattle's Cedar Grove compost—went on top.

**SNIPPING OFF FADED FLOWERS** *and overeager new shoots, Robyn Cannon keeps a minigarden of sun lovers fresh-looking and balanced. Set on wheels, the pot is rotated daily so that all plants get equal light.*

# Showy gardens in pots—for sun and shade

*Seattle gardeners share their secrets*

**J**UST AS BONSAI gardeners make forests in dishes, Robyn and Don Cannon wanted to make whole gardens in big terra-cotta containers. They did, setting them out on two large decks and a small patio they use for entertaining at their Seattle home.

**PLANT COMBINATIONS** *first take shape in the nursery, where it's easy to mix and match colors and textures.*

### DESIGNING THE GARDEN

Robyn chooses plants for the garden the way she selects fabrics for interior design: she picks a plant she likes—an apricot-colored begonia, for example—and walks it through a well-stocked nursery, choosing other plants that work well with it.

Her goal is a variety of textures, colors, and habits (upright to draping); she even takes fragrance into consideration. She chooses and freely mixes annuals, perennials, bulbs, and ground covers—whatever will work well for at least a season. Plants are also matched for exposure.

Then the planting begins.

## FROM PLANTS TO GARDENS

If the container gardens pictured here look nearly perfect, it's because each gets meticulous care. It starts when Don sprinkles the transplants with full-strength fish emulsion to help ease transplant shock.

Whenever the container starts to dry out, he waters alternately with plain water and with a quarter-strength dilution of the fertilizer.

For the first three weeks, he uses quarter-strength fish emulsion for even-numbered irrigations. In the fourth week, he switches to quarter-strength 20-20-20 fertilizer to force strong foliage development. In week six, he switches again, this time substituting quarter-strength bloom-formula fish emulsion.

Throughout the season, he supplements the fertilizer with a dash of micronutrients (sold in the fertilizer section of garden centers) every 10 days.

## BALANCED GROWTH: IT'S A QUESTION OF FINESSE

This steady, even feeding program pushes plant growth, which the Cannons direct by pinching and staking. Giving each container a half-turn every day prevents plants from leaning toward the sun. The Cannons deadhead flowers every day to keep new blooms coming and plants looking sharp.

On this schedule, plants come into their prime about two months after planting and stay that way until cold weather stops the bloom in fall. Last year, that was in late October.

After plants start looking shabby, the Cannons pull them out and cover the containers with tarps to protect them from frost damage during winter. Then, before replanting in spring, they replenish the potting soil by digging in new compost. ■

*By Jim McCausland*

### PLANTS FOR SHADE CONTAINERS

Astilbe
Browallia
Coleus
Coral bells
Fuchsia
Heliotrope
Lamium 'Variegatum'
Rex begonia
Semperflorens begonia
Strawberry begonia
  (*Saxifraga stolonifera*)
Tuberous begonia

**SHADE-LOVING PLANTS** *in a container include plenty of bright colors, whites, and variegation; all show well in both shade and low evening light. Purple heliotrope shows up behind the red tuberous begonia and at far right; it perfumes the air with a vanilla-like fragrance.*

# At Nixon library, the subject is roses

*May is the best month to see these Yorba Linda gardens*

JOHN HUMBLE

**FROM THE FORMAL GARDEN'S** *reflecting pool, visitors face President Richard Nixon's farmhouse birthplace. At right, pink 'Simplicity' rose and blue agapanthus are an especially successful spring combination.*

**BRILLIANT RED 'SHOWBIZ'** *and lemon yellow 'Sun Flare' floribunda roses dominate a terraced bed in The First Lady's Garden.*

THINK "ROSE GARDEN," and the Richard Nixon Presidential Library & Birthplace in Orange County probably isn't the first place to leap to mind. But former first lady Pat Nixon was an avid gardener, and the grounds of the 9-acre Yorba Linda museum honor her love of roses. They reign supreme both in mass plantings, including a new bed of 70 deliciously fragrant 'Double Delight', and in the intimate First Lady's Garden, where roses, irises, and perennials weave a luxurious tapestry. This month, when roses are in their glory, is the prime time to stroll the grounds.

## FRAGRANT LESSONS

The First Lady's Garden, inspired by the legendary White House Rose Garden, consists of terraced beds, each dominated by a single floribunda rose variety, 'Amber Queen', 'Angel Face', 'French Lace', 'Sun Flare', 'Simplicity', and 'Showbiz' among them.

The 4-year-old garden offers many lessons. Bright pink flowers of 'Simplicity' and blue flowers of agapanthus, for example, make a stunning color combination. To soften the look of concrete tiers, the gardeners planted cascading rosemary, which blooms blue in winter. Rosy lavender 'Angel Face' was found to be sensitive to crowding, while scabiosa, lamb's ears, and armeria proved to be good edging plants in the rose beds.

The Formal Garden, planted with traditional California plants including towering queen palms, kumquats, and clipped boxwood and myrtle hedges, features a 130-foot-long reflecting pool. The garden's ends are anchored by the library to the west and by the former president's birthplace, a 1912 farmhouse, to the east.

Near the pool's east end, glowing red, fragrant hybrid tea 'Mr. Lincoln' roses lead to a tiered garden amphitheater. Around the amphitheater's fringe, you'll find an assortment of roses. These include the burgundy red floribunda 'Pat Nixon' and a new planting of English roses including 'Abraham Darby', 'Cressida', 'Francine Austin', and 'Tamora'. Hundreds of 'Bonica' shrub roses ring the amphitheater like thick pink icing on a giant wedding cake.

Although roses are the main attraction at this time of year, don't overlook the nuggets of history revealed through other plants and garden ornaments on the grounds. The magnolia tree near the southeast corner of the amphitheater, for example, was originally planted by Mrs. Nixon at her California home, La Casa Pacifica, and transferred to the library garden in 1990. But the tree's roots go deeper than that: it is a seedling from a magnolia that Andrew Jackson brought from his home in Tennessee to the White House. Ornaments include the dove-of-peace weather vane in The First Lady's Garden, which is a replica of one George Washington ordered for his home in Mount Vernon.

The museum is at 18001 Yorba Linda Boulevard. Admission costs $4.95, $2.95 ages 62 and over, $1 ages 8 through 11. Admission to the gardens is free with museum admission. Both are open from 10 to 5 Mondays through Saturdays, from 11 to 5 Sundays. Guided garden tours are offered at 11 on Saturdays during May and June. For more information, call (714) 993-3393. ∎

*By Lynn Ocone*

**TALL BEARDED IRISES** *are at peak bloom in mid- to late May at Cooley's trial garden (above), where you can buy rhizomes. Sightseers at Schreiner's ride on a horse-drawn wagon.*

MICHAEL THOMPSON

# Iris time... head for the Willamette Valley

*Visit two world-class growers and two lively festivals in Oregon*

LIKE THE GRAND finale at a fireworks show, brightly colored iris blossoms seem to go off all at once this month in the Willamette Valley. The place to see them is between the Oregon towns of Keizer and Silverton, where the world's two largest iris growers have hundreds of acres of farm fields.

While you're there, you can take in any of several iris-related events, including fun runs, breakfasts, parades, and concerts.

## IRIS FARMS

Iris fields are spread around the valley, but since they're concentrated near each grower's headquarters, those are good places to start your tour. Iris bloom time varies from year to year, but the flowers are usually at their peak the third week in May. Call ahead to check.

While you're there, view the trial gardens and labeled cut-flower displays. If you see irises that you'd like, you can order on the spot for delivery during the summer planting season. Or you can order irises by mail through the growers' sumptuous catalogs ($4 each; call to order).

Both growers host elaborate and varied special events, mostly on weekends. Between them, you can expect barbecues, wine tastings, live music, and more.

*Cooley's Gardens,* 11553 Silverton Road N.E., Silverton; (503) 873-5463. To get to Silverton from the north, exit Interstate 5 at Woodburn and follow signs through Mount Angel to Silverton. Then take State Highway 213 (Silverton Road) about 2 miles west (toward Salem). Cooley's is on the right. From the south, take the Market Street off-ramp (exit 256) from I-5 at Salem, and head east on State 213 about 10 miles to Cooley's.

*Schreiner's Iris Gardens,* 3625 Quinaby Road N.E., Keizer; 393-3232. Heading south on I-5, take the Brooks exit (263) and head west about a mile to a four-way stop. Then go left (south) a mile on River Road N., and left (east) again on Quinaby another mile to the gardens.

## IRIS CELEBRATIONS

*Silverton.* The Silverton International Iris Jubilee combines a passel of weekend events in May ranging from runs and senior olympics to a pet parade. For a schedule of jubilee events, call the chamber of commerce at 873-5615.

*Keizer.* Iris Festival activities in Keizer include everything from a triathlon and a golf tournament to dances and a jazz festival. For a schedule, call the chamber of commerce at 393-9111. ∎

*By Jim McCausland*

A SILVER SWATH *of lamb's ears (Stachys byzantina) fronts an arbor with a red rose.*

# JUNE

# Sunset's
# GARDEN GUIDE

# June busts out all over the West. Enjoy the exuberance, shop for new garden ideas

What nature does effortlessly, students and instructors in the Ornamental Horticulture Department of Cal Poly San Luis Obispo have labored several years to duplicate. Tucked within Leaning Pine Arboretum is the result of their work—the California Collection, a small native planting that's rich with design and plant ideas for your home garden.

Instructor Dave Fross, who initiated and oversees the collection, says the garden is "designed with themes that are usable in suburban and urban gardens." All the plants are labeled and grouped in loose associations corresponding with natural ecosystems, including chaparral, oak woodland, redwood forest, and riparian meadow (pictured above right). The meadow grasses shown, including cane bluestem (*Bothriochloa barbinoides*), deer grass (*Muhlenbergia rigens*), and wild rye (*Elymus condensatus* 'Canyon Prince'), are appropriate for informal plantings and are most striking planted in clusters or massed.

The arboretum is at the north end of the Ornamental Horticulture Unit (building 48). Pick up a campus map and parking permit at the information building at the Grand Avenue entrance to campus. Hours are 8 to 5 weekdays, 9 to 5 Saturdays (except academic holidays). Admission is free. For more information, call (805) 756-2279.—*Lynn Ocone*

## A good month to go bananas

Need we say more? Well, perhaps: June is an excellent month to shop for and plant bananas in Southern California. And growing your own allows you to discover and enjoy dozens of unusual varieties—with fruits of many flavors, colors, and sizes—not found in most markets.

But before you buy, consider the basics. Bananas thrive in full sun and heat. Most are hardy down to 32° and grow best in *Sunset Western Garden Book* climate zones 21 through 24. Some varieties can tolerate temperatures as low as 27° for brief periods (with leaf burn). Some—'Cardaba', 'Dwarf Orinoco', 'Ice Cream', 'Manzano', and 'Raja Puri' among them—will produce in zones 19 and 20.

Bananas need plenty of water, and soil rich in nitrogen and potassium. They grow fast, and depending on variety and climate, most produce fruit anytime from 18 to 30 months after planting.

These four places in Southern California have good selections of bananas.

***Seaside Banana Garden,*** 6823 Santa Barbara Ave., Ventura 93001 (mailing address); (805) 643-4061. It's at the corner of Surfside Street and Carpinteria Avenue. Choose from more than 40 varieties in bare-root or in 5- and 15-gallon containers; $15 and up. Mail order or retail; catalog $2.

***Papaya Tree Nursery,*** 12422 El Oro Way, Granada Hills 91344; (818) 363-3680. Eight varieties in 5-gallon

CHAD SLATTERY

RIPARIAN MEADOW *at Cal Poly San Luis Obispo shows how cane bluestem, deer grass, and wild rye can be used in your garden.*

sulting in flower variations in future plantings.—*L. O.*

## Pastels paint a steep slope

Although June 21 marks the official start of summer, temperatures are moderate in many parts of the West, and hot days may be weeks away. This is fortunate for many flowering plants, because the milder temperatures can extend their bloom time.

The hillside garden of Bob and Rosie Heil, shown on page 140, makes the most of the season. This patchwork of colorful plants begins its succession of bloom in early spring and continues through summer. As garden designer Wendy Wilde found out, the steep, west-facing slope isn't

OFFICE LABELS *wrapped around stems of blooming sweet peas make it easy to differentiate flower color at seed-harvest time.*

containers; $24 to $36. Open by appointment only.

*Pacific Tree Farms,* 4301 Lynwood Drive, Chula Vista 91910; (619) 422-2400. Open 8:30 to 5 (9 to 3 Sundays); closed Tuesdays. More than 20 varieties of bananas in 5-, 15-, and 20-gallon containers from $30. Mail order and retail; catalog $2.

*Exotica Rare Fruit Nursery,* 2508 E. Vista Way, Box B, Vista 92084; (619) 724-9093. Open 9 to 5 daily. More than 20 varieties in 1-, 5-, and 15-gallon containers; prices range from $8 to $80. Mail order and retail; catalog free.—*L. O.*

## How to save sweet pea seed

Avid gardener and *Sunset* senior editor Kathy Brenzel knows a good thing when she sees it. That's why for the past five years she's been saving her sweet pea seeds so she can replant her favorite varieties. Because she likes to keep the color of each variety separate, she labels the immature pea pods late in the season. This is her technique.

Around June, when new flowers are smaller and have shorter stems, she labels the pods using ½- by 3½-inch sticky-back file folder labels (sold in stationery stores).

With indelible ink, she writes the variety on the label, peels off the backing, and wraps the label around the stem supporting the pod and flower (pictured at right). When the pods mature, they swell, turn brown, and dry. This is the time to collect the seed. Brenzel simply holds a paper bag under a pod and squeezes it so the seeds pop out.

If you wait too long to collect the seed, the pods will break open naturally and the seed will spill into the garden. And although peas usually self-pollinate, there is a chance that insects will cross-pollinate plants, possibly re-

**COLORFUL PATCHWORK** *of unthirsty plants thrives on a steep slope. Pink rockrose intermingles with gray lamb's ears and lavender. Snow-in-summer covers the upper slope.*

a site for pansies. After mild spring weather passes, it bakes in summer and is blasted by winds. It holds very little topsoil, mostly rock and clay. Only rugged plants survive here.

After one false start when half the plants died in the big freeze of 1990, Wilde finally found a combination of plants that thrive. Each one was planted in its own large hole with plenty of soil amendments.

The current hillside reflects the Heils' preference for pastels and other soft colors—lavender, pink, purple, and white. The show starts with Santa Barbara daisy, then white snow-in-summer lights up the slope. Purple iris, pink rockrose, and Spanish lavender follow. The floral extravaganza continues with pentstemon, daylilies, butterfly bush, and creeping thyme, which turns the steps bright laven-

der. Gray lamb's ears spreads between plants.

The best news is the plants require only minimum maintenance; the Heils use a hedge trimmer to deadhead the lavender, rockrose, and Santa Barbara daisy. Weeds used to be a severe problem, but they're under control since the plants have grown in.
—*Lauren Bonar Swezey*

## Make sure the manure is mature

Well-rotted horse or cow manure works wonders in the vegetable garden, adding valuable organic matter and essential nutrients to the soil all at once.

Fresh manure, however, is another story. It's been linked with human cases of *E. coli,* listeria, and salmonella. As if that weren't enough, it's bad for plants as well, burning tender roots and robbing

the soil of nitrogen as it breaks down.

The link between fresh manure and *E. coli* was reported in the August 1993 issue of *Lancet,* a British medical journal. The report cited the case of an American vegetarian whose family developed an *E. coli* infection after eating raw vegetables from her garden, which she had fertilized with fresh manure. *E. coli* bacteria were found in the woman's garden soil, and a child died from the infection.

In response to this report, Washington State University food specialist Val Hillers suggests that, besides avoiding fresh manure, you don't apply any manure to the vegetable garden within 60 days of harvest. And you should never use cat, dog, or pig manure, which can carry disease organisms as well as roundworms and tapeworms.—*Jim McCausland.*

## Wind up mum planting this month

With so much flowering right now and just about everything growing like gangbusters, you may not be thinking ahead to fall color. But June marks the end of the best planting season for one of the West's most valued autumn-blooming perennials—chrysanthemums.

Check nurseries now for *C. morifolium,* usually called florists' chrysanthemum or garden mum. It comes in many flower forms, colors, and growth habits. This group includes popular types like pompons, anemone, and daisy-flowered varieties. Although hard to find, small rooted cuttings not in flower are your best bet. One nursery that specializes in mums and offers bare-root plants by mail through June is Sunnyslope Gardens, 8638 Huntington Dr., San Gabriel, Calif. 91775; (818) 287-4071. The catalog is free.

Plant mums in fertile, well-drained soil in full sun. They require regular water, but young plants are sensitive to overwatering. Let the soil surface dry out between each irrigation. Feed mums in the ground monthly through the growing season with a complete fertilizer. Once buds show color, stop feeding.

When plants are established, about two weeks after planting, remove the tip of each plant to force three or more new shoots. For sturdy, bushy plants and larger flowers, pinch back all side shoots three or four times through August.—*L. O.*

## Hail to kale, and off we sow

Kale is one of those vegetables your mother tried to make you feel guilty for not eating. Finally, this nutritious green is getting some respect. It's appearing as a garnish and a vegetable at fine restaurants.

In cool- to mild-summer parts of the West, sow kale seed anytime this month in full sun and in rich, well-drained soil. Among the new hybrid varieties, ones with thick, curly leaves on short stems include 'Dwarf Blue Curled', 'Green Curled Scotch', and 'Squire'. The germination rate is fantastic, often 80 percent or better.

In about two months, leaves are ready to harvest. Plants will keep producing into the late fall; leaves can stay on the plant in cold storage to harvest through the winter. Once frost-bitten, leaves have a zestier flavor. (And, Mom, you were right. Kale tastes delicious, only I like mine stir-fried with some olive oil and garlic rather than steamed.)—*Steven R. Lorton.*

## Silver-leafed show-offs

The arbor pictured on page 136, bedecked with a climbing rose, gives this garden in Eugene, Oregon, a sense of visual depth. In the foreground is a drift of silver-leafed *Stachys byzantina,* commonly called lamb's ears. This old-fashioned perennial is currently enjoying a well-deserved comeback. It's easy to grow, quick to increase, drought tolerant, and has wonderful fuzzy leaves that give it its common name. The rosy purplish blooms appear this month; when they fade, you simply cut them off.

Silver foliage is great for lighting up a garden. Besides lamb's ears, other silver-leafed perennials include several artemisias: *A. ludoviciana albula* (silver king), *A.* 'Powis Castle', *A. schmidtiana* 'Silver Mound', and *A. stellerana* (dusty miller). They're all good candidates to shine in elegant contrast to green and other colors.—*S. R. L.*

## Ouch! Hot water from drip tubing can harm plants

When exposed to the sun, the black tubing used in drip-irrigation systems acts like a solar collector. Water that remains inside the tubing while the system is off can easily heat up to 110° or hotter. If you turn the system on in the afternoon, the first water out can be so hot it damages plants. If it hits the trunk of a young fruit tree, the resulting wound could invite borer infestation. Hot water can also harm roots and foliage, especially of young plants.

To prevent this kind of damage, cover the drip tubing with soil or mulch so it isn't exposed to the sun, and water in the morning before the tubing has a chance to heat up, or at night after it has cooled down.—*Lance Walheim*

## Building a better windbreak

When Gene Howard set out 12 years ago to build a windbreak to shelter his house and garden near Cheyenne, Wyoming, he started with year-old trees and shrubs and watered them only during the first two summers. Today, the windbreak is nearly 20 feet tall at its highest point (about half its ultimate height). How did he do it? His answer: "I just put into practice what I'd learned down at the station."

That "station" is the USDA's High Plains Grasslands Research Station in Cheyenne; Howard was its director for many years. Here are his keys to fast windbreak growth.

• Keep weeds and grasses down so windbreak plants won't have to compete with anything else for water.

• Plant in rows, with shorter, shrubby plants on the windward side, a second row of taller plants 12 feet back, and a third rank 12 feet behind that. Shrubs in the first row are 3 feet apart, while trees in the back two rows are 12 to 15 feet apart.

• Use drought-tolerant plants. For the exposed front row, Howard used Siberian peashrub (*Caragana arborescens*) and common buckthorn (*Rhamnus cathartica*); for the middle row, he chose Siberian elm (*Ulmus pumila*); and for the tall back row, ponderosa pine (*Pinus ponderosa*) and Eastern red cedar (*Juniperus virginiana*).

The rule of thumb is that a windbreak of medium density will reduce wind speed 50 percent or more on the ground behind it for about eight times the windbreak's height. So, a 25-foot-tall windbreak will protect ground-level plants for about 200 feet behind it.—*J. M.*

## It looks like lavender, smells like licorice

Korean licorice mint (*Agastache rugosa*) was a big hit last season in *Sunset*'s test garden in Menlo Park, California. Its stalks stretched up to 5 feet tall, and its dark green leaves filled the garden with a deliciously licoricelike fragrance. Then came 6-inch spikes of purple flowers that drew bees like honey. The leaves give salads a flavorful anise- or licorice-like zing, which may mystify guests who like what they taste but don't know what it is.

This plant comes from northeast Asia, where winter temperatures can get quite cold, and it is similar in appearance and habit to its American cousin, *A. urticifolia,* which is widely used in British gardens. This perennial should make it through winters in Sunset zones 7–9 and 14–24, but even if it doesn't, it's worth growing as an annual.

Plant seed this month (it needs warm soil to germinate). Give it full sun and rich, quick-draining soil. Water well until plants are established. Expect to be amazed by its rapid growth. The flowers start in late summer, and chefs use the flowers for gar-

nish or dry them for tea.

Seed of Korean licorice mint is available from Ornamental Edibles, 3622 Weedin Court, San Jose, Calif. 95132; (408) 946-7333 (catalog free). A packet of seeds costs $1.50, plus $3 shipping and handling for an order of any size.
—*S. R. L.*

## Alternative pest controls

As the weather warms up, check summer vegetables and fruits for pests ranging from aphids and mites to borers and hornworms. Using organic methods such as botanical insecticides and predatory insects to control these pests takes a variety of materials and techniques. Unfortunately, most nurseries don't carry a wide range of alternative pest controls. Here are four mail-order sources that specialize in them. Catalogs are free unless noted.

*Gardens Alive,* 5100 Schenley Place, Lawrenceburg, Ind. 47025.

*Integrated Fertility Management,* 333 Ohme Gardens

NORMAN A. PLATE

**FRAGRANT** *forest green leaves and rosy flower spikes make Korean licorice mint useful in both the landscape and the kitchen.*

NORMAN A. PLATE

## Tool of the Month

*Weed 'n Rake combines a hoe to uproot weeds and a six-tined rake to clean up debris. The standard model has a 12-inch handle, weighs just 19 ounces, and sells for about $13; the long model has a 56-inch handle, weighs 28 ounces, and costs about $16. Both models have retractable 6-inch rakes. If garden centers or hardware stores don't carry it, call the manufacturer at (800) 706-8665 for the nearest supplier.*

Rd., Wenatchee, Wash. 98801. Catalog $2.

*Necessary Trading Company,* Box 305, New Castle, Va. 24127. Catalog $2.

*Peaceful Valley Farm Supply,* Box 2209, Grass Valley, Calif. 95945.
—L. W.

## Wasp is latest weapon against eucalyptus borer

The eucalyptus longhorned borer is killing California's grand old blue gums (*E. globulus*), along with other eucalyptus trees, which have been part of the Golden State's scenery for 80 to 100 years. Some Californians aren't too sad to see them go. The trees have been blamed for everything from fires to sterilizing the surrounding soil.

Even though these trees are not natives, they have many admirers who view them as a vital part of the California landscape. UC Riverside researchers Larry Hanks, Jocelyn Millar, and Tim Paine are trying to save the stately trees by introducing tiny stingless wasps to parasitize and kill the beetles.

Releases were made where the borer has been wiping out trees in Southern California and on the Stanford University campus in Northern California. Although the borer hasn't reached other groves farther up the San Francisco Peninsula and in the East Bay, trees there are sitting ducks, according to Hanks.

So far, it looks as if the wasp is doing its job. Last year, up to 90 percent of the beetle eggs that were found by the wasps were parasitized. The main question the researchers hope to answer this spring is whether the wasps can live through winters and naturalize.

In the meantime, homeowners should keep their trees as healthy as possible (borers attack stressed trees). Deep-water trees at least once or twice in summer (once you start watering, continue every summer; discontinuing irrigation could stress trees more). Remove dead trees and clean up fallen branches; bag, bury, or chip them to prevent beetles from moving to other trees. If you keep the wood for firewood, wrap it in a plastic tarp until you use it. Prune only between November and March, when the beetles aren't active.—L. B. S.

## Electric 'Blue Panda'

At last February's Northwest Flower and Garden Show, noted plantsman Dan Hinkley of Heronswood Nursery in Kingston, Washington, really went out on a limb. He called *Corydalis flexuosa* 'Blue Panda' "the perennial of the decade, if not the century." Wow! Why?

'Blue Panda' was discovered in China, in the same environment where pandas live. It forms a tidy clump of ferny foliage that reaches 6 inches and spreads at a steady clip. But what gets this plant rave reviews is its flowers: electric blue masses of tiny blooms reminiscent of snapdragon blossoms, shooting up on long willowy stems from March through November.

Since this plant is comfortable in a cool, moist, coastal climate, and in light shade under tall conifers, it is perfect for the woodland garden. Set out nursery plants from gallon cans this month or whenever plants are available and the ground is workable.

Once established, 'Blue Panda' grows with little or no attention. Scatter a bit of complete granular fertilizer around it when you feed other perennials. In late autumn, cut back the foliage. The plant will leaf out early in the new year.—S. R. L.

## Battling Bermuda grass

It's taken over the flower beds, you can barely see the ground cover through the grass, you're tired of pulling out runners (which does little good anyway)—what are you going to do about the Bermuda grass that's taking over your yard?

It's time to get serious. You have several chemical herbicide options, each one very effective.

*Fluazifop-butyl* (Grass-b-gon) kills only grasses and can be sprayed over many ornamentals (check the label for which ones) without harming them.

*Glyphosate* (Round-up) is a broad-spectrum, systemic herbicide that will kill the entire plant when sprayed on the leaves. It can also kill or damage any plant it contacts. Use it only where the spray won't touch other plants, such as along walkways, edgings, paths, or on large patches of weeds. It's best used in late summer.

*Sethoxydim* (Poast) also kills only grasses but can be sprayed over a wider range of other plants, including flowering annuals and perennials, without harming them. It works best when applied in a fine spray.

Each herbicide is most effective in warm weather when the grass is growing vigorously. You'll probably need to make repeat applications. Follow label instructions exactly.—L. W.

## Drip system should grow with plants

Watering by drip irrigation is convenient, avoids water waste, and is normally beneficial to plant growth. But if you forget to adjust emitter placement after plants have been in the ground awhile, watering by drip may actually harm plants.

Roots normally grow from half to three times the diameter of the plant canopy (roots grow wider in sandy soil). When a system is installed, emitters are usually placed right on a plant's rootball only a few inches away from the stem or trunk. Once trees and larger shrubs start growing, the location and water supply aren't adequate to encourage root growth.

After plants have become established, emitters must be moved outward so roots continue to grow into the surrounding soil. It's best to remove the existing emitter and plug the hole so water doesn't puddle around the trunk or stem, which can encourage disease infection.

Place new emitters on existing tubing or on new sections added to the line. Depending on the size of the plant and its water requirements, you may need to add four, six, or (for large trees) even more emitters. Place them around the plant's drip line where the feeder roots can absorb the water. For trees and large shrubs, you will need to continue making adjustments as they grow.
—L. B. S.

# June Checklist

## ■ PACIFIC NORTHWEST

**BAIT FOR SLUGS.** They do the most damage on emerging seedlings and on plants with ornamental leaves like hostas. Bait to protect these vulnerable plants. Be careful to keep pets away from bait.

**CARE FOR HOUSE PLANTS.** Most are actively growing now. Feed them every two to three weeks with half-strength liquid fertilizer, and water as soon as the top ½ inch of soil dries out. Also, take plants outside and gently hose off any accumulation of dust. Spray plants in the shade, let them drip dry, then bring them back indoors, unless you're leaving them outdoors for the summer.

**CLIP HEDGES.** Leave the base of the hedge a few inches wider than the top. If you cut now, when plants are growing most, new foliage will quickly fill in gaps.

**CULTIVATE SOIL.** As we head into our driest months, get into the practice of cultivating around plants. Break up the crusty soil surface to make a mulch of soil that admits water but slows evaporation. Cultivating also keeps weeds down.

**CUT RHUBARB.** Stop harvesting as new stalks start to get noticeably thinner than old ones. This lets the plant put strength back into its roots for next year's harvest. Remove seed heads as they appear.

**DEADHEAD FLOWERS.** Rhododendrons will be winding up their bloom show this month. Break off flower heads as they fade. Also remove faded flowers on perennials and annuals to keep plants from setting seed and to encourage more flowers.

**FEED BEDDING PLANTS.** To encourage speedy growth, fertilize them lightly and frequently. Weekly feeding is not too often for plants in full sun. Use liquid plant food mixed at ½ to ¾ strength, or feed every other week at full strength.

**FERTILIZE PERENNIALS.** Feed plants as soon as they finish blooming. Scatter a half-handful of 12-12-12 granular fertilizer around the base of a plant with a crown the size of a dinner plate.

**FERTILIZE ROSES.** Feed plants after the first flush of bloom has faded, then again after the next bloom burst. Or use controlled-release fertilizer.

**GO AFTER MORNING GLORY.** To rid the garden of this invasive perennial, gently spade up the soil. Lift the long fleshy roots, pulling them out of the ground as close to the root ends as possible. Every little piece of root you leave in the ground will sprout. Keep at it. Total eradication may take several years.

**MAKE COMPOST.** As you clip, harvest, mow, and prune, turn organic matter into the center of the pile. Keep the pile moist and aerated by regular turning, and you'll have a pile that smells clean and breaks down quickly.

**ORDER SPRING BULBS NOW.** The Pacific Northwest is rich in commercial bulb growers. Order now, while the memory of what you like is fresh in your mind. Bulbs will be shipped quickly when fall planting time arrives.

**PLANT VEGETABLES AND ANNUALS.** April and May are the big bedding plant months, but you'll still find a fair selection to buy and plant now. Plant as soon as possible.

**REMOVE SUCKERS.** Rub off unwanted shoots as they appear on fruit trees and ornamentals. Suckers usually show up around the base of the tree and watersprouts next to pruning cuts.

**TEND HERBACEOUS BORDERS.** Clip faded blooms. Stake and tie up floppy plants and tall flower stalks.

**THIN APPLES.** By thinning apples, you'll get bigger, better fruit. After the June drop (the natural shedding of excess fruit), go over fruit clusters, thinning triples to two and doubles to one. Also remove any damaged or malformed fruits.

**WATER.** Pay close attention to any newly set-out plants as well as to plants in containers and ones under eaves or in sandy soil.

## June Checklist

■

### NORTHERN CALIFORNIA

■ **CARE FOR ROSES.** To encourage growth and additional flushes of bloom on repeat bloomers, remove faded flowers and feed plants with a complete fertilizer and iron chelate (if necessary). Mulch to conserve soil moisture and keep roots cooler.

On hybrid teas and grandifloras, snip off faded blooms ¼ inch above the first (from top) leaf with five leaflets. For a long-stemmed rose, cut above the second leaf with five leaflets.

■ **CHECK SPRINKLERS.** Inspect your sprinkler system to see that it is working properly and has no broken, malfunctioning, or misaligned heads. Turn the system on and inspect each head; replace broken ones. If a head bubbles or squirts irregularly, it may be clogged. Check slits for dirt or small pebbles. To readjust a misaligned head, turn it until it's spraying in the right direction.

The quickest way to measure sprinkler output and uniformity is to set five coffee mugs or cans of uniform size around your lawn area and run the sprinklers for 15 minutes. Then use a ruler to measure the depth of water in each container. If output is variable, adjust the flow (screw) on each head. In summer, lawns in warmer inland zones (San Jose, Santa Rosa) need about 1¼ inches a week.

■ **CONTROL MITES.** Mottled, dusty-looking leaves and possibly fine webbing indicate the presence of spider mites. To confirm infestations, look for minute whitish eggs and tiny mites on the undersides of leaves (a magnifying glass helps). Spray with insecticidal soap or horticultural oil (test oil on a small portion of the plant first; some plants may be sensitive to it). To help discourage infestations, periodically rinse theundersides of foliage witha strong spray of water.

■ **HARVEST VEGETABLES.** If you planted an early crop of beans, short-season corn, cucumbers, or squash, the harvest should be starting. Pick in the early morning when it's cool, and harvest vegetables at their peak maturity—firm, fully colored, and full flavored, but not too large. Harvest lemon cucumbers before they yellow; harvest beans before seeds swell. Zucchini and pattypan squash also can be harvested as baby squash when just a few inches long. Check corn

about four days after the silk turns brown (gently pull down husk and nick a kernel with a fingernail; cloudy milk should spurt out).

■ **MULCH.** To help control weeds, minimize water evaporation, and keep roots cooler, apply a 2- to 4-inch layer of organic material (use the deeper amount for larger plants) around shrubs, trees, and vines, and on flower and vegetable beds. Keep mulch several inches away from trunks.

■ **PLANT SUMMER BLOOMERS.** Less-thirsty choices to start now include coreopsis, gaillardia, globe amaranth, Madagascar periwinkle (vinca rosea), penstemon, perennial statice, portulaca, salvia, sanvitalia, sunflower, verbena, and zinnia. Good foliage plants for fillers are low-growing artemisias, dusty miller, and golden or purple sage. Plant late in the afternoon to give seedlings overnight to recover from transplant shock. In hot climates, shade young plants with cloth or boards until established.

■ **PLANT VEGETABLES.** No matter which zone you live in, June is prime vegetable planting time. Sow seeds of beans and corn. Set out transplants of cucumbers, eggplant, melons, okra, peppers, pumpkins, squash, and tomatoes.

San Rafael

Walnut Creek

Oakland

San Francisco

San Jose

Monterey

▨ Coastal (zone 17)

☐ Inland (zones 14–16)

■ **TRAIN TOMATOES.** For easy picking and to prevent fruit rot, support tomatoes off the ground with a cage or stakes. For large plants, make the cage 5 to 6 feet high and 2 feet in diameter (adjust height for smaller plants). Out of 6-inch concrete-reinforcing wire or galvanized mesh, cut a piece 76 inches long. Bend around plant and crimp ends. To stake, use two 8-foot 2-by-2s and set one on each side of the plant about 2 feet apart. As plants grow, tie them up with plastic ties.

**CHECK SPRINKLERS.** Inspect your sprinkler system to make sure it is working properly and has no broken, clogged, or misaligned heads. Turn the system on and inspect each head; replace broken ones. If a head is bubbling or squirting irregularly, it may be clogged (check slits for dirt or small pebbles). To readjust a misaligned head, turn it until it's spraying in the right direction.

**CONTROL PESTS.** Handpick or bait for snails and slugs. Monitor new growth for aphids. Finely mottled leaves with a dusty look suggest spider mites. Get rid of aphids and spider mites by hosing them off or spraying with insecticidal soap. To avoid borer infestations, keep trees watered and healthy.

**HARVEST HERBS.** For best flavor, pick individual leaves or sprigs before flower buds open.

**MULCH.** To prevent weed growth and water loss, spread a layer of organic material, such as compost, wood chips, or redwood bark, 2 to 3 inches thick (depending on plant size) under shrubs, trees, and vines, and on flower and vegetable beds. Keep mulch away from stems and trunks. To improve appearance and reduce dust, also mulch bare ground and pathways.

**PLANT SUMMER BLOOMERS.** Nurseries will have a good selection of seedlings in sixpacks and blooming plants in 4-inch pots and gallon cans. Good choices include cosmos, gaillardia, globe amaranth, Madagascar periwinkle (*Catharanthus roseus*), marigold, penstemon, portulaca, salvia, sanvitalia, verbena, and zinnia. You can still sow seeds of cosmos, marigold, sunflower, and zinnia.

**PLANT VEGETABLES.** You can still plant most summer vegetables, but don't wait too long. Since you're starting late, choose early-maturing varieties. Sow seed of beans, corn, cucumbers, melons, pumpkins, and squash. Set out transplants of eggplant, peppers, and tomatoes.

**REMOVE FIRE HAZARDS.** In fire-prone areas, clean up brush and debris to reduce fuel volume. When grasses turn brown, mow them to about 4 inches. Remove plant debris that may have accumulated on the roof. Prune dead and diseased wood from trees and shrubs. Prune tree limbs at least 20 feet off the ground. Cut branches back at least 15 to 20 feet from the house.

**REMOVE SPENT FLOWERS.** For better bloom and looks, cut off fading flowers from annuals, perennials, and flowering shrubs before they start to set seed.

**REVITALIZE HOUSE PLANTS.** Move them outdoors to a shady location and wash off dust. Leach salts from the soil by watering plants repeatedly. Apply a complete liquid fertilizer.

**TEND FRUIT TREES.** Support sagging fruit-laden limbs with sturdy stakes or 2-by-4s. If necessary to prevent limb loss, knock off excess fruit with a pole. To keep birds from fruit, cover tree with plastic bird netting or porous row-cover fabric.

**WATER.** Soak plants as needed in late afternoon or early evening to cool soil and give plants maximum time to absorb water before midday heat. If plants are prone to foliar diseases, water early in the morning so foliage will dry quickly. Irrigate deeply to soak the entire root zone. Save water by building watering basins around perennials, roses, shrubs, and trees.

**WEED.** Hoe, pull, or spray weeds before they spread seeds. Be diligent so weeds can't steal water and nutrients from desirable plants. For tips on controlling Bermuda grass, see page 142.

Redding

Lake Tahoe

Sacramento

Fresno

Bakersfield

Valley (zones 7–9, 14)

Mountain (zones 1, 2)

## June Checklist
### ■
### SOUTHERN CALIFORNIA

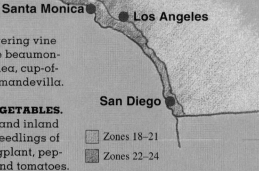

Santa Barbara
Pasadena  San Bernardino
Santa Monica  Los Angeles
San Diego

☐ Zones 18–21
☐ Zones 22–24

**CORRECT IRON CHLOROSIS.** In coastal, inland, and low-desert gardens (*Sunset Western Garden Book* climate zones 22–24, 18–21, and 13, respectively), take a look at your azaleas, camellias, citrus, and gardenias. If new leaves are yellowish with green veins, they lack iron; correct iron chlorosis with one of the many foliar sprays that contain chelated iron (and usually other micronutrients, too).

**GIVE NATIVES A LOW-WATER DIET.** You can kill sensitive native plants such as ceanothus and flannel bush by watering them in summer. If young plants must be watered, let water drip slowly over the rootball, away from leaves and trunk. Water at night or during cool weather, not in the heat of the day.

**KILL CATERPILLAR PESTS.** Petunias, geraniums, and nicotiana are favorites of geranium budworm (alias tobacco budworm). At first signs of the green larvae, spray with *Bacillus thuringiensis.*

**PAMPER CITRUS.** In coastal, inland, and low-desert gardens, feed with high-nitrogen fertilizer as directed on the label, then water thoroughly. To protect newly planted trees from sunburn, wrap trunks with burlap, cloth, or commercial tree wrap, or paint with white latex tree paint. To lessen June fruit drop, water mature trees deeply every two weeks through this month; water young trees weekly.

**PINCH AND SHAPE FUCHSIAS.** In coastal and inland gardens, if fuchsias are growing leggy, pinch off branch tips just above a set of leaves to force growth into side branches. Groom plants by picking flowers as they fade.

**PLANT FOR COLOR.** In coastal, inland, and high-desert (zone 11) gardens, some choices that aren't water guzzlers include amaranthus, bedding begonia, coreopsis, dusty miller, evolvulus, gaillardia, gazania, gloriosa daisy, Madagascar periwinkle (*Catharanthus roseus*), nierembergia, portulaca, scarlet sage, verbena, and yarrow. Plants that need more water, especially inland, include aster, coleus, impatiens, lobelia, melampodium, petunia, salpiglossis, and zinnia. Before planting, work in compost and a complete fertilizer.

**PLANT SUBTROPICALS.** In coastal and inland areas, this is a good month to plant citrus, floss silk tree, ginger, hibiscus, Natal plum, palms, plumeria, and bananas (see page 138). Flowering vine choices include beaumontia, bougainvillea, cup-of-gold vine, and mandevilla.

**PLANT VEGETABLES.** In coastal and inland areas, set out seedlings of cucumbers, eggplant, peppers, squash, and tomatoes. Sow seeds of beans, beets, carrots, corn, cucumbers, pumpkins, and summer squash where you want them to grow. In coastal gardens, you can still plant lettuce seeds and seedlings. In high-desert gardens, sow seeds of corn, cucumbers, muskmelon, okra, squash, and watermelon.

**TEND ROSES.** Feed roses after each bloom cycle and water regularly (do not let your roses dry out). Cut short- or long-stemmed flowers about ¼ inch above a leaf with five or more leaflets. If aphids or spider mites are a problem, wash plants frequently with soapy water, then rinse with clear water.

**THIN CORAL TREES.** In coastal and inland gardens, if your coral tree (*Erythrina*) grows in a lawn, it's probably overwatered, growing fast, and needs pruning now. Shorten long shoots by a third to a half, and remove any branches that cross. If possible, reduce the amount of water your tree receives. It will grow more slowly, need less pruning, and flower just as well or better.

**TURN AND MOISTEN COMPOST.** Turn compost—once for regular maintenance, more often for faster composting. Move material from bottom to top, from sides to center, so it decomposes quickly and evenly. Moisten the pile as you turn it.

**WATER WISELY.** Use an efficient irrigation system that doesn't mist, fog, or create runoff; drip irrigation, moisture sensors, soil soakers, and automatic shut-off valves for sprinklers and hoses are all good ways to save water. Don't overwater; let soil moisture and plant appearance be your guide. Pull moisture-stealing weeds. And don't forget to mulch.

## ANYWHERE IN THE WEST, TACKLE THESE CHORES:

**CARE FOR INDOOR PLANTS.** Warm weather and long days push the growth of indoor plants. Fertilize them at least monthly until winter, and pinch back tip growth to force compactness.

**HARVEST HERBS.** For best flavor, pick herbs before flower buds open, and harvest in the morning just after the dew has dried.

**MAINTAIN ROSES.** Cut off faded flowers, fertilize, then build a shallow moat around each plant to concentrate water around the root zone. Mulch each plant well.

**PRUNE HEDGES.** Clip the hedge so that its bottom is wider than its top. If you don't, shade from the top will make lower growth sparse.

**TREAT CHLOROSIS.** Iron deficiency (called chlorosis) is common in plants in areas with alkaline soil. Plants that suffer from it show yellow leaves with contrasting green veins. Treat the problem with iron chelate.

## IN THE INTERMOUNTAIN WEST, DO THESE CHORES:

**CHECK SPRINKLERS.** In these water-tight times, it's important to check your sprinkler system for clogged, misaligned, and broken heads. Repair them before you waste any more water (or parch your plants).

**MAINTAIN LAWNS.** Fertilize by applying about 2 pounds of actual nitrogen per 1,000 square feet. Water in well. Set your lawn mower at about 2 inches for most cool-season grasses (bluegrass, fescue, and rye); mow bent grass (a common choice for putting greens) at an inch or less.

**PLANT FLOWERS.** Some good choices of colorful summer-blooming plants include coreopsis, gaillardia, globe amaranth, Madagascar periwinkle, penstemon, statice, portulaca, salvia, sanvitalia, sunflower, verbena, and zinnia. For fillers, use artemisias, dusty miller, and golden or purple sage.

**PLANT VEGETABLES.** Do it as soon as possible this month. In short-season areas, start from nursery seedlings or you'll never get a crop. Beans and corn are usually available only as seed (corn is sometimes the exception), while cucumbers, eggplant, melons, okra, peppers, pumpkins, squash, and tomatoes are commonly sold as small plants.

**PROTECT FRUIT CROPS.** Birds love to eat small fruits like cherries and strawberries. Cover rows and small trees with bird netting or row covers until fruit is ready to pick.

## IN THE SOUTHWEST'S LOW AND INTERMEDIATE DESERTS, THERE'S MUCH TO DO:

**CHECK FOR SQUASH BORER.** Examine squash vines every few days, looking for tiny eggs. Rub them off, or the borers that hatch out will drill into the vine and weaken the plant.

**CONTROL BEET LEAFHOPPERS.** These greenish yellow, inch-long insects spread curly top virus to cucumber, melon, and tomato plants. They don't, however, like shade, so you can protect crops by covering them with shade-cloth. Remove infected plants; they're safe to compost.

**CONTROL SPIDER MITES.** These multiply ferociously on dusty plants in hot weather. They're almost too small to see, but mottled leaves and fine webs will tip you off to their presence. Blast mites off plants with a strong jet from the hose. If they get out of control, use a miticide.

**HARVEST VEGETABLES.** Each crop has its own picking instructions. *Cantaloupe:* Pick when the skin is well netted and the fruit slips from the vine with little pressure. *Corn:* After tassels turn brown, peel a husk partway back and pop a kernel with your fingernail: watery juice means you're too early, milky means you're right on time, and toothpasty cream means you're too late. *Eggplant:* Pick when the skin turns glossy. *Peppers:* You can pick bell and other peppers when they're green, but they're prettier and more flavorful after they turn color. *Potatoes:* Dig new potatoes just after plants flower, and full-size spuds when tops start to die down. *Watermelon:* Pick when the tendrils closest to the fruit begin to turn brown.

**MOW.** Cut grass often enough that you never have to remove more than a third of its height at once. Mow Bermuda, St. Augustine, and zoysia 1 to 1½ inches high. Keep hybrid Bermuda at about an inch.

**MULCH TREES AND SHRUBS.** Put a 2- to 4-inch organic or gravel mulch over the root zones of trees, shrubs, vines, flowers, and vegetables. It will keep weeds down, conserve moisture, and keep roots cool.

**PLANT PALMS.** This is the best month to plant or transplant palms. Move them into a hole that's the same depth as the rootball and twice as wide. Tie the fronds up over the bud to protect it. After new growth begins, cut the twine.

**PLANT SUMMER COLOR.** If you act early in the month, you can probably get away with planting cockscomb, firebush, globe amaranth, Madagascar periwinkle, portulaca, purslane, salvia, starflower, and zinnia. These will make it if you don't put them in the hottest part of the garden.

**PLANT VEGETABLES.** You can still plant black-eyed peas, melons, okra, peanuts, sweet potatoes, and yard-long beans.

**SOW FALL TOMATOES.** Plant seeds indoors for transplanting into the garden in late July. Some good varieties include 'Champion', 'Early Girl', 'Heatwave', 'Solar Set', and 'Surefire'.

**WATER.** Deep watering really helps plants during the hot months. Flood or drip irrigation both work, but if you use drip, flood once a month to wash salts out of the root zone.

# Grow a garden in a pocket planter

*Four new looks for the classic strawberry pot*

**F**EW THINGS IN THE GARDEN turn heads quicker than a strawberry pot overflowing with lush, berry-laden plants. But when planted with a mix of foliage types, this graceful clay pot forms a striking accent next to an entrance or when combined with other containers on a deck or patio. Plants can be chosen to create a particular look or for a location in sun or shade.

On these pages, this classic container billows with texture and exuberant colors in four unexpected looks. Follow one of the recipes or create your own combination.

## GETTING STARTED

The allure of the strawberry pot is matched only by its notoriety for being difficult to keep watered. The small, shallow pockets don't hold much moisture, and water poured into the top moves down the pot slowly and moistens plants unevenly.

When shopping for strawberry pots, look for ones with flared, cup-shaped pockets rather than barely bumped-out slits; they'll hold the plants, soil, and water better. Then use this tip from *Sunset*'s test gardener, Bud Stuckey. Cut a length of ¾-inch (inside diameter) PVC pipe so it's about 4 inches longer than the height of the strawberry pot. Drill ¼-inch holes through the pipe about every 2 inches, and cap the bottom end. Stand the pipe in the center of the pot, making sure not to

**AT PLANTING,** *herbs are poked into all the pockets of the jar. The PVC pipe in the center will make it easier to get water to the bottom of the pot. The herbs are shown in bloom on page 72.*

block the pot's drainage hole at the bottom. After filling the pot with soil and planting, water the soil on top and the planting pockets as usual, and then aim water into the pipe opening at the top. This distributes water to the plants more quickly and evenly.

## CHOOSING THE PLANTS

Pick a theme. Working around a design concept (like the ones labeled on these pages) or a color scheme will help you choose plants that complement each other.

Keep in mind plant shapes, textures, and ultimate sizes. Look for plants with long bloom time (most annuals), interesting foliage, or strong form. Be sure to choose plants with similar needs for light and water.

*Pocket plants.* Plants used in the small side pockets of the pot should be mounding, weeping, or cascading in

---

## Ingredients for a soft grass pot

Flowing shapes and subtle colors create this textured grass arrangement. In the top of the pot, arching pink, tail-like seed heads of purple fountain grass (*Pennisetum setaceum* 'Cupreum') and soft golden spikes of needle grass (*Stipa tenuissima*) form a spray behind the mounding velvety gray green foliage of *Helichrysum petiolatum*. Pockets are planted with blue fescue (*Festuca ovina glauca*), *Nierembergia* 'Purple Robe' together with snow-in-summer (*Cerastium tomentosum*), and white sweet alyssum.

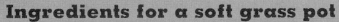

NORMAN A. PLATE

shape. In most cases, it works best to select two or three different types of plants and arrange them randomly one to a pocket; the textured grass pot on page 148 and the rose pot on this page were planted this way.

You'll have an easier time getting plants into the holes if you use cell-pack-size plants. If you combine plants or use ones bought in 4-inch pots, you'll have to squeeze or cut the root-balls or shake soil off the roots to make them fit, which can impair growth. Plants with big rootballs or small or flexible foliage can be popped into the pockets from inside the pot.

**Top plants.** Choose three or four plants for the top of the pot, combining mounding or cascading types with one or two upright ones for vertical accents. You can use plants bought in 1-gallon containers, provided some of the four are smaller.

## PLANTING THE POT

Begin by placing the watering pipe in the pot. Hold it upright while surrounding it with a porous, water-retentive soil mix; one part chicken manure, one part redwood soil conditioner, and two parts packaged potting soil works well. Be sure to mix in a controlled-release or complete granular fertilizer (such as 16-16-16).

The easiest way to plant the pot is tier by tier. Fill the bottom with soil mix up to the first tier of planting holes from the bottom, put in your plants, and fill in with soil from behind (inside the pot). Continue planting, going up the pot. Once plants are in, make sure they're properly anchored with soil in the planting holes, and not planted too deeply. The crown of the rootball should be flush with the soil line. ■

*By Emely Lincowski*

### Herb pot

This herb pot offers not only a culinary potpourri for the resident chef, but also the charm of a kitchen garden. At the top, intensely blue flowers of borage arch over tricolor sage, creeping rosemary, and lemon verbena. Pockets are planted with 'Purple Ruffles' and 'Dark Opal' basils, chives, lemon and English thymes, cinnamon basil, Greek oregano, and nasturtiums.

### Succulent pot

A blend of interesting plant shapes and subtle differences in foliage color—from whitish blue to gray green—make an attractive year-round display. Tall, pale pink, broccoli-like heads of *Sedum* 'Autumn Joy' stand behind cascading rosy red *Sedum* 'Ruby Glow' and magenta flowering portulaca. The pockets hold gray-foliaged *Sedum spathulifolium* 'Cape Blanco', sempervivum, *Crassula radicans,* and *Senecio kleiniiformis.*

### Rose pot

This delicate combination of pastel-colored flowers blends well with more formal settings, such as colonial-style houses with evergreen plantings. In the top of this strawberry pot, 'White Meidiland' rose rises among deep pink, double-flowered ivy geraniums (*Pelargonium* 'Sybil Holmes'). Randomly scattered in the planter pockets are 'White Lady' and 'Cobalt' lobelias, as well as *Ageratum* 'Blue Blazer'.

150

# Second act for dogwoods

*These summer bloomers thrive in the Northwest*

**SPRAYS OF WHITE** *cause Cornus kousa 'Summer Majesty' (left) to droop from the weight of its flowers. C. k. 'Snowflake' (above) has white blooms that turn to pink. Red-flowered variety (top), as yet unnamed, is due for fall release.*

MICHAEL THOMPSON

THE GREAT DOGWOOD flower show has two acts: after the North American natives put on their spring display, Oriental dogwood (*Cornus kousa*) takes the stage, bowing with blossoms in June and July.

This dogwood, native to China, Japan, and Korea, is easy to grow, thrives in the Northwest's acid soil and cool damp weather, and is not hard to find in nurseries. It's a mystery why we don't see more of it in gardens.

The tree has a handsome multistemmed form that eventually grows to 20 feet. In early spring, the tree wears a delicate veil of pale green leaves. In early summer, it blooms, with flowers followed by large red fruits resembling big strawberries. The slightly crinkly leaves remain dark green through summer, then blaze with vivid autumn colors, usually scarlet, dark red, or orange, before falling off. Come winter, the delicate limbs display mottled bark.

Another plus: Oriental dogwood seems unaffected by anthracnose, the fungal disease that sometimes plagues American native dogwoods (*C. florida* from the East, *C. nuttallii* from the West), causing black spots on leaves, cankers on branches and trunks, and occasionally tree death.

In the last two decades, Oriental dogwood has captured the interest of hybridizers and nursery owners, who have developed hundreds of crosses and selections that vary widely in flower and foliage color and form. Many of these plants are now ready for market. For example, the 1994 catalog of Greer Gardens in Eugene, Oregon, lists 25 varieties of *C. kousa*.

Along with the three shown above, the following are good choices for showy flowers or foliage. *C. k.* 'Milky Way' produces masses of white flower clusters. *C. k.* 'Satomi Red' has bright rose red flowers. *C. k.* 'Bon Fire', a new introduction, has white flowers and dark green leaves streaked with light green and gold; in autumn, the leaves turn crimson, red, and yellow. *C. k.* 'Snowboy', a dwarf form with white flowers, reaches 8 feet in height (with a 6-foot spread) and has variegated leaves that are pale gray green with irregular white margins and glowing splotches of yellow. A weeping form has also been introduced: *C. k.* 'Weaver's Weeping' has white flowers that shower down in June.

Plant Oriental dogwood from a nursery can when the soil is workable. Give it a spot where it will get full or partial sun. Keep a newly planted tree well watered; in the hottest, driest summers, even a mature tree will appreciate a twice-monthly soaking of the soil and leaves. To encourage a bumper crop of blooms, scatter a complete granular fertilizer around the base of the dogwood on the same schedule you use for other flowering trees and shrubs (mid-February, early April, late May, and early July). ■

*By Steven R. Lorton*

NORMAN A. PLATE

**GOOD GARDENING KNIVES** *include, from left,
an all-purpose stainless steel knife; a budding/grafting
knife (the hump on the end of the blade is for peeling bark
back); a horticultural knife with a sheepfoot blade for
general use such as deadheading flowers; and a
pruning knife with a hawkbill blade.*

# Knives for garden chores

*Pick the right blades
for cutting flowers,
pruning, grafting*

 good pocket knife is
a handy tool to carry
in the garden—for
cutting flowers,
pruning, grafting, and other
tasks. Here's a guide to
choosing the right knife for
the kinds of work you do.

When you shop for a knife,
you'll likely have three or
four blade shapes to choose
from. The all-purpose master
blade (the longest blade on a
multiblade knife), which is
usually curved to a point, is
most often a clip, spear, or
saber blade (the precise shape

determines the difference).
The straight-edged blade is
called a sheepfoot blade. The
hook blade, which may re-
mind you of a linoleum knife,
is called a hawkbill blade.
And the rather round-tipped
blade is a spey blade (if
you're a rancher, you'll know
about this one), which comes
standard on many good
pocket knives.

### HOW KNIVES CUT
### GARDEN TASKS

*Cutting flowers.* Sharpness
is the most important feature
for this task. A sheepfoot
blade is the best choice.
Florist knives and horticultural knives are well suited for
cutting and deadheading flowers; prices run from about $10
to $16.

*Pruning.* Until the middle
of this century, knives were
the most popular tools for
pruning trees and shrubs.
Experienced gardeners held
them in high esteem because,
on wood less than ½ inch in
diameter, an extremely sharp
knife makes a cleaner cut than

pruning shears or a saw.
That's important because
cleaner cuts heal faster.

The best blade for pruning
is a hawkbill, but sheepfoot
blades work well, too. Pruning knives range in price from
$12 to more than $50.

Try knife pruning on small
water sprouts or suckers no
thicker than drinking straws,
slicing quickly away from
yourself and to the right (if
you're right-handed). As you
get the feel of it, you'll become fast and effective.

When you're done, remove
the sap on the blade with
undiluted pine oil cleaner.

*Grafting and budding.*
Only the sharpest, cleanest
knives do these jobs well. An
oily blade spoils grafts by
contaminating the union of
the cambium on scion and
stock. Use a dead-straight
sheepfoot blade to make cuts
that are perfectly flat (a
curved blade can give you
sticks that won't mate well).
Do stick grafting in winter
and early spring.

Although you can do bud-
ding with any blade, it's nice
to have one with a hump at
the end to help peel back the
bark when you slip the bud
into the stock. Do bud grafting in August.

Grafting and budding
knives range in price from
$12 to $40. Left-hand models
of some knives cost slightly
more than right-hand models.
Contrary to conventional wis-
dom, grafting blades can be
made of any kind of steel;
high-carbon steel won't spoil
the scion-stock union, nor will
stainless steel improve the
success rate.

---

### MATERIAL CHOICES

*Blades.* Most blades are
made from either high-carbon
steel (about 1 percent carbon,
99 percent iron) or stainless
steel (commonly a mix of
iron, nickel, and chromium).

High-carbon steel takes and
holds an edge best. The blade
can be forged for added
strength (expect to pay more).
On the downside, it stains and

rusts easily, especially if you
get mild acid on it—like
sweat or the juice from an apple. When you cut fruit with
it, the blade leaves a slightly
metallic taste behind.

Stainless steel is a little
harder to get razor-sharp than
high-carbon steel and doesn't
hold an edge quite as well. If
you plan to cut a lot of fruit or
use your knife under wet conditions, stainless is a good
choice. Blades of high-carbon
stainless (or numerous other
formulas) are attempts to balance edge sharpness and
stainlessness.

Most knives are sharp
when you buy them; if they're
not, put an edge on them. Use
a good whetstone ($5 to $40)
for honing, and touch up the
blades often.

*Case.* Buy one with brass
liners, which don't corrode
easily.

*Handle.* Bone and horn
handles are rugged and good-
looking, but most have been
supplanted by plastic-based
synthetics. The synthetics are
functional but make your
hand sweat under prolonged
use. Wooden handles are designed to minimize the sweat
problem. Shape is important:
rounded handles are least
likely to blister your hands
during extensive use.

---

### KNIFE SOURCES

Garden centers and nurs-
eries rarely have good selections of horticultural knives.
Cutlery stores often have what
you need but (in our experience) may not know much
about them.

Mail-order suppliers are a
better bet. These two list a
good assortment of knives in
their catalogs: A.M. Leonard,
Box 816, Piqua, Ohio 45356
(800/543-8955); and Boker
USA, 14818 W. Sixth Ave.,
Suite 10-A, Golden, Colo.
80401 (800/992-6537). Smith
& Hawken (800/776-3336)
carries a good high-carbon
stainless steel horticultural
knife and a good carbon-steel
pruning knife. ■

*By Jim McCausland*

NORMAN A. PLATE

**TWO FAVORITE LARGE-LEAF** *green basils: 'Sweet' (left) has a fairly smooth, pointed leaf; the 'Napoletano' leaf is wider and very crinkled.*

# The best basil? It depends

*Sunset testers found some varieties perfect for pesto, others best fresh*

WHEN YOU LOVE growing and cooking with basil, nuances among green, large-leaf varieties can mean the difference between superb and merely good flavor.

Catalogs rave about all the varieties they sell, but basils with Italian names seem to garner the most superlatives. Are these basils really as good as everyone claims, or can you plant just about any basil and get the same result?

To find out, we grew seven varieties last summer in *Sunset*'s test garden—'Genova Profumatissima', 'Genovese', 'Broadleaf Sweet', 'Large Green', 'Lettuce Leaf', 'Napoletano', and 'Sweet'. These are traditional large-leaf basils commonly used fresh and for pesto.

Our panel of seven judges consisted of both foodies and gardeners who love to cook with basil. First, the judges tasted freshly harvested leaves. A few days later, each variety was made into a simple pesto and tasted with pasta (we puréed 2 cups packed fresh basil leaves, washed and well drained; 1 cup freshly grated parmesan cheese; and ½ cup olive oil in a blender).

## GROW ONE BASIL FOR FRESH USE, ONE FOR PESTO

Tasters were amazingly consistent in their preferences. The surprise was that the hands-down favorite for fresh basil—'Napoletano', chosen by six out of seven tasters—wasn't even a runner-up in the pesto category (most said it was too mild). Here judges preferred 'Sweet' by a margin of six to one.

When eaten fresh, 'Napoletano' was praised for its strong fragrance, good flavor with mild anise undertones, lack of astringency, and tender, handsome, crinkly leaves. A close second was 'Lettuce Leaf', sometimes sold as 'Lettuce-Leaved' ("sweet, mildly spicy, somewhat anisey, with a soft, crinkly leaf"). On the other hand, 'Sweet' was considered sweet but mild, with more fragrance than flavor—that is, until it was made into pesto.

As pesto, it elicited the following comments: "clear, sweet basil flavor and attractive color"; "the herb comes through strongly and pleasantly"; "mellow with nice aftertaste." Runners-up for pesto were 'Genova Profumatissima', 'Genovese', and 'Broadleaf Sweet', although two judges said all varieties are "more than acceptable" for pesto.

The clear message here is that it's best to grow at least two kinds of basil. Plant one, such as 'Napoletano', for using fresh in salads, on baked or barbecued fish, and in any dish that uses freshly harvested leaves. For pesto, flavors emerge stronger from completely different varieties, particularly 'Sweet'.

## WHERE TO ORDER SEEDS

Seeds of the panel's favorite varieties are available from the following catalogs (catalogs are free unless noted).

*Nichols Garden Nursery,* 1190 N. Pacific Highway, Albany, Ore. 97321; (503) 928-9280. 'Genovese', 'Lettuce-Leaved'.

*Shepherd's Garden Seeds,* 6116 Highway 9, Felton, Calif. 95018; (408) 335-6910. The catalog costs $1. 'Broadleaf Sweet', 'Genova Profumatissima', 'Napoletano', 'Lettuce Leaf'.

*Territorial Seed Company,* Box 157, Cottage Grove, Ore. 97424; (503) 942-9547. 'Sweet'. ∎

*By Lauren Bonar Swezey*

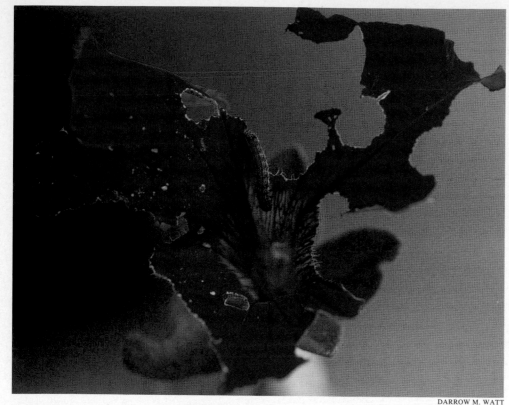

BUDWORM LARVA *devours a red petunia blossom, which turns its striped body reddish.*

DARROW M. WATT

# What's eating your petunias?

**NO BUDS OR BLOSSOMS** *(above) signals you should spray with Bacillus thuringiensis to halt budworm. Right, 2½ weeks later, plants bloom.*

**W**HY ON EARTH HAVE my petunias stopped flowering, when just a couple of weeks ago they were in glorious full bloom?" Any gardener who grows petunias is likely to ask this question come late spring or early summer.

No, it's not because you forgot to fertilize, although that may slow flowering; so can neglecting to deadhead. But in either case, you'll get at least some new flowers. When very few flowers open—and those that do are chewed—you're undoubtedly seeing the effects of the geranium budworm (*Heliothis virescens* or *Helicoverpa virescens,* also called the tobacco budworm).

This voracious ¼- to 1½-inch-long greenish or brownish light-striped caterpillar eats pinhead-size holes in buds of petunias (as well as of

NORMAN A. PLATE

garden geraniums, nicotiana, and border penstemon), which prevents the buds from opening. It also feeds on open flowers and foliage, often taking on the color of the flower it's been feeding on.

Geranium budworm used to be confined mostly to milder climates, but now even gardeners in cold climates such as Denver see its effects. The moth can survive not only through relatively mild winters, but also in protected areas around buildings and on geraniums brought inside for winter.

## ONE SPRAY OF BT WIPES 'EM OUT

What can a gardener do about this pesky creature? Some sources say budworm is difficult to control because the insect spends part of its life hidden in buds, but we had great success in *Sunset*'s test garden using *Bacillus thuringiensis kurstaki* (BT), a bacterial insecticide that is nontoxic to mammals.

For the best control, spray BT at the first sign of damage, when larvae are small (BT isn't as effective against large ones). Look for holes in buds, chewed leaves, and black droppings. You may also see larvae crawling around on leaves or inside buds.

Apply BT according to label directions and thoroughly spray buds and leaves (top and bottom) until the solution drips off. BT doesn't kill instantly, as harsher chemicals do. The larvae stop eating within a day after ingesting the bacteria on treated buds and leaves but continue moving around until they die from bacterial infection. Additional applications may be necessary. Monitor plants at least weekly and look for new damage, which is still green on the chewed edges (the old damage is brown and decayed).

You can also reduce budworm damage by handpicking and destroying insects and infested buds. ■

*By Lauren Bonar Swezey*

**RECYCLED CONCRETE** *cut into flagstone shapes is now a path through beds of succulents and grasses that require little water and maintenance.*

# Berkeley rubble lives on in the garden

IN A QUIRKY TWIST on the English concept of using local stone in the garden, landscape designers Jana Olson-Drobinsky and Marcia Donahue utilized what they consider the local stones of the Berkeley flatlands—broken concrete and old brick.

"I started with what the site provided—with what I call found material," explains Olson-Drobinsky, "and then used these typical castoffs as though they were stones and boulders." An old patio and driveway supplied the broken concrete. Some of the brick was on site; the rest came from an old retaining wall at another job site.

Homeowner Michael Doerr was all for it, and gave the designers freedom to follow their instincts. "You can't tell artists what to do. You have to trust their judgment," he says. But he made it clear that he didn't want an English flower garden with pinks, lavenders, and whites. He preferred warm colors that worked with the brick. He also wanted to reuse succu-

lents from an old garden and add horticulturally interesting plants. The designers gave Doerr just what he was looking for.

The backyard now incorporates a wonderful array of textures and colors from succulents, grasses, and spiky plants. To give height to the formerly flat yard, the planting bed just off the back of the house was raised. Pieces of broken concrete and mortared brick are strewn about as if tossed by an earthquake. Sedums, sempervivums, and echeverias grow between the cracks and crevices.

Throughout the rest of the bed grow *Agave parryi huachucensis, Aloe plicatilis,* desert spoon, honey bush, New Zealand flax, pampas grass, Mediterranean fan palm, *Stipa tenuissima,* and *Yucca recurvifolia.*

Nearby, dwarf bamboo (*Tleioblastus argentiostriatus*), weeping copper beech, *Heuchera maxima,* and sago palm prosper.

Since the plants grow in fairly heavy soil and the gar-

den is now well established, the plants need only infrequent watering—about once every 1½ weeks. The garden is low maintenance, too. Doerr weeds, deadheads flowers on the succulents when they fade, and cleans up the grasses once a year. ■

*By Lauren Bonar Swezey*

**MORTARED BRICK** *and concrete are strewn throughout the planting bed. Yellow-flowering sedum crawls over brick; sempervivums, echeverias, and aloes fill crevices.*

**REPLACING LAWN,** *this garden of water-thrifty plants provides plenty of summer color and fragrance. 'Hidcote' lavender (foreground), yellow-daisied senecio, and pink Mexican evening primrose are prominently featured. For more information, see page 160.*

# JULY

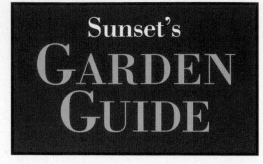

# Sunset's GARDEN GUIDE

## High summer brings on flowers, vegetables, and landscapes with tropical luxuriance

One of the unqualified delights of gardening in Southern California is the possibility of juxtaposing plants that conjure a tropical isle with those that evoke Anytown, U.S.A. The front yard in Santa Monica pictured at right is a good example of the range available to Los Angeles–area gardeners. Here, a stand of young king palms (*Archontophoenix cunninghamiana*) screens the house from passersby and street noise while providing a neutral counterpoint to flowering accents, including red kalanchoe (*Kalanchoe blossfeldiana*), yellow fortnight lily (*Dietes bicolor*), white 'Iceberg' rose, and pastel Santa Barbara daisies (*Erigeron karvinskianus*). Although the floral hues change with the season, the palms stay green year-round, giving the yard a luxuriant tropical feel.

Richard L. Mosbaugh designed and constructed the garden, choosing mostly shrubs and perennials, including an abundance of ground covers. Diminutive plants such as Corsican mint (*Mentha requienii*), creeping thyme (*Thymus praecox arcticus*), and isotoma (*Laurentia fluviatilis*) seem to ooze between the boulders that line the walkway.

Maintenance is moderate: about 4 hours of gardening a week, including deadheading, fertilizing, and watering, keeps the landscape in top shape.

### New book explains care and feeding of native shrubs

Summer is generally not a good time to plant California natives, but it's an excellent season to learn about them in preparation for fall planting. When it gets too hot to garden this month, sit back in your glider, pop a cool one, and dig into Glenn Keator's new book, *Complete Garden Guide to the Native Shrubs of California* (Chronicle Books, San Francisco, 1994; $16.95). Whether you already have a garden full of natives or are thinking of buying some, this book is a valuable resource.

In contrast to botanists' books on natives, which tend to be technical at the expense of practical information, this one offers gardeners useful advice on growing natives successfully. It covers basics like selecting a site, planting, mulching, and watering, as well as more specialized topics like plant propagation. The book also describes significant features of shrubs—their size, growing habits, leaves, bark, flowers, and fragrance—that can help you make informed decisions when designing your garden. Comprehensive lists of shrubs for specific situations like containers, hedges, and barriers are also provided.

At the heart of the book is an encyclopedia describing 500 shrub species, 60 of which are illustrated. This is perhaps the book's one

CHAD SLATTERY

you can't find it, call the company at 612/941-4180 for a source in your area). It comes both ready to use (24 ounces for $6, 64 ounces for less than $10) and concentrated (16 ounces for less than $8; makes ¾ gallon).

## When is a tomato not a tomato?

When it's a tree tomato (*Cyphomandra crassicaulis,* usually sold as *C. betacea*). You may have run across this plant in newspaper ads claiming, "60 pounds of tomatoes every year for life ... amazing tree tomato towers up to 8 feet tall, yields fruit nonstop up to seven months a year ... incredibly intense flavor that makes ordinary tomatoes seem washed out and wimpy!"

Sounds pretty good. But native New Zealander and San Francisco resident Keren Abra knows better. She's been growing a tree tomato for five years.

Tree tomato is native to tropical areas and is grown commercially in New Zealand, where it's known as tamarillo. It can be grown outdoors in *Sunset Western Garden Book* zones 16, 17, and 22–24, and, when given overhead protection, in zones 14, 15, and 18–21.

In Abra's sheltered, sunny garden, her tree produces more than 100 pounds of fruit—but not seven months a year. Fruits start ripening in October and are finished by February. The 2- to 3-inch-long, red, egg-shaped fruits are intensely flavored with a slight tomato taste that is tart, even bitter, and deep red-purple juice that leaches out, making them unsuitable for salads and sandwiches. "They seem to be an acquired taste,"

limitation—photographs would have been more helpful. Still, as a companion on trips to your favorite botanic garden or nursery, Keator's book is hard to beat.

## Environmentally safe herbicide controls weeds

Weeds are the bane of every gardener. If you don't control them, they suck moisture and nutrients from the soil and compete with your ornamental plants.

Controlling weeds without using toxic chemicals is usually a tedious affair—hand-pulling and hoeing are the typical choices. But there is another alternative that's both environmentally safe and less labor intensive than pulling and hoeing. It's called Safer Superfast Weed and Grass Killer. Ringer Corporation has introduced this new, environmentally sound herbicide made from a combination of fatty acids. It's an improved version of an old product that worked most effectively at

high temperatures. This one doesn't have the temperature limitations of its predecessor, and kills weeds within hours of application. Since the herbicide breaks down quickly, you can replant within 48 hours of spraying.

The product destroys the leaf's cuticle layer, causing it to dehydrate and die. It will not translocate to roots of surrounding plants, making it safe to use around vegetables, flowers, and landscape plants.

Superfast is available at nurseries and home centers (if

**BURSTING WITH BLOOM,** *'Black Eyed Stella' daylily is a superb performer both in pots and in borders.*

says Abra. "I have yet to convince my family to enjoy them, but my friends from New Zealand love them."

Since the skin is tough and bitter, you can't eat the fruit right off the tree; most people scoop out the flesh and eat it with sugar.

But Abra thinks a tree tomato is worth growing, given the right conditions. It needs ample water and fertilizer, regular pruning, and protection from snails. Branches need support as the fruit

ripens. And since the tree drops fruit, it should be planted away from patios.

You can order a tree from MBT Nursery Sales, 1401 Lakeland Ave., Bohemia, N.Y. 11716 ($6.99 plus $1 postage and handling).

## All-America Daylily for 1994: 'Black Eyed Stella'

Over the past few years, mail-order catalogs have been raving about 'Stella de Oro' daylily because of its long bloom season and compact growth habit. But it's not the best plant for mild-winter climates because it's deciduous for three months. It also doesn't do well in hot, dry climates.

But now mild-climate gardeners can get great performance from an evergreen offspring of 'Stella de Oro' called 'Black Eyed Stella'. This patented plant was chosen over 6,000 other plants as the All-America Daylily for 1994.

'Black Eyed Stella' has 3-inch-wide, bright yellow flowers with red eyes that bloom in six- to eight-week flushes from about April to November in mild-winter

regions (with the greatest show in spring). The 12-inch-tall foliage is a dark blue-green and the flower stalks grow 14 to 22 inches high.

Plants may be available in some nurseries; if not, you can order by mail from these sources.

*Caprice Farm Nursery,* 15425 S.W. Pleasant Hill Rd., Sherwood, Ore. 97140; (503) 625-7241. Catalog $2, deductible from order. Sells double fan-size plants for $12.50 plus $4.50 shipping.

*Greenwood Daylily Gardens,* 5595 E. Seventh St., Box 490, Long Beach, Calif. 90804; (310) 494-8944. Catalog $5, deductible with order. Sells double fan-size plants for $12 plus $5 shipping.

## A good rock garden plant for containers

*Lewisia cotyledon* is native to Northern California and southern Oregon, where it grows in natural mountain rock gardens. In Southern California's heat and dryness, it's easiest to grow lewisia hybrids in containers.

*L. cotyledon* has clusters of flowers, each an inch or more across, rising on 10-inch stems above rosettes of oblong, fleshy evergreen leaves. Flower colors range from white to pink to pale orange. Sometimes flowers are multicolored, banded with pink or red. They bloom most heavily from spring to early summer, year-round on the coast.

Lewisias need fast-draining soil. The plant rots when its crown or roots stay wet, so let the soil dry out a little between waterings.

Plants are usually sold in 4-inch containers for less than $5 and in 1-gallon containers for less than $7.

## To import plants from Canada, follow the rules

As Northwesterners flock across the border to Canada this summer, many will visit nurseries and public gardens.

Inevitably, some gardeners will see plants they'd like to bring home.

In order to enter the United States, any plant grown in Canada must have a Phytosanitary Certificate. This certifies that Agriculture Canada has inspected the plant, found it free of pests and disease, and approved it to leave the country.

Some nurseries will help arrange an inspection if you plan to be in Canada for two or more days. You can select the plants you want, let the nursery make an inspection appointment, then pick up the plants before you return to the United States.

You can also have plants inspected from 8 to 4 Mondays through Fridays at the Agriculture Desk of the Customs and Immigration Building at the border crossing on Provincial Highway 15, which merges with Interstate 5 about 2 miles inside the United States. Before you head for the border, call ahead (604/538-3656) to make sure an inspector will be on hand.

Do not attempt to import plants without the proper papers; undocumented plants are confiscated at customs.

## Plant or divide iris now for blooms next spring

The tall bearded iris is most spectacular in May, when the perennial spends much of the month sending up its fleur-de-lis blossoms. But this is one spring-flowering "bulb" (technically a rhizome) that has a summer planting season.

*If you're planting,* check nursery bins for rhizomes of named iris varieties. Their pictures should be on the package—or the crate, if you're buying bulk stock.

*If you're dividing iris,* do it during summer, six weeks or more after flowering. Dig clumps, shake or wash off soil, then cut rhizomes apart at their natural junctures. Discard old, leafless rhizomes from clump's center. Cut back

**A ROCK PLANT CONTAINED:** *lewisia does well here in pots.*

young husky plants to 6-inch, pointed fans, replant so that roots project downward at about a 45-degree angle and rhizomes are just barely covered with soil. Water in well.

## New book for San Francisco–area food gardeners

If you're looking for a comprehensive book on vegetable gardening, *Golden Gate Gardening: The complete guide to year-round food gardening in the San Francisco Bay Area & Coastal California,* by Pam Peirce (agAccess, 603 Fourth St., Davis, Calif. 95616, 1993; $24.95), may be just the one.

It's primarily directed at gardeners along the coast and in San Francisco (climate zone 17 in the *Sunset Western Garden Book*), particularly the information about what vegetables can and can't be grown in various microclimates (it splits San Francisco into seven). But all of the general information is suitable for the entire Bay Area.

The 397-page book has no color photographs and just a few simple drawings. But it has a tremendous amount of solid information about what you can grow in various microclimates, how to plan your garden, how and when to start seeds, how to evaluate and amend soil, and how to deal with weeds, pests, and diseases. Most of the last half of the book is devoted to describing vegetables and fruits that grow well in the area.

The book is available in bookstores or directly from the publisher for $29.76, including tax and shipping; call (800) 235-7177.

**FLAMBOYANT FLORAL CIRCUS** *captures the spirit of summer. Bed of multicolored zinnias is centered by hot pink cosmos.*

## Annuals for late-summer color

July in California's Central Valley brings an abundant harvest of ripe tomatoes and sweet fruit, and a rainbow of summer color from heat-loving plants such as crape myrtle and zinnias.

To avoid a late-summer lag in color, you can sow seeds of many annuals this month. Cosmos, marigolds, sunflowers, sweet alyssum, zinnias, and other warm-season annuals germinate quickly and fill the void as spring-planted annuals fade. Sow the seeds directly in the ground where you want them to grow, even around your existing blooming plants. You can also start seeds indoors in flats, but seed sown in the ground will adapt more quickly to summer heat. Gently remove existing plants as they decline.

After sowing, lightly cover the seed with soil and keep the bed moist (you'll probably have to water more than once a day). As soon as the seedlings are a couple of inches high, spread a mulch around them to keep roots cool and moist.

*PROFUSION OF PALMS sets tropical mood in Northern California garden. At top left is Guadalupe palm (Brahea edulis), at top right is windmill palm (Trachycarpus fortunei). Woman's hand is resting on a Mediterranean fan palm (Chamaerops humilis); above and behind her are a pindo palm (Butia capitata) and a queen palm (Arecastrum romanzoffianum).*

Most of these plants get by with very little water; the palms receive no irrigation other than rainfall. The cycads and jacaranda are a bit thirstier.

## Visit a historic garden in Seattle

One of Seattle's oldest gardens is now open to the public by reservation. Named the E.B. Dunn Historic Garden Trust (for the garden's chief benefactor), the 2.7-acre garden, with its adjoining 4 acres of lawn and landscaped grounds, dates back to 1915, when the Olmsted Firm designed the country estate of the Arthur Dunn family. The owner supplemented the design with his own plantings.

Now nearly 80 years old, the north Seattle garden offers a chance to see venerable specimens of trees and shrubs.

Call (206) 362-0933 to make reservations and get directions. Admission costs $5; children under 12 are not admitted.

## Water-thrifty plants replace lawn

When you consider that the fragrant drifts of lavender and thyme pictured on page 156 replaced a little-used, labor-intensive front lawn, you have to think that Gary and Kathy Winans of Seattle made a good trade.

Motivated by frequent summer water restrictions in their area, the Winanses thumbed through seed and plant catalogs, choosing plants that

## Tropical-looking garden in Northern California

A great place to appreciate the long, warm days of summer is in a cool, tropical-looking setting like Gerry and Gus Panos's Hillsborough, California, garden, pictured above. Planted only five years ago, just before a killing freeze, the garden has evolved into a lush environment full of mature trees and shrubs.

The Panoses wanted a garden reminiscent of the warm climates they love to visit—the Caribbean, Greece, Hawaii, and Mexico. Gerry Panos and landscape designer Michael Postl, of Living Green Plantscape Design in San Francisco, chose cold-hardy plants that would survive the Northern California climate, but offer a lush and tropical appearance.

Two 40-foot-long flatbed trucks carried in specimen plants from Southern California, including agaves (the only plants that were killed by the freeze), aloes, bougainvillea, cycads, golden goddess bamboo, honey bush, jacaranda, Mediterranean fan palm, Mexican blue palm, pindo palm, queen palm, and timber bamboo.

would serve as good-looking, water-thrifty turf replacements. In addition to the several lavenders and thymes that cover most of the garden, they also grow ornamental grasses, evening primroses, and other drought-tolerant perennials. The whole plot is watered with a drip-irrigation system.

You can shop for these plants this month, picking varieties that grow well in your area.

### Victoria's hanging baskets on video

Each summer, visitors admire the many handsome hanging baskets that line the streets of Victoria, British Columbia. Now, noted nurseryman Brian Minter has come out with a new video that takes viewers through the process of assembling one of these baskets.

*Hanging Baskets of Victoria and How to Make Them* offers a simple step-by-step approach. The 45-minute VHS tape tells what materials you need, what to plant, where to put the basket, and how to care for it.

The video is produced by MetroMedia, Box 46050, Victoria, B.C., Canada V8T 5G7. Cost of $26.95 (Canadian) includes shipping and handling. To order by credit card, call (604) 380-0926.

### A shady way to cut summer electric bills

If you follow the path of the summer sun as it moves across the sky this month, and pay attention to the ever-changing shadows it casts around your home, you can use this information to conserve energy and cut your utility bills.

In California's Central Valley, for example, utility companies report that properly positioned shade trees can cut typical summertime electrical bills (mostly from air conditioning) by as much as 20 percent. While you should wait until the cooler months of fall

to plant, now is the time to plan where trees should go.

Take a stroll around your house several times during the day. In the morning, the sun shines on the east side of the house. At noon the sun beats down on the roof. In the afternoon, the hottest part of the day, it shines on the west side. Stand close to the walls and note how your shadow falls, particularly on windows, so you'll know where to plant shade trees.

To provide the most cooling, plant medium-size (25- to 50-feet-tall) deciduous trees with a spreading habit, within 5 to 10 feet of the east and west sides of your home. Shading windows is particularly important, since sun shining through can quickly warm the house. It also pays to shade the south side of the house. Just make sure to plant deciduous trees so you don't block the warm winter sun.

### Rose of Sharon is back in fashion

Victorians planted whole hedges of rose of Sharon, and Depression-era women pinned the flowers in their hair. Now, this old-fashioned deciduous shrub is enjoying renewed popularity with gardeners. The northern cousin of the tropical hibiscus, rose of Sharon (*Hibiscus syriacus*) is hardy enough to withstand the West's coldest winters; it's also disease and pest resistant. Like lilac, it seems to do best after sharp, cold temperatures.

Flowers are single, semidouble, and double. The simple single-flowered varieties seem to enjoy the greatest popularity. 'Diana' has pure white flowers; 'Helene', white flowers with rose red centers; 'Aphrodite', deep rose pink blooms with deep red centers; 'Minerva', shell pink blooms with deep rose centers; and 'Blue Bird', rich blue blossoms. Double-flowered kinds include rich pink 'Blushing Bride' and purple lavender 'Collie Mullens'.

Plant rose of Sharon from

containers now in a spot that gets full sun or part shade. It's not fussy about soil. Once established, this plant will tolerate summer drought, but it flowers best when given ample water. To ensure a good flower crop and vigorous growth, fertilize on the same schedule, with the same plant food, that you use for other flowering shrubs.

### Plywood den for garter snakes

Docile and nonpoisonous, garter snakes are welcome visitors, especially in Pacific Northwest gardens. They like to be where they have access to warm, moist, dark places. And from these hideouts they roam in search of all kinds of critters—like slugs, insects, and mice—that they love to

eat and you don't want in your garden.

Robert Holbrook of Concrete, Washington, makes certain his vegetable garden always has plenty of these pest police. At the south end of the plot, Holbrook lays out a 4- by 6-foot sheet of ¾-inch plywood. The plywood gets full sun, and the ground under it stays moist and warm. Whenever he lifts up the plywood to take a peek, Holbrook finds half a dozen fat and happy garter snakes curled up below.

### Eugenia on rebound, thanks to a hungry wasp

*Tamarixia,* a tiny parasitic wasp the size of a pepper flake, may be accomplishing what no pesticide could: it's beginning to control the euge-

**RELIABLE ROSE OF SHARON** *is colorful substitute for tropical hibiscus in climates that experience subfreezing winters.*

nia psyllid, the sucking insect that creates those ghastly galls on the leaves of eugenia (*Syzygium paniculatum*). The stingless wasp lays its egg between the eugenia leaf and the abdomen of the psyllid nymph. The egg hatches, and the larva feeds on the psyllid, killing it. Then the larva pupates and turns into an adult wasp, which exits through a tiny hole it chews in the psyllid's back.

We can thank Professor Donald Dahlsten of UC Berkeley's Division of Biological Control for introducing the wasp to Southern California. He found *Tamarixia* in its native Australian homeland in 1991, and in July 1992 he released scarcely a thimbleful—102 wasps—in Anaheim at Disneyland (which has a sizable investment in eugenias).

So far, *Tamarixia* has successfully overwintered and is spreading throughout the region, consuming psyllids as it goes. It's been found in Glendale, Pasadena, Los Angeles, Pacific Palisades, Santa Mon-

ica, Irvine, and Riverside. In May 1993, additional wasps were released at the San Diego Zoo.

Dahlsten is optimistic about *Tamarixia*'s success, although he says it can take 3 to 5 years to know for sure whether the wasp has the psyllid under control. And we still have a lot to learn about caring for eugenias in ways that encourage the wasp and discourage the psyllid. For now, if you see any signs of *Tamarixia,* don't spray pesticides lest you kill the beneficial wasp. Although the wasps are hard to see, you should be able to spot their handiwork— look for a psyllid nymph with a hole in its back on the underside of the leaf.

Pruning practices may make a difference, too. Dahlsten suggests that if you find many tiny yellow psyllid eggs on new growth, cut the plant back 2 to 3 inches. Leave prunings under the trees for a week or so. The psyllids die when their nutrient source is cut off, and if *Tamarixia* is present, it will continue feeding on psyllid nymphs.

JACK CLARK

**IF YOU SEE** *a psyllid with a hole in it, don't spray your eugenia with pesticides.*

## Walla Walla Sweet onions: taste now, plant later

Noted for its sweet onions, Robison Ranch in Walla Walla, Washington, is also one of the nation's largest producers of shallots. The ranch grows asparagus, garlic, and rhubarb as well. You can order a 10-, 25-, or 50-pound box of their Walla Walla Sweet onions this month. In August, the ranch starts shipping shallots, then garlic. It also sells seed garlic and shallots, as well as onion sets, asparagus crowns, and rhubarb.

Garlic can be planted in the fall. Rhubarb, asparagus, shallots, and onion sets should go in early next spring. For a price list of produce, edible or for planting, write or call Robison Ranch, Box 1018, Walla Walla, Wash. 99362; (509) 525-8807.

## Homemade mildew control

Researchers at Cornell University in Ithaca, New York, have come up with a simple treatment to prevent powdery mildew on roses and other plants. Mix 2 teaspoons of baking soda and 2 teaspoons of lightweight horticultural spray oil (Cornell uses Sunspray) with 1 gallon of water.

Apply a fine spray of the solution weekly to prevent mildew and other fungus. Reapply the spray to new growth (test the spray on a single leaf to check for leaf burn).

The treatment is thought to work, at least partially, by changing the pH of the leaf surface.

## Children's garden in San Jose, California

Kids love to touch, smell, feel, and learn about plants. And they can do all these things at the new Drought Tolerant Demonstration Garden/Children's Garden in Emma Prusch Memorial Park. The garden, planted last spring, is growing, blooming, and attracting kids (and lots of adults).

The garden is home to well over 100 kinds of plants suited to our dry climate. Along with trees and shrubs— including Chinese pistache, crape myrtle, osmanthus, and toyon—plantings include a Sensual Garden full of fragrant and fuzzy plants (a favorite with youngsters) and a colorful perennial border. All of the plants are labeled. A meadow of unmowed fine fescue is adjacent to the perennial garden.

Cupertino landscape consultant Heidi K. Johnson of Yamagami's Nursery designed the garden, which is maintained by Santa Clara County UC Master Gardeners and the city of San Jose. The garden surrounds the Ethel and William Prusch Jr. Multicultural Arts Center, to the

NORMAN A. PLATE

**Tool of the Month**

*Moving heavy container plants can be an arduous task. The WheelAround Cart shown above easily totes pots and trash cans up to 19 inches in diameter. The heavy-duty steel cart carries loads up to 200 pounds, and the wide wheels run smoothly over gravel paths. WheelAround Cart costs $69.95 plus shipping. For a brochure or to order, call the manufacturer at (800) 335-2278.*

left of the park's main entrance.

Other areas to visit at Prusch Park are the Rare Fruit Orchard, Small Animal Area (with chickens, ducks, geese, and rabbits), International Grove of trees, and farmhouse. A picnic area has two large barbecues.

To get there from U.S. 101, take Story Road ¼ mile east, turn left onto King Road, and turn left into the park. From Interstate 280, exit at King Road, continue ½ block, and turn right into the park. The park is open 8:30 to sunset daily. Admission and parking are free. The entire park is wheelchair accessible. For more information, call (408) 926-5555 between 8:30 and 4:30 weekdays.

*By Steven R. Lorton,*
*Jim McCausland, Lynn Ocone,*
*Lauren Bonar Swezey,*
*Lance Walheim*

# July Checklist
## ■
### PACIFIC NORTHWEST

**CLIP AND FEED GROUND COVERS.** Once bloom is finished, shear back plants to keep them compact, then scatter a complete granular fertilizer over the beds and water well.

**DIG SPRING-FLOWERING BULBS.** Once the tops have shriveled and dried, you can dig and divide those bulbs that need it, then replant or store for fall planting.

**FEED LAWNS.** To keep lawns green and healthy, fertilize with ½ to 1 pound of actual nitrogen per 1,000 square feet early this month. Water well.

**FILL IN WITH ANNUALS.** Set out marigolds, salvias, and zinnias from 4-inch pots. Pop them into beds or containers for a quick midsummer perk-up.

**FUSS WITH FUCHSIAS.** Water regularly and thoroughly. Snip off faded blossoms before they form fruits. Snip back leggy branches. Feed plants monthly with a complete liquid fertilizer (12-12-12 works well) mixed at full strength according to manufacturer's instructions.

**GROOM ROCK GARDENS.** Once flowering has finished, cut bloom stalks back. If leaves are dusty, spray them with water early in the morning (giving them time to dry out during the day prevents mildew). Shop nurseries for healthy plants to add to your rock garden.

**GROOM STRAWBERRIES.** Remove dead leaves and stems, and rid beds of accumulated debris. Fertilize thoroughly and water plants well. To start new plants, pin down runners with wire staples (you can make them from clothes hangers). They'll root quickly.

**MONITOR HOUSE PLANTS.** Check plants that are summering outdoors for aphids and signs of other unwanted visitors. Check daily to see that soil is adequately moist. Watch foliage for signs of sunburn; if normally green leaves take on a bronzy look, move them to a shadier spot.

**PLANT DAHLIAS AND MUMS.** Shorter varieties of dahlias and chrysanthemums are sold now as bedding plants. Use them to fill gaps in beds for late summer and autumn bloom.

**PRUNE AZALEAS AND RHODODENDRONS.** Cut back leggy or misshapen growth early in the month.

**SOAK HANGING BASKETS.** Exposed to wind and sun, hanging baskets tend to dry out quickly. During hottest weather, you may have to water them twice daily.

**SOW VEGETABLE SEEDS.** There's still time to sow seeds of beets, broccoli, bush beans, carrots, chard, Chinese cabbage, kohlrabi, lettuce, peas, radishes, scallions, spinach, and turnips.

**TEND CAMELLIAS.** So that water will quickly get to the shallow roots, gently rake soil around plants and mulch well. A 2- to 3-inch layer of well-rotted sawdust or fir needles extending from the trunk of the plant out to the drip line works well. To help ensure a big flower crop next spring, apply a final feeding, at midmonth, of a granular fertilizer high in phosphorus and potassium (5-10-10 is a good choice).

**TEND ROSES.** Keep plants fed and well watered. When you cut hybrid tea roses, snip them off just above a five-leaflet leaf.

**WATER FLOWERING SHRUBS.** Plants are setting buds for next year's bloom right now, so make sure they get enough water.

**WORK THE COMPOST PILE.** In hot weather, keep the pile moist. Add grass clippings, prunings, and pulled weeds.

# July Checklist

■

## NORTHERN CALIFORNIA

### CARE FOR FRUIT TREES.
Support limbs of apple, peach, pear, and plum trees that are overladen and sagging with ripening fruit. Cover trees with bird netting to protect your crops.

### CARE FOR LAWNS.
Keep the mowing height high during the heat of summer; mow when the grass is about a third taller than the recommended height. For bluegrass and fescue, mow when the grass is 3 to 4 inches tall, with your mower set at 2 to 3 inches. Cut Bermuda grass when it's 2 inches tall with the mower set at 1 inch.

### CONTROL TOMATO HORNWORMS.
Inspect tomato plants for chewed leaves and black droppings, then hunt through foliage and handpick and destroy the large worms. To destroy smaller ones, spray plants with *Bacillus thuringiensis* (BT).

### CUT BACK FLOWERS.
Deadhead annuals and perennials such as daisies, daylilies, geraniums, marigolds, and penstemon. If it's too time-consuming to deadhead plants such as marguerites and verbenas, shear off flowers with grass clippers. Cut back petunias and fertilize to encourage a new flush of growth.

### DIVIDE BEARDED IRIS.
Dig up old clumps with a spading fork, then cut or break the rhizomes apart at their natural junctures. Replant the younger, vigorous rhizomes (see page 160).

### FEED CYMBIDIUMS.
To encourage flower formation for next winter's bloom, feed cymbidiums with quarter-strength liquid fertilizer every time you water plants.

### PLANT LONG-SEASON BLOOMERS.
Nurseries still have a wide variety of summer flowers that will bloom into fall. Choices include ageratum, celosia, dahlias, marigolds, petunias, portulaca, salvia, sweet alyssum, and zinnias.

### POLLINATE MELONS, SQUASHES.
If you're not getting good production (zones 14–16), high temperatures may be inhibiting fruit set. To aid pollination, use an artist's brush to gather yellow pollen from freshly opened male flowers and dust it onto the stigma in the center of female flowers, which have slightly enlarged bases. You can also pull off male flowers, gently remove petals, and shake the flowers directly over the female flowers.

### PRUNE CANE BERRIES.
After harvesting fruit, remove old raspberry canes as they begin to die; cut off blackberry and boysenberry canes that have fruited and tie new canes to a trellis.

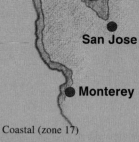

San Rafael
Walnut Creek
Oakland
San Francisco
San Jose
Monterey

▨ Coastal (zone 17)

▢ Inland (zones 14–16)

### START PERENNIALS.
To get ready for fall planting, take cuttings of dianthus, geraniums, scabiosa, Shasta daisies, verbena, and other herbaceous perennials, dip them in rooting hormone, and plant them in a mixture of two parts perlite to one part peat moss. Also sow seeds of campanula, columbine, coreopsis, delphinium, forget-me-not, foxglove, purple coneflower, and rudbeckia in the same growing medium.

## CARE FOR FRUIT TREES.
To prevent breakage, support fruit-laden limbs of apple, peach, pear, and plum trees. Cover trees with bird netting to protect ripening fruit.

## CARE FOR LAWNS.
Keep the mowing height a bit higher during summer's heat to keep roots cool by protecting them from hot sun. For bluegrass and fescue, set mower at 2½ to 3 inches. Also hold off fertilizing these cool-season lawns until September. Mow Bermuda grass lawns to a height of ¾ to 1 inch and continue your fer

tilizer program. If you are not already aware of local watering restrictions, check with your water department, and ask for evapotranspiration (ET) guidelines.

## CONTROL FLOWER-CHEWING WORMS.
If your nicotiana, petunia, and penstemon plants appear healthy but have no blooms, budworms are probably eating flowers before they open. To control them, spray affected plants every 7 to 10 days with *Bacillus thuringiensis*. BT can also help control young tomato hornworms (handpick the big ones).

## CUT BACK CANE BERRIES.
After harvesting June blackberries and boysenberries, cut spent canes to the ground. Tie up this year's new canes; they'll bear fruit next year, if not this fall.

## FERTILIZE.
Keep vegetables and summer-flowering annuals growing vigorously with regular applications of high-nitrogen fertilizer.

## MULCH.
To conserve moisture, discourage weeds, and keep roots cool, cover the soil around plants with a 2- to 3-inch layer of organic mulch.

## PLANT FOR FALL BLOOM.
You'll see a wide variety this month in nurseries, including ageratum, celosia, cosmos, dahlias, marigolds, petunias, portulaca, salvia, and zinnias. Plant begonias and impatiens in light shade.

## PLANT VEGETABLES.
You can still plant warm-season vegetables, including corn, snap beans, summer squash, and tomatoes.

## WATER.
Continue to use water wisely. If necessary, rebuild soil basins and furrows to direct water to plant roots.

Redding

Lake Tahoe

Sacramento

Fresno

Bakersfield

Valley and foothills (zones 7–9, 14)

Mountain (zones 1, 2)

## WEED.
Hand-pull or hoe weeds before they starve plants of water and nutrients, go to seed, or get too large and hard to eliminate. For the really tough ones, such as Bermuda grass, spot-spray with an herbicide.

## July Checklist

### SOUTHERN CALIFORNIA

**CARE FOR CYMBIDIUMS.** In coastal (*Sunset Western Garden Book* climate zones 22 through 24) and inland (zones 18 through 21) areas, water weekly and feed this month and next with high-nitrogen fertilizer. Apply it according to label instructions.

**CHECK MOWING HEIGHT.** Cut Bermuda lawns short, an inch or less high, preferably with a reel-type mower. If you have tall fescue or a similar cool-season lawn, use a rotary-type mower set at 1½ inches.

**DIVIDE IRISES.** In coastal and inland gardens, lift old, overgrown clumps of bearded irises, and cut or break apart rhizomes at their natural junctures. Discard old, leafless centers and replant large, healthy rhizomes 1 to 2 feet apart; barely cover with soil.

**FERTILIZE SELECTIVELY.** Warm-season annual flowers and vegetables, warm-season lawns, and all azaleas and camellias need feeding now. It's also time to feed subtropicals such as bananas, bird of paradise, bougainvillea, hibiscus, and lantana. Water plants thoroughly a day or two before feeding, then deep-water again immediately afterward.

**HARVEST FLOWERS AND VEGETABLES.** To encourage more flowers, cut off seed heads of cosmos, dahlias, marigolds, rudbeckias, and zinnias. For a continued vegetable harvest and attractive plants, pick heat-loving vegetables such as beans, cucumbers, eggplant, peppers, and squash at their prime; some vegetables, like summer squash, should be checked daily.

**MULCH.** To suppress weeds, cool the soil, and reduce evaporation, spread a 2- to 3-inch layer of compost, ground bark, weed-free straw, or dried grass clippings around vegetables, fruit trees, shrubs, roses, and perennials. Keep area around stems and tree trunks clear.

**PLANT QUICK COLOR.** In coastal, inland, and high desert (zone 11) gardens, set out soon-to-bloom annuals in full sun; choices include globe amaranth, Madagascar periwinkle (vinca rosea), marigolds, portulaca, salvia, verbena, and zinnias. Be sure to water regularly.

**PLANT VEGETABLES.** In coastal and inland gardens, you can still plant some vegetables for a late extra harvest—if you water diligently. Plant seeds of beans, carrots, corn, cucumbers, and summer squash. Set out seedlings of cucumbers, eggplant, melons, peppers, pumpkins, squash, and tomatoes.

**TEND ROSES.** Feed after each bloom cycle, and water deeply as needed. Cut flowers just above a leaf node with five or more leaflets. Check for aphids and spider mites. If you find any, wash plants with a strong jet of water from the hose, or use an insecticidal soap.

Santa Barbara
Pasadena
San Bernardino
Santa Monica
Los Angeles
San Diego

☐ Zones 18–21
▨ Zones 22–24

**THIN TREES.** In low-desert (zone 13) areas, prune to open up top-heavy trees such as acacia, Brazilian pepper, mesquite, and olive; thin branches and suckers so wind can pass through. Stake or guy young trees to support them in wind.

**TIP-PRUNE.** Gardeners in coastal and inland areas can force more branching and encourage bushier plants by pinching off the tips of chrysanthemums, fuchsias, and recently planted marguerites.

## July Checklist

**HERE IS WHAT NEEDS DOING**

## ANYWHERE IN THE WEST, TACKLE THESE CHORES:

**HARVEST VEGETABLES, FLOWERS.** As vegetables mature, pick them often to keep more coming, and to keep ripe ones from becoming overmature (cucumbers, zucchini) or downright rotten (tomatoes). With flowers, pinch back or shear off flowers before they go to seed to encourage continued bloom.

**MAINTAIN ROSES.** After each bloom cycle, remove faded flowers, cutting them off just above a leaf node with five leaflets (nodes closest to the flower have three leaflets). Then fertilize and water deeply to stimulate the next round of bloom.

**MULCH.** Apply a 3-inch layer of organic mulch around permanent plants to reduce soil evaporation and suppress weeds. You can use leaves, shredded garden waste, lawn clippings, even tree limbs that have gone through a grinder.

**PRUNE CANE BERRIES.** In all but the coldest parts of the West, cut out old, drying raspberry canes after the harvest. On everbearing kinds, cut off the half of each cane that bore fruit. Cut off blackberry canes that have fruited, and tie new canes to a trellis. In cold-winter areas, do it in August.

**TEND CYMBIDIUMS.** To help build buds for next year's bloom, apply quarter-strength liquid fertilizer every time you water.

**WATER.** Water annual flowers and vegetables only after the top inch of soil has dried out. Basins and furrows help direct water to the roots. Deep-rooted permanent plants can be watered less often, but water them deeply whenever you do irrigate.

## IN THE INTERMOUNTAIN WEST, DO THESE CHORES:

**CONTROL BUDWORMS.** Budworms eat through the buds of geraniums, nicotiana, penstemons, and petunias, preventing flowering. If they're in your garden (look for holes in the buds), spray plants every 7 to 10 days with *Bacillus thuringiensis* (BT).

**CONTROL TOMATO HORNWORMS.** Look for these green worms if you see chewed tomato leaves spotted with black droppings. Handpick large hornworms (they can be finger size or larger); when they're small, you can control them with BT.

**PLANT VEGETABLES.** In all but the highest-altitude areas, plant beets, broccoli, cabbage, carrots, cauliflower, green onions, leaf lettuce, peas, radishes, spinach, and turnips for fall harvest. Plant winter squash among the spinach; as you harvest spinach, the squash will quickly fill in gaps.

**TIP PRUNE.** To make them bushier, pinch out the tips of chrysanthemums, fuchsias, and recently planted marguerites.

## IN THE SOUTHWEST'S LOW AND INTERMEDIATE DESERTS:

**PLANT VEGETABLES.** You can still plant pumpkins if you act early in the month (otherwise they won't be ready for Halloween). Set out beans, corn, and all kinds of squash any time this month.

**POLLINATE MELONS AND SQUASH.** In hot-summer areas, high temperatures inhibit fruit set on squash. You can improve the situation by dabbing pollen-from male flowers with a small artist's brush, then painting the pollen onto female flowers; you can identify female flowers by their swollen bases.

**SOLARIZE SOIL.** You can put the sun to work cleaning weed seeds out of your soil if you act now, during the hottest part of the year. Till the soil, rake and water it, and cover with clear plastic weighted down along the edges. Leave it in place three weeks, then turn the soil again and repeat the process. The intense, trapped heat will kill weed seeds and seedlings, making weed control easier next time you plant.

**SOW TOMATO SEEDS.** Sow tomato seeds around mid-July. Plants will come up and flower by September, and fruits should follow through frost.

**THIN TREES.** Prune top-heavy acacia, Brazilian pepper, mesquite, and olive trees. Take out suckers; dead, diseased, or injured wood; and branches that run closely parallel to each other.

# Avant Gardens

## Bold colors, sculptural forms, unusual textures...and some plants, too

By Peter O. Whiteley

Most garden designers subscribe to a familiar school of style. Some lean toward the free-form charm of English cottage gardens, while others prefer the spartan serenity of Japanese landscapes. But, as in any field of creative endeavor, there are those designers who choose to explore new directions.

One of the strongest trends is to rely on manmade forms as well as nature's own to achieve an exciting interplay of texture and color. The designers featured here have not, however, lost sight of the important tenet that gardens are for people. These are functional but visually surprising spaces that invite you to come outside and enjoy their beauty.

## A sculptured garden

It's not unusual for a garden to contain a piece of sculpture or two, but the garden created by the San Francisco firm of Delaney/Cochran/Castillo *is* the sculpture. Running through the rectangular yard are brightly colored stucco walls, welded-metal trellis walls, rows of handmade concrete tiles, a trapezoidal courtyard of lavender calico rock, bands of pink concrete, and swaths of massed plants. Designer Topher Delaney even considered the passage of time—the shapes of shadows

Uplighted monolithic walls make a theatrical backdrop for alfresco meals, and hide a small work center covered by a corrugated metal roof (bottom below). The two tall walls and a pair of low ones edge a small patio. The crisp lines and vivid colors of these manmade elements contrast with the natural forms of oaks and a bed of spiky lavender, which echoes the color of the walls and boulders surrounding a curvaceous metal gate (top below).

PETER CHRISTIANSEN

DAVID DUNCAN LIVINGSTON

Wisteria-bearing bamboo trellis screens a delightfully disparate garden. Ceramic columns flanking the entrance are filled mostly with concrete, then topped off with potting soil, which sprouts flames of variegated New Zealand flax. Crowns of copper cut to have jagged, flamelike profiles reinforce the fire motif. Other eclectic elements include a false-front garden shed with shards of colored mirror embedded in its stucco façade (below, and above left) and a deconstructed stone lantern from an old entrance to a Korean city (below left).

PETER O. WHITELEY

DAVID DUNCAN LIVINGSTON

cast by walls, and the changing color of vines trained on the welded-metal trellis walls—as an essential component of the garden's plan.

The vibrant colors of the freestanding walls were drawn from a Mediterranean palette of ocher, lavender, and dark blue. The owners used a complementary terra-cotta color on the back wall of their house.

Large groupings of carefully selected plants complement the oversize scale of the garden's "hardscape" elements. The massings emphasize the forms of particular plants and increase the visual impact of their blossoms when they flower. Plants were chosen for their drought tolerance as well as their aesthetic appeal. They include *Salvia clevelandii,* 'Tuscan Blue' rosemary, Italian cypress, bougainvillea, trumpet vine, lavender, and dwarf agapanthus.

## International funk

Bits of Mexico, Korea, Southeast Asia, England, grade-school playground, and contemporary funk are mixed together in the small backyard garden created by San Jose landscape designer Cevan Forristt for owners Michele and Rickson Sun. The garden is divided into seven zones, each with a distinct function and look. The details and diversity of the garden enrich it to the extent that, as Michele put it, "if all the plants died, it would still look good."

The garden entry is flanked by freestanding columns made from celadon-glazed flue tiles. Electrical and drip-irrigation

## Avant Gardens

Giddily colorful walls and plants screen a front yard in Santa Monica. The low, powder blue wall has a purple planter along its base and a series of terra-cotta–colored beam ends projecting from its top (left). The taller, tawny yellow stucco walls (below) stair-step to display potted plants along the curving entry area.

PETER O. WHITELEY

CHAD SLATTERY

lines run through the columns to lights and plants placed in their crowns.

Beyond the columns is a raised patio consisting of square concrete modules that make it look like a giant chessboard. The patio is edged with a band of concrete and made with pre-cut squares of terra-cotta–colored Arizona flagstone and soft gray Connecticut bluestone. A set of four copper chairs, a circular table, and some handmade plant containers are the only pieces on the "board."

Other garden zones include a berm with a low fountain ringed by "ruins" made from pieces of a granite lantern, a private sitting area shrouded by bamboo and screened by sheets of copper overlaid with manzanita branches, a barbecue area with a counter that cantilevers from the garage wall, and a play structure for the kids.

## Behind bright walls

An overexposed front yard got a bright face-lift when owners Diane and George Mkitarian of Santa Monica masked it with walls that warm the neighborhood with cheerful colors. Before, the corner lot and house lay open to views and noise from a busy street. To cut down on visual and acoustical intrusions, the owners constructed thick concrete-block walls along the sidewalk. The sculptural walls curve in and out and step up and down, ranging in height from 3½ to more than 6 feet.

The audacious walls have cut down on street noise and provided a sheltered yard for the Mkitarians and their children. The colorful garden also has had one unexpected side benefit for the whole neighborhood: "It has been our contribution to slowing down traffic," says Diane. ∎

# How to choose the right garden hose

*In general, you get what you pay for, but don't let price be your sole guide*

FOR MOST OF US, A hose is a hose is a hose, as long as it transports water from the faucet to the garden. But if you've ever struggled with a cheap hose—one that's hard to maneuver and a wrestling match to coil, that kinks at the faucet and sprouts leaks after just a few years— you know there is more to a good hose than meets the eye.

## THINGS TO CONSIDER

**Price.** The old saw, "you get what you pay for," generally applies to hoses. Money isn't too much of an object, since the price for a 50-foot, ⅝-inch hose tops out at about $30—choose one guaranteed for life. As you'd expect, the ones in the $20 range are usually better than the less-expensive models, although an

article in the May 1993 *Consumer Reports* cited a Sears Craftsman hose as a pretty good deal at only $8.

**Materials.** All hoses are not created equal. Depending on the manufacturer, a hose may be made of rubber or vinyl or a combination of the two. The best hoses incorporate multiple layers of reinforcing fabrics such as nylon or rayon. However, the number of layers in a hose can be misleading because manufacturers count and bond the layers differently, and, in some cases, a layer may not have any impact on quality. Just because a hose has five plies doesn't mean it's necessarily better than a hose with four.

**Fittings.** Hose couplings and swivels can be another quality indicator. The strongest couplings are made of brass—the thicker, the bet-

ter—and the best swivels are hexagonal (as opposed to round). The angular shape of a hexagonal swivel makes gripping and attaching the hose to the faucet easier. Also, look for a protective collar just below the coupling—it's designed to prevent the hose from kinking at the faucet.

**Potability.** We've all drunk water from a hose—you know the taste. But only a few hoses are made from "drinking-water-safe" materials approved by the FDA, although the agency's blessing applies only to a hose's construction, not to the quality of water that flows through it. Not surprisingly, most hoses in this category are geared to the boating and RV markets. The Gilmour Boat & Camper (about $19) and the Teknor Apex Boat & Camper (about $16) are two examples. Some of the garden hoses in Colorite's Water-Works line ($15 to $25) also use FDA–approved materials.

**Suggestions.** There are many high-quality hoses on the market that are readily available in the West, are kink resistant, coil easily, have heavy-duty couplings, and come with lifetime guarantees. One that's worked well for a few of our garden writers is the Flexogen hose from Gilmour Group (about $24). A comparable hose is the Teknor Apex Ultra Flexible (about $17).

## RESOURCES

The hoses listed above can be found in most garden supply stores. For the dealer nearest you, call the manufacturer: Colorite Plastics, (201) 941-2900; Gilmour Group, (800) 458-0107; Teknor Apex Company, (800) 556-3864. ∎

*By Lynn Ocone*

NORMAN A. PLATE

**AN UNREINFORCED HOSE** *(left) is made of a less-flexible grade of vinyl that kinks when bent. The reinforced hose bends without kinking.*

LAST SUMMER WE phoned a nursery to ask whether they had any blueberry plants laden with fruit. "Yes," the manager answered, "if our employees haven't eaten them all." That's the thing about blueberries: it's well-nigh impossible to pass by without plucking some, since you don't have to peel or seed them before popping a few into your mouth.

In addition to producing delicious fruit, blueberry plants excel in the landscape, adapting successfully to both shade and sun, and producing colorful fall foliage.

Breeders and nurseries have done remarkable things with blueberries in recent years. Now there are varieties for most Western climates, with plants ranging in habit from ground covers to tall shrubs, and fruits that run from pea to cherry size.

Though most of the blueberries mentioned here are self-pollinating, they bear most heavily when other varieties are nearby for cross-pollination. Plants grown in sun have more compact growth and yield bigger crops.

## PICK THE RIGHT PLANTS

**Western Oregon and Washington.** This is prime blueberry country, so you can succeed with almost any variety that's sold. When most people think of blueberries, they envision northern highbush (*Vaccinium corymbosum*) varieties, since that's the kind you usually find at the supermarket. Unless otherwise noted, the following are northern highbush varieties.

Full-size blueberry shrubs give the most fruit. Choose a mix of early, midseason, and late varieties. Three good

**GRAPE-SIZE** *'Elliott' blueberries are great for eating fresh.*

# For pancakes and landscapes

*Blueberries are easy to grow—if you pick the right plants for your climate and get them off to a good start*

PHIL SCHOFIELD

**ALREADY BEARING FRUIT,** *a blueberry bush goes into garden soil generously amended with peat moss. Summer and fall foliage colors differ by variety.*

choices would be 'Spartan' (early), 'Olympia' (midseason), and 'Jersey' (its small, late berries are the perfect size for pancakes and muffins). 'Elliott' is another strong late-season variety, bearing tart, tasty berries from late summer to first frost.

For extra-large berries, try 'Darrow', a plant that grows well but can't handle extreme cold. Each of its tangy berries is the size of a 50-cent piece. If you can't find 'Darrow' (growers have a hard time starting it), try 'Toro', a new large blueberry with outstanding flavor. Its large, grapelike fruit clusters grow among huge leaves that turn brilliant red in fall.

Good choices for small, non-highbush border or container plants include 'North Country', 'Northsky', 'Top Hat', and 'Northblue', all of which top out at 1½ to 3 feet tall.

For an ornamental ground cover, consider *V. crassifolium* 'Wells Delight', a flat, spreading evergreen that produces just enough fruit to keep your garden's birds happy; or the wild lowbush blueberry, *V. angustifolium*.

Southern highbush blueberries (see page 178) also work well in the coastal Northwest.

**East of the Cascades and the Sierra.** You can grow most northern highbush blueberries in most gardens in the intermountain West. But if you have to contend with much heat or extreme cold in your garden, you'll have to choose varieties carefully.

In the coldest, snowiest areas, try 'Northsky', 'North Country', 'Northblue', or 'Northland' (up to 4 feet tall). Though 'Northland' has a spreading form, its pliable branches shed snow well. 'Patriot' is another good choice, since it can also grow in

**CLUSTERS** *of 'Bluecrop' bear fruit over a long season. This variety is considered one of the best all-around highbush blueberries.*

FALL CREEK FARM & NURSERY

**DEEP BLUE** *'Northland' is an early-bearing variety and the most cold-hardy highbush blueberry.*

poorly drained soil.

Where summer heat is a problem, try 'Bluecrop', 'Bluejay', 'Blueray', 'Jersey', or 'Northland'. With the exception of 'Northland', these all become full-size blueberry bushes; expect them to grow about as tall as you.

***Northern California.*** There are northern highbush blueberry farms in the Sacramento Valley, so it's no surprise that you can succeed with them in your garden if you choose the right varieties ('Bluecrop', 'Blueray', and 'Bluetta', for example) and supply enough peat to maintain soil acidity.

Another option is to plant one of the promising new southern highbush blueberries. These combine the superior flavor of northern highbush berries, the soil adaptability of *V. darrowi,* and the heat-tolerance and low-winter-chill requirements of rabbiteyes (*V. ashei*). The result is an excellent blueberry you can grow from Canada to Mexico.

'O'Neal' is a very early, very sweet berry that may just be the best of the southern highbush. Others to try are 'Cape Fear' and 'Georgia Gem'. All these plants reach 4 to 6 feet tall at maturity.

'Sierra' is a new northern highbush cross with some southern highbush blood. It grows very fast to 6 feet (consider using it as a hedge), and produces quarter-size berries. It hasn't been grown long enough in California to have much of a track record.

## GIVE PLANTS THE RIGHT START

Many nurseries sell a variety of blueberries in pulp pots this month. Cut off the pulp before you set out plants in your garden.

When you buy, nursery workers will probably try to sell you peat moss as well. "The rule of thumb," says one nurseryman, "is to sell a bag of peat for every blueberry bush that goes out the door." Why the peat? Blueberries like slightly acid soil—a pH of 5.5 is about right—that holds water well, and peat acidifies soil and improves its water-holding capacity.

Dig a hole as deep as the plant's rootball and five times as wide. Amend the backfill soil with 50 percent peat, set the plant in the hole, fill in with the amended soil, and mulch well around the plant.

Blueberries are water lovers. After you plant, soak them to help settle the rootball. You can put your plants on drip irrigation, as some California blueberry farmers have done.

To keep plants growing well, apply an acid azalea or rhododendron fertilizer twice in spring; March and May are good months.

The only disease you may encounter is mummy berry, which occasionally shows up in western Oregon and Washington. When berries should be shifting from green to blue, they turn salmon or pink and fall to the ground, dry and mummified inside. If that happens to your plants, spray twice during next spring's bloom with Funginex.

You can also buy blueberry bushes as bare-root plants in winter.

---

## SOURCES

Two good mail-order sources for blueberry plants are ***Bear Creek Nursery,*** Box 4114, Northport, Wash. 99157, (509) 732-6219 (catalog $1, refundable with first order); and ***Northwoods Retail Nursery,*** 27635 S. Oglesby Rd., Canby, Ore. 97013, (503) 266-5432 (free catalog). Plants cost $5.20 to $9.50 each. ∎

*By Jim McCausland*

**BLUEBERRY PLANTS** *are grown for wholesale nursery stock (foreground) and for retail fruit market (background) at Fall Creek Farm & Nursery in Lowell, Oregon.*

**FRESH, SUCCULENT** *leaves of Italian oregano impart a mild flavor to chicken and fish.*

# The best garden oreganos for cooking

THE GREEKS VALUED IT for medicinal purposes even before its famous marriage with lamb. French and Italian cooks use it to impart a spicy, robust flavor to their favorite dishes. And pizza aficionados can't live without it. Oregano is an herb that's found in almost everyone's spice cupboard.

But if you've ever tried to grow oregano (*Origanum*), its taste may have disappointed you. What's sold in the nursery as culinary oregano is often *O. vulgare*, a rather bland, tasteless type that V. J. Billings of Mountain Valley Growers describes as a "culinary zero."

Many gardeners and cooks don't realize that there are other oreganos they can grow with tastes that range from spicy and pungent to mild and flavorful.

## SUIT YOUR TASTE BUDS

Each of the seven oreganos shown below has a distinctive flavor and intensity. The powerful, spicy flavor of Cretan oregano may be too intense for some, craved by others. Sweet marjoram is on the opposite end of the flavor scale, with a sweet, floral taste that some may find soapy. Italian and Sicilian oregano are hybrids, with mild flavors somewhere between a strong-flavored oregano and sweet marjoram.

You may want to consider growing two kinds—one strong, the other milder—and blending them to suit the dish or your taste buds. The following types are listed in order of potency, from strongest to lightest flavor.

**Cretan** (*O. onites*). Gray-green woolly foliage. Grows to 18 inches tall.

**Greek** (*O. vulgare hirtum*, sold as *O. heracleoticum*). Considered to be the best cooking oregano. Sturdiest plant of all, handles many soils. Grows to 3 feet tall.

**Syrian** (*O. syriacum*, usually sold as *O. maru*). Similar in flavor to Greek, but plant not as sturdy. Grows to 2 feet tall.

**Kirghizstan** (*O. vulgare gracile*, usually sold as *O. tyttanthum*). More ornamental than others; pink flowers. Grows to 2 feet tall.

**Sicilian** (*O. majorana*). Green, rounded leaves. Grows to 2 feet tall.

**Italian** (*O. majoricum*). Bright green foliage. Grows to 2 feet tall.

**Sweet marjoram** (*O. majorana*). Good for potpourri, too. Grows to 1 foot tall.

## OREGANOS THRIVE IN FULL SUN

Plant in well-drained soil or in a raised bed. Since oregano is native to the Mediterranean, it needs only moderate water. Allow plenty of room to spread; most oreganos become good-size plants. To keep foliage succulent (leaves on woody growth are not good for cooking), cut the plants back severely two or three times a year. Don't let plants go to seed or you'll have oregano sprouting where you don't want it. Also, plants from seed may not be the same as the parent.

You may find some of the oreganos listed above in the herb section at your nursery. Or you can order these oreganos by mail.

*Mountain Valley Growers, Inc.,* 38325 Pepperweed Rd., Squaw Valley, Calif. 93675; (209) 338-2775. The catalog is free. This nursery sells all seven kinds of oregano.

*Richters,* 357 Highway 47, Goodwood, Ont., Canada L0C 1A0; (905) 640-6677. The catalog costs $2. The nursery sells six kinds. ■

*By Lauren Bonar Swezey*

## CULINARY OREGANOS HAVE DIVERSE ORIGINS AND FLAVORS

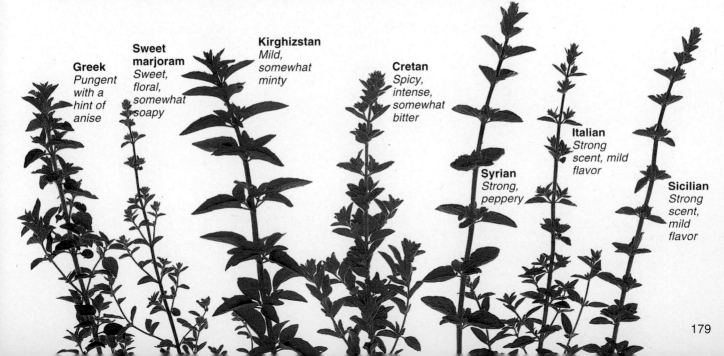

**Greek**
*Pungent with a hint of anise*

**Sweet marjoram**
*Sweet, floral, somewhat soapy*

**Kirghizstan**
*Mild, somewhat minty*

**Cretan**
*Spicy, intense, somewhat bitter*

**Syrian**
*Strong, peppery*

**Italian**
*Strong scent, mild flavor*

**Sicilian**
*Strong scent, mild flavor*

# Southern California dream stone

**BOUQUET CANYON STONE** *gives this new Southern California pool, designed by Nick Williams and Associates, a timeworn, natural feel.*

**B**OUQUET CANYON stone: it's as ubiquitous in the Southern California home landscape as citrus and camellias. That's probably Vic Williams's fault. Since 1945, Williams has been hauling stone from his Bouquet Canyon quarry in Angeles National Forest to his Newhall sales yard 30 miles to the south. He's the last remaining operator to extract the prized blue-gray micaceous schist with its rust-colored veins from the canyon so that we might use it in our patios, fireplaces, walkways, and walls.

The commercial use of Bouquet Canyon stone began in 1922 when H. A. Jones, Sr., hauled some out of the canyon, loaded it on a wagon, and delivered it to clients in Beverly Hills and Pasadena, more than 40 miles away. When Williams staked his first claim in 1945, he

**VIC WILLIAMS**

was one of four prospectors working the canyon below Del Sur Ridge.

Competition back then was stiff, "a dog-eat-dog thing," says Williams, who's pushing 80. For years, the business barely squeaked by. And it was hard work, to boot: using just a pick and shovel, on a good day Williams and his one employee would personally handle as much as 7 tons of stone.

All that changed in 1954 when Williams staked the claim he still works today, "the best claim of all." It sits high on the ridge and has a seemingly inexhaustible supply of retrievable rock. Williams's crew of men and machinery works about 20 acres of the ridge; the United States Forest Service, which sets the quarry's boundaries, leases the land to Williams, and receives royalties on the excavated stone.

## STONE-AGE TECHNIQUES

Although the quarrying process remains much the same as it was in the old days, today's excavator does have a few powerful tools at his disposal. Bulldozers, not shovels, push away dirt and mud, known in the stone biz as overburden, to reveal ledges of the sought-after stratified rock. Mammoth skip loaders then scoop up immense buckets of boulders—and there the technological advances basically end. Preliminary sorting and grading is done on site by keen-eyed quarry workers. Only about 25 percent of the recovered stone has commercial value, and, as Williams dryly notes, "There's no machine that can pick out a good rock from a bad rock."

After sorting and grading, the stone is loaded on large dump trucks and hauled to the sales yard. On a typical day, 50 tons of stone make the trip to Newhall. There, workers split the stone, again by hand, using hammers and chisels. After it's split, the stone is sorted by size, stacked on pallets, and made ready for customer pickup. Sizes range from 1-inch-thick flagstone for walkways to 3½-inch-thick stones for wall veneers to 5-inch-thick slabs for waterfalls and driveways. Williams sells to wholesalers only—by the ton.

## WHAT THE FUTURE HOLDS

According to official estimates, the quarry has another 23 years or so of stone in it. In contrast to the early days in Bouquet Canyon, government agencies—from the county to the federal level—now exert a strong influence on the quarry's operations and mining practices. Environmental controls include a reclamation

plan, which is regularly reviewed and reapproved by the Los Angeles County Planning Commission.

Even without the new environmental regulations, mining stone is a tough trade. Every so often a rumor will circulate that Williams is out of business (he imagines it's started by a competitor). And then there are the quarries in the San Bernardino Mountains that, according to Williams, are selling inferior stone and calling it Bouquet Canyon. But the stone business is not for the thin-skinned, and Williams takes these snags in stride, happy to still be working the stone that has been his life for almost half a century.

For a distributor in your area, call Vic Williams Bouquet Canyon Stone Co. Inc. at (805) 259-3939. ■

*By Lynn Ocone*

CHRISTOPHER GARDNER

**AT THE QUARRY,** *bulldozers remove overburden to reveal ledges of blue-gray micaceous schist. At the stone yard, workers split the rock by hand. It's then sized and stacked.*

SUMMER-BLOOMING *perennials flourish even in the parkways outside Lauren Springer's northern Colorado house.*

# Sidewalk surprise

*A horticulturist and author plants to weather all the elements—including neighborhood kids*

S HE CALLS THEM HELL strips, but Lauren Springer's parkways—the ribbons of earth between the street and the sidewalk—look more like little slices of heaven.

Springer, a professional horticulturist and author, gardens at her home on a ⅓-acre corner property in northern Colorado. With winter temperatures that dip to 30° below, summer highs that top 100°, and only 12 inches of precipitation (including snow) a year, it's astonishing to see the broad range of plants she grows in the parkways—all without irrigation.

Springer chose mostly informal plants, relying on those best adapted to full sun and her "lean," as she calls it, somewhat sandy soil. The plants are drought and child tolerant—when classes let out of the elementary school down the street, children parade by, and sometimes through, the sidewalk garden.

When Springer and her husband, Michael Pavsek, bought their house four years ago, the strips were solid bindweed. After the arduous task of eliminating the weeds, Springer planted mostly grasses, perennials, and bulbs. Some hardy cactus and self-sowing annuals such as desert bluebells (*Phacelia campanularia*) and blazing star (*Mentzelia lindleyi*) mingle throughout.

## BULBS AND BUFFALO GRASS

Buffalo grass (*Buchloe dactyloides*) dominates the most-traveled portion of the parkways. Springer jokes, "I chose the plant so I wouldn't weep when the kids rode their bikes over it." This warm-season grass is slow to green up in spring, but spreads rapidly by surface runners once it's established.

Thousands of bulbs are planted within the grass in this 10- by 75-foot strip. Among them are several different species tulips, as well as *Iris reticulata* and *Crocus chrysanthus.* In contrast to large-flowered hybridized bulbs, these diminutive plants bloom like wildflowers.

The bulbs peak in spring while the grass is still dormant. The dark, brilliant colors of flowers such as magenta *Tulipa humilis* show up best against the winter beige of the grass. In early summer, when the bulbs' foliage dies, Springer rakes it away. She mows the grass once a year, in November.

## BLUE GRAMA PRAIRIE

This 10- by 75-foot prairielike section combines blue grama grass (*Bouteloua gracilis*) with perennials, including blanket flower (*Gaillardia grandiflora*), butterfly weed (*Asclepias tuberosa*), *Penstemon barbatus,* and *Thelesperma filifolium.* The fine-textured grass is clumping, not spreading, which makes

BLUE GRAMA GRASS *combines with blanket flower, butterfly weed, and Thelesperma filifolium in prairielike planting.*

LAUREN SPRINGER

MAGENTA TULIPA HUMILIS *brightens buffalo grass.*

interspersing perennials easy.

The grass grows to a foot tall—on windy days, it looks like an undulating sea of green, spangled with colorful perennials. Come August, flowers rise above the unmown grass and persist through winter. In late winter or early spring, just before a surge of new growth, Springer mows the grass and uses the resulting "haystack" to make compost.

## PERENNIAL PATCHWORKS

The 6- by 75-foot strip in front of the house is divided into two perennial plantings; in one, pastel colors are prominent, and in the other, hot colors such as orange and red reign. The hot-colored plants reach peak bloom a little later in the summer than the pastels, giving the strip an extended bloom season.

Plants with contrasting forms and textures add depth and help distinguish one another amid the shout of color. Tucked in among velvety poppy petals, for example, are little thorny cactus such as *Coryphantha,* which has shocking pink flowers. In the pastel planting, pink penstemons with upright spikes of tubular flowers contrast with such mounding plants as pinks (*Dianthus*) and stonecress (*Aethionema coridifolium*).

## RESOURCES

Springer gets seed from regional sources, such as Plants of the Southwest (Agua Fria, Route 6, Box 11A, Santa Fe, N.M. 87501; catalog $3.50), and from plant societies' seed exchanges, including American Penstemon Society (1569 S. Holland Court, Lakewood, Colo. 80232) and American Rock Garden Society (Box 67, Millwood, N.Y. 10546).

To learn about the rest of Springer's garden, look for a copy of her new book, *The Undaunted Garden* (Fulcrum Publishing, Golden, Colo., 1994; $29.95). ∎

*By Lynn Ocone*

PETER CHRISTIANSEN

**VEGETABLE SEEDLINGS** *above, purchased late (on July 1), are leggy and yellowish. Six weeks after planting, most are filling in; beans and squash are starting to produce.*

# Is it too late to plant summer vegetables?

*Not if you start right away*

 UDDENLY IT'S JULY, AND YOU realize you haven't started your summer vegetable garden. Is it too late to plant? Do nurseries still have vegetable seedlings? And what kind of production will you get if you do plant now?

After hearing these questions from some of our staff here at *Sunset,* we decided to shop around at local nurseries, find out what's available, then grow the vegetables in our test garden to determine whether the harvest is worth the effort.

What you get depends on where you live, but for gardeners in much of California it's not too late to plant most summer vegetables.

## LOOK FOR HEALTHY SEEDLINGS

In Northern California, seedling selection in nurseries at this time of year isn't the greatest. By now, wholesalers are getting ready to move into cool-season vegetables, so retail nurseries are beginning to close out summer vegetables. What you're likely to find are tomato, squash, cucumber, pepper, and melon seedlings that are overgrown and root-bound.

In spite of their ragtag appearance, however, most of the seedlings we bought performed well enough to make planting worthwhile. When you do shop, try to find deep green seedlings that are not overgrown for the size of the pot. Before planting, pinch off any flowers or fruit so energy goes into developing healthy foliage. Plant vegetables in rich soil well amended with organic matter and compost.

We discovered that beans and squash are best started from seed. A short-season variety of zucchini, 'Raven', that we planted from seed (42 days to harvest) was more productive than an 'Ambassador' (51 days) we purchased as a seedling.

In Southern California, nurseries carry seedlings of warm-season vegetables much later in the season. You'll still be able to find high-quality seedlings this month—even later on the coast.

If you live in a cold-winter climate, it's too late to put in warm-season vegetables. You should be getting ready to plant cool-season crops like broccoli.

## EXPECT A SMALLER HARVEST

The biggest downfall of cantaloupes, cucumber, and crookneck squash in our garden was mildew, a severe late-summer problem in many areas. The cantaloupe produced just two fruit, and the cucumber and squash only half a dozen each, before succumbing.

Our zucchini, 'Italian Bush' beans, 'Serrano' pepper, and 'Big Boy' tomato developed good-size crops. The 'Patio' tomato wasn't quite as productive, but both tomatoes produced into November. The zucchini finally quit the first of November because of mildew. 'Dusky' eggplant and 'Yolo Wonder' pepper didn't put on enough foliage to develop large crops (each produced only a few fruit), but both would probably be more successful in warmer climates. ∎

*By Lauren Bonar Swezey*

COLORFUL PALETTE *of South African bulbs for mild-winter climates includes lavender Gladiolus carneus, yellow Lachenalia mathewsii (bottom right), white L. unifolia (bottom left), and orange and purple Watsonia laccata. For more information, see page 188.*

# AUGUST

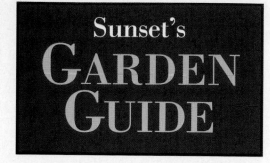

# Sunset's
# GARDEN GUIDE

## August's a month of exotic blossoms, ripening crops, planting for fall

**DOUBLE ROSE FORMS** *of tuberous begonia, in pink and cardinal red, add splashes of color to the summer and fall garden. Behind the begonias are pink impatiens, purple and blue lobelia, and gray green wallflower foliage.*

Tuberous begonias are among the most colorful flowers you can grow in shade, producing big red, yellow, white, pink, or orange flowers over lush, large leaves. Now, while begonias are covered with a profusion of flowers, is the time to learn and note what you like.

Some kinds bear extremely large, upright flowers, while others are loaded with hanging flowers. Get the upright kind for planting in beds, and the hanging kind for containers.

Any plants you buy now will give you a good show for the rest of the summer if you apply quarter-strength fertilizer weekly. Alternate doses of a bloom fertilizer (lower in nitrogen, higher in phosphorus) with applications of a complete fertilizer. Mist plants several times a day (misting heads on timer-controlled drip-irrigation systems make this easy).

When the foliage begins to yellow in fall, reduce watering until all the leaves have died. Then pull them off, lift and clean the tubers, and dry them in filtered sun for three days before storing in a dark, frost-free place for winter.

### Extra-hardy garlic: Order bulbs for fall planting

This fall, you can buy a new garlic bred for cold climates. German Extra-hardy Garlic is a stiff-necked variety, too tough to braid after harvest. Order bulbs now for planting in the garden in September.

At planting time, divide the bulbs into individual cloves and plant them scar-ends down in well-drained, fertilized soil. The garlic will spend the winter sending out roots, foliage will emerge in the spring, and full-size bulbs should be ready for harvest next July or August, depending on your climate.

Water planting beds and mulch them heavily. In spring, after danger of hard frost is past, pull the mulch back to give tops room to grow.

The bulbs are standard in size and potency. You can order from Johnny's Selected Seeds, 310 Foss Hill Rd., Albion, Maine 04910; (207) 437-4301. Cost is $5.25 for three heads (20 to 30 cloves), $9.95 for six heads (40 to 60 cloves).

### Tips for success with containers

As summer marches on and planting activities in your garden slow to a crawl, you may want to turn your attention to brightening up the patio or deck. A few well-placed pots filled with colorful bedding plants like petunias and marigolds can do wonders for the sometimes austere surfaces of wood and concrete.

Planting a couple of containers takes less than an hour. For lasting results, you should plan your pots carefully and treat their contents well. Here are a few tips:

• Combine plants that have the same light requirements. Especially inland, don't mix plants that need shade, like

THOMAS HALLSTEIN

be here today and gone tomorrow. While hornworms can be 4 or 5 inches long, they're hard to spot because their bright green coloring blends with the foliage. The black pellets they excrete do show up on leaves and around plants; if you see pellets or defoliated stems, look for hornworms feeding on the undersides of leaves.

The two types of hornworms are both the larvae of sphinx moths: the tomato hornworm has a black and green horn on its rear; the tobacco hornworm has a red horn.

Handpicking hornworms usually provides sufficient control. If you choose to spray, apply *Bacillus thuringiensis* (BT), a biological control that kills leaf-feeding caterpillars. BT is most effective on young hornworms, which stop feeding soon after ingesting the spray. Follow the label directions, and for maximum control, reapply every few days while the hornworms are active.

Nature has its own way of controlling hornworms. The hornworm pictured below has been parasitized by a natural enemy, the *Braconid* wasp. The wasps develop in the hornworm; when they emerge, they remain attached and spin tiny pale cocoons. The wasps eventually kill the worm.

BILL ADAMS

impatiens and coleus, with sun-loving plants, such as cosmos and zinnias.
• Use a lightweight, fast-draining potting mix. Garden soil is too heavy for containers. It forms a dense mass that is slow-draining and hard for roots to penetrate.
• Moisten the potting soil thoroughly before putting it in the container. Mix it with water in a tub or wheelbarrow if necessary.
• Fill the container with soil to

1 inch below the top. If you fill the container too full, it is difficult to water.
• Space plants appropriately. Overcrowding increases water consumption and can promote disease.
• Water thoroughly immediately after planting; saturate the soil until excess water runs from the drainage hole. Containers dry out quickly, so check the soil and water daily if necessary.
• Feed plants regularly during

the growing season with a complete fertilizer. Never fertilize when the plants are dry.

## The big green pests of the West

With their voracious appetites, hornworms can wreak havoc on tomatoes, and sometimes peppers and eggplants, by consuming leaves and gnawing green fruit. If hornworms are feeding on your tomato plants, the foliage may

**WHITE COCOONS** *of Braconid wasp on its back mean doom for this hornworm.*

BEN DAVIDSON

## Tip of the Month

*This homemade PVC sprinkler rig can serve as a portable irrigation system for a lawn or garden. The rig is made with 1-inch-diameter PVC pipe, joints, and end caps, all glued with PVC cement. The 10-foot-long horizontal section is supported near each end by crosspieces made of short lengths of capped pipe. Two vertical pieces of pipe capped with "micro" sprinkler heads (many sizes are available) sprout near the crosspieces. The rig attaches to a garden hose using a threaded end piece.*

## Southern California's special bulbs

South African bulbs must feel right at home during Southern California's long, dry summers. These colorful and diverse bulbs require no summer watering, making them perfect companions to similarly unthirsty natives. The problem, though, is that many of our gardens are irrigated year-round. That's why home for many South African bulbs is a container with sandy soil and no summer water.

Most nurseries sell South African bulbs in the fall to coincide with the planting season. The selection, however, is usually limited. Not so at UC Irvine Arboretum's annual summer bulb sale. At the arboretum, which boasts the largest collection of South African bulbs outside their native country, you can choose from hundreds of species, including bulbs shown in the photo on page 184.

The bulbs range from 50 cents to $10 each, depending on rarity. Photographs of the plants in bloom are displayed, growing information is provided, and trained volunteers are on hand to answer questions. A connoisseur's table holds a display of rare bulbs, including the pendulous and evergreen *Agapanthus walshii* and various species of *Cyrtanthus,* whose lilylike flowers come in shades of red.

Although you can plant the bulbs now in containers (or beds that you aren't planning to water), it's not a bad idea to keep them in a cool, dark, and dry place until fall. If your garden has heavy clay soil, it's best to plant the bulbs in a raised bed or a container—the bulbs require quick-draining soil.

The arboretum is on the north campus, one block south of the corner of Campus Drive and Jamboree Road. From Interstate 405, take the Jamboree exit and head west. Parking and admission are free. For more information, call (714) 856-5833.

## Start cool-season vegetables now for harvest this fall

It's hard for many gardeners to accept the fact that the best time to plant cool-season vegetables is in the heat of summer. Started this month, young plants grow fast in the warm days of late summer, then produce their crops during the cooler days of fall. By planting now, you avoid some of the problems of spring planting; cole crops such as broccoli and cauliflower hardly ever bolt, and root crops, such as radishes, are crisp and sweet, not hot or bitter.

Early in the month, sow seeds of beets, broccoli, brussels sprouts, cabbage, carrots, cauliflower, endive, kale, kohlrabi, onions, parsnips, radishes, and turnips. You can keep sowing root crops into September. About midmonth, set out transplants of cole crops. Wait until September to start lettuce and peas.

Work the soil well before planting, adding organic matter and a complete fertilizer. Don't let seeds or seedlings dry out. You will probably have to water at least once a day until young plants become established.

## Pick pears when they're still firm

Unlike many fruits, pears can't just be plucked from a tree and eaten. If you let a pear ripen on the tree, it will be soft and mushy. So how do you tell when a pear is ready to pick?

Commercial growers use a pressure tester, but most homeowners don't have access to one. The second best way to determine readiness is by using estimated harvest date guidelines and to test how easy it is to remove the pear from the tree.

Harvest dates vary according to climate and season, but most pears ripen between late July and early October. 'Bartlett' should be harvested in late July (or later in cooler climates). 'Anjou' is usually ready in mid- to late August; 'Bosc' and 'Comice' are ready to pick around mid-September to early October. You should be able to get harvest dates for other pear varieties from a local nursery or U.C. Cooperative Extension Master Gardeners.

Don't wait for fruit to start dropping from the tree. As the harvest period approaches, check every few days by lifting up a pear horizontally, grabbing it so your index finger and thumb are on the stem. If the fruit snaps off cleanly from the twig, the pears are ready to harvest in three to seven days (the shorter time in warmer weather). Keep in mind that fruit growing on the ends of the branches at the top of the tree often ripen earlier than fruit in shadier areas.

## Squeeze more bloom from summer annuals

Many annual flowers can be coaxed out of their late-summer doldrums and into another round of bloom by first cutting them back with pruning shears, then stimulating them with an extra dose of fertilizer. This technique can work with fibrous begonias, cosmos, impatiens, marigolds, petunias, and zinnias.

Cut back plants by a third to a half. Don't be afraid to use hedge shears; this is not artistic pruning. Make sure you cut off most of the bloom and all the seedheads. Next, go on an intensive fertilizer program, applying a high-nitrogen liquid fertilizer once a week according to label instructions. Water regularly.

Some plants can't handle the stress (a few may die), but others should produce new growth in a week or two. Once they start blooming again, go back to the normal feeding program. ■

*By Steven R. Lorton, Jim McCausland, Lynn Ocone, Lauren Bonar Swezey, Lance Walheim*

**BAIT FOR SLUGS.** Just like people, slugs go for the cool spots when hot weather hits. Set bait in dark, moist areas: around and under large rocks, along the foundation of the house, in ground covers such as ivy and *Vinca minor*, around and under large planters and low decks. Take care to keep pets (especially dogs) away from the bait.

**BUD FRUIT TREES.** Add new varieties to existing fruit trees by budding. Bud this month for new growth next spring. For complete instructions, consult the *Sunset Western Garden Book*.

**CONSERVE WATER.** Even if supplies are ample, water frugally. Use soaker hoses or drip irrigation. Or build shallow watering basins around the trunks of trees and deep-rooted shrubs and run a garden hose slowly to soak the soil well.

**DEADHEAD SPENT FLOWERS.** Unless you want seed to form, clip spent blooms. This allows one-time bloomers to focus their energy into foliage production and it induces repeat bloomers to keep on flowering.

**DIVIDE PERENNIALS.** You can dig, divide, and replant early-blooming perennials such as bearded irises and Oriental poppies. Dig a circle around the plants with a spade or shovel, pop them out of the ground, and then with a sharp knife cut small clumps in half, large clumps in quarters, and replant.

**FERTILIZE.** If you want continued bloom, keep feeding fuchsias, geraniums, petunias, marguerites, and marigolds. Feed them monthly with full-strength liquid plant food, or apply a half-strength dose every two weeks.

**HARVEST HERBS.** Flavors will be stronger if you harvest herbs in the morning just after the dew has dried. If you want to dry them, put the herbs on a screen and set them in a shady spot.

**PROPAGATE SHRUBS.** Many shrubs can be propagated from semihardwood cuttings taken this month. Candidates for cuttings include evergreen azaleas, camellias, daphne, elaeagnus, euonymus, hebe, holly, hydrangea, magnolia, nandina, rhododendron, and viburnum. With a clean, sharp knife, take 4- to 6-inch cuttings from ends of stems, strip the leaves off the lower ends of the cuttings, dip the ends in rooting hormone, and put the cuttings in pots filled with potting mix (equal parts of humus and sand work well). Water cuttings and place them in a bright spot, but out of direct sun. Keep cuttings moist by misting daily or by covering them with a plastic bag. When cold weather sets in, move the cuttings to a frost-free place.

**PRUNE CANE BERRIES.** Remove canes that bore fruit in June. On everbearing plants, remove the half of the cane that has already produced fruit.

**WEED.** Pull weeds now before they set seed and scatter it around the garden. Compost the plants you pull.

# August Checklist

**■**

## NORTHERN CALIFORNIA

**CARE FOR FLOWERS.** To keep warm-season annuals blooming through the end of summer and into fall, water and fertilize regularly with fish emulsion or other fertilizer. Remove spent flowers before they go to seed.

**CHECK FOR NUTRIENT DEFICIENCIES.** Inspect leaves for signs of nutrient deficiencies. If leaves have an overall pale yellow cast, plants need a dose of nitrogen fertilizer. If leaves are yellow but the veins are green, plants are suffering from chlorosis; treat it by applying chelated iron.

**DEEP-WATER LARGE TREES AND SHRUBS.** Trees and shrubs that aren't on an irrigation system may need a deep soaking now. Use a soaker hose, deep-root irrigator, or standard hose (flowing slowly into a watering basin), and irrigate until the soil is well-soaked under the dripline of the plant. Check moisture penetration by digging down into the soil with a trowel.

**HARVEST FRUITS AND VEGETABLES.** Check the garden daily to see what's ready to pick. Search bean, summer squash, and tomato plants thoroughly so you don't miss ripe produce. If you want to preserve tomatoes by canning them, harvest while they're still firm; soft tomatoes may contain harmful bacteria. Cut herbs and hang from rafters in a clean, dry place.

**PICK UP FALLEN FRUIT.** Collect off the ground decaying fruit that could be harboring insects and diseases. If fruit looks suspect, toss it in the garbage; don't compost it.

**PLANT FOR SUMMER-FALL BLOOM.** Perennials that bloom now into fall include begonias, coreopsis, dahlias, daylilies (some), fortnight lily, common geranium, lantana, *Limonium perezii*, Mexican sage, Peruvian verbena, and yarrow. For annuals, choose cosmos, celosia, Madagascar periwinkle, marigolds, sweet alyssum, and zinnias.

**REMOVE BUDS ON MUMS.** For bigger blooms on chrysanthemums this fall, pinch off all but one bud per stem now. Stake and tie plants to keep them from flopping over and breaking.

**SOW EARLY-BLOOMING SWEET PEAS.** To get a crop of flowers by December, sow seeds of early-flowering types (called Early-Flowering Multiflora or Early Multiflora) this month. These will bloom when days are short. Protect new growth from slugs and snails and provide support for the vines.

**START COOL-SEASON VEGETABLES.** Start seeds of broccoli, brussels sprouts, cabbage, and cauliflower; they need six to eight weeks to reach transplant size. Sow seeds of carrots, chard, lettuce, peas, and radishes (wait until next month in zone 14) directly in the ground.

Coastal (zone 17)

Inland (zones 14–16)

**TEND ROSES.** To get good fall bloom from rosebushes, give them plenty of water during August's hot days. Also, feed bushes with a complete fertilizer and, if necessary, apply iron chelate to correct chlorosis; water nutrients in thoroughly. Snip off old blooms or rose hips; lightly shape plants if necessary.

## August Checklist

■

### CENTRAL VALLEY

☐ **CARE FOR ROSES.** Cut off faded flowers and water as necessary. Feed lightly to encourage repeat bloom. Remove any suckers and unwanted branches.

☐ **CUT BACK PERENNIALS.** Some perennials will give a second flower show if you cut spent flowering stems back now to about 6 inches. Good candidates for repeat bloom include coreopsis, delphinium, fleabane, Jupiter's beard, and penstemon.

☐ **DEEP-WATER LARGE TREES AND SHRUBS.** If they depend on rain instead of irrigation, they may need a deep soaking now. Apply water with soaker hoses, a slow-running sprinkler or hose, or a deep-root irrigator until the soil is well soaked at least to the plant's drip line. Check moisture penetration by digging down with a trowel.

☐ **DIVIDE IRISES.** If iris rhizomes are crowded, dig up and divide them now for better bloom next spring. It's also a good time to go shopping for new kinds in retail nurseries.

☐ **FERTILIZE.** This month is your last chance to fertilize tender fruit trees such as citrus and avocado. Camellias and azaleas are setting next year's flower buds; apply an acid fertilizer now to boost bloom. Keep using liquid fertilizers on container plants. If plants have yellow leaves with green veins, apply chelated iron.

☐ **GET BEDS READY FOR FALL PLANTING.** Cultivate the soil at least 12 inches deep (if possible) and then work in a 2- to 3-inch layer of organic matter, such as compost, and a complete fertilizer. Rake planting beds smooth.

☐ **GROOM PLANTS.** To prolong bloom on annuals, perennials, and flowering shrubs, remove spent flowers before seeds form.

☐ **MULCH.** Add fresh mulch as needed to keep soil and roots cool, save moisture, and discourage weeds. Lay down at least 2 to 3 inches of material, and up to 5 to 6 inches around larger plants. Keep mulch several inches away from trunks so they stay dry.

☐ **PICK UP FALLEN FRUIT.** Collect decaying fruit that could harbor insects and diseases. If fruit looks suspect, toss it in the garbage; don't compost it.

☐ **PLANT OR SOW ANNUALS.** Start seeds of fall- and winter-blooming annuals, such as calendula, Iceland poppy, pansy, primrose, snapdragon, stock, and viola.

☐ **PLANT VEGETABLES.** This is the best month to plant many cool-season vegetables for fall and winter harvest. See item on page 188.

☐ Valley and foothills (zones 7–9, 14)

☐ Mountain (zones 1, 2)

☐ **WATER AS NEEDED.** Keep a close eye on maturing vegetables; letting them dry out now could ruin the harvest. Also watch newly planted seeds and container plants; they'll need frequent watering in hot weather. Rebuild soil basins around fruit trees as needed.

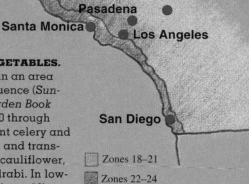

## August Checklist

■

### SOUTHERN CALIFORNIA

**CUT FLOWERS.** To groom annuals and perennials and encourage more blooms, cut fading flowers.

**DIVIDE AND PLANT BEARDED IRISES.** If you have established plants (3 years old or more), divide them now for more flowers next spring. Dig up plants, cut away old, leafless rhizomes, and replant the youngest, most vigorous divisions. If you are just starting out, look for rhizomes that begin arriving in nurseries this month. Plant them 1 to 2 feet apart in an area that gets at least a half-day of sun. In cool coastal areas, rhizome tops should show just above the soil surface. In hot areas, lightly cover tops with soil to prevent sunburn. Water immediately after planting.

**FERTILIZE ANNUALS AND VEGETABLES.** Continue feeding warm-weather performers every two to four weeks, especially if they are growing in containers.

**HARVEST VEGETABLES.** Zucchini and cucumbers should be harvested almost daily so you can enjoy them at peak flavor, and so plants will continue to produce. As you harvest tomatoes, watch for fruit-laden branches that need bracing.

**KEEP MULCHING.** Use mulch to reduce weeds, conserve moisture, and improve soil. Spread a 2- to 3-inch layer of compost or ground bark around plants, keeping it away from stems and tree trunks. Add fresh material as necessary.

**PLANT VEGETABLES.** If you live in an area with ocean influence (*Sunset Western Garden Book* climate zones 20 through 24), you can plant celery and peas from seed, and transplant cabbage, cauliflower, celery, and kohlrabi. In low-desert gardens (zone 13), sow seeds for corn and snap beans by mid-August, cucumbers by early September. In late August, start seeds of cool-season crops— such as broccoli, cabbage, cauliflower, and leaf lettuce—indoors or in an area protected from intense sun and heat. Transplant seedlings in September or October. In high-desert gardens (zone 11), sow seeds of carrots, spinach, and turnips; set out plants of cabbage, chard, kale, and lettuce; and plant potato eyes.

**PREPARE PLANTING BEDS.** After pulling up spent summer crops, prepare the beds for fall planting by turning the soil and working compost into the top several inches.

**START WINTER BEDDING PLANTS.** In coastal areas, sow seeds of calendula, Iceland poppies, nemesia, and pansy in flats for transplanting in late September.

Zones 18–21
Zones 22–24

## August Checklist
### ■
### HERE IS WHAT NEEDS DOING

## ANYWHERE IN THE WEST, TACKLE THESE CHORES:

**CARE FOR ANNUALS.** Shear or pinch off fading flowers of long-blooming annuals, then water and fertilize to encourage bloom through the end of summer.

**CHECK FOR CHLOROSIS.** If leaves are yellowish, but veins are green, apply chelated iron to correct iron deficiency (chlorosis). If leaves are simply yellowish and you can spot no insect or other problems, apply a complete fertilizer.

**DEEP-WATER TREES AND SHRUBS.** Permanent landscape plants that rely mainly on rain may need supplemental irrigation now. Water with a soaker hose, deep-root irrigator, or hose running slowly into a watering basin built around the plant.

**HARVEST FLOWERS FOR DRYING.** Pick them with long stems, strip off the leaves, bundle them together, and hang upside down indoors to dry.

**PICK RIPENING FRUIT.** By picking fruit as soon as it matures, you encourage the production of more, and thwart the rot and insects that invade over-ripe fruit.

**RUB OUT WATER SPROUTS.** Shoots that pop up along the horizontal branches of fruit trees (especially apples and pears) are easy to remove now, before they get long. Just rub them out with your thumb, or cut them out with a sharp horticultural knife.

## IN THE INTERMOUNTAIN WEST, DO THESE CHORES:

**DIVIDE PERENNIALS.** You can divide and replant bearded irises early this month, and Oriental poppies any time. Once such perennials are dug up, use the opportunity to pick out weeds that are in the beds. Amend beds with compost or peat moss before replanting.

**HARVEST HERBS.** Pick them in the morning, after dew has dried. You can use most kinds fresh. If you want to dry them, lay them on a screen in dry shade, or put them in a dehydrator.

**MAKE COMPOST.** As you pull out spent annuals and early vegetables, put them in the compost pile, keeping it well turned and watered. By frost, you'll have enough compost to dig into empty garden beds.

**PLANT IRISES AND AUTUMN CROCUS.** Iris rhizomes and autumn crocus (*Colchicum*) corms are in nurseries now. Plant immediately. The irises will flower next year, the crocus within a month.

**START VEGETABLES.** If the first killing frost doesn't come until October in your area, sow seeds of beet, carrot, spinach, and radish; crops should mature by then.

## IN THE SOUTHWEST'S LOW AND INTERMEDIATE DESERTS:

**CARE FOR LAWNS.** Mow at least weekly, cutting common Bermuda at about 1½ inches and hybrid grasses at ¾ inch. Cut zoysia and St. Augustine at 1½ to 2 inches. If you have cool-season grasses (such as fescue, Buffalo grass, and Kentucky bluegrass), cut them at 2 to 3 inches.

**CARE FOR ROSES.** To give roses a push for strong fall bloom, acidify the soil with soluble sulfur (Disper-Sul), fortify it with a complete fertilizer, and apply iron chelate to correct chlorosis. Water soil amendments in thoroughly.

**CONTROL CORN BORERS.** If translucent patches are showing up on your corn leaves, leaving them skeletonized, Southwestern corn borer larvae are the likely culprits. They can also kill the plant's growing tip. Spray plants, especially the places where leaves join the stalk, with *Bacillus thuringiensis* (BT).

**FERTILIZE SHRUBS.** After monsoon rains have come and plants perk up again, give shrubs a half-strength application of a complete fertilizer, watering it in well, to help them recover from heat stress.

**PLANT VEGETABLES.** In mild-winter areas (Phoenix and Tucson), plant beans, corn, cucumbers, squash, and tomatoes for a late harvest. Late in the month, set out transplants of beets, broccoli, cabbage, carrots, cauliflower, chard, and spinach. Mulch and shade the transplants to protect them from late summer's hot weather.

**PREVENT FRUIT SPLIT.** Citrus, melons, pomegranates, and tomatoes can split when monsoon rains or irrigation give them too much water after summer drought (their skins can't stretch enough to accommodate the extra water inside). You can minimize this problem by keeping soil evenly moist around these plants as fruits near maturity.

**PRUNE SPRING-PLANTED PEPPERS, TOMATOES.** In hot-summer, mild-winter areas, you can encourage a fall crop on many kinds of peppers and tomatoes by pruning them. Cut back tomatoes by about a third, and lightly prune peppers. Use shade-cloth to protect the newly exposed stems from sunburn. Be sure to discard any split fruit.

PETER CHRISTIANSEN

**ENGLISH VINE TRELLIS** (*64 inches tall by 29 inches wide*) *supports a potato vine* (Solanum jasminoides) *in a cottage garden brimming with perennials.*

B
LANK, VERTICAL GARDEN walls cry out for lush green vines and colorful climbers to soften stark lines. The easiest and most attractive way to support twining and vining plants is with one of the new handcrafted trellises that are available by mail. Catalogs carry an impressive array of trellises—from hand-forged metal to woven wood—that are as much a focal point for the garden as a support for plants.

The trellises are extremely simple to use. Most come ready to install: just push the feet into soil next to a wall or in a planter box, plant a vine near them, and wrap the stems around the supports (use plant ties when needed). A few need minor assembly, and two wooden ones without feet need to be anchored to a wall.

Plant low-growing vines, such as dwarf sweet peas, black-eyed Susan vine (*Thunbergia alata*), or small clematis, on the short trellises, and any taller vines on the others. Rampant growers, such as silver lace vine (*Polygonum aubertii*) and wisteria, should be used only on the large redwood trellis pictured below.

---

**WHIMSICAL TO CASUAL**

---

The woven wooden trellises bring a casual touch to the garden, while the

# Decorative trellises add charm to the garden

*Latticework frames for plants range from rustic to formal*

NORMAN A. PLATE

**ARCHITECTURAL CUPOLA** *trellis* (*54 inches tall by 15 inches wide*) *at left shows gardeners the way with the points of the compass. Redwood trellis system above (about 78 inches tall by 54 inches wide) makes a handsome foil for roses.*

METAL TRELLISES *come in many shapes and sizes (left to right): shell trellis (26 inches tall by 23 inches wide), Josephine's fountain antique trellis (62½ inches tall by 30 inches wide), architectural urn trellis (54 inches tall by 13 inches wide), Lisbon wall trellis (94 inches tall by 25 inches wide), and wrought-iron trellis screen (72 inches tall by 24 inches wide).*

metal ones are generally more formal in appearance. Choose a look that's right for your surroundings.

For a cottage garden of colorful perennials that overflow their beds, consider the English vine trellis or Palladian vine arch. The vine trellis is more secure if attached to a wall; the vine arch, which has three pieces, must be mounted to a wall by nails, screws, or hook-and-loop (Velcro) fasteners.

The reclaimed redwood trellis is part of a modular system that brings a classic French tradition to the garden. As a freestanding trellis with posts, it can be used as a backdrop for roses and perennials. Without the posts, it can be anchored to a wall (use purchased wall brackets).

The metal trellises range from whimsical architectural shapes decorated with urns or points of the compass to traditional ones like the Josephine's fountain antique trellis fashioned by an Arkansas blacksmith.

The architectural trellises, the Josephine's fountain trellis, and the shell trellis are made of steel. Each is finished slightly differently: the architectural trellises are of galvanized steel, the shell trellis is dark with a hardened oil finish, and the antique trellis—also with a hardened oil finish—has been covered with lacquer.

The wrought-iron trellis screen is finished in a dark green weather-resistant epoxy; the Lisbon trellis is of uncoated copper tubing that weathers to a handsome verdigris.

## WHERE TO GET TRELLISES

The trellises shown here can be purchased by mail from the catalogs below. Catalogs are free.

*Gardeners Eden,* Box 7307, San Francisco, Calif. 94120; (800) 822-9600. Sells the architectural trellises ($48 each) and the wrought-iron screen trellis ($78).

*The Natural Gardening Co.,* 217 San Anselmo Ave, San Anselmo, Calif. 94960; (415) 456-5060. Sells the Palladian vine arch ($95).

*Plow & Hearth,* Box 830, Orange, Va. 22960; (800) 627-1712. Sells the Lisbon wall trellis ($149).

*Smith & Hawken,* 2 Arbor Lane, Box 6900, Florence, Ky. 41022; (800) 776-3336. Sells two types of antique trellises ($85 each), the English vine trellis ($32), and components for the redwood trellis system shown ($323; other pieces available).

*Wayside Gardens,* 1 Garden Lane, Hodges, S.C. 29695; (800) 845-1124. Sells the shell trellis ($39.99). ∎

*By Lauren Bonar Swezey*

PALLADIAN VINE ARCH *trellis (60 inches tall by 36 inches wide) made from wild vines comes in three pieces and must be mounted to a wall.*

PETER CHRISTIANSEN

A MOVABLE FEAST: *Growing lettuce in a wheelbarrow allows you to rotate tender greens into or out of the sun or shade.*

PETER CHRISTIANSEN

# Lettuce in a wheelbarrow

*How a crazy idea became a reality, and why it might not be so crazy after all*

**L**ETTUCE IN A wheelbarrow? Don't look at me—it wasn't my idea. Blame it on Caroline. I didn't even plant the stuff. Blame that on Bud.

The idea evolved innocently enough from a conversation last summer with a friend named Caroline. She and her young family had recently moved into a stately old house whose gardens were in even worse shape than the gutters. All summer long the yard was in an uproar. One day, during a lull in the landscaping, I noticed a rusty old wheelbarrow filled with bushy heads of green and red leaf lettuce. The vegetable garden, it seems, was being dug up to make way for the pool.

"I'm a little worried about the vegetables," said Caroline, unable to suppress a chuckle at the collection of salad-to-go before her. "Leave 'em like that" was my typically smart-aleck response. "They look fine in a wheelbarrow."

Instantly, Caroline's wheels started turning. "If you grew lettuce in a wheelbarrow," she mused, "you could move it around to catch the afternoon sun." Sun, in fact, is a problem in her yard, which is shaded by mature redwoods and oaks.

## OKAY, BUT WHY LETTUCE? WHY A WHEELBARROW?

Enter Bud Stuckey, *Sunset*'s resident horticulturist and ace gardener. Bud quickly got into the spirit of things. He filled a beat-up wheelbarrow with potting soil and compost fertilized with fish emulsion, then planted it with various kinds of lettuces as well as endive, parsley, nasturtium, basil, and chives.

Truth told, Bud took the concept of lettuce in a wheelbarrow a whole lot more seriously than Caroline and I had. Bud's idea was to create a gourmet salad bar on wheels. Like Caroline, he considered portability a key benefit of this mobile propagation technique, although he used the wheelbarrow to roll his tender crops *out* of the harsh afternoon sun rather than into it. To foil slugs, he parked the wheelbarrow in a slightly different spot in the *Sunset* test garden each night. Gophers? No problem here, he announced with a smile. Drainage? Rust had taken care of that. And Bud knew that the short root systems of lettuces and similar plants lent themselves perfectly to the average wheelbarrow's shallow dimensions.

Meanwhile, back at my house, the family lettuce patch was producing so much that we were buying balsamic vinegar by the gallon. Unwittingly, our older son, Sam, added the final element to this mobile gardening story. As most children do, Sam took great pride in the garden he helped plant. He enjoyed the gentle act of harvesting ("Prepare to die!" he'd bellow as he hacked at the heads). Most of all, he loved washing the newly picked greens. His method was, and is, singular—a rinse with the garden hose in a child-size plastic shopping cart. After an invigorating spin around the lawn, he would pronounce the lettuce washed—and drained. Call me indulgent, but if that's all it takes to get him to eat his greens, so be it.

Now, if I could just figure out a way to make eggplant fun… ■

*By Ben Marks*

**SAM DEMONSTRATES** *his washing technique in a child-size plastic shopping cart.*

CROCUS SATIVUS *is lovely to look at—and you can harvest the stigmas for saffron, too.*

# August planting for fall color

## Bulbs breathe life into autumn gardens

LOOKING FOR A QUICK return on a garden investment? Try autumn-blooming bulbs. If you plant these bulbs in the middle of this month, you can expect to see blooms just weeks later. The refreshing flowers are a welcome lift to gardens languishing in hot, dry weather. Under the right conditions, most come back annually.

For best results, plant autumn-blooming bulbs by mid-September. If you plant later, they likely won't bloom until the following year. The bulbs require well-drained soil. Water deeply when you plant, then sparingly until the fall rains come. After that, they'll need no additional water.

Once the fall bloom is over, leaves emerge in winter and spring. The bulbs lie dormant in summer and do fine without water. In fact, too much water during dormancy may cause them to rot, so it's best to put your bulbs in among similarly unthirsty plants. If your garden requires watering in the summer and has heavy clay soil, it's a good idea to grow the bulbs in containers.

LYCORIS RADIATA *is exotic and somewhat unpredictable.*

### FOUR FOR FALL

*Colchicum (meadow saffron, autumn crocus). C. autumnale* has large crocuslike flowers in white or shades of pink and purple. The corms, which are poisonous, can bloom with or without soil or even water, although the flower colors are more intense when planted outdoors. In the ground, clusters of long-tubed flowers bloom shortly after planting, growing as much as 8 inches high and 4 inches wide. Two especially showy varieties are 'The Giant', with its lavender-to-violet flowers, and 'Waterlily', a double-petaled violet. In mild-winter areas, bulbs usually flower for only a couple of seasons.

*Crocus (fall-flowering).* These species crocus grow as tall as 5 inches and are attractive planted in clusters. The showiest is *C. speciosus,* with deep blue violet flowers; it multiplies rapidly. The variety called 'Conqueror' has blue 1½- to 2-inch flowers. The long-tubed, scented flowers of *C. goulimyi* are pale to dark purple; the bulb naturalizes especially well in Southern California. *C. kotschyanus*

(also sold as *C. zonatus*) has lilac flowers with yellow throats. Flowers of fragrant *C. karduchorum* are lilac with white throats. And *C. sativus* is the saffron crocus; harvest its orange red stigma for seasoning.

*Crinodonna (Amarcrinum).* This hybrid of *Amaryllis belladonna* and a *Crinum* species produces a cluster of pink trumpet-shaped flowers, each 4 to 5 inches wide and equally long; they bloom atop bare 2½-foot stems. The flat, straplike leaves, which make inviting runways for snails, are mostly evergreen.

*Lycoris (spider lily).* These are the most unpredictable of the autumn-blooming bulbs. Even if planted by mid-September, there's only a 50 to 75 percent chance your *Lycoris* will bloom this year. Also, the plants do well when crowded, so don't disturb the roots for several years. *L. radiata* is the most exotic of the group. It has coral red flowers, with long upward-curving stamens, that bloom in clusters on bare stems growing as tall as 1½ feet. Other flowers in this group include *L. albiflora* (white flowers on 1-foot stems), *L. aurea* (golden yellow funnel-shaped flowers on 2-foot stems), *L. sanguinea* (red flowers on 2-foot stems), *L. sprengeri* (purplish pink flowers on 2-foot stems), and *L. squamigera,* which looks like a petite *Amaryllis belladonna* (rose pink trumpet-like blooms on 2-foot stems).

### BULB SOURCES

You'll find autumn-blooming bulbs available at most garden centers and nurseries. *Colchicum* arrives this month; most others arrive in early September. With the exception of *Crinodonna* and *Crocus* 'Conqueror', they are all also available by mail order from McClure & Zimmerman, Box 368, Friesland, Wis. 53935; (414) 326-4220. Order now (catalog is free); shipping begins in late August. ∎

*By Lynn Ocone*

BLOOMING TRUMPETS *of Black Dragon lilies stand out against sprays of pink Astilbe 'Cattleya' in July.*

MICHAEL THOMPSON

# She blazes trails through floral bounty

*Lilies, roses, and perennials provide nonstop summer color in this Eugene, Oregon, garden*

I DON'T BELIEVE YOU should walk past flowers—you should walk *through* them." This, says Elizabeth Lair, is the guiding principle behind the garden she created in her backyard in Eugene, Oregon.

First, she enclosed the area with a 6-foot-high cedar fence, leaving a 5- by 20-foot space at the rear for composting (see plan on facing page). Then Lair built a toolshed at the northeast corner of the garden, where it wouldn't shade the rest of the plot. A big arbor was constructed in the garden's southwest corner to diffuse the harsh sunlight of summer afternoons. Lair added a tiny deck on the south side of the property. Then she laid out the paths of pea gravel that wind around planting islands.

## BLOOMING ISLANDS

Each of the island beds is home to a cornucopia of

DANGLING BELLS *of a perennial foxglove (Digitalis mertonensis) add a splash of color beside a path.*

plants suited to the amount of light that spot gets. The mix of plants for each bed was selected to provide continuous summer bloom.

Perhaps most interesting, Lair ignores the advice of designers who say island beds should have low growers around the edges, intermediate plants behind, and tall growers in the center. "I'll put tall growers right at the edge of the path. It adds to that feeling of walking through the plants."

In the delphinium island, the big, bold blue flower spikes stand tall in June. After their blooms fade, the delphiniums are cut back and fertilized, and the next set of spikes rises to provide a second show in August. In July and August, phlox come into flower. Throughout the summer, Asiatic hybrid and Oriental lilies pop up. And in pockets all across the island, plants like meadow rue (*Thalictrum rochebrunianum*), *Cimicifuga racemosa,* and *C. simplex* fill in with white foamy flowers on long stems.

In the bed intersected by the dry creek, roses line the path, and tall-growing impatiens (*I. glandulifera*) bolt up in summer, having self-sown from the previous year's crop. These 5-foot-tall annuals form a leafy screen for astilbe, epimedium, ferns, hostas, and other shade plants behind.

Lair loves hybrid tea roses and chooses those with big, richly colored blossoms and strong fragrance. "They never look sticklike," she explains, "because I plant bushy perennials like gypsophila next to them that grow into and through the canes and hide them." Among her favorite hybrid teas are 'Fragrant Cloud', 'Mister Lincoln', and 'Just Joey'. For shrub roses, she likes David Austin's English roses—'Abraham Darby', 'Constance Spry', and 'Fair Bianca' merit a spot where their long-blooming flowers and handsome foliage show to best advantage.

At the end of the dry creek, there's a small pond. A Japanese maple and a Japanese snowdrop tree (*Styrax japonicus*) canopy the pond to shelter a mix of moisture-loving plants including *Acorus gramineus* with its fanlike leaves, purple-stemmed taro (*Colocasia esculenta*), more astilbe, assorted ferns, digitalis, hostas,

and even sea oats (*Chasmanthium latifolium*).

Vines scramble along the fence and over two arbors. Clematis, honeysuckle, and climbing roses flower throughout the growing season.

## ORGANIC NOURISHMENT, CONSTANT CARE

Lair composts everything, and adds well-rotted dairy-cow manure bought by the truckload. As soon as a plant has finished its cycle, she cuts it back and liberally piles compost around the crown and anywhere soil shows. In March, lilies get a couple of big handfuls of cottonseed meal and a sprinkling of bone meal. Lair waters on all dry days (local water ordinance permitting) with a hose and watering wand at the base of plants (overhead watering encourages mildew).

On her daily rounds in the garden, she is never without pruners in hand. The minute a bloom fades, it's snipped off.

Plants that have grown too big are dug up and divided between late October and late February. Extra plants are moved to bare spots in the garden or given to friends or charitable plant sales. ■

*By Steven R. Lorton*

**SIDE VIEW OF PLANTER WALLS** *shows how they slope down to low benches. Stucco and brick detailing blend the walls with the house and center path.*

PETER O. WHITELEY

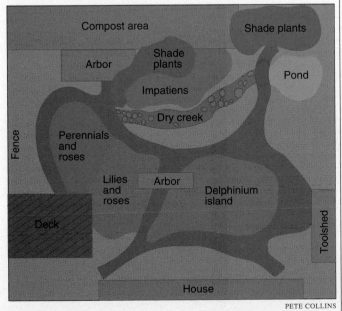

PETE COLLINS

**WINDING PATHS** *lead from the back of the house past islands and around beds of perennials and roses en route to arbors.*

# More than a garden wall

THE WALLS RUNNING ACROSS this remodeled front garden have multiple personalities. Viewed from the street, they appear to be simple, low barriers that frame the front entry walkway and serve to separate private property from a public sidewalk. Step between them, though, and you'll see they play more complex roles. The street-facing walls wrap around raised planters, then slope down from 24 inches in height to 12 inches where they become broad, brick-topped benches.

The walls are made of concrete block with a stuccoed surface. Bricks capping the walls add a contrasting color and a visual tie to the brick walkway that runs between them. The west-facing planter beds, which contain rich, well-drained soil and built-in irrigation, make ideal locations for growing flowers and vegetables.

Page Sanders of Palo Alto, California, designed the planter walls as one of a series of parallel bands of plants and paths that replaced her front lawn. They're bracketed by plant beds that run along the street and the front of the house. ■

*By Peter O. Whiteley*

**BEFORE:** *A mass of oaks and scrub blankets the steep slope below a Berkeley Hills home.*

**AFTER:** *Clearing out the brush and thinning the oaks have made the slope much more firesafe.*

# Landscaping for fire safety

*A specialist gives fire prevention tips*

I N THE IMMEDIATE aftermath of the 1991 Oakland Hills fire storm, a few types of trees were blamed for much of the disaster. Not long afterward, however, the community's emergency pre-

**PRUNING A LARGE TREE** *is a complex task and usually requires the skill of a professional arborist.*

paredness task force concluded that it's much more important to maintain yards on a regular basis and alter landscape designs than to place blame on, and remove, one or two species of trees.

Task force member and arborist Elan Shapiro, of Brende & Shapiro Tree and Shrub Care in the East Bay, has been donating hundreds of hours to educate the public on landscape fire safety. We followed him on two landscape renovation projects to learn how to make gardens more firesafe.

## ASSESSING YOUR LANDSCAPE

When Shapiro visits a landscape, the first item of business is to identify and evaluate the potential areas of fire danger. The key to a firesafe landscape is to interrupt *fire pathways* (horizontal paths of foliage that allow fires to move quickly from one plant canopy to another); eliminate *fire ladders* (arrangements of plants that provide a continuous fuel supply from the ground into the tree canopy and back); and reduce *biomass,* or *fuel load* (the leaves, bark, twigs, and branches—dead or alive—that accumulate in a plant).

"The Oakland Hills used to be oaks and grasslands but we turned it into a thick forest,"

explains Shapiro. "If we want to live here, or in other places like this, we have to maintain the plants regularly. So we're constantly trying to find a middle ground between our privacy needs, safety, and plant health. There are levels of improvement you can make in any garden—and doing something is always better than doing nothing at all."

For instance, you can prune a wide-canopied tree between houses into a fan shape to reduce the biomass, or remove a dense mass of vegetation and replace it with a stucco wall or wrought-iron fence and plant vines to cover.

Shapiro recommends avoiding measures that are too drastic, such as completely clearing a lot on a slope. If you suddenly strip out all of the plants that hold the slope in place, erosion could be a serious problem the following winter.

"The ideal situation when considering fire safety is to think in context of the entire neighborhood, which can generate a great deal of cooperation," says Shapiro. "If everyone reduces their fire hazards by 20 to 30 percent, the entire neighborhood benefits."

It's best to have an arborist come in each year. Although most trees need pruning only every two to four years, fast-growing shrubs need mainte-

nance at least annually—and you'll spread out the cost of maintenance if you prune trees in alternate years rather than all at once.

## BERKELEY SLOPE GARDEN

After a number of years without maintenance, the steep slope below the Berkeley Hills home pictured above was a dark jungle of oak trees and scrubby vegetation. To correct this severe fire hazard, Shapiro recommended clearing out most of the bushy vegetation and pruning the more than 20 trees.

First, all of the scrubby underbrush, including the Scotch broom, coyote brush, and poison oak, was removed. Next, an oak that grew under a suspended wooden deck (creating a fire ladder to the house) was cut down.

Then the crew pruned the oak branches up off the ground, cut back branches to create spaces between the trees (while maintaining their natural lines), and pruned out deadwood. Since oaks are sensitive to overpruning, they were careful not to remove more than 15 percent of the foliage (other types of trees generally tolerate having as much as 25 percent of their foliage removed).

Later, the slope will be planted with drought-tolerant,

low-flammability ground covers, such as ceanothus and wild strawberry.

## OAKLAND HILLSIDE HOME

In the Oakland garden shown below, accommodating the homeowner and maintaining privacy were as important as pruning for fire safety. The major hazards were a wall of four large pittosporums against a neighbor's garage and back fence (a fire pathway); a fire ladder formed by a dense configuration of a camellia, magnolia, and redwood against a redwood deck; and a mass of foliage between the house and the next-door neighbor's house. In addition, a huge cedar hanging over the front of the house required pruning for both fire and storm safety.

Shapiro and his crew decided to remove three of the pittosporums and to lightly thin out the remaining one so it still provides screening. To eliminate the fire ladder created by the camellia, magnolia, and redwood (shown below left), they pruned to separate the vegetation. First, the camellia was trimmed lower and the magnolia foliage was thinned on one side to balance it with the other, where it is sparse because of

overhanging redwood branches. Lightly trimming the top of the magnolia and removing the lower branches of the redwood then separated the two trees. Finally, highly flammable dead redwood leaves were cleaned out from the plants growing beneath it.

Since the next-door neighbor didn't want to lose privacy, the bay and cedar trees remain between the houses, but they were cut back about 3 feet from each house, and about 15 percent of the remaining biomass was thinned. In the front yard, the lower branches of the large cedar (which is highly flammable) were pruned about 10 feet away from the roof; the remaining branches were thinned out all along their lengths, not just at the interior part of the limbs. This prevented branches from becoming too heavy at the tips, in addition to reducing the biomass.

When pruning trees, it's important to make sure that foliage is removed all around the tree rather than just on the side where it hangs over a house, because a lopsided tree may be unstable. Also, if you prune off too many low branches, a tree will become top-heavy. ■

*By Lauren Bonar Swezey*

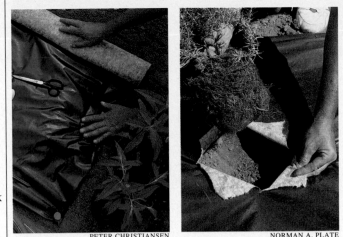

PETER CHRISTIANSEN        NORMAN A. PLATE

**UNROLL FABRIC,** *then use scissors or a knife to cut slits for plants. Tuck the flaps back in around the bases of plants.*

# Landscape fabrics screen out weeds

F EW GARDEN CHORES must be done with such irritating regularity as weeding around permanent landscape plants. But there is an alternative to chemical controls and constant labor. You can install landscape fabrics over the soil and around plants. The best of these synthetic fabrics provide a much more effective barrier to weeds than organic mulch alone.

The fabrics are made of woven polypropylene, spunbonded polyethylene, or a combination of other synthetic materials.

The denser the fabric the better it suppresses weeds. However, because the fabric is porous, it allows air, water, and nutrients in solution to reach the soil. The density and porosity of the fabric vary by manufacturer.

Landscape fabrics are best used in permanent plantings around trees and shrubs. They aren't really suited for use in beds where you change plants often (annuals and

vegetables for example).

You can install these fabrics around existing plants or cut slits in them to accommodate new plants.

## INSTALLATION

Before you install the fabric, make sure the soil is free of weeds. Eliminate them by repeated cultivations or by applying an herbicide such as glyphosate.

Wait for a calm day to install the fabric (on windy days, it will sail around).

Unroll the fabric and estimate where to cut the material. Use a sharp knife or scissors to cut slits (Xs work best), then carefully fit the fabric over or around the plant. Overlap seams by at least 3 inches to close any gaps. To anchor the outer edges of the fabric to the soil, you can use plastic pegs, nails, or heavy wire staples.

After installation, cover the fabric completely with 2 to 3 inches of a weed-free organic mulch such as shredded bark. The mulch protects the fabric from ultraviolet degradation and helps conserve soil moisture. Keep the mulch free of weeds. Use liquid fertilizer to feed plants through the fabric.

Landscape fabrics are sold in nurseries and garden supply centers. They are available in various widths and lengths; a 3-foot-wide, 50-foot roll costs about $13. ■

**BEFORE:** *A wall of pittosporums in this Oakland garden surrounds a neighbor's garage; redwood, magnolia, and camellia in the foreground create a fire ladder.*

**AFTER:** *To open up the garden, all but one pittosporum has been cut down. Pruning has separated the vegetation and broken up the fire ladder.*

PETER CHRISTIANSEN

CHINESE CABBAGES *are spaced so they barely touch when mature. The bed is framed with poured concrete capped by pressure-treated 2-by-12s.*

PHIL SCHOFIELD

# Raised beds breed success

*Cool- and warm-season vegetables thrive at the Food Garden in Vancouver, British Columbia*

**P**USHING THE LIMITS of Northwest vegetable and fruit gardening is the driving force behind the Food Garden at the University of British Columbia Botanical Garden in Vancouver. Home gardeners can harvest some good ideas during a visit.

Tucked into ¾ acre, the Food Garden is a patchwork of a dozen raised beds, each 1 foot high, 6 feet wide, and between 30 and 60 feet long. Each year in late February or early March, the staff amends the beds by spading in 21 cu-bic yards of mushroom compost. A supplement of organic fertilizer is occasionally necessary.

The cornucopia of crops begins in March when over-wintered broccoli wakes up and starts to form heads; soon, leeks, kale, and parsnips are ready for harvest. From then on, the planting schedule is brisk: peas, onions, leaf crops, and potatoes go in early, followed by tomatoes, peppers, corn, and eggplant. By early August, the garden is in full fruit and harvest is underway.

## COAXING THE MOST OUT OF WARM-SEASON CROPS

The garden achieves surprising success with warm-season crops, such as cantaloupes, that are notoriously difficult to grow near the coast. In May, the melon beds are covered with black plastic sheeting to warm up the ground. In early June, slits are cut into the plastic and seedlings of 'Earligold' cantaloupe are set in. With their roots in warm soil and their leaves receiving heat radiated by the black plastic, the plants quickly set fruit. Big, sweet melons are harvested into early autumn.

Peppers, too, flourish in the raised beds. Besides bell peppers ('Early Cal Wonder', 'Golden Bell', and 'Staddon's Select'), the garden harvests sweet peppers ('Anaheim College 64' and 'Eastern Rocket') and even hot chili peppers ('Early Jalapeno', 'TAM Jalapeno', and 'Ser-rano Red Chile'). Seed for many of these varieties comes from Territorial Seed Company in Cottage Grove, Oregon. "These seeds are developed for our cool, moist climate," says Food Garden curator Murray Kereluk.

The staff uses mostly organic gardening techniques. Soap sprays are used to control aphids, and dormant spray is applied to fruit trees to eliminate scale and overwintering pests.

One of the few problems with the raised beds is their 6-foot width. Ideally, a bed should be no wider than 4 feet so that a gardener can reach to the middle from either side.

Around the perimeter of the garden, you'll see dozens of espalier methods and a wide assortment of plants in containers. Apples, peaches, pears, cherries, and plums are trained into elaborate fences or whimsical shapes, or planted in half-barrels, demonstrating how little space it takes to grow fruit crops and how ornamental they can be.

The garden is open from 10 to 6 daily, till 7 in July and August. Entry to the Food Garden is included in admission to the 70-acre UBC Botanical Garden; fees start at $4 Canadian, with discounts for students, seniors, and ages 6 through 12.

From Provincial Highway 99 on the south side of Vancouver, exit at Marine Drive W. and follow it to the UBC campus. The UBC Botanical Garden is north of the intersection of S.W. Marine Drive and 16th Avenue. Park in the free lot and follow the path through the tunnel to the Food Garden. For information, call (604) 822-9666. ∎

*By Steven R. Lorton*

**CUT-FLOWER CROPS** *(far left) also are grown at the Food Garden; they include nasturtiums (foreground), marigolds, and hollyhocks. Paths of crushed rock 4 inches deep run between the beds and around the garden.*

202

**TWO-PART SIFTER** *has a tray with screening and a wooden frame that fits over a wheelbarrow. As tray slides back and forth, fine-textured compost sifts into wheelbarrow, ready to push to the garden.*

PETER CHRISTIANSEN

# Build a compost sifter on wheels

*It's easy to build and easy to use*

COMPOST BINS ARE a free source of the best organic material for your garden beds. Just toss in garden clippings and kitchen scraps, and soon you'll have nutrition-rich plant food. However, to get top-quality compost, you need to separate twigs, rocks, and undecomposed vegetable matter from the good stuff.

The best way to do that is to use a sifter with a wire mesh bottom. Most sifters require you to hold them up as you shake them back and forth. The wood-framed sifter shown here gets a vigorous workout in *Sunset*'s test garden, but, since it rests on a wheelbarrow, it puts little strain on backs and arms.

The sifter consists of two parts: a frame that straddles most wheelbarrows (lengthwise or sideways), and a tray with a bottom made of metal

screening. You fill the tray with material from the compost bin, slide it back and forth in the frame, and dump the leftovers from the tray after the good compost has fallen into the wheelbarrow.

## HOW TO MAKE IT

Our sifter was built with redwood, but you can use fir, cedar, or a pressure-treated wood. You'll need:

- 6 feet of 1-by-1
- 10 feet of 1-by-2
- 5 feet of 1-by-4
- 16 feet of 2-by-4
- 46 #6 2-inch drywall screws
- 8 #10 3½-inch drywall screws
- 1 2- by 3-foot piece of ½-inch-square galvanized metal screen
  Galvanized 14-gauge staples
- 2 sturdy metal handles
  Sandpaper
  Clear polyurethane
  Candle

For tools, you'll need a handsaw, combination square, drill, hammer, screwdriver, tin snips, and paintbrush.

Cut the wood according to the dimensions in the drawings. Assemble the frame by screwing the 1-by-1s flush to the bottom of the inside face of the 2-by-4s with the 2-inch screws (predrilling will help prevent splitting). Screw the two 1-by-4 crosspieces to the bottom of the 2-by-4s.

Screw the tray's 2-by-4 side and end pieces together using 3½-inch screws. Cut the screen to size with tin snips and secure it to the bottom of the 2-by-4s with galvanized staples. Screw the 1-by-2s to the tray's bottom, and screw a handle to each end.

Sand the wood surfaces and seal the frame and tray with polyurethane. The final step is to rub a candle on the bottom of the tray and the tops of the frame's 1-by-1s so the tray slides easily. ∎

*By Peter O. Whiteley, Bud Stuckey*

20¾"    36"

1x2
2x4    Screen    Handle
1x2

2x4

1x4    1x1

36"    27"

**EYE-CATCHING DISPLAY** *of cool-season spring annuals starts with planting in early fall. See page 208 for details on these colorful containers.*

# SEPTEMBER

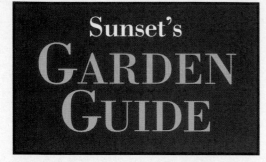

# Cooling weather, shorter days, usher in West's prime planting season

In many parts of the West, September nights can get downright frosty. But there's a way to extend the harvest of leafy vegetables: use a frost-protection structure such as the cloche pictured here. Chef Kyle Fulwiler uses it to grow lettuce and other salad greens at the governor's mansion in Olympia, Washington.

Fulwiler's salad cloche, as she calls it, is made from a sheet of 6-mil plastic stretched over arched sections of ½-inch-diameter PVC pipe. The enclosure, which covers a 4- by 30-foot raised bed, provides crops complete protection from chilly nights, and allows them to survive otherwise killing frosts. If you build a similar structure, be sure to pull back the plastic during the day, or plants will cook when the air inside heats up.

## Small daffodils with big impact

When shopping for daffodils, bigger isn't always better. Four reliable garden performers that display modest-size flowers include *Narcissus* 'Hawera', 'Jack Snipe', 'Peeping Tom', and 'Tête-à-Tête'. Look for these varieties at well-stocked nurseries or in mail-order bulb catalogs. Plant them all this fall, and you'll have two months of daffodil blooms next spring.

'Tête-à-Tête' is first to bloom in early spring, producing yellow flowers on 10-inch stems. This variety has *N. tazetta* genes, which make it a little less hardy than some of the others, but which are also the source of its wonderful fragrance.

'Peeping Tom' is another yellow kind, and starts flowering a week or two after 'Tête-à-Tête'. It grows to about 12 inches tall; blooms have no fragrance.

**TENTLIKE CLOCHE** *protects bumper crops of lettuce and other greens used in salads by chef Kyle Fulwiler. She also uses the golden petals of calendula flowers in salads.*

DON NORMARK

'**Jack Snipe'** blooms a week or two after 'Peeping Tom'. It grows to 12 inches tall, producing white-petaled flowers with yellow cups; they have no fragrance.

'**Hawera'** is the last to bloom, with fragrant, nodding yellow blossoms on 10-inch stems.

## Wildflowers: why and how to sow seeds now

Scattered in garden beds in autumn, wildflower seeds spend the winter absorbing the chill and moisture they need to germinate in spring. Those you sow now will come up days or weeks ahead of any spring-sown seeds.

To prepare a seedbed, loosen the soil with a spading fork and add soil amendment to boost organic matter. Take out the biggest rocks, then rake the area and water it well. When weeds come up, hoe them out. Then rake, water, and hoe again. When you think you've eliminated the weeds, scatter the wildflower seed, rake it in, and let nature take its course. Next spring, your biggest job will be keeping spring weeds out of the wildflowers.

You can buy wildflower seed from many suppliers. One good source that offers relatively inexpensive bulk wildflower seed in both regionalized mixes and pure lots is the Natural Gardening Company, 217 San Anselmo Ave., San Anselmo, Calif. 94960; (415) 456-5060. Catalog is free.

## A mannerly grass from the Japanese forest

Japanese forest grass (*Hakonechloa macra* 'Aureola'), pictured above, is one of the most vigorous yet well-behaved grasses that you can put in your garden. It can be grown in all Western climates.

Give it rich soil with good drainage, normal water, and a spot in light shade, and you'll

MICHAEL THOMPSON

**BRIGHTLY STRIPED** *Japanese forest grass is shown here with vine maple leaves.*

have a handsome 1-foot-high clump of bright green leaves with creamy to golden yellow stripes. Leaves pop up in April and last through the first hard frost. This grass has good manners: it forms an increasingly larger clump but doesn't become invasive as many grasses do.

Look for plants in 1-gallon cans at nurseries now. Plant immediately. This grass also does well in containers.

## Fall roundup for house plants

If your potted tropical plants have been spending their summer vacation outdoors, they should be lush and green by now. In all but the mildest regions, it's now time to move them back into the house for winter. Before you do, gather them on the patio table for a thorough checkup.

Prune out dead, damaged, or diseased leaves and stems. Then inspect the plants carefully for any insects that might have attached themselves. Cover the soil in each pot with plastic, put the plants into the shower, and rinse them thoroughly with lukewarm water, washing the dust off the stems and tops and undersides of all the leaves.

Take the plants back outside to dry, then treat those that have insect infestations with an insecticide (if you use insecticidal soap, dilute it

207

with distilled water). After plants have been treated and dried, bring them indoors and put them in a bright spot.

## Cool-season bloomers in pots

For the biggest show of flowers in spring, there's no better time to plant cool-season annuals than in early fall. You can plant them in the garden or in containers. The 20-inch pots shown on page 204 are stuffed with colorful combinations of orange, red, and pink schizanthus; orange and yellow snapdragons; antique shades of pansies; and white sweet alyssum.

To plant, fill containers with a good potting soil. Start with sixpacks of annuals and select ones that aren't root-bound. Stuff plants about 4 to 6 inches apart in pots—much closer than you'd plant them in the ground. Since plants will be competing for root space, water the containers often to keep the soil moist and fertilize regularly. This coming winter and next spring, you'll be rewarded with a dramatic display of blooms.

## A guide to discouraging deer

When you see a family of deer munching grass in a wild meadow, it's easy to look at them and say, "Gee, they're cute." But when deer browse in your garden, you're more likely to exclaim, "Oh no, my roses!"

There are ways to discourage deer from feeding in your garden. Nurseryman Bob Tanem, drawing on 30 years of gardening experience and research throughout California, has published a guide called *Deer Resistant Planting*. This 16-page booklet lists 75 trees, 121 shrubs, 85 perennials, and 18 annuals that deer almost never eat or rarely eat, or that are noted because established plantings have been observed in areas with heavy deer traffic. Tanem also offers advice on

how to keep deer out of small vegetable and rose gardens.

To order a copy, send $5.95 to Bob Tanem, 273 N. San Pedro Rd., San Rafael, Calif. 94903.

## Great gardener tells all

If you enjoyed Allen Lacy's garden columns in the *Wall Street Journal* or the *New York Times,* you'll be delighted to know that this gifted writer is now publishing his own garden newsletter, *Homeground.*

This 16-page quarterly is an eclectic compilation of gardening, tool, and plant notes; quotes; and extensive book reviews. It's well illustrated with drawings and black-and-white photographs. Lacy writes most of the text, but he includes articles by other writers as well.

You can subscribe to *Homeground* for $38 per year, or get a sample copy for $10. Send a check payable to Allen Lacy's *Homeground,* Box 271, Linwood, N.J. 08221.

## Good news for water conservation in California

Another summer has nearly passed, and you've done your utmost to limit water waste. If you're wondering what more you can do to conserve water, help is on the way. Come November 8, graywater use will be legal in all California communities (it's already legal in some).

Graywater is the term for water reclaimed from showers, bathtubs, sinks, and washing machines. Since most residences produce 20 to 40 gallons of graywater per person each day, using it to irrigate the landscape can mean significantly less water consumption (and lower water bills).

In the meantime, you can get information on graywater rules and collection methods by calling the California Department of Water Resources

at (916) 327-1620. Ask to be put on the mailing list to receive future publications.

## New method for planting trees

Not so long ago, planting a tree called for digging a hole 6 inches wider and deeper than the rootball and mixing amendments such as peat moss into the soil. Because these practices were implicated in the declining health of trees, American Forests has developed new guidelines for tree planting.

The new method is recommended for all trees but is particularly suited to those planted around newly constructed homes where earth-moving equipment has compacted the soil.

First, choose a species that is suitable for your climate and a specimen that is in good health. Select an appropriate site, in sun or shade, that allows plenty of room for the tree to grow.

Dig a planting area the same depth as the tree's rootball and three to five times the diameter of the rootball, assuming there's sufficient space and other plants will not be disturbed.

Score the sides of the rootball to prevent circling roots. Set the rootball in the center of the planting area and fill in around it with existing soil (no amendments are needed). Gently pat—but don't overpack—the soil. Use water, not your feet, to settle the soil.

Rake the soil to level it, and cover with 4 to 6 inches of mulch, such as wood chips or leaf mold (replenish mulch annually). Don't wrap the trunk with protective tape.

Stake the tree only if you live in a very windy area. If staked, make sure the tree can sway in the wind; movement encourages strong trunk development. Remove stake and ties after one year.

If your soil is not compacted, Richard Harris, professor emeritus at UC Davis

and author of *Arboriculture: Integrated Management of Landscape Trees, Shrubs, and Vines,* says digging a planting hole twice the diameter of the rootball is adequate. However, new houses built on former agricultural land may be sitting on a plow pan—a compacted 1- to 2-inch layer of soil 8 to 12 inches below the soil surface. According to Harris, this layer should be broken up with a shovel before planting.

## Sow some winter greens

It's very satisfying to go into the garden in the dead of winter and harvest a crop of fresh greens. If you'd like to do that this winter, now is your last chance to get leaf crops going. Early this month, weed and cultivate planting beds and enrich with organic matter. Then sow seeds of chard, kale, mustard, and spinach, as well as beets and turnips for their greens. Germination is tricky in hot, dry weather. Keep the seed bed moist by watering daily, then keep the water coming if the weather remains dry. When fall arrives, these crops will be well established, ready to flourish in the damp chilly weather they love.

Here are some varieties to try; the initials following the name are keyed to seed sources that follow the list.

*Beet:* 'Lutz Green Leaf' (WAB).

*Kale:* 'Red Russian' (NG), 'Siberian' (TS).

*Mustard:* 'Red Giant' (NG), 'Tah Tsai' (TS).

*Spinach:* 'Cold Resistant Savoy' (SS), 'Olympia F1' (TS).

*Swiss chard:* 'Fordhook Giant' (SS, TS, WAB), 'Silverado' (SS).

*Turnip:* 'Shogoin' (NG, TS).

**Seed sources:**

**NG** Nichols Garden Nursery, 1190 N. Pacific Highway, Albany, Ore. 97321; (503) 928-9280.

**SS** Stokes Seeds Inc., Box

548, Buffalo, N.Y. 14240; (905) 688-4300.

**TS** Territorial Seed Company, Box 157, Cottage Grove, Ore. 97424; (503) 942-9547.

**WAB** W. Atlee Burpee & Co., 300 Park Ave., Warminster, Pa. 18991; (800) 888-1447.

## New directory of Northwest garden sources

Where can you find a stone lion's head, a yellow-flowering magnolia, or salal grown from seed? Tracking down certain garden materials, plants, and seeds can be frustrating. Now Nan Booth Simpson has produced a book to ease your detective work: *Great Garden Sources of the Pacific Northwest* (TACT, Portland, 1994; $15.95).

Simpson, a landscape architect and native Texan, moved to the Northwest five years ago. She was overwhelmed by the availability of good things for Northwest gardeners. So she catalogued them in an informative, easy-to-use directory.

In its pages, you'll find nurseries that specialize in Northwest natives, a chapter on edible landscapes (including where to find the fruits, berries, and nuts to go in them), sources for alpine plants, garden furniture, and ornaments, even a listing of public gardens to visit.

You can find this guide in bookshops and many garden centers, or you can order it from the publisher: TACT, Box 25211, Portland, Ore. 97225; (503) 297-0873. Add $2 for postage and handling.

## Landscape with unthirsty plants

In California's Central Valley, September marks the beginning of prime planting season for permanent landscape plants. Keep water conservation in mind when you select plants. Keith Morse, owner of the Fresno garden pictured

SCOTT ANGER

**WATER-THRIFTY FRONT YARD** *in Fresno, California includes a drift of pink Mexican evening primrose, a dry streambed, yellow santolina, and a chitalpa tree.*

above, replaced his front lawn with a water-thrifty landscape designed by Gary Jones of Good Earth Landscaping. Morse was tired of mowing weekly and watching irrigation water run down the gutters, so Jones recontoured the yard to improve drainage, added a "dry streambed" of stones, and planted an array of colorful but unthirsty plants. Jones chose blue oat grass, California fuchsia, Mexican evening primrose, *Salvia greggii* (see item on page 212), santolina, and yarrow,

as well as a selection of culinary herbs including lemon thyme and lavender. For shade, he planted two chitalpa trees (a hybrid of catalpa and desert willow).

## How tuna can catch earwigs

An earwig's lifestyle makes it an easy critter to trap. Feeding mostly at night, the earwig chews on dahlia flowers and soft fruits and eats notches out of leaves (it also feeds on some insect pests). During the

day, it hides out in cool, moist places—under boards, clods of dirt, or plant foliage. The common method of trapping earwigs is to place rolled-up newspapers in the garden at night, let the pests congregate in the papers in the morning, and then dispose of them during the day.

Another method of trapping earwigs is suggested by Mary Louise Flint, author of the University of California's *Pests of the Garden and Small Farm, A Growers Guide to Using Less Pesticide.* In her

Sacramento garden, Flint puts out several empty, shallow tuna or cat food cans filled with about ¼ inch of vegetable oil. The fishy odor attracts the earwigs, which fall into the oil and drown. Every few days, she dumps out the bugs and refills the cans. If the cans you use don't smell fishy, add a few drops of bacon grease to the oil.

## Plant now for winter-through-summer blooms

Mid-September marks the beginning of the fall planting season in many parts of the West. And if you plant the right combinations this fall, your garden can bloom from winter through summer. Pam Morgan of Pasadena, California, knows this. Her garden, (shown at right) in spring, combines annuals, perennials, and flowering shrubs; all thrive when fall planted.

Because heat-loving perennials such as coreopsis and pink penstemon are in a lull during winter, Morgan plants cool-season annuals in the fall. Bachelor's buttons, pansies, sweet alyssum, lobelia, English daisies, and Iceland poppies interspersed with *Linaria macrocarpa* fill gaps in the bed with clouds of color. The blue and purple bachelor's buttons are prized for their height, while the English daisies are one of Morgan's favorite low-growers. In late spring, as the perennials fill out the bed and come into bloom, Morgan starts pulling out the annuals, which by then are declining.

Shrubs add dimension to the bed, as well as provide consistent color through the seasons. Ceanothus blooms from late winter into early spring, lavatera peaks in late spring, and blue hibiscus and anisodontea bloom practically year-round.

With so many flowers coming in and out of bloom, deadheading is the most frequent gardening task. Some of the profuse bloomers, including

GREY CRAWFORD

**THE SECRETS** *of the winter-to-summer blooms in Pam Morgan's garden are fall planting and flowering shrubs.*

coreopsis and scabiosa, look best with weekly, or even daily, clipping during spring and summer. Other perennials, such as penstemon and heliotrope, need only occasional deadheading.

## Try neem oil to control pests on ornamentals

Neem oil, derived from the neem tree (*Azadirachta indica*), is what is called a "biorational" pesticide: it has low toxicity to mammals and does not persist in the environment. It is effective against many insect pests, including aphids, caterpillars, loopers, mealybugs, thrips, and whiteflies, as well as diseases such as mildew and rust.

Although neem oil has been used in other states for several years now, the Cali-

fornia EPA Department of Pesticide Regulation has only recently approved the use of neem on ornamental plants.

Neem targets insects at several stages, but its primary function is as an insect growth inhibitor, preventing insects from reaching maturity. Neem is also somewhat effective against adult insects as an antifeedant (preventing feeding so insects starve to death) and a repellent. It's best to alternate insecticidal soap or pyre-thrum with the neem spray; this gives you an effective way to kill insects in two stages of development. Neem should be applied two to three times in succession, every 7 to 10 days, or possibly every 3 to 4 days for heavy infestations.

Safer's BioNEEM liquid concentrate costs $9.99 for 8 ounces, $19.99 for 16 ounces,

and $33.99 for 32 ounces. Mix 6⅔ tablespoons concentrate with 1 gallon water. The product is available at many nurseries and garden supply stores; if you can't find it, call Ringer Corporation at (800) 654-1047 for a local supplier.

## Digger pine has its own climate zone, but does it belong in your garden?

With its lacy silver needles and forked trunk, the digger pine (*Pinus sabiniana*), also called gray or foothill pine, is native to the foothills of California. The tree is identified with climate zone 7 of the *Sunset Western Garden Book.* This zone surrounds the Central Valley, and is also called California's Digger Pine Belt.

A fast-growing tree of undeniable beauty, the digger pine tolerates drought, thriving on dry hillsides where few other trees will grow.

If you have the right spot, it's worth planting. Reaching 40 to 50 feet high, digger pine is best planted with other natives in large gardens. It is known for weak wood and breaking limbs.

You can buy container-grown digger pines from nurseries that offer native plants. The trees are also easy to grow from seed sown in fall: Just pick up a recently fallen cone that's still closed, put it in a warm, dry place (next to a heater, for example) until it opens, then pick out the seeds. Sow seeds directly in the ground; protect them from rodents with a screen cage, and let winter rains do the rest.

## Let the sun weed your garden

If you're planning to sow wildflower seeds later this fall (see item on page 207), soil solarization is a good non-chemical way to clear your landscape of weeds. Soil solarization is a process in which the sun's heat is trapped under sheets of clear plastic. The top 2 to 6 inches of soil bakes, killing weeds, weed seeds, and disease organisms.

Soil solarization is most effective at controlling cool-season weeds and grasses. It weakens rhizomatous grasses like Bermuda, but may not eliminate them. Occasionally, a plant such as white clover will thrive under the plastic. The process also controls many soil organisms harmful to plants, including fusarium and verticillium fungi.

Start cooking now while there's still plenty of sun and the days are hot. If the average maximum temperature in your area hovers between 85° and 90°, the process takes about six to eight weeks. If it's cooler, allow eight to ten weeks.

Begin by tilling or cultivating the plot. Break up clods, remove rocks, and level the soil. Work in amendments and compost if needed. Moisten to a depth of 1 foot, and then cover the area with clear plastic sheets (preferably UV stabilized so they won't break down) or with bubble plastic. Smooth out the plastic so it makes contact with the soil at edges; this helps keep it from flapping in the wind. Bury the edges of the plastic in 4-inch-deep trenches. Bubble plastic resists wind better than sheet plastic.

If you want to use sheet plastic (it's cheaper) in windy areas, it may be necessary to lay soil-filled plastic sandwich bags or some other weight on top of the sheets to help hold them down. When you remove the plastic, work only the top several inches of soil so you don't churn up viable weed seeds below.

### The victory garden grows again—in Portland

Immediately after World War I, the victory garden became a symbol of American spirit when citizens were asked to dig in and grow food for Europe's hungry.

When the United States entered World War II, the Department of Agriculture urged citizens to return to their gardens. The rationale was simple: if the home front could feed itself, industry could send more food overseas to U.S. soldiers and sailors. Americans responded to the call with patriotic zeal: by 1943, more than 30 percent of all fresh vegetables consumed in the U.S. came from some 20 million small home plots, school lots, or similar spaces.

Today, you can see a functioning model of a victory garden in the courtyard of the Oregon History Center in Portland. The exhibit, which opened on June 6—the 50th anniversary of D day—is called *Home Front: Oregon in World War II*.

The garden was designed to be space-efficient, highly productive, and, as one of the creators puts it, "as filling to the spirit as it is to the stomach." Vegetables such as cabbage, carrots, chard, tomatoes, and peppers (in four colors) fill the rows. The summer garden will flourish through this month, then the late-season garden will be planted and maintained by volunteers. Produce is harvested and given to agencies that feed Portland's hungry.

The Oregon History Center is at 1200 S.W. Park Avenue in downtown Portland. It's open 10 to 5 Tuesdays through Saturdays, noon to 5 Sundays. Admission costs $4.50, with discounts for seniors, students, and children.

### Aquasocks for puttering

Most gardeners have two kinds of gardening shoes: clodhoppers for mowing, spading, and other heavy work; lighter shoes, like sneakers, for weeding and puttering around the garden. Bainbridge Island, Washington, gardener Joe Sullivan has the perfect puttering footwear. He dons aquasocks, the slip-ons used by divers and windsurfers.

Light and easy to get on and off, they wash easily and dry out quickly when wet. They conform to your feet and have a treaded rubber sole, so you don't slip around as you walk on pavement or wet lawn. Sullivan normally wears his aquasocks over bare feet. But if the weather is cold or he's working in a spot where there are sticks or stones, he slips them over a pair of heavy wool socks.

A pair of aquasocks costs from $10 to $40. You can buy them at shops that sell athletic gear or at most larger department stores.

### Flowering perennials that hug the ground

Gardeners looking for low-growing, long-blooming perennials will appreciate *Diascia vigilis* and Santa Barbara daisy (*Erigeron karvinskianus*). You can plant both this month.

*Diascia* is a South African native with attractive, ½-inch-wide, light pink flowers that appear on the ends of sprawling stems that turn up about 6 inches as flowers develop. The biggest show is in spring, but flowers will appear all summer if old flowers are cut off after bloom.

***Santa Barbara daisy*** is a vigorous perennial with dainty ¾-inch pinkish or pur-plish white flowers. The 10- to 20-inch-tall trailing plant spreads rapidly to about 2 feet, making it a great filler between larger shrubs and perennials. Santa Barbara daisy self-sows readily; if seedlings aren't removed, you'll have a pretty ground cover popping up around the garden.

Both plants prefer full sun and moderate to little water. Diascia dies in winter if planted in heavy, wet soil.

Santa Barbara daisy is available at most nurseries. *D. vigilis* is a little harder to find; more widely available is its cousin *D.* 'Ruby Field', which has darker flowers and smaller leaves.

### Vegetable seed paradise in downtown Stockton

Walking into Lockhart Seeds in Stockton, California, is like stepping back in time. Sacks of bulk seed crowd the floor, and bins stretch from floor to ceiling; each is labeled with an old-fashioned seed packet. Behind the long front counter, friendly faces await your questions. This is a vegetable gardener's paradise.

Lockhart Seeds has been in business for about 47 years, and is one of the last true seed stores left in the West. The firm specializes in vegetable varieties adapted to the Cali-

K. BRYAN SWEZEY

**LOW-GROWING PERENNIALS:** *Pink-flowered Diascia vigilis and Santa Barbara daisy clamber over a boulder. Design: Maile Arnold, Sebastopol, California.*

## Tool of the Month

*Digging into clay soil or spading down into root-filled soil is easier with the sharp-toothed Super Shovel. It's made of 13-gauge carbon spring steel for hardness and flexibility and has a wooden handle that's available in two lengths: short (26 inches) or long (48 inches). The shovel costs $29.95 plus $6 shipping and handling; order from Super Shovel, Inc., 9471 Alberta Rd., Richmond, B.C., Canada V6Y1T7.*

fornia's Central Valley. If you're planning to plant cool-season crops, the store is worth a visit. But if you can't stop by, write or call for their mail-order catalog. It lists a tantalizing array of broccoli (10 kinds), cabbage (14 kinds), carrots (6 kinds), and lettuce (20 kinds), as well as herbs and grasses.

The store is at 3 North Wilson Way in downtown Stockton. Hours are 8 to 5 weekdays, 8 to 1 Saturdays. For a catalog, write or call Lockhart Seeds, Box 1361, Stockton 95201; (209) 466-4401. Minimum mail-order purchase is $10.

## This buddleia's for you

With a musky fragrance and a floriferous habit, buddleia is known for its ability to attract butterflies—it's commonly called butterfly bush. New introductions and newly available old-timers seem to be fluttering forth like the migrating insects these deciduous shrubs were named for. Offerings go way beyond the handsome but standard old purplish blue cones of blossom that you sometimes see along a country road. Most are varieties of *Buddleia davidii.* Look for 'African Queen' (rich lavender scented flowers), 'Black Knight' (deep, dark purple), and, colored as their names imply, 'Pink Delight', 'Purple Prince', 'Glasnevin Blue', and 'White Bouquet'.

During summer, nurseries sell blooming buddleias in 1- to 5-gallon cans. All the varieties named here are available from Heronswood Nursery, 7530 288th St. N.E., Kingston, Wash. 98346. Catalog costs $3.

Buy plants while they're blooming, slip them into decorative containers, and display on a deck or near an entry. Keep plants well watered. Buddleias tolerate drought, but if you let them go dry, especially when they're confined to a container, you'll shorten the bloom period. When autumn arrives and plants head into dormancy, transplant them to beds where they'll get sun or light shade.

## Shopping time for salvias

The genus *Salvia* includes many herbs, California natives, and colorful flowering perennials. Most thrive in hot-summer climates and require little water. September is an ideal month to shop for and plant salvias, since many will be in bloom. Here are some best bets.

*Salvia greggii* is near the top of most lists of favorite flowering perennials. It's an airy, shrublike plant that reaches 3 to 4 feet tall, producing long spikes of small flowers in shades of pink, red, crimson, light yellow, or white. It blooms in spring and fall.

*S. farinacea* (mealy-cup sage) is often sold as an annual, but it may overwinter where frosts are light, producing dark blue or white flowers on 2- to 3-foot-tall plants.

*S. leucantha* (Mexican bush sage) is a graceful, arching perennial with white or purple flowers on long, velvety purple spikes. It grows 3 to 4 feet tall and at least as wide. If spent flowers are cut off, Mexican bush sage will bloom from summer into late fall.

*S. officinalis* (garden sage) is a popular cooking herb as well as an ornamental plant. It grows 1 to 2 feet tall and produces dark blue flowers. 'Tricolor' has purple and white foliage; 'Icterina' has yellow and green leaves.

With the exception of *S. officinalis,* these salvias are not reliably hardy above the 1,500-foot elevation.

## Choosing a caretaker for your trees

A good arborist offers a wide range of services, including pest and disease control, pruning, bracing, and fertilizing. If the trees in your landscape show signs of stress or disease, an arborist can diagnose the problem and often help correct it. Since trees can be worth thousands of dollars in replacement costs (to say nothing of their sentimental value), it pays to shop for the right caretaker. Here are a few suggestions to help you find a competent arborist.

• Don't be swayed by door-to-door solicitation. A good reputation is the best indicator. Talk with neighbors and nurseries to get recommendations. If you have a city arborist, call for referrals.

• Check the person's work for yourself. If possible, visit the homes of former clients.

• Get at least three estimates. Talking with different candidates will give you a better understanding of the tasks at hand, the individuals' capabilities, and reasonable prices.

• Be wary of arborists who suggest topping trees; this practice is rarely called for and usually does more harm than good.

• Consider credentials. The International Society of Arboriculture (ISA) offers a voluntary certification program. A certified arborist must have at least three years' experience, pass a comprehensive examination, and participate in continuing education. Certification does not guarantee an outstanding arborist, but it does indicate a serious professional. To find a certified arborist in your area, call the ISA's Western chapter at (602) 955-5315.

• Select an arborist who is insured and offers proof of coverage for personal injury, property damage, and liability.

## Sunscreen for soaker hoses

Summer sun is a soaker hose's worst enemy. The sun's ultraviolet light can cause a hose to deteriorate in a few years; the warmer the climate, the faster a hose will crack. One soaker hose manufacturer, Aquapore Moisture Systems, has just received a patent for a UV inhibitor that protects the soaker hose from sun damage and extends its life.

Aquapore's Moisture Master hoses are composed of 65 percent recycled tire rubber and 35 percent polyethylene. The recycled rubber contains carbon black, a natural UV inhibitor. A UV stabilizer is added to the polyethylene. Aquapore guarantees its products for seven years.

Moisture Master hoses are sold at many garden and home improvement centers. If you can't find them, you can call the manufacturer at (800) 635-8379 for the retail outlet nearest you.

*By Steven R. Lorton, Jim McCausland, Lynn Ocone, Bud Stuckey, Lauren Bonar Swezey, Lance Walheim*

## September Checklist

### ■

### PACIFIC NORTHWEST

**BUY AND PLANT BULBS.** Spring-flowering bulbs, including daffodils and tulips, will show up in nurseries soon after Labor Day. Shop early to get the best selection. Plant bulbs immediately after purchase so they won't dehydrate.

**COMPOST.** Start a new pile with the prunings, spent annuals, and vegetable waste you take from your garden this month. Turn and water your existing pile.

**DIVIDE IRIS.** Pacific Coast native iris can be dug this month, divided, and replanted. Use a sharp knife to cut plants apart. Replant at once and water well. Early next spring, you can scatter a light application of a complete granular fertilizer around each plant.

**FEED, MOW, AND OVERSEED LAWNS.** Grass lawns surge into active growth in early fall, and they need food: apply about a pound of actual nitrogen per 1,000 square feet of turf. Mow regularly to keep grass from looking shaved and brown.

To overseed lawns, first rough up bare spots with a rake. Scratch in grass seed; a good blend for the Pacific Northwest contains perennial ryegrass, fine fescue, and perhaps some bent grass and Kentucky bluegrass to provide a quick cover and prevent erosion. Cover the seeded area with mulch and water well, and don't let the surface soil dry out.

**KEEP ON FUSSING WITH FUCHSIAS.** Continue to clip back faded blossoms, snip off errant shoots, water, and keep up with your regular feeding program.

**MULCH.** As cold weather becomes a threat to marginally hardy plants, weed around them thoroughly, then apply a layer of mulch such as compost. The mulch helps insulate the roots and minimizes soil erosion.

**SHOP FOR BERRY COLOR.** Trees, shrubs, and ground covers with handsome fall berries abound in nurseries this month and next. Shop for plants now and set in the ground immediately.

**TEND ROSES.** Cutting roses at this time of year means pruning. Remove stems just above a five-leaflet branch. Shape the plant as you cut. Also, let a few roses form hips (seed pods) late this month. Hips encourage the plant to head into dormancy, they are ornamental, and many of the smaller kinds make good winter food for birds.

**WATER.** Be especially attentive to plants that may dry out quickly: those growing in pots and under eaves.

**WINTERIZE GREENHOUSES.** Before frost threatens, clean out seedbeds and flats. Check heating vents, watering systems, glass or plastic windows and panels, and examine weather-stripping.

## September Checklist

### NORTHERN CALIFORNIA

**CARE FOR LAWNS.** Late September is a good time to renovate bluegrass, fescue, and ryegrass lawns. Dethatch, aerate, fertilize with a complete lawn fertilizer, and water well. If you need to reseed bare patches, prepare the area by digging in organic matter, then firm down the soil, water well, scatter seed, and cover lightly with mulch. Water several times a day to keep the seed moist; cut back water when new grass is well rooted.

**CHECK FOR SPIDER MITES.** These tiny pests suck juices from plant leaves, causing stippling; tiny white eggs on the undersides of leaves and fine webbing may also be noticeable. Control infestation by spraying the tops and undersides of leaves thoroughly with a lightweight horticultural oil or insecticidal soap, following label instructions.

**CONTROL POWDERY MILDEW.** This white, powdery disease infects many vegetables and plants including dahlias, roses, and zinnias. Spray foliage with a mix of 2 teaspoons baking soda, 2 teaspoons lightweight horticultural spray oil, and 1 gallon water (reapply to new plant growth); or dust with sulfur at first sign of mildew. Sulfur can damage some melons and squash; test by dusting a leaf and waiting a few days. Do not apply sulfur to roses when temperatures will exceed 90°.

**DIVIDE PERENNIALS.** Now through October is the time to divide many perennials, such as agapanthus, candytuft, coreopsis, daylilies, and penstemon, that are either overgrown or not flowering well. Perennials can also be divided to increase the number of plants. Use a spading fork or shovel to lift and loosen clumps. With the shovel or a sharp knife, cut clumps into sections through soil and roots. Replant sections in well-amended soil; keep moist.

**PLANT ANNUALS.** To get cool-season annuals off to a good start so they bloom this winter and early next spring, plant after midmonth in zones 15, 16, and 17, at month's end in zone 14. If the weather is hot, shade new seedlings temporarily. Keep the soil moist. Set out calendula, forget-me-nots, larkspur, Iceland and Shirley poppies, ornamental cabbage and kale, pansies, primrose, snapdragon, stock, sweet peas, toadflax, and violas. In coastal areas, plant cineraria, nemesia, and schizanthus.

**PLANT VEGETABLES.** Set out seedlings of broccoli, cabbage, cauliflower, lettuce, and spinach. Sow seeds of beets, carrots, leeks, onions, peas, radishes, and turnips.

Coastal (zone 17)

Inland (zones 14–16)

**PREPARE TO LANDSCAPE.** Before planting a lawn or a bed of flowers or vegetables, prepare the soil. Use a rotary tiller or dig the soil, add plenty of compost or other organic matter, and mix in a complete fertilizer, if necessary. If the area is weedy, water to sprout weed seeds, then hoe them down.

**SET OUT PERMANENT PLANTS.** September marks the beginning of the fall planting season. Nurseries should be well stocked with a variety of trees, shrubs, ground covers, and vines (wait until spring to plant frost-tender plants such as bougainvillea and citrus).

## September Checklist

■

### CENTRAL VALLEY

☐ **BUY SPRING-BLOOM-ING BULBS.** Buy early to get top-quality bulbs. Plant anemone, crocus, daffodils, Dutch iris, freesia, homeria, ixia, leucojum, lycoris, oxalis, ranunculus, scilla, sparaxis, tritonia, and watsonia. Buy hyacinths and tulips now but wait to plant; their bulbs need chilling in the refrigerator for at least six weeks before planting. Do this by placing bulbs in a well-ventilated paper bag in the crisper section, away from apples.

☐ **CARE FOR LAWNS.** After a dry summer, cool-season lawns such as bluegrass, fescue and ryegrass can be renovated. Renovation removes thatch, improves water penetration, and invigorates the turf. Dethatch, aerate, and apply a complete fertilizer.

☐ **CHECK FOR WILDFIRE HAZARDS.** September is peak wildfire season in the foothills. Check your property to identify hazards and reduce the potential fuel load. Make sure you have a 30- to 100-foot defense zone around your home. Cut branches back to 15 to 20 feet from the house. Trim tree limbs so they're at least 20 feet above the ground; prune out dead limbs. Remove dead plants and cut back field grasses. Clear leaf litter from the ground, rooftop, and gutters. If there's sufficient water, keep plants close to the house moist until the weather cools.

☐ **CONTROL MITES.** Discourage spider mites by keeping plants clean and free of dust (a strong spray from a hose works). Or spray with insecticidal soap or lightweight horticultural oil according to label directions.

☐ **DIVIDE PERENNIALS.** Now through October is a good time to divide many perennials that are crowded or not flowering well. Dividing is also a good way to increase plants such as agapanthus, candytuft, coreopsis, daylilies, Mexican evening primrose, and penstemon. Use a spading fork to lift and loosen the clumps. With a sharp knife, cut sections through soil and roots of plants. Replant divisions in well-amended soil; keep moist.

☐ **FERTILIZE.** Make sure fall-planted vegetables get the nutrients they need: apply a complete fertilizer at planting time; follow up with another dose in three to four weeks.

☐ **MAKE AND USE COMPOST.** As summer flowers and vegetables give way to fall plantings, add debris to a new compost pile for amending soil next spring.

☐ **PLANT ANNUALS.** Get winter flowers going now: they'll bloom better during the upcoming cool weather and next spring. After midmonth, sow seeds of California poppy, clarkia, and *Dimorphotheca*. Set out transplants of calendula, Iceland poppy, larkspur, pansy, primrose, snapdragon, stock, and viola. If weather is hot, shade new seedlings temporarily.

☐ **PLANT PERENNIALS.** After summer heat subsides, plant campanulas, candytuft, coreopsis, delphinium, dianthus, foxglove, gaillardia, geum, Mexican evening primrose, penstemon, phlox, salvia, and yarrow.

☐ **PLANT VEGETABLES.** There's still time to plant most cool-season vegetables. Set out transplants of broccoli, cabbage, cauliflower, chard, kohlrabi, and lettuce. Sow seeds of beets, carrots, lettuce, onions, peas, radishes, spinach, and turnips.

☐ **PREPARE TO PLANT.** Clean planting areas and cultivate, adding soil amendments and a complete fertilizer if necessary. Before planting, water soil to sprout weed seeds, then hoe the young weeds.

☐ **WATER.** September can be one of the hottest, driest months. Watch plants for signs of water stress, especially container plants, which dry out quickly.

▨ Valley and foothills (zones 7–9, 14)

▨ Mountain (zones 1, 2)

Redding

Lake Tahoe

Sacramento

Fresno

Bakersfield

**PLANT BULBS FOR SPRING COLOR.** In coastal and inland areas (*Western Garden Book* climate zones 22, 23, and 24 and 18 through 21, respectively), daffodils, Dutch irises, freesias, homeria, ornamental oxalis (also called shamrock), ornithogalum, sparaxis, spring star flower (*Ipheion uniflorum*), and watsonia are in nurseries this month. Plant Dutch irises and daffodils in October; plant the others as soon as you can. In the high desert (zone 11), it's time to plant anemones, crocus, daffodils and other narcissus, Dutch irises, freesias, hyacinths, ranunculus, scillas, and tulips.

**PLANT FOR WINTER-SPRING COLOR.** Cool-season annuals appear in nurseries in coastal, inland, and low desert (zone 13) areas in mid- to late September. Start early for blooms from Thanksgiving through April. After midmonth (mid-October in the low desert), set out seedlings of these annuals: calendula, candytuft, Iceland poppy, nemesia, pansy, snapdragon, stock, and sweet alyssum. Also set out biennials or perennials treated as annuals: delphinium, English daisy, foxglove, sweet William, and viola. A heat wave could stress or kill new plants; shade and water them well. In the high desert, annuals appear in nurseries in early September, but selection is more limited.

**PLANT (OR SOW) COOL-SEASON VEGETABLES.** In coastal and inland gardens, when weather cools, set out seedlings of broccoli, brussels sprouts, cabbage, cauliflower, celery, chives, kale, and parsley. Sow seeds for beets, chard, chives, collards, kale, kohlrabi, parsnips, peas, radishes, spinach, and turnips. Plant garlic, onions, and shallots. In the low desert, when temperatures drop below 100°, sow seeds of beets, carrots, celery, green onions, kale, leaf lettuce, leeks, parsley, parsnips, peas, potatoes, radishes, spinach, and turnips. Sow lettuce and cole crops in flats or in containers to transplant in October. In warm areas of the high desert, such as Las Vegas, plant all cool-season crops listed for low desert. In cooler areas, plant lettuce and spinach seeds or plants, and radish seeds.

**PROTECT PLANTS FROM WIND.** Santa Ana winds usually blow this month. Take down hanging baskets to protect them from drying out in the hot winds. Support young trees with strong stakes and ties that don't girdle trunks.

**SHADE SEEDLINGS.** Protect transplants from intense sun with temporary shade. Lay a window screen, supported by four stakes, over a group of plants in a garden bed. Shadecloth or an old sheet stapled between two stakes on the south side of plants also works.

**SPREAD MULCH.** Hot fall days can be hard on heat-sensitive plants such as azaleas, camellias, and gardenias. To protect them, renew organic mulch in a layer as deep as 3 inches. Keep mulch away from the trunks of trees and shrubs.

Santa Barbara
Pasadena
San Bernardino
Santa Monica
Los Angeles
San Diego

Zones 18–21
Zones 22–24

**START A FIRST VEGETABLE GARDEN.** For a winter crop of vegetables, plan and prepare beds now. Choose a site in full sun for most or all of the day. Rough out a planting plan so you know how much space you need. Cultivate or till new ground; break up clumps and remove all weeds. Work in compost, aged manure, and other amendments.

**WATER WISELY.** Check the soil moisture before watering; use a trowel or soil sampling tube. Established plants need less water than newly planted ones. If possible, deep-water shrubs, trees, and ground covers before hot, dry Santa Ana winds arrive. Water during cool early morning or evening hours.

## ANYWHERE IN THE WEST, TACKLE THESE CHORES:

☐ **BUY BULBS.** Spring-flowering bulbs, including daffodils and tulips, arrive in nurseries just after Labor Day. Shop early for the best selection. In cold-winter areas, plant immediately.

☐ **FERTILIZE LAWNS.** Apply about one pound of actual nitrogen per 1,000 square feet of turf.

☐ **MAKE COMPOST.** Compost the weeds, vegetable remains, spent bean vines, grass, and leaves that come out of your garden. Make a pile about 4 feet in diameter, putting down alternating layers of green (grass clippings, for example) and brown matter (dried leaves). Water to keep the pile as moist as a squeezed-out sponge, and turn the pile weekly with a pitch fork. You should have usable compost in about six weeks.

☐ **PLANT PERENNIALS.** Moderate temperatures and, in most places, the approach of winter rains make this a good time to plant most perennials, including campanula, candytuft, catmint, coreopsis, delphinium, dianthus, diascia, foxglove, gaillardia, geum, penstemon, phlox, salvia, and yarrow. Set them out in well-prepared garden soil and water well. If you live in a cold-winter part of the West, spread mulch around plants to keep them from heaving when the ground freezes.

☐ **SOLARIZE FIREWOOD.** Green firewood can harbor bark beetles that pose a threat to garden trees. Eliminate beetles by piling wood into stacks no more than 4 feet high, wide, and deep. Cover each stack with a clear plastic sheet. Bury the edges of the plastic and tape the seams; sunlight will do the rest, cooking the beetles within a few weeks.

## IN THE INTERMOUNTAIN WEST, DO THESE CHORES:

☐ **CLEAN UP THE GREENHOUSE.** Clean out seedbeds and flats, scrubbing them out with a weak dilution of bleach. Then check and replace weatherstripping, broken glass, and torn plastic. Finally, check vents, filters, and heaters, replacing or repairing broken components before hard frosts come.

☐ **HARVEST CUCUMBERS, MELONS, AND SQUASH.** Cantaloupes are ready when skin is well netted and the fruit slips easily from the vine. Pick watermelons when tendrils near the fruit start to turn brown. Pick cucumbers and summer squash any time; they're excellent when young and tender. Pick winter squash when rind colors up and hardens.

☐ **MULCH PLANTS.** If freezes come early where you live, you should lay down a 3- to 4-inch layer of organic mulch around plants now to protect roots from freezing. You can use straw, shredded leaves, or rough compost.

☐ **WATER.** Sometimes cooler days make it easy to forget watering. Pay special attention to plants growing under eaves and in containers, as well as new plantings.

## IN THE SOUTHWEST'S LOW AND INTERMEDIATE DESERTS:

☐ **BUY AND CHILL BULBS.** In warm climates, certain spring-blooming bulbs including crocus, hyacinths, and tulips need a few weeks of chilling to flower well in spring. Buy them now, put them in paper bags, and store at 40° to 45° for at least six weeks before planting in garden beds around Thanksgiving. (You can store them in the crisper section of the refrigerator, away from apples.)

☐ **CARE FOR LAWNS.** If you plan to overseed your Bermuda grass lawn, stop feeding it. If you don't plan to overseed, apply high-nitrogen fertilizer (½ pound 20-0-0 per 100 square feet) now and water it in well to keep the grass actively growing for as long as possible.

☐ **PLANT COOL-SEASON VEGETABLES.** As soon as temperatures drop below 100°, sow beets, carrots, celery, chard, endive, green onions, kale, kohlrabi, leeks, parsley, parsnips, peas, potatoes, radishes, spinach, and turnips. Sow lettuce and cole crops (broccoli, brussels sprouts, cauliflower) in flats now for transplanting in October.

☐ **SOW CORN AND BEANS.** If you live in the low or intermediate desert and like a Thanksgiving harvest of fresh corn, sow seeds as soon as temperatures drop below 100°. Plant in dense blocks to aid pollination. At the same time, plant a final crop of beans adjacent to the corn and let them climb.

# All-season color

*Perennials, annuals, and bulbs keep this coastal Southern California garden blooming year-round*

**Winter** *Three views of the same bed are shown here. In winter, tulips are the focal point, but not at the expense of the pansies, violas, stock, and Chrysanthemum paludosum.*

**Spring** *Cool-season annuals, including larkspur and Canterbury bell, are planted in the fall for spring bloom. Note how the bed gently curves into the lawn.*

**Summer** *Dahlias, golden fleece, and impatiens bring a variety of shapes and colors to the bed. A lone sunflower is an important element in the composition. "I like things scrambled, not uniform," says designer Scott Wright.*

IMAGINE A FLORAL bouquet occupying an entire front yard. As old flowers fade, new ones magically take their place. The arrangement never dies; it just evolves. Landscape designer Scott Wright has created such a living bouquet in Laguna Beach, California. Thanks to a carefully choreographed succession of blooming perennials, annuals, and bulbs, the landscape has color virtually year-round.

The backbones of Wright's

CHAD SLATTERY

of color. He uses specific combinations of shapes, colors, textures, and plant forms to create a desired look and mood. He even considers the beds—the frames for the plants—which have curved lines rather than straight ones. Even a narrow bed along a picket fence has a gently undulating outer edge.

Height is another factor. Wright generally keeps short plants, such as alyssum and golden fleece, in front and taller ones, such as cosmos and dahlias, toward the back. He also weaves a few low-growing plants in among those that are slightly taller to add depth within the bed.

For added drama, Wright plants in drifts, grouping plants of the same type and color. The result is a color scheme that seems to shift wholesale with the season. In winter, for example, blocks of tulips in brilliant, contrasting colors brighten overcast days. The garden is more subdued in spring as cool blues and purples of delphinium and larkspur dominate. Things warm up again in the summer when warm-color harmonies of red, orange, and yellow fill the beds.

## TIPS AND TECHNIQUES

Except for the bulbs, Wright plants mostly seedlings from cell-packs. Seedlings give quick color, are less vulnerable than seeds, and leave little room for weeds.

Plants such as dahlias, larkspur, and delphiniums require staking. Wright uses easily camouflaged green bamboo stakes and green twist-ties to hold the stems in place.

Tulips receive special care at planting time. Wright digs trenches 8 to 9 inches deep and adds bulb food. He covers the fertilizer with a 1- to 2-inch layer of sand and positions the bulbs. Finally, Wright covers the bulbs with soil amended with compost and aged chicken manure.

To sustain high-impact color throughout the year,

garden are perennials, although it takes a steady supply of annuals to keep the color show going. In addition to successive waves of planting throughout the year, the maintenance routine includes fertilizing, watering, staking, and deadheading.

The two major planting periods in Wright's gardening calendar are late November, for autumn perennials, bulbs, and cool-season annuals, and late May, for summer perennials and warm-season annu-

als. The three peak bloom times are winter (dominated by tulips), spring (dominated by cool-season annuals and perennials), and summer (dominated by warm-season annuals and perennials). October through early November is the quietest color period, with only a few blooms lingering on the perennials. During this time, Wright lets perennials die back and go to seed. Then he pulls the last of the summer annuals, amends the soil, and gives it a rest.

### HOW TO BEGIN

Now is a good time for beginning year-round gardeners to get started, since September is the perfect month to prepare new beds for planting in the fall. Don't worry about scale. The principles behind all-season color are the same whether you are planting a single bed or landscaping an entire yard.

One of the secrets of Wright's success is that he does more than simply fill a garden with dizzying splashes

**Spring** *The hard edges of a brick walkway are softened by larkspur, alstroemeria, and Mexican bush sage, which are allowed to spill out of their bricked-in beds.*

**Summer** *After the larkspur is spent, dahlias and cosmos come to the fore. The Mexican bush sage persists. "The beds are never all wiped out at once," says Wright, pictured above.*

Wright regularly feeds both the soil and the plants. During the brief period in early fall when the beds are "resting," he amends the soil again. When plants are pumping color, he fertilizes weekly, alternating between aged manure, a complete granular fertilizer, and a flower fertilizer.

Finally, the flower beds are irrigated with bubbler sprinklers rather than overhead spray, which would beat down the flower stalks. ■

*By Lynn Ocone*

## PLANT & BLOOM CALENDAR

The Scott Wright–designed garden is in *Sunset Western Garden Book* zone 24, which runs in a band along the coast from the Mexican border to Point Conception. The calendar and planting suggestions below will work best in similarly mild climates.

### September & October
*What's in bloom:* dahlias, tuberoses, warm-season annuals, heat-loving perennials.

### November
*What to plant:* perennials, tulips (early, midseason, and late), anemones, daffodils, narcissus, ranunculus, and the bulk of the cool-season annuals—when weather cools, by Thanksgiving.

### December
*What's in bloom:* the first of the cool-season annuals, and narcissus.

### January
*What's in bloom:* cool-season annuals, narcissus, early tulips.

### February
*What to plant:* cool-season annuals and perennials to fill between bulbs.
*What's in bloom:* cool-season annuals, perennials, anemones, daffodils, and tulips.

### March
*What to plant:* cool-season annuals and perennials as fillers.
*What's in bloom:* cool-season annuals, daffodils, delphiniums, and tulips.

### April
*What to plant:* the last of the cool-season annuals for quick filler color, dahlias, tuberous begonias, Madonna lilies, tuberoses.

*What's in bloom:* cool-season annuals and perennials, ranunculus.

### May
*What to plant:* perennials, Madonna lilies, tuberoses, tuberous begonias; then, at month's end, the majority of the warm-season annuals.
*What's in bloom:* cool-season annuals at their peak; perennials and self-sown warm-season annuals.

### June
*What to plant:* tuberous begonias.
*What's in bloom:* dahlias, Madonna lilies, warm-season annuals, tuberous begonias, perennials.

### July & August
*What's in bloom:* warm-season annuals, heat-loving perennials, dahlias, Madonna lilies, tuberoses, and tuberous begonias, all at their peak.

## PLANTS FOR ALL SEASONS

*Cool-season annuals for fall planting and blooms in fall, winter, and spring:* alyssum, Canterbury bell (biennial or annual), *Chrysanthemum paludosum*, delphinium (perennial treated as annual), larkspur, lobelia, pansy, snapdragon, stock, viola.

*Warm-season annuals for spring planting and blooms in spring,* summer, and early fall: blue bedder salvia (lives on as perennial), *Chrysanthemum paludosum*, cosmos, golden fleece.

*Spring perennials:* alstroemeria, coreopsis, delphinium, Mexican evening primrose, society garlic.
*Summer perennials:* alstroemeria, busy Lizzie (*Impatiens wallerana*), coreopsis, gloriosa daisy, Mexican bush sage, Mexican evening primrose, society garlic.

*Autumn perennials:* coreopsis, gloriosa daisy, Mexican bush sage.
*Self-sowing volunteers:* alstroemeria, alyssum, busy Lizzie (*Impatiens wallerana*), *Chrysanthemum paludosum*, cosmos, larkspur, lobelia.

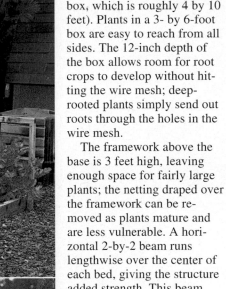

NORMAN A. PLATE

*A GROW BOX is a raised bed with a frame around it. Elements can include a trellis, bird netting, and an irrigation system.*

# How does her garden grow? In a box

*A reader uses a homemade design to get the most out of her small garden*

THERE'S RARELY A bare spot in Evani Lupinek's compact, 100-square-foot vegetable garden at her home near San Luis Obispo, California. "I've got to have something to eat from the garden every night," says Lupinek. "Besides, I hate the look of bare dirt." To get the most from her precious space, and to keep things perpetually green, she has designed several simple grow boxes of various sizes, complete with pest barriers and irrigation systems. Her intensive gardening techniques and the enabling mild coastal climate result in an abundant year-round supply of organic vegetables.

## BUILDING THE BOX

Lupinek gardens in a narrow 10-foot-wide side yard bordering a wild canyon. Though insect pests are few, deer, gophers, raccoons, rabbits, cats, and birds pose quite a challenge. Her boxes, which resemble raised beds once in place, are made of 2-by-12s anchored in the soil; sheets of ½-inch wire mesh stapled to the bottom of the boxes keep burrowing critters out. A framework of 2-by-2s over the boxes supports bird netting that keeps grazers and diggers at bay.

Having built three boxes out of different kinds of lumber and of various dimensions, Lupinek has determined that the optimal box would be 3 by 6 feet and constructed from redwood or cedar (although she still uses her first box, which is roughly 4 by 10 feet). Plants in a 3- by 6-foot box are easy to reach from all sides. The 12-inch depth of the box allows room for root crops to develop without hitting the wire mesh; deep-rooted plants simply send out roots through the holes in the wire mesh.

The framework above the base is 3 feet high, leaving enough space for fairly large plants; the netting draped over the framework can be removed as plants mature and are less vulnerable. A horizontal 2-by-2 beam runs lengthwise over the center of each bed, giving the structure added strength. This beam also keeps netting from sagging and holds irrigation tubing in place. Lupinek uses a row of micro-spray emitters, spaced 24 inches apart and attached to the beam's underside. A drip-irrigation line on the surface of each bed supplements the spray system.

The final element in the large box is a 70-inch-high trellis made of 2-by-2s and 1-by-1s. It runs the length of the box and sits 6 inches in from the edge. Within the trellis, Lupinek used two techniques to support her plants. In the center of the trellis, she strung heavy-gauge fishing line up and down for climbing plants such as beans. For easy assembly, Lupinek strung her line through 1-by-1s that were predrilled (the holes are 3 inches apart) and then nailed to the inside top and bottom of the trellis.

On the sides of the trellis, she stapled nylon netting to 1-by-1s before attaching them to the inside surfaces of the 2-by-2s. The netting, with its vertical and horizontal lines, works well for plants such as cucumbers. ∎

*By Lynn Ocone*

ROBYN CANNON

**REMODEL IN PROGRESS:** *New plants go into the bed.*

**AFTER REPLANTING,** *the whole garden is accessible from brick walkways and paths made of concrete pavers cast to look like flagstones.*

ROB CASEY

# Fine-tuning a perennial garden

**BELLFLOWERS RISE** *behind hot pink astilbe in the rejuvenated garden.*

ROBYN AND DON Cannon wanted a handsome entry to their Seattle home, so they set to work on a large flower bed between the walkway and patio. They amended the soil, fertilized, and planted vigorous perennials. The resulting garden thrived, blooming for eight seasons. Then the Cannons decided to rip it all out and start fresh.

What did they learn from the first garden that made them want to do it all over again? Here are some lessons.

### DON'T OVERCROWD PLANTS; ALLOW EASY ACCESS

There's much to be said for planting perennials so densely that there's simply no room for weeds. But by the time they dug it out, the Cannons' first garden was so crowded that plant growth was suffer-

ing, and not even the owners could get in.

Before replanting, they amended the soil with compost, then divided the perennials they wanted and tossed out the ones they didn't. All digging, dividing, and replanting were done during last year's growing season.

As a final step, they had concrete pavers cast and installed, forming the paths shown in the photos above. It's made maintenance much easier: most plants are now within easy reach of the walkway or paths.

### KEEP PLANT SIZES, COLORS IN MIND

When the Cannons planted their first perennial garden, organization tended to be casual: plants were set into whatever empty spaces remained. On replanting, the Cannons followed the simple, proven formula of putting taller plants in the back, shorter ones up front. They also paid close attention to

coordinating textures, colors, and bloom seasons.

While planting, they left irrigation courses between perennials. Then, with plants in place, they laid in ooze-type soaker hoses, setting them 2 to 4 inches below the soil surface. The ends of the soakers poke up out of the soil, so the Cannons can attach a hose whenever they need to water.

Soakers irrigate a swath about a foot wide, so courses between plants have to be planned accordingly. And since the hoses are laid loosely in the soil, their routes can be shifted as plantings change over the year. If you install a system like this, use unmarked plant labels to mark soaker locations so you don't slice through the hoses when you plant and transplant new perennials.

For ongoing maintenance, the Cannons fertilize every two weeks between May and October, and water whenever soil starts to dry out. ■

*By Jim McCausland*

PETER O. WHITELEY

**PLANT FREESIAS** *next to walkways and other high-traffic areas where you can enjoy their fragrance. Here, candytuft helps keep freesia stems from flopping.*

NORMAN A. PLATE

**FRESHLY CUT FREESIAS** *were tested for fragrance. In this batch, Tecolote red (front, center), Tecolote yellow (behind), and 'Snowdon' (right rear corner) were the most intense.*

# Freesias get the sniff test

*Of 21 kinds tested, 4 came out tops*

RENOWNED FOR THEIR heady fragrance, freesias are one of the highlights of a spring garden. So imagine how disappointed you'd be if you planted a swath of freesia corms in fall, only to discover the following spring that they had practically no fragrance.

If you choose the wrong variety of freesia, this scenario could easily happen to you. Although gardeners associate fragrance with freesias, not all of them emit the strong, spicy-sweet scent that we expect.

Which freesias are a gardener's best bet for fragrance? To find out, we grew 21 single- and double-flowered types in *Sunset*'s test garden in Menlo Park, California. The following March, we put our sniffers to the test.

## FROM KNOCKOUTS TO DISAPPOINTMENTS

On a warm, sunny spring day, we selected freshly opened blooms from each of the 21 types of freesias and inhaled deeply. We then arranged them into four categories according to degree of fragrance: intense, medium, mild, and faint to none.

*The most intensely fragrant* were 'Safari' (yellow), 'Snowdon' (double white), Tecolote red, and Tecolote yellow. When arranged in a vase and placed indoors, these freesias will permeate the air with sweet fragrance.

*Those with medium fragrance* included 'Oberon' (red, yellow center), 'Golden Crown' (double yellow), 'Talisman' (soft orange pink), Tecolote pink, Tecolote white, and 'Washington' (double orange red, gold center).

*Only mild fragrance* was noted in 'Adonis' (double rose), 'Flamingo' (double salmon pink), 'Florida' (rose pink), 'Matterhorn' (white), 'Rossini' (double rose red, yellow center), and 'Silvia' (double blue).

*Fragrance was extremely faint* in 'Bloemfontein' (double pastel pink), 'Blue Navy' (purple), 'Royal Blue', Tecolote blue, and 'Wintergold' (golden yellow).

Keep in mind that your results could differ somewhat from ours when you grow freesias at home. According to Dan Davids of Davids & Royston Bulb Company in Gardena, California, all noses are different. "Some noses are more sensitive to fragrance than others. Also, time of day, humidity, and sunlight all affect the intensity."

## SHOP AT NURSERIES FOR FREESIAS

The best place to get freesias by name is at full-service nurseries and other gardening stores that sell a wide variety of bulbs. Freesias will grow outdoors in *Sunset Western Garden Book* zones 8, 9, and 12 through 24; elsewhere, plant them in pots indoors.

Choose a site in full sun with well-drained soil. Plant the corms pointed ends up about 2 inches deep and 2 inches apart. If planted too shallowly, the plants will tend to flop when in bloom. Also, avoid windy locations and keep soil moist. ∎

*By Lauren Bonar Swezey*

# Sowing a classic look

*Plant old-fashioned annuals from seed this fall for variety and economy*

**SHIRLEY POPPIES** *and corn cockle are good full-sun companions.*

N EARLY EVERYONE likes old-fashioned annuals. Their lavish blooms and graceful forms bestow even the most urban landscapes with romantic country charm. As a bonus, these old-time favorites are excellent in fresh-flower bouquets, and a few dry beautifully.

Although you can buy a few types of old-fashioned annuals as seedlings in nurseries every spring, far more varieties are available by seed. In fact, some of these annuals—love-in-a-mist and corn cockle, for example—are usually available only by seed. Others, including larkspur and Shirley poppies, grow taller and are more vigorous when sown in place than when purchased and transplanted. With seed, you can sow at prime time, resulting in plentiful blooms over

**LARKSPUR** *produce 4- to 5-foot spikes of color. Give them partial shade inland.*

an extended period. And finally, seeds are more economical than plants: a packet of 1,000 godetia seeds costs only about $2.25 compared with a sixpack of godetia for around the same price.

## BEST BETS FOR OLD-FASHIONED CHARM

**Corn cockle** (*Agrostemma githago*). 'Milas' is an outstanding variety with satiny 3-inch plum-colored flowers veined with deep purple and fading to white in the center; excellent cut. Wispy plants with grassy foliage reach 2 to 3 feet tall. Sow in fall in warmest climates only; spring everywhere else. Reseeds. Full sun.

**Godetia** (*Clarkia amoena, Godetia grandiflora*). Many varieties to choose from, with plants ranging in height from 4 to 5 inches to 3 feet. In spring, clustered upright buds open to cup-shaped 2-inch flowers; they may be single or double, frilly or not. Flowers are white and shades of pink, lavender, and crimson—usually overlaid with contrasting streaks. Tall varieties are best for cutting. Sow in fall if winters are mild; spring in cold climates. Sun.

**Larkspur** (*Consolida ambigua*). Upright, branching stems of strains such as Giant Imperial give height (4 to 5 feet) to beds and borders. Spring-bloom spikes are dramatic in white, blue, purple, pink, salmon, and carmine; spikes dry well. For best germination, plant fresh seed. Thin for biggest flowers. Sow in fall. Sun; partial shade inland.

**Love-in-a-mist** (*Nigella damascena*). Attractive both fresh and dried, the lacy 'Persian Jewels' has 1½-inch double flowers in blue, white, and rose. Eighteen-inch-tall plants come into bloom quickly, followed by attractive swollen, papery seed capsules valued

for dried arrangements. *N. hispanica* has 2½-inch deep blue single flowers with bright orange anthers and dark seed capsules. 'Oxford Blue' grows to 30 inches. Sow in fall. Sun or part shade.

**Shirley poppy** (Flanders field poppy, *Papaver rhoeas*). Slender stems (2 to 5 feet tall) with elegant crepe paper–like flowers (2 inches or more across) and divided silver green leaves. Flanders field poppy usually refers to the scarlet ancestor of Shirley poppies, which are commonly white, red, pink, orange, and bicolors. 'Mother of Pearl' are delicate pastels. Sow spring through summer for continuous bloom. Full sun. Reseeds.

**Stock** (*Matthiola incana*). Spikes of fragrant single or double 1-inch flowers in cream, pink, lavender, purple, red, or white. Column types are ideal for cutting, with a single but impressive 2- to 3-foot-tall flower spike. Also good for cutting is the Giant Imperial strain, with multiple spikes on branching plants to 2½ feet. Sow in fall. Full sun.

**Sweet peas** (*Lathyrus odoratus*). Among the dozens of choices is the exceptionally fragrant climber 'Painted Lady' (carmine pink and white), introduced in the 18th century. Other fragrant climbing varieties are 'Antique Fantasy' (mixed), 'Lady Fairbairn' (lavender rose), and 'Royal Wedding' (white). 'Snoopea' (mixed) is a sweet-smelling bushy type to 30 inches. In warm areas, plant this month for winter bloom. In *Sunset* zones 7, 8, 9, and 12 through 24, plant between October and January. Sun.

## SEED SOURCES

Together, these two companies offer all the varieties described here (catalogs free):

Thompson & Morgan, Box 1308, Jackson, N.J. 08527; (908) 363-2225.

Park Seed Co., Cokesbury Road, Greenwood, S.C. 29647; (800) 845-3369. ■

*By Lynn Ocone*

PHIL SCHOFIELD

COVERED *by grapevines, this arbor becomes a walk-in cornucopia during the harvest.*

# Shady arbor is a grape factory

*It supports six vines and produces bunches of seedless fruit*

POSTS AND BEAMS *tie the arbor together; six grapevines climb along and atop wire.*

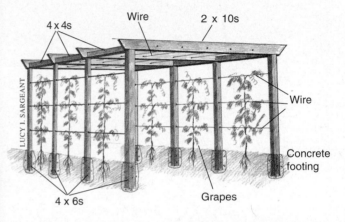

LUCY I. SARGEANT

*Diagram labels:* 4 x 4s · Wire · 2 x 10s · Wire · Concrete footing · Grapes · 4 x 6s

**T**HE PERFECT GRAPE arbor is a high-volume fruit factory as well as a shady refuge when the weather turns hot. The one pictured here produces both plentiful fruit and shade. Built five years ago by fruit scientists at Washington State University's Mt. Vernon Research and Extension Unit, it's completely covered with six grapevines, supplying a harvest that stretches from September into October.

The structure is made from eight 9-foot-long pressure-treated 4- by 6-inch posts. Each post is anchored in an 18-inch-deep concrete footing. The posts are set 6 feet apart in two parallel rows, with 12 feet between the rows. Four 2- by 10-inch tie beams connect the rows, while the four posts in each row are connected by 4-by-4s.

On each side of the arbor, strands of heavy-gauge wire are strung horizontally through the 4-by-6s at three heights: one 2 feet above the ground, one 4 feet, and one 6 feet. These support the hori-

zontal vines. Wire also runs at 2-foot intervals across the top of the arbor for the vines to clamber over.

The vines are planted midway between the posts, three to each side. They produce five varieties of seedless grapes: one plant each of 'Canadice' (red fruit with flavor like that of 'Concord'), 'Einset Seedless' (light red), 'Interlaken Seedless' (greenish white), and 'Reliance' (light pink fruit with slightly foxy flavor); and two plants of 'Vanessa' (reddish purple fruit like 'Flame').

When the fruit matures, clusters of grapes hang down from the top and sides of the structure, so they're easy to see and pick. To protect the fruit, WSU horticulturists completely cover the arbor with bird netting. The arbor floor is carpeted with fescue, one of the most shade-tolerant lawn grasses. ■

*By Jim McCausland*

DENSE CLUSTERS *of ripe seedless grapes are protected from birds by netting draped over the entire arbor.*

ANN SUMMA

**VINTAGE ROSE** *specializes in casual country touches. Offerings at other shops and nurseries run the gamut from 19th-century English iron urns to contemporary Italian tiles.*

# Looking for garden accents?

*Eight places to shop, each within an hour of downtown L.A.*

I F PLANTS ARE A garden's bread and butter, then ornaments and accessories are the sugar and spice. When skillfully chosen and placed, these human touches can transform even the most ordinary planting into something unique.

Shopping for just the right piece should be as enjoyable as living with your found treasure. To help you in your search, we've selected eight shops and nurseries of various specializations and sizes. All are within an hour's drive of downtown Los Angeles.

## SMALL BOUTIQUES

If you believe that good things come in small packages, then specialty shops are for you. **The Malibu Florist,** in the Malibu Colony Plaza, sells more than just flowers. Choose from a collection of hand-painted Italian tiles and pots, hand-forged candlesticks, beveled-glass hanging vases, and concrete angels and hearts.

**Hollyhock,** in Larchmont Village, is primarily an interior design store and gift shop, with a small courtyard in back featuring garden indulgences that are either quite old and mellowed or new and made to look antique. English hand-thrown terra-cotta pots, faux lead plaques etched with poetry, and early 19th-century English iron urns decorate the walls and floor.

For those with tastes tending toward the rustic and the quaint, **Heard's Country Gardens,** in Westminster, offers weathered birdhouses, folksy garden signs, antique wooden planting crates, mirrored-glass gazing balls, and willow trellises. The accessories are displayed amid a wide assortment of perennials and herbs. **Vintage Rose,** next door to Heard's, also specializes in the casual country look, with hand-painted signs, refurbished iron plant stands, and white picket window boxes.

## ONE-STOP SHOPS

At the opposite end of the size spectrum are these four independent nurseries, each of which sells practically everything for the garden. At **Sperling Nursery,** in Calabasas, you'll find a good selection of water ornaments, including brass frogs, cement lion heads, and resin fairies.

**Armstrong's Home and Garden,** in West L.A., is a rambling home-and-garden center whose offerings range from purely functional indoor light bulbs to decorative outdoor lights.

An assortment of weather vanes in animal and sports motifs sits on a catwalk near the ceiling of the gift shop at the **Palos Verdes Begonia Farm,** in Torrance. Don't miss the painted mailboxes, tuned aluminum wind chimes, and colored concrete steppingstones imprinted with botanical designs.

Finally, there's the grand-daddy of them all, **Rogers Gardens,** in Corona del Mar. You'll find plants set in and among towering rusted-iron obelisks and antique iron beds and chairs. The colorful glazed pots from Provence are suited to both garden and patio. ■

*By Lynn Ocone*

### GARDEN SPOTS

● The Malibu Florist, 23823 W. Malibu Road, Malibu, (310) 456-1858.

● Hollyhock, 214 N. Larchmont Boulevard, Los Angeles, (213) 931-3400.

● Heard's Country Gardens, 14391 Edwards Street, Westminster, (714) 894-2444.

● Vintage Rose, 6424 Maple Avenue, Westminster, (714) 373-4547.

● Sperling Nursery, 24460 Calabasas Road, Calabasas, (818) 591-9111.

● Armstrong's Home and Garden, 11321 W. Pico Boulevard, West Los Angeles, (310) 477-8023.

● Palos Verdes Begonia Farm, 4111 242nd Street, Torrance, (310) 378-2228.

● Rogers Gardens, 2301 San Joaquin Hills Road, Corona del Mar, (714) 640-5800.

JEFF BARBER

**TEAK BENCHES** *near the Rockland Border offer restful views of perennial color.*

**ROSES CLIMB** *on metal trellis.*

# Regal sights at Government House Gardens

*Visit a grand estate in Victoria, British Columbia*

FOR NEARLY 130 YEARS, Victoria's Government House has served as the residence of the lieutenant governor of British Columbia. But in recent years, the estate's gardens had been neglected.

Then, in 1988, David C. Lam was appointed lieutenant governor, and he and his wife, Dorothy, both zealous gardeners, set out to rectify the situation. Restored and enhanced, the gardens look grander than ever. If you visit this month, you can still see some late-summer floral majesty and the first royal flushes of autumn color.

Today, you can stroll through 11 different gardens spread over the 36 acres that surround the house. Enter through the main gate and walk directly to the front door of Government House. Next to the guest register, pick up a map for a self-guided tour of the front gardens. Here are some highlights.

***English Country Garden.*** If you think summer is over, you'll get a pleasant horticultural surprise at this garden just inside the entry gate. Even now, the English Country Garden should be a riot of colorful blooms.

***Sunken Rose Garden.*** In Victoria, the last rose often opens around Christmas, so the hybrid teas should be blooming vigorously in September. Climbing roses clamber and tangle over long wooden arbors, creating welcome shade on hot days.

***Flower Garden.*** Flowers are grown here as crops for use in bouquets. You'll find both common and rare flowers: *Artemisia lactiflora, Aster frikartii* 'Mönch', Japanese anemone, Joe Pye weed (*Eupatorium purpureum*), and purple smoke tree (*Cotinus coggygria* 'Royal Purple').

***Rockland Border*** is a fine example of a traditional English border garden. Running the length of two city blocks and backed by a tall, handsome iron fence, the border mixes shrubs, perennials, and even a few annuals.

***Victorian Rose Garden*** is an elegant link between England and North America. A gift from the Lams to the people of British Columbia, this new garden is patterned after the rose garden at Warwick Castle in England. Most of the antique roses will be past their bloom, but look for a good show from the collection of David Austin's English roses.

Government House is at 1401 Rockland Avenue, about 1 mile north of downtown Victoria, and an easy walk from the Empress Hotel. The gardens are open during daylight hours year-round, except on the rare occasions when the Royal Canadian Mounted Police close them for a visiting head of state. Admission is free. ■

*By Steven R. Lorton*

**TUDOR INFLUENCE** *shows in façade of Government House, a 125-room mansion completed in 1959. In front, a 1907 porte cochere survived 1957 fire that destroyed an earlier structure.*

**FALL-PLANTED PERENNIALS** *put on a colorful show in spring. For more on these bountiful bloomers, see page 233.*

# OCTOBER

# Pick a pumpkin, prepare for winter, plant for spring

**A SEED** *this size can produce a monster like the 727-pound 'Atlantic Giant' at right.*

**P**umpkins will be piled high at grocery stores and roadside stands this month. And in Clackamas, Oregon, growers of the Northwest's biggest pumpkins will compete in a weigh-off at the Great Pumpkin Harvest Festival. In 1993, Kirk Mombert of Harrisburg, Oregon, drew a crowd with the 727-pound pumpkin pictured at right. The festival is usually held on the first Saturday in October; for details, call (503) 654-7777.

If you admire a particular pumpkin this fall and want to grow one like it next year, try to find out what variety it is. Order fresh seed for the best chance of growing a monster. Pumpkin varieties range from behemoths such as 'Atlantic Giant' (200 to 400 pounds and more) to diminutive ones such as 'Baby Bear' (1½ to 2½ pounds). There's even a spooky, white-skinned variety called 'Lumina', with delicious, deep golden flesh inside. Wait until next spring to sow seeds or set out transplants in warm garden soil where plants will get full sun.

If you attend the festival, you can buy seeds extracted from the giants. If you can't make it to Clackamas, you can order seeds of 'Atlantic Giant', 'Baby Bear', and other kinds from Nichols Garden Nursery, 1190 N. Pacific Highway, Albany, Ore. 97321; (503) 928-9280. Catalog is free.

## Moving time for peonies

Peonies ordinarily don't like to be disturbed. But this month as plants are going dormant, you can move clumps or divide some to establish new plantings. Dig up the clumps; cut the stems back to 4 to 6 inches long (just so stalk is left to show you which side is the top). If you're simply moving the clump, replant it in a well-cultivated bed enriched with organic matter. Position it so that uppermost growth eye is no more than 2 inches below the soil surface, and water well. To divide a clump, first hose soil off the roots. Then, with a sharp knife,

cut the clump into divisions; each should have 3 to 5 growth eyes and a good root system. Plant as directed above.

About mid-February, scatter dry fertilizer around plants: apply lightly around new clumps, heavily around established ones. Peony grower Rick Rogers of Caprice Farm Nursery in Sherwood, Oregon, recommends a low-nitrogen fertilizer (5-10-10 is a good choice).

## The right way to sow wildflowers

Gardeners who sow wildflower seeds in fall may envision a springtime scene of brightly colored blossoms billowing in the breeze, with butterflies and bees dancing from bloom to bloom. But sometimes when spring arrives, weeds—not wildflowers—steal the show.

"The most common mistake when planting wildflower seeds is not getting rid

soil and tamp it for good soil contact.

Wait for fall rains to germinate the seeds. If rains don't come, water to keep the soil moist and continue watering through bloomtime. When the plants have dried and dropped their seed, cut old stalks to 3 to 6 inches high.

Wildflower Seed Co. will send you a free catalog; write or call the firm at Box 406, St. Helena, Calif. 94574; (707) 963-3359.

### Seed-hunting in vacant lots

This month, when Harold Johnson of Seattle walks the family dog, he'll be carrying two plastic bags with him: one for tidying up after the dog, and the other for collecting seeds.

All through the summer, with his trusty canine companion in tow, Johnson tracks mysterious plants in vacant lots. He identifies the plants in reference books, and determines if and where they belong in his garden. When seed pods split open, he shakes the seeds into a bag, takes them home, and either plants them or labels and stores them in a cool, dry place until early spring. Among Johnson's prize finds are a huge hollyhock with creamy lemon flowers, some unusually deep blue nigella, and some strapping big yellow water iris (*I. pseudacorus*).

DAVID FALCONER

### A true blue poppy for cool, moist regions

In the garden's concert of color, few flowers sing the blues better than *Meconopsis betonicifolia,* commonly called the Himalayan poppy. The mood it sets is simple, strong, and riveting. The plant looks especially sultry standing tall in some shaded spot in the garden, against a background of glossy evergreen leaves or needles.

This native of western China adapts well to the cool,

of the existing weed and native grass seeds that are in the soil and germinate along with the wildflowers," says Michael Landis, president of the Wildflower Seed Company in St. Helena, California. "These fast-growing weeds and grasses smother out the slower-growing wildflowers," he adds. For a more successful planting, Landis recommends that gardeners take the time to eliminate the competition.

First, choose a site in full sun. To get rid of existing weeds, hand-cultivate the soil to a depth of 3 to 4 inches and remove all weeds; this is the method with the least environmental impact. You can also spray weeds with an herbicide, such as glyphosate, and then cultivate the soil after the weeds have died.

The next step is crucial: Soak the soil thoroughly, then wait for the weed seeds to germinate. When they do,

spray with glyphosate or lightly cultivate the soil to a depth of *not more than* 1 inch; deeper cultivation exposes more weed seeds that will germinate along with wildflower seeds.

Before sowing the wildflower seeds, rake the soil to form shallow grooves. To ensure even distribution of seed, mix with four times its volume of sand or vermiculite and broadcast by hand. Then rake the seed lightly into the moist climate and acid soil of the coastal Northwest and Northern California. Plants grow about 4 feet tall, with blue-green, slightly fuzzy, oblong leaves up to 6 inches long. The four-petaled blossoms stand atop long, straight leafless stems.

Treat this plant as a short-lived perennial. Give it light shade or filtered sun in a cool spot out of strong winds. It needs rich, loose, acid soil with plenty of moisture in the growing season and quick-draining, slightly dry soil in winter.

This month is a good time to hunt for the Himalayan poppy out of flower at some nurseries; plant immediately.

You can also grow plants from seed. But if you were to ask 10 gardeners who have grown blue poppy from seed about their experiences, you would be likely to get 10 different reactions, ranging from "a snap" to "nearly impossible."

Seed is available from Thompson & Morgan, Box 1308, Jackson, N.J. 08527; (800) 274-7333. A package of 100 seeds costs $3.15. You can sow seeds directly in the ground this fall or start them indoors in late winter.

***To direct-sow,*** scatter seeds now onto well-cultivated, organically rich soil. Cover the seed with a light layer of soil; water. With luck, seedlings will pop up in spring; protect them from slugs by spreading bait.

***To start seeds indoors,*** sow them in flats or pots of fast-draining, sterile soil. Keep them in a bright spot, out of direct afternoon sun (an east- or north-facing window is best) where there is good air circulation to help prevent damping off, a fungus disease. Keep the soil constantly moist. When seedlings are up and frost is no longer a threat, move flats outdoors into a lightly shaded area. When plants are about 3 inches high, they're ready to transplant into garden beds.

To ensure that the plant

MOODY BLUE *flowers of Himalayan poppy open 2 to 3 inches across with yellow stamens.*

DON NORMARK

gets well established, don't allow it to bloom the first year. When you see the flower stalk emerge (usually in the fall for first bloom), pinch it off. In its second year, cut faded blooms to prevent seed pods from forming. If you want to collect the seed (but risk losing the plant), the best seeds are said to come from the uppermost pod. Fertilize this poppy at the same time you do other perennials.

## A new twist on an old favorite

For the past six years, Teddy Colbert's Garden in Ventura County, California, has been supplying the country with do-it-yourself kits and ready-made living wreaths composed of colorful, easy-care succulents. These

beautiful, unique decorations can adorn doors and walls for years, and can be brought inside to serve as festive centerpieces for holiday tables.

Now Colbert has branched out, offering a living-wreath kit of gourmet greens. What could be fresher than a salad picked right at the table?

The custom mesclun mix is supplied by Le Jardin du Gourmet, the Vermont seed company specializing in European vegetables and herbs. Seedlings emerge from the wreath of soil and moss within a week. In about a month, you have a vivid display of color and texture: the port wine shade of 'Red Sails', feathery chicory, fluffy-leafed chartreuse 'Black-seeded Simpson', blue green romaine, spoon-shaped leaves of *mâche*. There's even a wreath

kit of crinkly, dark green 'Bloomsdale' spinach. Greens, it seems, come in all hues.

When not pressed into service at the table, the salad wreath should be situated in sunlight or partial shade, depending on your climate, and periodically dunked in water. When the lettuce plants have been consumed, implant with more seeds, or, for a permanent wreath, simply plant succulents (a discount coupon for 200 cuttings comes with each salad wreath kit).

Living salad wreath kits cost $38.50, plus tax and shipping. All materials and instructions are included. For a catalog of other living wreaths, call Teddy Colbert's Garden at (800) 833-3981.

## Split citrus? Check your watering habits

Just when your citrus fruits, figs ('Kadota' and 'Mission'), grapes, and pomegranates have reached maturity, you notice that they've split open while still on the tree. The fruit is ruined, and you wonder what you did wrong.

Chances are it's nature's doing. When early rains coincide with ripening fruit, the plant absorbs large quantities of moisture, causing the fruit to expand rapidly and crack.

Irregular irrigation can also cause the problem. If the plant is stressed, then suddenly watered heavily, the fruit can split, particularly if the weather has been warm. You can't control rainfall, but you can make sure that plants get regular watering.

## Drain and unhook those hoses

In colder parts of the West, now is the time to drain hoses and irrigation systems, and to insulate exposed outdoor hose bibs.

If you use a freeze-resistant hose bib, remember that it works only when there is no hose attached. This bib is designed with the valve well inside the wall of your house, where the temperature presumably never drops below freezing. But when you leave a hose attached, the water in the hose freezes, expands back toward the valve, and bursts the pipe inside the wall.

## Planting time for perennials

Fall planting can lead to wonderful spring surprises. Just look at the colorful jumble of flowering perennials pictured on page 228 in the garden of landscape designer Maile Arnold in Sebastopol, California. This mix of cascading ground covers includes orange sunrose (*Helianthemum nummularium* 'Stoplight'), yellow basket-of-gold (*Aurinia saxatilis*), and light pink *Saponaria ocymoides*. Taller dark pink Jupiter's beard (*Centranthus ruber*) and European columbine (*Aquilegia vulgaris*) grow behind. Look for these plants in nurseries that sell a wide assortment of perennials.

If planted this fall, the perennials will be well rooted by spring. These plants put on their best flower show in April, May, and June. You can get a second flush of bloom from basket-of-gold by shearing off the old flowers after about 80 percent of the blossoms have opened.

## Lock up those pesticides

Many adults are careless when it comes to storing pesticides. The *National Home and Garden Pesticide Use Survey,* recently put out by the Environmental Protection Agency, found that in households with youngsters under 5 years old, about 47 percent of the households stored at least one pesticide within reach of children—less than 4 feet off the ground and not locked in a cabinet.

To prevent accidents, always keep pesticides in their original containers and store in a locked cabinet. When you remove a pesticide to use in the garden, take only the amount you need, then immediately replace the container in the cabinet and lock it up.

## Start ranunculus in nursery packs

Tulips are spectacular, if short-lived, in mild-winter parts of the West, and daffodils are sunny reminders of warmer days ahead, but no spring bloom can match the prolific production of bright-colored ranunculus, particularly for cut flowers. A large tuber can easily produce 50 to 75 blooms for weeks on end in colors that range from creamy whites to berry reds.

But when to plant them? Planting now in your garden beds could mean digging up flowers that might still be producing fall color. Planting too early in the rainy season can cause the tubers to rot. And if you plant too late, your blooms will coincide with warm temperatures that shorten flower production and make plants look wilted and washed out. What to do?

Plant now in recycled six-pack nursery containers to prevent overwatering and get a jump on spring. Here's how. Half-fill recycled sixpack containers with moist sand. Set tubers, prongs downward, in containers, cover with potting soil, and water thoroughly. Unless the weather is unusually hot and dry, you won't need to water again until the first green sprouts appear, in 10 to 14 days.

By placing the sixpacks in old nursery flats, you can move the plants under cover during the first fall downpours. To protect the tender sprouts from birds, cover the flats with netting. In November, transfer young ranunculus directly to the garden, planting them 6 to 8 inches apart. The rich rainbow of ranunculus flowers pictured below grew in a Southern California raised garden bed that produces vegetables in summer

DAVID LANSING

**MANY-HUED RANUNCULUS** *will enliven mild-winter gardens during winter and early spring before hot weather arrives.*

before being converted into a cut-flower garden in the fall. In spring, when the ranunculus plants die down, tubers are lifted out one at a time and replaced with salad crops.

## Undemanding perennials for the Southern California coast

October is a great time of year for planting perennials such as the sun-loving show-offs in the Summerland garden shown below. By planting around midmonth, you miss summer's extreme heat but catch a month or so of remaining warm weather. Roots grow quickly in the still-warm soil, plants continue their growth through the cool winter months, and come spring and early summer, they burst into bloom.

In this berm planting, designer Ron Rollosson combined undemanding perennials well suited to coastal Southern California's sea breezes and summer heat. At center is tall, airy *Verbena bonariensis,* with its clusters of lilac flowers atop branching stems, which grow to 4 feet and taller. The subtle silver foliage of *Artemisia arborescens* (behind the verbena) and the yellow flowers of dusty miller (*Senecio cineraria*) create a neutral counterpoint to the dark purple flower spikes of Mexican bush sage (*Salvia leucantha*). The brilliant yellow flowers in the background are Mexican tulip poppies (*Hunnemannia fumariifolia*), self-sowing perennials most often treated as annuals. They thrive in soil that drains well and die out if overwatered. *Chrysanthemum anethifolium* forms mounding white cushions in the foreground. This short-lived perennial blooms from spring to fall. It grows fast and is best replanted each year, but it can be hard to find. A good substitute is marguerite (*C. frutescens*), which looks very similar, performs comparably, and is widely available in nurseries.

## Late fall means early greens

The end of October, when Santa Anas cease and soil cools, is the perfect time for starting mesclun in Orange County.

Mesclun is any combination of mild and piquant greens meant to be harvested young. Since the greens don't mature, seeds are usually sown more thickly than normal and are often broadcast mixed together rather than in separate rows.

The result is a pretty crop that yields a steady supply of premixed gourmet greens for as long as eight weeks. You can begin scissoring off the first tender leaves when they are no more than 3 inches tall and continue snipping regrowth until the greens turn bitter. Then pull out the entire bed and start from scratch.

Mesclun does well in broad, shallow containers (10 inches deep or more), or you can sow it directly in the ground. Amend the top 6 inches of soil with compost or worm castings. Scatter the seed on top of the bed, and dust lightly with topsoil. Keep the soil consistently moist until seeds germinate. Continue to water frequently and fertilize regularly with fish emulsion or a complete fertilizer.

You can put together your own combination of greens, but starting with a product already mixed is easier; it's also a good way to discover your preferences. Shepherd's Garden Seeds sells a California Mesclun Mix Set, which contains arugula, cress, endive, mustards, and several green and bronze leaf lettuces. For a free catalog, call (408) 335-6910. Mesclun in containers at nurseries often consists of this mix. Another good source for mesclun mix is The Cook's Garden. The catalog costs $1; call (802) 824-3400.

## Head to Planet Earth to see Australian natives

Planet Earth Growers Nursery, near Kerman, California, about 15 miles west of Fresno, is a great place to learn about drought-resistant plants.

Six years ago, owners Cathy and John Etheridge

RUSS A. WIDSTRAND

**SPRINGTIME PERENNIAL DISPLAY** *is reward for timely fall planting. White chrysanthemums and lemon yellow Mexican tulip poppies contrast with the purples of upright Verbena bonariensis and Mexican bush sage. Silvery artemisia and yellow-flowerd dusty miller complete the picture.*

founded this nursery specializing in Australian plants and started planting a demonstration garden next door. Today that garden—filled now with water-thrifty acacias, eucalyptus, melaleucas, myoporums—is considered to be the second largest collection of Australian plants in the United States. Named the M. Young Botanic Garden in honor of Cathy's grandfather, it has been recognized by the American Association of Botanical Gardens and Arboreta.

In addition to selling Australian plants, Planet Earth now features California and Southwestern natives.

Planet Earth and the M. Young Botanic Garden are located at 14178 W. Kearney Boulevard, just outside Kerman. Hours are 9 to 6 Tuesdays through Sundays. Admission is free. For directions, call (209) 846-7881.

## Insulate lilies from deep freezing and hungry rodents

Lying just under the soil's surface, plump lily bulbs make wonderful winter forage for rodents, who tunnel beneath the mulch you've applied to protect lilies from deep frost.

You can foil the rodents and insulate the lilies by waiting to mulch until the top ½ to 1 inch of soil has frozen. Then lay down the mulch (autumn leaves or pine needles, for example) to prevent deeper freezing—the kind that causes soil to heave. The mulch also keeps the surface soil frozen hard enough to make it difficult for rodents to dig into it.

## The tall Westerner with long spurs: columbine

Columbine is one of the most delicate and beautiful woodland wildflowers grown in North America, and it is among the most favored for perennial borders. Several native species excel in the

CHARLES MANN

**GOLDEN-SPURRED COLUMBINE** (*Aquilegia chrysantha*) is native to Arizona and New Mexico. Its flowers can reach 3 inches across, with 2½-inch-long spurs.

garden. Unlike European and Asian varieties, all have long spurs.

For perennial borders, use tall columbine (the many short varieties are better suited to rock gardens). Some good choices include red-and-gold Canadian (*Aquilegia canadensis*), 1½ to 2 feet tall, and Western columbine (*A. formosa*), 1½ to 3 feet; yellow (*A. canadensis* 'Corbett'), 1½ feet; golden-spurred (*A. chrysantha*), 3 to 4 feet, from New Mexico and Arizona; and *A. longissima* 'Maxistar', 2½ to 3 feet, from the Southwest; and the purple-blue Rocky Mountain columbine (*A. caerulea*), 1½ to 3 feet. All but Canadian and 'Maxistar' have white forms as well.

These plants are short-lived—three to five years at most—but all self-sow freely. They also crossbreed shamelessly; if you want seedlings to be like their parents, plant only one kind of columbine. If you want multiple species, keep them as far apart as possible, but expect some crossbreeding anyway.

Columbine's ferny foliage is susceptible to mildew and may start to look ratty after flowers fade, so it's best to use this plant in mixed borders. Interplant it with campanulas, bleeding heart, poppies, iris, ferns, daisies, foxglove, and short kinds of yarrow.

You can sow any kind of columbine seed now for flowers next summer. Scatter seed in a place that gets filtered sunlight (in woodland edges and under trees, for example).

The soil should have good drainage but contain enough organic matter to keep moisture around plant roots at bloom time.

If you miss fall-planting season, you can buy plants next spring from nurseries or mail-order sources. One seed source for various hybrid and species columbines is J. L. Hudson, Seedsman, Box 1058, Redwood City, Calif. 94064; catalog $1.

## A dwarf form of maiden grass

When it comes to big, bold grasses, *Miscanthus sinensis* and its varieties are hard to top, producing graceful clumps that can stretch up to 6 feet, sometimes 10. Their long, handsome blades are topped by numerous long wands holding bursts of seed. This giant grass is often too large, however, for many gardens.

Recently a dwarf form has come on the market: *M.s.* 'Yakushima' is a 3- to 4-foot-high version of *M.s.* 'Gracillimus', which is commonly called maiden grass. 'Yakushima' has a free-flowering habit that starts at an early age. It forms a tidy burst of fine foliage that adds interest in perennial plantings. It also adds a pleasant change of texture when planted among evergreen shrubs. The foliage turns brown after the first hard frost. Most gardeners leave it standing through the winter, then cut everything back to near ground level early in the spring before the plant sends out new growth.

Give this plant good garden soil. This is an excellent grass for a large container. Water it well the first two summers to get it established (it is, however, quite drought tolerant). Fertilize it lightly, on the same schedule as you do perennials, to promote a good flower crop. You can buy plants in full flower in 1-gallon cans this month; plant them immediately.

## Plant butterfly weed now to lure monarchs to your garden

The ranks of the royal air force might be a bit slim this year, but make no mistake: the monarchs are coming. If these imposing orange-and-black butterflies haven't shown up in your neighborhood yet, they'll fly in soon.

Veteran butterfly-watchers cite two reasons for their low numbers. Late-spring storms two years in a row took a toll on northward returning flocks. More worrisome in the long run, however, is the loss of habitat. The stands of trees along the coast where monarchs roost in winter, as well as the butterfly weed plants they feed on as caterpillars in spring, are diminishing.

You can lure wintering monarchs into your yard—and help ensure their presence again next year—by planting any form of *Asclepias* (known

JOEL ZWINK

**MERRITT DUNLAP** *in his Fallbrook cactus garden with some of his Haageocereus aureispinus (foreground).*

as butterfly weed or milk-weed) now. *Asclepias* provides both nectar for adult butterflies and fodder for their young caterpillars.

*A. tuberosa* and *A. curas-savica* are the most typically planted species. The first is North American in origin, the latter South American. Both perennials form small clumps of dark green, narrow-leafed foliage 1 to 3 feet tall. Broad umbels of small bright orange flowers appear summer through fall.

*A. curassavica* holds a slight edge over *A. tuberosa* among experienced growers for its slightly darker flowers (easier to incorporate into a border) and less rigidly upright form.

If neither species is available through your local nursery, *A. tuberosa* plants can be ordered from either Wayside Gardens (800/845-1124) or Park Seed Co. (800/845-3369). *A. curassavica* and *A. tuberosa* seeds are also available from Park.

Gardeners who dislike orange blooms might prefer 'Hello Yellow', a solid yellow *A. tuberosa* hybrid recently introduced by Wayside. Native California milkweed, with its white and cream flowers, is even subtler. The Theodore Payne Foundation in Sun Valley, Calif. (818/768-1802) sells *A. fascicularis* seeds and plants (it's a narrow-leafed milkweed), as well as other varieties. Tree of Life Wholesale Nursery in San Juan Capistrano, Calif. (714/728-0685) will also have native *Asclepias* for sale this year. The nursery, at 33201 Ortega Highway, is open to the public on Fridays.

## Tips from Fallbrook's cactus man

Merritt S. Dunlap has been collecting cactus for 65 years. At present, his ½-acre garden in Fallbrook, California, overflows with 820 species from eight regions of the Americas. The 88-year-old retired engineer and building contractor

started many of his rarest specimens from seed, and he rattles off their botanical names (such as *Weberbauero-cereus winterianus*) with the facility of a true cactophile.

Among his most intriguing varieties are a woolly white-haired cactus from Peru and a smooth, spineless cactus from Baja California, the latter now thought to be extinct in the wild. These and the rest of his collection, Dunlap says proudly, will be given to Lotusland in Santa Barbara, where 2 acres have been set aside for them.

Dunlap has no difficulty cultivating cactus in north San Diego County's avocado belt (*Sunset Western Garden Book* zone 23). The plants enter dormancy as summer ends and cooler weather begins, and this slowdown lasts until temperatures rise in the spring. "I don't water substantially after September, and I don't fertilize," Dunlap says, adding that dormancy helps cactus handle frost. He begins watering and fertilizing regularly again in March, at the start of the growing season.

Here are a few more of Dunlap's cool-weather tips:
• Cactus should be protected from severe frost, although many large specimens will tolerate night temperatures as low as 28° provided days are warm (the flesh absorbs enough heat to last through a nighttime chill).
• Cactus have shallow feeder roots; pull weeds by hand to avoid disturbing the soil (don't hoe). Avoid using chemical weed killers.
• Protect from snail damage, which can cause permanent scars. Handpick or bait.

And if you're looking ahead to spring, Dunlap's got one more bit of advice. Take cuttings at the narrowest part of the mother plant; set cuttings aside for about two weeks or until healed before planting in fast-draining soil mix. Dunlap's recipe: 3 parts Supersoil to 1 part agricultural pumice (available by the bag at Grigsby Cactus Gar-

dens, 2326–2354 Bella Vista Drive, Vista; 619/727-1323). Protect cuttings from afternoon sun.

## Kitty doesn't like catnip? Time for cat thyme

Many herb gardeners are familiar with germander (*Teucrium chamaedrys*). This neat, compact plant is used in classic knot gardens and as a small hedge. Less widely known are germander's close cousins, which are all attractive, hardy evergreen plants that thrive in milder-winter regions of the West (*Sunset Western Garden Book* zones 7–9, 14–24).

Cat thyme (*T. marum*) is one germander relative that's irresistible to many felines. The small 1-foot-high plant has tiny gray leaves and bright maroon flowers—that is if any of the leaves and flowers are left, since many cats chew it right down to ground level.

Other interesting kinds include creeping germander (*T. chamaedrys* 'Prostratum'), which grows to a height of only 6 inches and has pretty pink flowers; yellow germander (*T. flavum*), up to 2 feet tall with glossy foliage and yellow blooms; and curly wood sage (*T. scorodonia crispum*), with wavy-edged leaves that look good in dried bouquets.

All germanders grow best in full sun and well-drained soil. Once established they need little water.

One mail-order source that sells more than 10 kinds of germander is Mountain Valley Growers, Inc., 38325 Pepperweed Rd., Squaw Valley, Calif. 93675; (209) 338-2775.

## For a final rose show in California's Central Valley

Weather permitting, many roses growing on the floor of the Central Valley keep on blooming into December. There are some steps you can

**WHITE FLOWERS** *with yellow centers bloom on prostrate sageleaf rockrose from mid- to late spring.*

SCOTT ANGER

take now to encourage your roses to end the season with a blaze of floral glory.

First, apply a complete fertilizer according to label directions, then water deeply. Be diligent about deadheading: cut off faded blossoms and any hips (seed pods) that may have formed. If miniatures or floribundas are at the end of a bloom cycle, remove spent flowers with pruning shears. With hybrid teas, grandifloras, and climbing roses, cut back individual stems to at least the first leaf with five leaflets. Make sure the plants don't dry out if the weather stays warm.

### Showy rockroses that grow low

The rockrose genus (*Cistus*) includes many plants that make wide-spreading ground covers, but most of them grow 3 to 4 feet tall. Only a few kinds stay low to the ground. Two of the showiest are *C. salviifolius* 'Prostratus' and *C.* 'Warley Rose'; both make good bank covers and grow well in poor, rocky soils. In regular garden soil, they need good drainage. In mid- to late spring, these rockroses put on a profuse flower show.

*C. salviifolius* **'Prostratus',** the prostrate sageleaf rockrose, pictured above, grows 1 to 2 feet tall and 6 to 8 feet wide. White flowers, 1 to 1½ inches wide with yellow spots at the base of each petal, appear amid small, gray-green leaves.

*C.* **'Warley Rose'** grows about 1 foot tall and spreads 3 to 4 feet wide. Small dark cerise to magenta pink flow-ers are set off by crinkly dark green leaves.

### A laboratory called Casa Pacifica

One of the privileges of being at *Sunset* is getting to meet people like Lew Whitney of Rogers Gardens in Corona del Mar. And one of the great things about people like Lew Whitney is that they get you into the most amazing gardens.

Last spring, at Whitney's urging, we spent a day touring and photographing at Casa Pacifica, the former home of the late Richard Nixon. Whitney has been directing the planting at this San Clemente landmark for more than a decade. "What I like best about it," he says, "is the freedom the owners give me to experiment. It's almost like a laboratory. It's a true garden in that it evolves."

Although the Casa Pacifica grounds are probably a bit grander in scale than most people's backyards, the lessons to be learned there can be applied to any garden. That's why, during the next few months, we'll be sharing with you some of the photographs Bill Aron took there.

This month we focus on ladybells, or *Adenophora*. "This is a true perennial," says Whitney of this violet beauty. "Just let it come up and bloom, and then cut it back." Although reference books usually describe *Adenophora* as a summer bloomer, Whitney says that in coastal Southern California the fragrant species *A. liliifolia* will bloom in winter and spring. Sow seeds now in well-drained, fertile, slightly alkaline soil. It will do fine in light shade.

### Water-efficient plants for the desert

We don't often recommend research papers as reading for home gardeners, but *Ten-year Research Findings on Water-Efficient Ornamental Plants for the Coachella Valley* (Coachella Valley Resource Conservation District, Indio, and Desert Water Agency, Palm Springs; 1993) is an exception. This 32-page booklet tells how 70 trees and shrubs performed in a 10-year trial at Palm Springs, California (the same low-desert climate zone as Phoenix).

Many plants did well in the trials. Arizona cypress (*Cupressus arizonica*) and river she-oak (*Casuarina cunninghamiana*) grew so strongly that they've now been planted by the thousands for desert windbreaks. These top choices grow exceptionally well with little water.

All plants included in the trial are listed in charts, and many are illustrated with excellent color photos. But read carefully: a number of plants get fairly glowing reports, but are noted as being eaten by rabbits before the trial ended.

On the whole, however,

BILL ARON

**VIOLET-FLOWERED ADENOPHORA** *at Casa Pacifica: plant now for colorful display next year.*

this booklet is a valuable contribution to desert-gardening literature, with detailed information about drip irrigation, fertilization, and more. To order a copy, send a check for $6.50 to Desert Water Agency, Attn: Plant Book, Box 1710, Palm Springs, Calif. 92263.

## Onions that keep on producing

Most gardeners think of onions as an annual crop, but bunching onions will give you a continuous crop of mild-tasting stalks year after year if you harvest them carefully. They're also known as Japanese bunching onions, Welsh onions, spring onions, or sometimes scallions (although scallions can refer to any onion in the green onion stage).

If you leave some stalks in the ground (see the photo below), offshoots will develop that will continue to grow. Harvest older stalks by gently pulling them up so the young shoots are left undisturbed.

NORMAN A. PLATE

**BUNCHING ONIONS** *are ready to harvest when stalks are ⅓ to ½ inch across; allow very young ones to continue growing and multiplying.*

Bunching onions can be used in cooking just like any green onion.

Plant seeds in full sun and well-drained soil this month so you'll have a crop that's ready to harvest next spring. Seeds are available from the following sources.

*Southern Exposure Seed Exchange,* Box 170, Earlysville, Va. 22936; (804) 973-4703. Sells 'Evergreen Hardy White Bunching' and 'White Spear'; catalog $2.

*Sunrise Enterprises,* Box 330058, West Hartford, Conn. 06133; (203) 666-8071. Sells 'Multi-Stalk 9', 'Long White Tokyo', and 'Red Beard' (outer skin is red); catalog $2.

## Book offers tips on landscaping to cut utility bills

How can you use plant material to reduce the cost of heating, air conditioning, and water bills? You'll find advice in *Energy-Efficient and Environmental Landscaping: Cut Your Utility Bills by up to 30 Percent and Create a Natural, Healthy Yard,* by Anne Simon Moffat, Marc Schiler, and the staff of Green Living (Appropriate Solutions Press, 1994; $17.95).

This book explains many simple and useful ways you can use plants to save energy—such as planting tall trees to shade the east and west sides of a house (not the south), or using windbreaks to block winter winds and funnel summer breezes toward the house.

The first section of the book discusses the basic principles of energy-efficient landscaping and identifies specific principles for various climates: temperate; cool; hot, arid; and hot, humid. The second section offers advice on water-efficient landscaping, lawn care, native plants, recycling garden waste, and environmentally sound pest management.

A third section provides tips on design, installation, and maintenance. Appendices

NORMAN A. PLATE

### Tool of the Month

*For centuries, Japanese gardeners have used bamboo brooms to sweep up garden debris. These take no te brooms are unsurpassed at sweeping fallen leaves and twigs from uneven surfaces such as ground covers and pebble-covered paths. To sweep with these brooms, you use a light flicking action. The brooms are made in a small Japanese village and imported. You can order them by mail from Take No Te, 415 26th Ave. E., Seattle, Wash. 98112; (800) 246-2910. Cost is $20 plus shipping and handling.*

in the fourth section give details on plant hardiness, solar angles, and tree densities. Numerous line drawings illustrate the basic concepts. The book is available directly from the publisher; send $19.95 (postage included) to Appropriate Solutions Press, Dover Road, Box 39, South Newfane, Vt. 05351, or call (802) 348-7441.

## For strawberries next June, plant soon

Planting strawberries as early as possible in fall ensures a large crop next spring. Start looking in nurseries now or order bare-root plants by mail.

There are two basic types of strawberry plants: June-bearing and everbearing. June-bearing varieties produce most of their fruit in spring and early summer; they are considered the highest quality strawberry. Everbearing varieties bear fruit over a long period from spring into fall, but produce fewer ripe berries at any one time.

*June-bearing* varieties recommended for Northern California are 'Douglas', 'Pajaro',

and 'Sequoia'. 'Tioga' does well in warm inland areas (zone 14); 'Chandler' produces well in cool, damp climates (zone 17).

*Everbearing* varieties for Northern California include 'Ozark Beauty' and 'Quinault'.

Plant strawberries in the ground as soon as you get them. Choose a site in full sun with well-drained soil. Space plants 1 to 2 feet apart with 2 to 4 feet between rows (use the shorter spacing for everbearing varieties). Plant the crown (base of plant) at soil level; don't plant too deep or too high. For bare-root plants, spread roots out at planting time, don't crowd them together.

If you can't find strawberry plants at local nurseries, here are two mail-order sources: J. M. Enterprises, Box 802, Anderson, Calif. 96007, (916) 365-5680; and Peaceful Valley Farm Supply, Box 2209, Grass Valley, Calif., 95945, (916) 272-4769.

*By Debra Lee Baldwin, Sharon Cohoon, Linda Estrin, David Lansing, Steven R. Lorton, Ben Marks, Jim McCausland, Lynn Ocone, Lauren Bonar Swezey, Lance Walheim*

## October Checklist
### ■
### PACIFIC NORTHWEST

**ACCUMULATE COM-POST.** As you rake up fallen leaves and cut back spent perennials and annuals, turn them into the compost pile. If new garden debris is mixed into well-worked compost, it should be broken down and ready to spread on beds by early spring.

**BUY AND PLANT BULBS.** Shop early for the best selection of spring-blooming bulbs; choose ones that are plump and firm. Crocus, daffodils, grape hyacinth, hyacinth, scilla, and tulips can all go in the ground now. Shop later for bargains, but avoid soft or shriveled bulbs.

**FLUSH DRIP SYSTEMS.** Turn your system on full blast one last time. Check each emitter. Clean or replace any that aren't functioning at the proper rate. Then remove end caps and flush the system with water to push any sediments out of the line. Drain the lines. Take aboveground systems indoors for the winter. Disconnect buried systems.

**CARE FOR HOUSE PLANTS.** Plants that have spent the summer outdoors should come indoors by midmonth to avoid a damaging chill. Cover the soil in each pot with plastic, put the plants in the shower, and rinse them thoroughly with lukewarm water, washing the dust off the stems and tops and undersides of all the leaves. Take them back outside to dry. Clip off damaged or yellowed leaves. Use a kitchen fork, chopstick, or small hand-cultivator to loosen the soil in the top of the pot. Water plants well and bring them indoors.

**DIVIDE PERENNIALS.** When perennials look lackluster, it is often because they are crowded. With a spading fork, dig up clumps of perennials such as Shasta daisies, daylilies, *Centaurea*, Siberian iris, and phlox. Cut the clumps into pieces about the size of a cup saucer, and replant them. Cut foliage back to about 4 to 6 inches from the ground and water well. Feed perennials in late February and early April to promote bloom.

**GROOM LAWNS.** To have a neat-looking lawn through winter, mow and edge the lawn well as the growing season for grass comes to an end. Rake up fallen leaves; if you let them accumulate, they'll get wet, mat up, and smother the lawn. Early in the month, overseed bald spots.

**MULCH.** Spread a 3- to 4-inch layer of mulch over the roots of tender plants to help them survive winter cold snaps.

**PLANT GROUND COV-ERS.** This month and next are the best time to get ground covers established.

**PREPARE PLANTING BEDS.** Once you've pulled the last of the summer vegetables and flowers, spread on generous amounts of compost, shredded leaves, and well-rotted manure, then dig or rotary-till it into the soil.

**PREPRUNE FRUIT TREES.** Once leaves have dropped, prune out dead, diseased, or injured limbs. Dispose of diseased wood. Most books say to prune active growth on fruit trees in late winter or early spring (about the time you prune roses), but in the mild climate of the coastal Northwest, you can do this anytime from now on without fear of plant damage from hard freezes.

**STORE PRODUCE.** Members of the squash family should be stored with at least 2 inches of stem left on the fruit in a cool, dry, preferably dark place. Store them so fruits don't touch and air can circulate around them. Onions, shallots, and nuts should go in mesh bags or slotted crates. Check all stored produce regularly for signs of rot.

**UNTANGLE POTBOUND ROOTS.** Perennials and shrubs you've been using as container plants can go into the ground now. Before you transplant, pull apart the tangle of roots that has wound around the sides of the pot. Dig a generous planting hole in the ground and add organic matter and plant, spreading the roots out in the hole as much as possible. Firm soil over roots and water.

**WRAP YOUNG TREE TRUNKS.** The low winter sun can burn tree trunks and cause cracking by thawing the trunks quickly after a freeze. Trunk wrap is sold at garden stores or through mail-order catalogs. Burlap (or any coarse fabric) also works well. Wrap the fabric around the trunk, gently spiraling from bottom to top. Tie twine around the trunk at 2-foot intervals to secure the wrap.

## October Checklist

**NORTHERN CALIFORNIA**

**CONTROL SNAILS AND SLUGS.** They mount a full attack in cool, damp fall weather. After dark, use a flashlight to conduct a search-and-destroy patrol around plants in the garden and in containers. Handpick the culprits and crush them or discard in a closed container. If they're too numerous for handpicking, use a liquid or dry bait.

**DIVIDE PERENNIALS.** If your perennials appear crowded or have smaller blooms this year, it's time to divide them. Candidates include asters, bellflowers, callas, daisies, daylilies, helianthus, heliopsis, rudbeckia, and yarrow. Dig each clump so the rootball remains intact. Wash or gently shake off excess soil, then cut divisions using a sharp knife. Each division should have leaves and plenty of roots. Plant immediately.

**FEED ANNUALS.** Get flowers off to a strong start and early bloom by feeding plants with a high-nitrogen fertilizer according to package directions. Make sure the soil is moist before fertilizing. If you use a dry fertilizer, water thoroughly after applying it.

**PLANT ANNUALS.** For winter through spring bloom, plant cool-season annuals now, so they get established and start blooming before the weather turns cold. Set out seedlings of calendula, pansies, Iceland poppies, primroses, snapdragons, stock, and violas. In zones 15, 16, and 17, you can also plant calceolaria, cineraria, nemesia, and schizanthus. Sow these from seed: baby blue eyes, forget-me-nots, sweet alyssum, sweet peas, and spring wildflowers. If you plant from nursery sixpacks, remove the seedlings and loosen roots by gently pulling apart the bottom third of the rootball; new roots will grow from broken ends into surrounding soil instead of just circling around the existing rootball.

**PLANT LAWNS.** Before planting, rotary-till the soil and add plenty of organic matter and a lawn fertilizer for new grass.

**PLANT FOR PERMANENCE.** This is one of the best months for setting out any kind of plant that's not frost tender. Ground covers, shrubs, trees, and most perennials benefit from fall planting. They get off to a fast start in still-warm soil and then develop a healthy root system during the cool months ahead.

**PLANT VEGETABLES.** There's still time to plant onions, radishes, spinach, and turnips. Lettuce can be planted year-round in many parts of zone 17.

**POT UP BULBS.** A 16-inch pot with flared sides will hold 40 to 50 bulbs of daffodils, hyacinths, or tulips. Set bulbs snugly on a base of potting soil just deep enough so their tops are about 4 inches below the pot rim. Cover bulbs with soil, leaving about 1 inch at the top for watering space. Set the pot in a cool shady area, wet the soil, and top off the pot with wood shavings; dampen the shavings. Move pots into full sun when leaves develop. Flowers appear about four months after planting.

**TIDY UP.** Remove fruit and leaf litter under trees. Compost only pest-free plant debris. If you suspect pests, bag up the debris and toss it in the garbage.

**WATER.** If rains don't come this month, or if rainfall is sporadic, continue to water even if the weather gets cold. Cold, dry winds take moisture out of leaves, and roots can't provide more moisture if the soil is dry (many plants that died in the severe 1990 freeze were victims of dehydration, since rains had been almost nonexistent that fall). Check soil moisture by digging down with a trowel.

San Rafael

Walnut Creek

Oakland

San Francisco

San Jose

Monterey

Coastal (zone 17)

Inland (zones 14–16)

# October Checklist

## CENTRAL VALLEY

**BUY AND PLANT SPRING BULBS.** Choose from crocus, daffodil, Dutch iris, freesia, grape hyacinth, leucojum, ranunculus, scilla, and tulips. Lesser-known bulbs are babiana, ixia, sparaxis, tritonia, and watsonia; they multiply and come back in greater profusion each year.

**COMPOST.** As you remove spent annuals and vegetables, incorporate them into the compost pile along with other disease-free garden debris. Keep the pile moist, but not soggy; add a small amount of nitrogen fertilizer to speed decay. Turn the pile every few weeks.

**CONTROL SLUGS AND SNAILS.** Cooler, dewy nights bring out slugs and snails en masse. After dark, use a flashlight and search out these pests. Handpick and crush or dispose of them in a closed container. If they're too numerous for handpicking, set out bait.

**DIG UP BULBLIKE PLANTS.** After foliage has withered, dahlias, gladiolus, and tuberous bogonias are ready for digging. Carefully clean corms and tubers, then store in a cool, dry, frost-free place during winter.

**DIVIDE PERENNIALS.** If you noted smaller blooms this season, chances are plants are overcrowded. Dig up clumps of agapanthus, asters, daylily, perennial candytuft, Shasta daisy, and yarrow. Divide the clumps by slicing through the rootball with a shovel or prying the clump apart with your hands or a spading fork.

**ORDER BARE-ROOT PLANTS.** If you want to try special varieties of fruit or shade trees, or berries, order plants soon through mail-order suppliers so you'll be sure to get the ones you want in time for bare-root planting.

**PLANT COOL-SEASON COLOR.** Set out nursery plants of calendulas, pansies, Iceland poppies, primroses, snapdragons, stock, and violas. Sow seeds of bachelor's button, Johnny-jump-ups, sweet alyssum, and sweet peas. Try interplanting annuals in beds of spring-blooming bulbs.

**PLANT COOL-SEASON CROPS.** There is still time to plant some cool-season vegetables on the valley floor (zones 8, 9, 14). Sow seeds or set out transplants of peas and lettuce; sow seeds of onions, radishes, spinach, and turnips.

**PLANT LAWNS.** Plant cool-season lawns, such as bluegrass, tall fescue, and perennial rye. Fertilize existing lawns. If you have Bermuda grass, dethatch, aerate, and overseed with ryegrass or tall fescue. Mow grass to 2 to 3 inches high.

**PLANT PERENNIALS.** Nurseries now offer a wider variety of perennials than ever before, and you're more likely to find them in economical sixpacks. Choices include campanula, columbine, coral bells, coreopsis, delphinium, felicia, gloriosa and Shasta daisies, candytuft, penstemon, salvia, and yarrow.

**PLANT FOR PERMANENCE.** Many trees, shrubs, ground covers, and vines can be planted this month. But wait until spring to plant frost-tender subtropicals such as citrus and bougainvillea.

Redding

Lake Tahoe

Sacramento

Fresno

Bakersfield

◩ Valley and foothills (zones 7–9, 14)

▢ Mountain (zones 1, 2)

**SOW WILDFLOWERS.** Fall is the best time to sow wildflowers for spring bloom. Prepare the soil by watering to germinate weed seeds, then kill the weeds by hoeing or using a contact herbicide. Then broadcast wildflower seed and lightly rake it into the soil. Let winter rains supply the water.

# October Checklist

## SOUTHERN CALIFORNIA

Zones 18–21
Zones 22–24

**CARE FOR AZALEAS AND CAMELLIAS.** Right now, azaleas and camellias are developing their flower buds for spring. A thorough, deep soaking will help ensure a good spring flower display. To promote larger camellia blooms, pinch off excess buds, leaving one or two at the end of each stem.

**CLEAN DECAYING MATERIAL FROM PLANTS.** To keep trees and shrubs disease-free, remove decaying fruits and flowers from under the canopy. Fungal spores will continue their cycle of disease and may contaminate your garden if allowed to remain. Infected material should be disposed of rather than composted.

**CLEAR GROUND FOR NEW PLANTINGS.** "Grow and kill" is a valuable defense against annual and perennial weeds and is widely recommended in preparation for fall plantings. As cool-season weeds begin to germinate, encourage their growth by watering, then pull or treat with an herbicide. Repeat treatment again a few weeks later. Afterward, weed competition should significantly decrease.

**CUT BACK GERANIUMS (PELARGONIUMS).** For compact growth and better blooms next spring, trim now by one-half to one-third. Use cuttings to start new plants.

**DIVIDE PERENNIALS.** Plants growing in crowded clumps should be divided; crowding inhibits bloom, and division is an ideal way to propagate new plants. Dig up plant, shake soil from rootball, cut divisions with a sharp knife, and replant immediately. Plants to divide now include bearded irises, callas, daylilies, fortnight lilies, ginger, and yarrow. Wait to divide asters, coreopsis, and Shasta daisies until they finish blooming. Kaffir lilies, however, prefer crowding— wait to divide until tuberous roots push themselves out of the ground.

**FEED ROSES FOR WINTER BLOOM.** Give roses one last feeding early in October; continue watering and deadheading to promote a final bloom cycle.

**FERTILIZE DROUGHT-TOLERANT PLANTS.** At lower elevations, October begins the season of active root growth for drought-tolerant plants. Apply balanced time-release fertilizers to fortify root systems and to promote spring-time growth. Put off fertilizing frost-sensitive plants until spring.

**LAWN TIPS.** Feed fescues and other cool-season lawns with a complete fertilizer containing at least 6 percent nitrate nitrogen. Nitrate-based fertilizers also help keep warm-season lawns, such as St. Augustine and Bermuda grass, greener longer. Overseed and mulch Bermuda grass before it goes dormant. For St. Augustine lawns, switch to a warm-season fertilizer such as 16-6-8 with ammoniac nitrogen in March.

**MANAGE PESTS.** As the temperature cools, pest populations multiply. To control aphids and white-flies, hose plants off or spray with insecticidal soap; repeat every three to four days. To guard against slugs and snails, handpick at night, and wrap trunks of citrus with copper bands.

**PLANT COLOR IN SHADE.** Replace tired impatiens with English or obconica primroses. If you like tall spiky flowers, you'll enjoy the striking show of color you'll get with masses of 'Rocket' snapdragons, which grow as tall as 3 feet. Ornamental kale is fun and different—as weather cools, its lavender, purple, and creamy white leaves become more deeply and brightly colored.

**PLANT EDIBLE FLOWERS.** Sow seeds of calendulas, chives, pansies, and violets amid your fall vegetables to dress up your salads as well as your planting beds.

**PREPARE FOR FALL PLANTING.** Throughout Southern California, October signals the arrival of the year's best planting time for most trees, shrubs, and perennials. Exceptions include bare-root roses and deciduous trees (not available for planting until later), and cold-sensitive tropical and subtropical plants, such as avocado, bougainvillea, citrus, and hibiscus. Expect the fall cooling trend by the start of the month at high elevations, by mid-month along the coast, by Halloween inland. Plants started now will not show much top growth until spring, but roots will be getting established.

**PREPARE HIGH-ELEVATION GARDENS FOR WINTER.** Thinning and staking evergreen shrubs prevents fragile stems from snapping under winter's heavy snows. Piling a 4- to 5-inch teepee of pine-needle mulch around stems of perennials, as well as shrubs such as rhododendrons and roses, keeps soil temperatures relatively even and prevents root damage.

**SOW FLOWER SEEDS.** Cool-season annuals to start this month from seed are alyssum, baby blue eyes, candytuft, forget-me-not, linaria, Shirley poppies, and sweet peas.

**TEND CHRYSANTHEMUMS.** For fewer but larger blooms, remove side buds on plants with developing buds (not open flowers). Check for aphids. Withhold fertilizer when buds show color, and tie stems to stakes to support heavy blooms.

**WATER FOR SANTA ANA WINDS.** Plants that droop during these two- and three-day dry spells will perk up if misted occasionally. Keep soil moist and protect roots with a layer of mulch. Especially sensitive are azaleas, camellias, ferns, fuchsias, impatiens, and tuberous begonias; in warmer inland areas, cover with shadecloth.

## ANYWHERE IN THE WEST, TACKLE THESE CHORES:

☐ **DIVIDE PERENNIALS.** When blooms on previously healthy perennials become smaller and plants seem weaker, overcrowding is often the cause. Cure it by dividing perennials and re- planting them in freshly amended beds. Use a sharp spade or pruning knife to make divisions, depending on which kind of perennial you're working with; each clump should have plenty of roots and leaves.

☐ **KEEP A GARDEN JOURNAL.** If you don't have one, now is a good time to start. Write down this year's successes and failures, and note plants you want to include in next year's garden, including fall fruits and vegetables you sample from other gardens now.

☐ **PLANT FLOWER BULBS.** Buy them now for planting right away. They'll provide the first color in spring, and many will naturalize in your garden (see page 244).

☐ **SOW WILDFLOWER SEEDS.** There are many commercial mixes available; you'll do best with one that's tailored for your area. Prepare soil and sow now for emergence early next spring (details on page 241).

## IN THE INTERMOUNTAIN WEST, DO THESE CHORES:

☐ **AMEND SOIL.** This is a great time to do advance preparation for next spring's garden beds. You can dig in uncomposted barnyard manure now with impunity: by next spring it will all have rotted.

☐ **COMPOST EVERYTHING.** Put leftover vines, stalks, and leaves in a compost pile, or dig leafy remains directly into garden soil (this is called sheet composting). Sheet composting isn't as successful with corn stalks, but you can simply knock them down and let them lie where they fall; you'll be able to till them in by spring before you plant. (Corn left standing all winter is still too dry, fibrous, and woody to sheet compost in spring.)

☐ **FLUSH DRIP SYSTEMS.** Turn on drip systems one last time, taking note of clogged or damaged emitters. Order replacements for those you can't repair. Take end caps off main lines and run water through them, then drain and replace end caps. Take ooze tubing up after flushing and store it in a garage or basement over winter.

☐ **ORDER FRUITS, NUTS, AND BERRIES.** If you plan to set out any rare or unusual varieties during bare-root season, order now from mail-order sources or retail nurseries.

☐ **PICK UP FALLEN FRUIT.** Compost dropped fruit and fallen leaves before insects invade.

## IN THE SOUTHWEST'S LOW AND INTERMEDIATE DESERTS:

☐ **FEED LAWNS.** Apply 1 pound actual nitrogen per 1,000 square feet of lawn. For newly seeded winter lawns, fertilize after they're 6 weeks old.

☐ **HARVEST VEGETABLES.** You should be harvesting mature, summer- sown beans, lettuce, and radishes now. Also harvest fall-sown seedlings as soon as they come up, thinning them out to the distance recommended on the package.

☐ **MANAGE PESTS.** As fall flowers and vegetables start putting on tender new growth, aphids, whiteflies, and snails often move in to feast. The secret is to control pest populations before they get out of hand. Hose off plants invaded by aphids and whiteflies, then spray insecticidal soap to get remaining insects. Bait for snails, or handpick them.

☐ **OVERSEED LAWNS.** Mow Bermuda lawns closely (at about ½ inch) and overseed with perennial rye.

☐ **PLANT COOL-SEASON ANNUALS.** Nurseries have lots of choices for winter color: calendula, dianthus, English daisy, Iceland poppy, lobelia, nemesia, ornamental cabbage and kale, pansy, primrose, schizanthus, snapdragon, stock, and viola.

☐ **PLANT COOL-SEASON VEGETABLES.** You have many choices, including beets, cabbage and its close relations (bok choy, broccoli, brussels sprouts, cauliflower, Chinese cabbage, kale, kohlrabi), carrots, garlic, lettuce, onions, parsley, peas, radishes, and turnips.

☐ **PLANT FLOWER BULBS.** Plant amaryllis, anemone, calla, crocus, daffodils, harlequin flower, oxalis, ranunculus, and watsonia. Chill bulbs of crocus, hyacinths, and tulips in the refrigerator for at least six weeks before planting.

☐ **PLANT GROUND COVERS.** Try *Acacia redolens*, Baja and Mexican evening primroses, *Dalea greggii*, dwarf rosemary, gazania, lippia, low-growing junipers, snow-in-summer (*Cerastium tomentosum*), and verbena.

☐ **PLANT NATIVES.** This is the best month to set out all kinds of native plants. Prepare soil well, digging a hole the depth of the rootball and three to five times as wide for trees and shrubs. For seeds, dig soil at least one spit deep (the depth of a spade blade) and amend soil with organic matter before sowing.

☐ **PLANT PERENNIALS.** Set them out right away for spring bloom.

☐ **PLANT SHRUBS AND TREES.** Plant everything except those (like bougainvillea and hibiscus) that won't tolerate cold.

☐ **PLANT STRAWBERRIES.** Set them out after midmonth for a crop next spring. 'Sequoia' and 'Tioga' do well here.

☐ **TEND ROSES.** Prune them back by about a third, feed, and water to encourage one more round of bloom by Christmas.

☐ **WATER.** Everything needs watering if nature doesn't provide it, especially anything you've sown or planted this fall. Check soil moisture with a trowel, watering when the top inch of soil has dried out.

# Bulbs
# Forever

*Plant them now and these
naturalizers will brighten your
garden winter into summer…
year after year.*

By Jim McCausland and
Lauren Bonar Swezey

**LIKE WILDFLOWERS,** *ranks of
'Ice Follies' daffodils come up
spring after spring, bearing
bicolored, flat-cupped flowers.*

You planted them on a fall day several years ago, and every winter they take you by surprise: almost overnight, fat green spears push up out of the ground and into the cold air. A few weeks later, your first bulbs are in bloom, and the progression of color—from crocus to daffodils to lilies—continues into summer.

Call them naturalizers or perennializers: these are the bulbs that do so well they keep coming back year after year. Some even multiply. Most of them succeed because they're made for the West's wet-winter, dry-summer climate. They shoot up when rainfall is abundant, then go dormant when summer drought reaches its peak.

To find the best performers for fall planting, we talked to gardeners and growers all over the West. Pick the right bulbs for your area, and they should brighten your garden for years to come.

Along with naturalizing, consider the other merits of bulbs: they're easy to plant, relatively pest-free, and come in an amazing array of flower forms, colors, and heights. With bloom times ranging from late winter into summer, bulbs can give you a carefree pageant of color that lasts more than half the year.

DOUG WILSON

AMONG *the earliest signs of spring, Dutch crocus carpet a Northwest lawn.*

NORMAN A. PLATE

SUMMER SHOW-OFFS *in a 9- by 16-foot perennial bed, lilies include regal (white), 'Tristar' (red), and 'Connecticut King' (yellow).*

## The landscaper's dilemma

Bulbs look best when their flowers are massed in plain sight. They look worst when their dying foliage is massed in plain sight. But if you cut back the foliage before it fades, you cut back the life of the bulb. Here are four landscaping solutions that show off bulbs to best advantage and encourage naturalizing:

**Overseed bulbs with annuals.** Use tall, lacy-leafed summer annuals such as cosmos and baby's breath. They'll conceal declining foliage without blocking the light it needs. Avoid types that need abundant summer irrigation, which is bad for dormant flower bulbs. Whenever you dig bulbs to divide (see page 252), you'll need to tear out the annuals too.

**Overplant with ground covers.** We've seen daffodils push up through English ivy year after year, though in the long run, aggressive ground covers win the survival contest. Innumerable Western pastures are studded with daffodils, and many Northwest lawns sport colorful spots of crocus. To keep bulbs healthy, plant swaths you can mow around until foliage dies down. Bear in mind that ground covers make bulb division a bleak prospect.

**Plant clusters in flower beds.** Even small groups of bulbs provide impressive spot color. Eleanor Christensen, of West Shore Acres Bulb Farm in Washington, recommends planting bulbs in a kidney-shaped pattern. "It's so adaptable: you can stretch it out or wrap it around other flowers, perennials, or small shrubs, and you can do it with almost any number of bulbs." The only caveat is to dig bulbs every three years or so, as much to clear away invading roots as to divide the bulbs.

**Naturalize in mulched earth.** Nursey owner Dianne Bell planted 10,000 daffodil bulbs on a conifer-shaded hill. "On the first day, I dug holes and spaced bulbs 6 inches apart, sprinkled in bulb starter, and set each bulb top up. I was less precise the second day. By the third day, I was flinging bushels of bulbs over the hillside, dragging soil and mulch over them, and not even thinking about fertilizer. The amazing thing is that, five years later, I can't tell the difference between the beds I planted the first day and those I planted the third."

Covering bulbs with mulch improves soil, keeps down weeds, retains moisture, and lends a natural effect well suited to a relaxed landscape; the warmer the climate, the thicker the mulch should be.

# Best bets for naturalizing

More important than how you plant is what you plant. The following are good naturalizers in all or most of the West, and they're readily available this month in nurseries and through catalogs. Bloom times are approximate: expect earlier bloom in Southern California and the low desert, later in northern and high-elevation areas.

## Scilla or Bluebells (*Endymion*)

There are two groups called bluebells or scilla. Spanish bluebells (*E. hispanicus*) come mostly in blue (though there are white, pink, and rose forms available), grow well almost everywhere, and look like loose woodland hyacinths. Their 20-inch flower stalks rise above grassy foliage in spring.

The true scillas include Peruvian scilla (*Scilla peruviana*), which naturalizes along the California coast and in most of Southern California, and Siberian squill (*S. siberica*), which naturalizes only in the Northwest and the high desert. Peruvian scilla has a full dome of blue flowers that rise to the top of 10-inch, strappy leaves in late spring. Siberian squill is low—less than 6 inches high—and has a looser stalk of spring flowers in shades of blue, white, and purplish pink. Both kinds do well in light shade. Plant bulbs 3 to 4 inches deep and 6 inches apart.

## Calla (*Zantedeschia*)

From Seattle to San Diego, callas are widely known and sold both as dormant rhizomes and as nursery plants. Plants do best in mild coastal climates, where they're evergreen; in colder areas, foliage dies down in winter. The rhizomes develop clumps you can divide every few years. Plant 4 to 6 inches deep and 1 to 2 feet apart to allow room for the large arrow-shaped leaves.

In spring and early summer, the common calla (*Z. aethiopica*) bears 3-foot stems, each topped by a large white flower (spathe) with yellow, fingerlike spadix in the center. Dwarf and colored (pink, yellow, and purple) callas are less vigorous.

NORMAN A. PLATE

## Crocus

Dutch crocus (*C. vernus*) naturalize in areas with pronounced winters; that excludes much of California. In late winter through early spring, the lawn-high, urn-shaped flowers—white, yellow, lavender, purple, or striped—appear just above grasslike foliage. Plant bulbs 2 to 4 inches deep and 4 inches apart, arranging them in masses or in highly visible clusters along walkways and borders. Go light on water in summer (often not possible if you plant crocus in lawns).

## Daffodil (*Narcissus*)

Drive through Western farmland and you'll see daffodils growing along the edges of fields and pastures, as they have for decades. Don't be misled into thinking all daffodils naturalize: some may give a great show the first year but then decline. You'll do best with mixes sold for naturalizing or by buying any of the following varieties.

Large trumpets or cups for bloom from early to midspring: 'Carlton', large-cupped yellow; 'Ice Follies', early flat-cupped bicolor that fades to cream; 'King Alfred', the best-known type of yellow trumpet (the name is so popular it's used to identify similar daffodils, including 'Dutch Master' and 'Unsurpassable'). Plant large-flowered types 4 to 6 inches deep, 6 to 8 inches apart.

Cyclamineus hybrids (single, medium-size flowers with swept-back petals), early spring: 'February Gold' and (somewhat later) 'Peeping Tom', both yellow. Multiflowered daffodils (the most fragrant): 'Thalia', an early-spring, white triandrus hybrid; 'Suzy' (midspring) or 'Trevithian' (late spring), both yellow jonquilla hybrids; 'Cheerfulness' (white) or 'Yellow Cheerfulness', late-spring doubles. In mild parts of California, single or double paperwhites and the related gold-cupped, yellow 'Soleil d'Or' flower all winter. In the Northwest, the best tazetta is the somewhat hardier 'Geranium', whose red-orange corona and white petals appear in early spring. Set small-flowered types 3 to 4 inches deep, 4 to 6 inches apart.

Most daffodils grow 1 to 2 feet high. If your garden gets a lot of rain or wind in spring, avoid tall and double-flowered kinds, which get knocked down more easily than singles and short varieties.

(Continued on page 248)

## Freesia

Only mild-winter parts of Arizona and California have a climate benign enough to convince freesias to naturalize. While they reproduce reliably there, their fragrant flowers are smaller the second year. Comeback is iffier in the San Francisco Bay Area and comparable climates, and freesias are one-season plants in the Northwest.

Spindly stems, 12 to 18 inches tall, tend to flop over from the weight of their multiple blossoms, which bloom in succession from late winter to early spring. To prop up the flower stalks, interplant freesias with strong-foliaged annuals or perennials they can lean on.

Hybrid freesias come in all colors. If you don't deadhead spent flowers, they may self-sow—and the offsprings' flowers usually revert to cream color marked with purple and yellow. For best fragrance, try 'Safari' (yellow), 'Snowdon' (double white), Tecolote red, and Tecolote yellow. Plant corms 2 inches deep, 2 to 3 inches apart.

## Grape hyacinth (*Muscari*)

The pea-size blue flowers of *Muscari armeniacum* bunch together like clusters of grapes atop 6-inch stems with grassy leaves. The white form is *M. botryoides* 'Album', which also naturalizes well.

For a bold swath of spring color, start with at least three or four dozen bulbs, and set them 2 to 3 inches deep, 3 inches apart. Use them to create a cool riverine corridor that plays up the hot colors of surrounding tulips and daffodils.

## Bearded iris

Tall bearded irises come in almost every color and perform well in all climate zones. The tendency among breeders now is to develop strong-stemmed, shorter varieties—in the 3-foot range instead of 4 feet and taller—so they stand up to bad weather and fit easily into the perennial border. There are plenty of varieties with ruffles, great colors, and abundant blooms to choose from. All bloom in April or May.

Breeders charge as much as $40 per rhizome for new varieties, but older varieties run $2 to $5. By dividing rhizomes every three years, you can really stretch your investment. Breeders have also been working on reblooming varieties, which flower in both spring and fall; they have a ways to go in reliability and flower color range, but you might want to experiment with them.

Mail-order sources generally stop shipping bearded irises by the end of September, but you should still find stock in nurseries in October. Place rhizomes 1 to 2 feet apart, with the top just below the soil surface and the roots spread out.

## Dutch iris

They come in a wide range of colors and grow in all zones. In the mildest parts of Southern California, naturalizing results are mixed—you may lose some or even all of your bulbs after the first year or two. The farther north you are, the better the return, as long as the ground doesn't freeze down to bulb level.

You can choose from about 12 varieties of Dutch iris in shades of yellow, white, blue, and purple, with some stunning bicolors; all behave about the same. We like the planting scheme of Lew Whitney (of Rogers Gardens in Corona del Mar, California), who sets out pure drifts of 8 to 12 bulbs of each variety he can get his hands on; they flower over about a month, late spring into early summer. Plant bulbs 4 inches deep, 3 to 4 inches apart.

## Leucojum

Sometimes called summer snowflake, leucojum is often confused with snowdrop (*Galanthus nivalis*). Leucojum grows everywhere and has lots of little bell-shaped white flowers on 18-inch stalks; snowdrop, which grows only where winters are chilly, has slightly larger white flowers on plants that are less than a foot tall.

Leucojum takes well to life under deciduous trees and in mixed shrub or perennial borders. Plant bulbs 3 to 4 inches deep, 3 to 4 inches apart. Don't disturb them for the first few years, then divide them. Flowers appear in winter in mild climates, in early spring in colder areas.

NORMAN A. PLATE

## Lily

Lilies come in an enormous array of sizes, colors, and bloom seasons (the ones listed here flower in early summer). All are temperate-zone plants, and most are readily available in fall.

A Northwest grower gave us a good tip: "If you want to naturalize lots of lilies, buy the cheaper ones on any grower's list. They're cheap because they multiply so quickly for us."

Asiatic lilies naturalize well in most of the West. Some good Asiatics to try are yellow 'Mary Bernard' or 'Connecticut King', orange 'Enchantment' or 'Pretender', deep peach 'Tiger Babies', red 'Tristar', and white 'Brushstroke', 'Nepal', or 'White Sails'.

Among Oriental lilies, good perennializers include 'Casablanca' (white), Imperial Gold, Imperial Silver, 'Rubrum' (pink to reddish), and 'Stargazer' (red and white), a favorite of almost every grower we talked with. In warm areas, plant these bulbs in light shade and mulch well.

Other good choices are regal lily (*L. regale,* fragrant white), *L. pumilum* (fragrant, coral), and trumpet-flowered lilies. These don't need much winter chill to keep coming back.

Avoid tiger lily (*L. lancifolium*), which is the Typhoid Mary of the group: without showing symptoms, it carries diseases that can affect other bulbs in your garden.

Give lilies even moisture and cool soil; a thick layer of organic mulch helps. Space bulbs about 1 foot apart, setting small bulbs 2 to 3 inches deep, medium ones 3 to 4 inches, and large ones 4 to 6 inches. Keep beds well weeded; lilies can't compete with grass runners. And bear in mind that lilies are a feast for gophers, squirrels, and deer.

## Watsonia

You can grow this South African native in all mild parts of the West, but it's most successful in coastal California. Almost all plants labeled watsonia are *W. pyramidata,* which bears 4- to 6-foot spikes of red, white, lavender, or pink flowers that bloom in late spring and early summer. The deciduous leaves, which grow in fall and winter, reach about 2½ feet tall.

The rare species *W. beatricis* is evergreen, with flower colors that range from peach and apricot to scarlet. Bloom time is mid- to late summer.

Both kinds produce fine, long-lasting cut flowers and survive with little extra summer water. Given their height, watsonias lend themselves to the back of a garden bed. Plant them 4 inches deep, 6 inches apart.

## The Bulb Family

We group them together as bulbs, but only some are true bulbs, with fleshy scales usually surrounded by a papery tunic. (Because they lack this tunic, lily bulbs are more susceptible to drying out.) Corms have solid center tissue instead of scales. Rhizomes are thickened stems that usually grow horizontally near the surface of the soil. Tubers and tuberous roots are also commonly grouped with bulbs.

These pictures represent typical shapes for the leading naturalizers. We show them oriented the way you should plant them, but if you're still puzzled by which end goes up, setting bulbs on their sides is a good way to hedge.

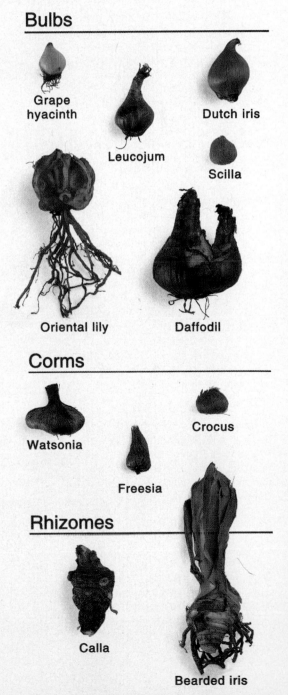

### Bulbs

Grape hyacinth

Leucojum

Dutch iris

Scilla

Oriental lily

Daffodil

### Corms

Watsonia

Freesia

Crocus

### Rhizomes

Calla

Bearded iris

# Other choices for naturalizing

Many of the following may not be well known or widely available, but they're all good naturalizers in at least part of the West.

• **African corn lily** (*Ixia*). This drought-tolerant plant grows in all mild-winter parts of the West, desert included. The 18-inch stems bear spikes of dark-centered red, yellow, cream, pink, or orange flowers that are good for cutting. Leaves are swordlike, upright. As time passes, you'll get more plants naturally from seed, and by lifting and dividing corms in summer (replant in autumn—3 to 4 inches deep and apart).

• **Allium.** This ornamental onion relative produces striking, globe-shaped flowers. Good naturalizers include *A. moly* (10 inches tall, bearing yellow flowers in late spring), *A. neopolitanum* (15 inches tall, white, midseason), *A. sphaerocephalum* (20 inches tall, reddish purple flowers, early summer). Of these, *A. neopolitanum* is the only one that's tender, but even it will survive in mild parts of the Pacific Northwest. Depending on bulb size, plant 3 to 8 inches deep and apart.

• **Baboon flower** (*Babiana*). Easy to grow and widely available, plants bear 12-inch-tall flower spikes. Hybrids flower red, cream, blue, white, and lavender, while species flower blue, purple, white, and lavender (*B. stricta*) or deep red and royal blue (*B. rubrocyanea*). Corms naturalize where soil is well drained and relatively warm; set them 4 inches deep, 3 inches apart.

• **Daylily** (*Hemerocallis*). Despite their tuberous roots, daylilies didn't make our main list of bulbs simply because they're more commonly sold as plants in nursery cans. These classic do-gooders grow almost everywhere under almost all conditions. Flowers rise above a fountain of grasslike foliage that's usually 2 to 3 feet tall. True to their name, individual flowers last a day (rarely two) but open in succession to give a tremendous amount of summer bloom for little effort. Space plants about 1½ feet apart.

• **Harlequin flower** (*Sparaxis tricolor*). This is a Southwestern special, well suited to mild areas of California and the intermediate and subtropical deserts of Arizona. Plants have sword-shaped leaves on 1-foot stems that bear small, bright, usually tricolor flowers, as the botanical name suggests. Set corms 2 to 3 inches deep and 2 to 4 inches apart.

**ALLIUM MOLY**

**HYBRID DAYLILY**

**HARLEQUIN FLOWER**

**NAKED LADY**

**CANDIA TULIP**

• **Naked lady, or belladonna lily** (*Amaryllis belladonna*). Leafless, pink, lily-like flowers appear in summer on 2- to 3-foot stems; foliage follows in fall and winter. Excellent for mild-winter California. Foliage is damaged at about 20°, but bulbs usually survive temperatures that don't go below the teens. In dry California climates, bulbs need only occasional water. Set bulb tops even with the soil surface, and 8 inches apart.

• **Ornithogalum.** Star of Bethlehem is the common name for two related plants. *O. umbellatum,* the hardiest, produces white flowers on foot-tall stems; plant 2 to 3 inches deep, 6 to 8 inches apart. *O. arabicum* produces clusters of white flowers on 2-foot stems; it needs summer heat to bloom well (in the coastal Northwest, put plants against south-facing walls). Chincherinchee (*O. thyrsoides*) is a South African native that likes mild Southern California best. Plant the latter 5 to 6 inches apart and barely cover the tops with soil.

• **Spring star flower** (*Ipheion uniflorum*). You'll find its blue star flowers blooming in mild-winter gardens from San Diego to Seattle; survival depends on minimum temperatures above 15° or so. Short, grassy foliage and a tendency to multiply make it a successful ground cover in sun or part shade. It will grow in almost any soil and isn't fussy about water, but attracts slugs and snails. Plant 3 inches deep, 3 inches apart.

• **Tritonia.** Naturalizing in mild-winter California gardens, it grows little more than a foot tall, with brilliant clusters of warm-toned flowers. Though these bulbs need regular watering until flowers fade, they can go dry during summer. Set them 2 to 3 inches deep, 2 to 4 inches apart.

• **Tulip species.** Sometimes called botanicals, these are much smaller than hybrid tulips (5 to 12 inches tall), but still have charm. The best bets for mild climates are lady tulip (*T. clusiana* 'Cynthia') and its relation *T. c. chrysantha, T. greigii* varieties and hybrids, *T. hageri, T. kaufmanniana* varieties and hybrids, *T. praestans,* Candia tulip (*T. saxatilis*), and *T. sylvestris*. Plant 4 to 6 inches deep and 3 inches apart.

• **Windflower** (*Anemone*). These low growers with daisylike flowers do well everywhere except the desert, and naturalize well in the Pacific Northwest. The most common is blue *A. blanda,* which also has pink and white forms; plant tubers 1 to 2 inches deep, 2 inches apart in full sun (flowers close in the shade). *A. coronaria* strains are fine single-season choices, but they don't naturalize.

# Bulb Basics

**BULB SIZES** *of 'King Alfred'-type daffodils are graded DN #3 (one flower per bulb), DN #2 (one or two flowers), DN #1 (two or three flowers), and Jumbo (three or four flowers).*

## Grades of bulbs

Like eggs, bulbs are graded by size. Generally, the bigger the circumference, the more flowers you get. The most common sizes of narcissus (daffodils) range from DN #1 down to DN #3. The largest 'King Alfred' types are called jumbos. Narcissus smaller than DN #1 may be labeled in centimeters (typically 14 centimeters and smaller).

Dutch irises and lilies are graded in centimeters. Dutch irises range from 6 to 12 centimeters or larger; 8 to 9 centimeters is typical. Lilies run from 12 to 20 centimeters.

Sizes vary according to variety, too. For instance, large-cupped and trumpet daffodils produce larger bulbs than species and miniatures; blue Dutch iris bulbs are larger than the purple and yellow kinds.

When you're planting a large quantity for the long haul, choosing midsize bulbs makes economic sense. But beware of mail promotions that offer a large quantity of bulbs for just a few dollars: you may end up with undersize bulbs that produce few flowers.

Look for a note in catalogs that indicates the size and quality of bulbs; it may simply say top-size bulbs. When shopping locally, buy early in the season and choose firm bulbs that aren't sprouting. Generally, they should still have their outer skins intact (although sometimes pieces fall off in the box—common with freesias).

## Soil preparation

Good soil drainage is the key to long bulb life. "If you can't dig in it, you can't expect a bulb to live in it," says Dan Davids of Davids & Royston Bulb Company. Where soil is poorly drained, plant on a slope or in raised beds.

Before planting, add organic amendments if your soil is clayey, sandy, rocky, or low in nutrients. Your best bets are leaf mold, redwood soil conditioner, compost, or similar products; unless it's well aged, manure can burn bulbs. If the soil is low in organic matter, spread about 3 inches over the planting area and dig it in; use only an inch or so if the soil is already fairly loose and loamy. In acid soil in the Pacific Northwest, you may need to add lime to make the soil neutral.

At planting time, mix into the soil a bulb food or a balanced fertilizer, such as 10-10-10; these are generally better sources of nutrients than bonemeal. Fertilize again at bloom time or just when flowers fade. The following seasons, broadcast fertilizer over the soil and rake it in when flowers first emerge. When using a dry fertilizer, water it in well unless rain is expected.

## Planting

By laying out bulbs on top of the soil before you dig the first one in, you can fine-tune your planting scheme and distribute bulbs evenly. Or, for a natural random effect in a field or large planting area, just toss the bulbs onto the ground and plant them where they land.

In well-prepared or sandy soil, one of the easiest ways to plant is to use a trowel as shown below. A bulb planter works best in moist soil that's clayey enough to hold the soil together when the planter is removed. Push the planter into the soil and twist it slightly as you remove it. Some bulb planters have a release mechanism that opens the sides so the soil drops out easily. Otherwise, you have to knock the soil out.

For planting depth, the standard guideline is to set bulbs so they're covered with soil three times as deep as the bulb's diameter. But there are exceptions. In hot climates or sandy soil, plant slightly deeper than recommended; in heavy soil, plant slightly shallower. Some types of bulbs should be planted

**TO DIG PLANTING HOLES,** *grip trowel as shown, stab it into loose soil, and pull toward you; drop in the bulb and cover with soil.*

LUCY I. SARGEANT

just below the soil surface, as our listings note.

Bulbs can handle a tremendous amount of crowding; for a show-stopping effect in *Sunset*'s gardens, we mass them in pots so they're touching. But if you want bulbs to naturalize for a few years without having to divide them, don't jam them together.

## Watering

Water bulbs well at planting time and then water as needed to keep the soil moist (but not saturated) through winter and spring while roots are growing and flowers blooming. A layer of mulch over the soil will help maintain soil moisture.

Right after petals have faded or fallen off, remove the flower stalks so bulb energy isn't diverted into seed formation. Let the foliage remain and continue photosynthesizing, so bulbs will store up nutrients for next season's show. Bundling the foliage is not recommended; as Cynthia VanLierop of Van-Lierop Bulb Farm says, "Foliage is like arms and legs to bulbs; don't tie them up!" Wait for foliage to turn limp and yellow, then cut it back to 4 to 6 inches above the soil; pulling it off too soon can damage the bulb. Or wait until foliage dries up and then pull it off.

## Bulb division

Many bulbs can be left undivided for years. If bulbs aren't blooming well because of overcrowding, then it's time to divide. Daffodils may need dividing every three to five years, bearded irises every three or four years.

Lift most true bulbs in summer after the foliage dies down. Using a spading fork, carefully dig up and separate clumps into individual bulbs; each new bulb should include a piece of basal plate—the area from which new roots arise.

Divide bearded irises between July and the end of October (the earlier date in cold climates). Use a sharp knife to divide rhizomes, discarding the woody center. Plant only healthy sections with good fans of leaves; allow cuts to heal for several hours or up to a day before replanting.

Divide lilies in spring or fall. You can also propagate them from bulb scales that you pull off the main clump (see illustration below), or from bulblets. Scales and bulblets take at least three years to flower.

Corms (such as freesias) wither each year and grow new ones to replace the parent. They also produce cormels, or small corms, at the base; you can pick these off and replant them, but they generally won't bloom for the first two years.

## Troubleshooting

If bulbs decline prematurely, the problem is more likely to be overwatering than disease. In cool, moist weather, botrytis blight may damage lilies, causing leaf spots and stem rot,

but it usually doesn't affect the bulbs. A similar disease may rot narcissus flowers and bulbs. To prevent infection, plant where there's plenty of air circulation, keep beds free of debris, and keep soil dry when bulbs are dormant. Remove and destroy infected plant parts and rotting bulbs.

In mild climates, aphids can be a problem in spring. You can gently wash them off with water (hard blasts can damage flowers) or spray with insecticidal soap or other insecticide.

Gophers go after most bulbs except daffodils. So do mice, which follow mole tunnels to reach bulbs. To ward off these critters, use hardware cloth to surround bulbs or to line an entire bed. You can fashion a protective basket by bending two rectangles of hardware cloth into U shapes and nesting one inside the other so you have wire on all four sides; bury the basket so the edges are at soil level.

## Where to get bulbs

This month you'll find a good selection of bulbs in nurseries and garden centers around the West. But if you can't find what you want locally, try any of the Western mail-order sources listed below; all sell a wide selection of spring-flowering bulbs. For a list of specialty sources, including Western growers who focus on lilies, irises, daylilies or novelty daffodils, send a self-addressed, stamped envelope to Bulb Sources, *Sunset Magazine,* 80 Willow Rd., Menlo Park, Calif. 94025. It's late in the year for orders, so act quickly to have bulbs shipped for planting this fall.

For catalogs, contact ***Jackson & Perkins,*** Box 1028, Medford, Ore. 97501, (800) 292-4769; ***Marde Ross & Company,*** Box 1517, Palo Alto, Calif. 94302, (415) 328-5109; and ***Peaceful Valley Farm Supply,*** Box 2209, Grass Valley, Calif. 95945, (916) 272-4769 (also sells wire mesh planting baskets).

For phone orders (or on-site purchase) this month, try ***RoozenGaarde,*** 1587 Beaver Marsh Rd., Mount Vernon, Wash. 98273, (800) 732-3266; ***Van-Lierop Bulb Farm,*** 13407 80th St. E., Puyallup, Wash. 98372, (206) 848-7272; and ***West Shore Acres Bulb Farm,*** 956 Downey Rd., Mount Vernon, Wash. 98273, (206) 466-3158. ■

**DIVIDE DAFFODILS** *(above) by separating one or more healthy noses from the clump. Divide lilies by separating bulbs, or by peeling off scales (as shown at left) or bulblets along the stem.*

LUCY I. SARGEANT

GRANITE BOULDERS *and ornamental plants border a pool in the rock garden. A deck (below) off a bedroom overlooks the scene. Cattails and water lilies grow in the water; green tufts of fountain grass stand at poolside.*

# A trio of gardens surrounds a house with beauty, bounty

MICHAEL THOMPSON

ENTRY WALK *is a patchwork of salvaged stone slabs and old paving blocks. In the food garden (right), sweet corn and other crops thrive in raised beds.*

FITTING A HOUSE AND three different gardens into a 90- by 375-foot lot can be challenging, especially when the property sits high on a ridge. But as owners Don and Sylvia Campbell discovered, it can be done—beautifully. Architect George Suyama and landscape architect Robert W. Chittock joined forces to design and execute the project for the Campbells in Vancouver, Washington.

The contemporary house is surrounded by a trio of gardens: a woodsy entrance garden, a rock garden, and a high-production food garden. The landscape blends aspects of Oriental design with plants that thrive in the Pacific Northwest.

The entrance garden is essentially an open forest of Hinoki cypress underplanted with low-growing evergreens, ferns, and ground covers. A walk made of randomly shaped stones and pavers leads through the forest to the front door.

The rock garden resembles a mountainscape. Paths lead through outcroppings of rock in which perennials are planted in pockets of soil. The centerpiece of the rock garden is a pool fed by a recirculating stream.

The food garden occupies a space not more than 20 feet wide and 40 feet long on the west side of the house. Here, the Campbells grow a variety of their favorite vegetables, berries, and other fruits. These include several kinds of corn, bush and snow peas, Chinese cabbage, kohlrabi, Swiss chard, blueberries, everbearing raspberries, strawberries ('Benton', 'Hood', and 'Tristar'), and seedless 'Himrod' grapes. The vegetables are grown in 4-foot-wide, 16-inch-high raised beds made of pressure-treated lumber. The beds are watered by drip irrigation.

The Campbells' compact orchard consists of a dozen dwarf and espaliered fruit trees, including several varieties of apple, apricot, Asian pear, Italian plum, nectarine, peach, and 'Rainier' sweet cherry. ■

*By Nancy Davidson*

WILLIAM B. DEWEY

**DROUGHT-TOLERANT,** *low-fuel-volume plants used on this California slope for fire safety and to control erosion include artemisia (foreground), St. Catherine's lace (right), 'Yankee Point' ceanothus (center), and flowering trailing lantana.*

**EXISTING LARGE BOULDERS,** *as well as many smaller stones unearthed during construction, keep roof runoff from eroding the slope. Plant on the left is a 'Concha' ceanothus.*

planted. Two years later, the slope is doing fine, held in place by a combination of drought-tolerant and fire-resistant plants and erosion-control techniques.

## STARTING FRESH? NOT QUITE

The busy couple that owns the house wanted something colorful and easy to care for on the back slope. Rob Lane, of Rockrose Landscapes in Santa Barbara, took the couple's thinking further by adding his own requirements—erosion control, drought tolerance, fire safety.

Lane's task was complicated by the house builder,

whose crews had left the slope bare, exposing fragile topsoil to the elements. Fortunately, the barren slope included a number of large boulders, which at least gave Lane a starting point for his landscaping. Unfortunately, the builder had channeled runoff from the roof into a 6-inch-diameter drainpipe that emptied onto the bare slope. "I knew I had to do something at the end of this gaping pipe to prevent the water from creating a Grand Canyon in the middle of the landscaping," Lane says. His solution was to transform an ugly pile of native sandstone rocks—leftovers from construction and grading—into a good-looking dry streambed that would break the force of the water and direct it harmlessly to a nearby creek.

The patios and terraces posed a different problem. The builder had graded the slope adjacent to the patios to

# Slope strategies

*October marks the end of the dry season, the coming of the rains. How one designer planted for both*

**S**TEEP SLOPES POSE steep challenges for gardeners. Slopes erode, they are usually in fire zones, and they are often hit by high winds.

The owners of this attractive new hillside house in Santa Barbara knew these risks all too well—their last home on this same site was destroyed in the Painted Cave blaze of 1990. By 1992, the owners had rebuilt and re-create terraces for plants, but Lane realized that water running off the patios would sit in the heavy clay soils of the terraces, killing anything he planted there. His solution was a second creek bed for drainage. Lane's crew dug shallow ditches in gently curving natural shapes, then placed the rocks directly on the soil in a random pattern. The creeks have met the challenge of two very wet winters and several intense storms.

## PLANTING FOR FIRE AND RAIN

Throughout the slope, Lane planted with the principles of fire-wise landscaping in mind—the creation of defensible space, the use of low-fuel-volume plants, the elimination of highly flammable plants. Although all of the plants on the slope would burn in a fire, their low profile is designed to keep flame lengths manageable.

To control erosion, Lane turned to large, dense, and deeply rooted plants. It is the root system of a plant that most effectively knits the soil together, especially if it's encouraged to run deep by the use of a drip system rather than overhead sprinklers. Aboveground, dense canopies of foliage can dissipate the energy of rain before it reaches the soil, as well as help keep weeds down. "I use wide-spreading woody plants wherever possible, ones that grow from a single stem rather than many," says Lane. Unlike creeping, herbaceous ground covers, single-stem plants are sturdy and easy to drip-irrigate.

All of the plants were planted from inexpensive 1-gallon containers—these plants grow better than larger sizes and are much easier to plant. "We had to use a jackhammer on nearly every planting hole to break through the rock-hard soil," recalls Lane. "There was no way I was going to use 5-gallon plants!" Using smaller plants

also made it possible to eliminate the unsightly basins so often seen on slopes.

Lane used drought-tolerant California natives throughout the slope. Ceanothus (*C.* 'Concha' and *C.* 'Ray Hartman') were planted because of their erosion-control properties but kept away from the house due to their relative flammability. Even the low-lying *C. griseus horizontalis* 'Yankee Point' was kept a respectable 30 feet away. Elsewhere, St. Catherine's lace (*Eriogonum giganteum*), Canyon Prince wild rye (*Leymus condensatus*), and *Artemisia* 'Powis Castle' showcase shades of gray while lending a natural feel to the lower creek bed.

Other plants include Mediterranean-climate species that are well adapted to the tough local conditions. Rockrose (*Cistus skanbergii*) and trailing lantana (*Lantana montevidensis*) were planted in masses. A row of virtually fireproof white oleanders (*Nerium oleander*) was planted at the property line to create a visual boundary, as well as to control any grass fires that might start on the other side. Low 'Petite Pink' oleander and upright rosemary (*Rosmarinus officinalis* 'Tuscan Blue') were planted near the patios. And at the top of the slope, a row of bright green *Pittosporum tobira* 'Wheeler's Dwarf' was planted to give definition to the living spaces.

The final erosion strategy was to cover exposed sections of the slope with a 2-inch layer of gorilla hair, an oddly named but very effective mulching material made from shredded redwood bark. Though it has since decomposed, the mulch protected the exposed soil from the rain during the critical first winter.

## DIFFERENT SLOPES FOR DIFFERENT FOLKS

Of course, all slopes are not created equal. The methods employed here by Lane might

WILLIAM B. DEWEY

**THE TOP OF THE SLOPE** *is marked by paving stones surrounded by Dymondia and a barrier of tobira. A row of white oleanders was planted at the property line to slow grass fires.*

not be adequate on steeper slopes or ones with sandy soils that erode more easily. Jute and other kinds of erosion-control netting, retaining walls, and temporary cover crops are good examples of alternative slope stabilization approaches. If you're not sure what to do, call a licensed professional; the consequences of making the wrong decisions can be irreversible.

The thing you *can* control is the state of your slope after

it's been planted. Make sure your irrigation system is as efficient as possible, lest you wash away all your hard work. And don't let your slope get too wild. Good maintenance is just as important as good design in a fire-wise landscape; notice the absence of dead leaves and flammable refuse on Lane's slope. In this case, an ounce of prevention is worth far more than a pound of cure— it could save your house. ∎

A **SPARKLING WALKWAY** *is formed by diamonds and triangles of glass pavers filled with ground glass cullet.*

**DOUG WILSON**

**LEAF AND BERRY MOTIFS** *ornament pavers cast of Milestone.*

**RECYCLED STEEL** *table has top of glass and cultured stone.*

# The ultimate recycled garden

A T FIRST GLANCE, THE front yard didn't look out of the ordinary. A handsome walkway led past beds of flowers and ornamental plants to a house with a French provincial façade. Then, as you looked closer, touched the objects, and consulted the exhibit brochure, you discovered that everything in this landscape design, except the plants, consisted of recycled materials—from the glass pavers in the walkway to the plastic timbers around the planting beds to the soil composted from garden waste.

The exhibit, called Jardin Encore, attracted thousands of visitors at the 1994 Northwest Flower and Garden Show in Seattle. The display garden demonstrated that recycling solid waste is already paying off in the form of attractive and useful materials with many applications in the home landscape.

Sponsored by the King County Commission for Marketing Recyclable Materials and the King County Solid Waste Division, the exhibit was a team effort that tapped suppliers in California, Oregon, and Washington. Landscape designer Madelyn Katzman designed and coordinated the garden with help from recycling department project coordinator Joyce Gagnon.

## REBORN BARREL, FAUX STONE

Some of the recycled materials in Jardin Encore were familiar: salvaged and remilled lumber for trellises, broken concrete for retaining walls, patio furniture made from recycled scrap metal, and a born-again whiskey barrel to catch rainwater from a downspout. Other items, such as a trellis made of rebar, demonstrated new ways to use old materials.

Still other objects weren't quite what they appeared to be. The "stone" pillars flanking the front porch entry looked real but were actually designed and created by artist Terry Eagan, using Milestone, a new material invented by Don Miles that combines ground recycled glass, Portland cement, and resins.

The walkway, too, used recycled glass in surprising ways. Diamond-shaped lattices formed by glass pavers

DOUG WILSON

**A TRELLIS** *wrought of recycled rebar supports a bougainvillea vine. Plastic timber (right) edges a vegetable bed.*

**ONCE A WALK,** *now a wall, recycled concrete stacks up for garden enclosure.*

were filled with sparkling glass cullet, a gravel-like material that resembles fine beach pebbles. The glass, much of which comes from recycled bottles, is crushed mechanically, then tumbled to smooth sharp edges. The cullet comes in assorted colors—greens, deep amber, and clear.

### PLASTIC LUMBER, FAKE SHAKES

Perhaps the most surprising items were made from recycled plastic. The timbers used to frame the beds were really plastic lumber look-alikes. Much of the plastic stock is high-density polyethylene recycled from bottles that once held milk and liquid detergents. Large timbers are formed by injection molding—shooting hot plastic into a mold. Smaller ones are formed by extruding hot plastic from a mold in much the same way that toothpaste is

squeezed out of a tube. The timbers are textured and colored to resemble wood, or pigmented to look painted. An 8-foot length of 6-by-6 plastic timber costs about $56. Manufacturers claim the plastic lumber will last hundreds of years.

Up on the roof, what looked like cedar shakes were actually thermoplastic shingles. Made with plastic recovered from cast-off computers, these high-tech shingles are large panels formed by injection-molding. One hundred square feet, installed, costs about $375. When properly installed, these thermal plastic shakes can earn a Class A fire rating in California.

Even the exterior house coloring was recycled household paint incorporated into Milestone. And the window box up on the wall? Just another encore for recycled plastic wood. ■

*By Steven R. Lorton*

## RESOURCE DIRECTORY

Below are the suppliers of recycled materials for Jardin Encore whose products are mentioned or shown in this story. Most of these businesses can send out brochures about their products; call during weekday business hours. To find out more about recycled materials of all kinds, you can call the King County Commission for Marketing Recyclable Materials at (206) 296-4439.

CONCRETE
*Recycled-concrete wall:* The Wall, Portland, (800) 228-9255.
*Tile and steppingstones:* First Impressions, Renton, Washington, (206) 228-8452.

GLASS
*Bricks:* Hot Stuff Glass, Bellingham, Washington, (206) 733-0539.
*Cullet and pavers:* Clean Washington Center, Seattle, (206) 389-2549.
*Decorative glass tiles:* New Design, Seattle, (206) 633-0154.

PAINT
*Recycled paint:* Major Paint, Torrance, California, (310) 542-7701, ext. 2260.

PLASTIC
*Landscape timbers:* Charles R. Watts Co., Seattle, (206) 783-8400.
*Shake roof panels:* Eiger West, Inc., Bellevue, Washington, (206) 462-1644.
*Window box:* Recycled Products, Tacoma, (206) 588-4685.

ORNAMENT
*Faux stone:* Terry Eagan, of Art Effects, Seattle, (206) 522-6247.
*Patio table:* Decorative Stone Concepts, Kirkland, Washington, (206) 821-4819.
*Rebar trellis:* Perrin Designs, Seattle, (206) 781-8346.

JAMES FREDERICK HOUSEL

**A TAPESTRY** *of drought-tolerant vegetation, including ivy and ornamental grasses, fills this slope. A small deck (lower left) perched at the top offers a quiet spot for reading.*

# Multilevel face-lift for a really steep lot

THE HOUSES THAT perch on the hills of many Western cities are much loved for their great views. But the steep ground around these houses makes lawns impossible and gardening a challenge. Consequently, these plots often become neglected tangles of blackberries or other obstreperous plants.

Seattle landscape designer Micheal Moshier faced the challenge of a 40°-plus slope on a 40- by 50-foot lot. He started by stripping the slope, taking out all but one large shore pine (*Pinus contorta*). To control soil erosion during construction, he covered the bare ground with black plastic sheeting.

Moshier kept an existing 4-foot-high concrete retaining wall topped by a hedge of English laurel at the top of the slope. Working from there, he built a series of small wooden decks and stairs that zigzag down the slope to the house. For the stairs, he used a mix of materials for utility and visual variety: concrete at the

top and bottom of the slope, where street access made it easy to pour; and in the middle of the slope, where the grade is the steepest, pressure-treated wood and steel decking anchored in concrete piers.

At the bottom of the slope, he removed soil to make a level terrace at the rear of the house, and used backfill soil to plug the gap between the slope and another 4-foot-high retaining wall. He installed a small pond at one end of the terrace.

In replanting the slope, Moshier chose plants needing little water or maintenance. English ivy and sword ferns carpet the steepest areas. Farther down the slope, dwarf cotoneasters and *Rubus calycinoides* cover the ground. Glacier ivy crawls downhill and spills over the retaining wall, displaying its blue-green and cream leaves.

Clumps of ornamental grasses are scattered along the slope. The big roundish leaves of hostas and the spiky foliage of irises pop up here

and there where a change of texture is needed.

Closer to the terrace, *Artemisia* 'Powis Castle' displays its fragrant, silvery leaves. The waxy, celadon leaves of *Sedum* 'Autumn Joy' poke up topped by rich coral blossoms that turn a handsome nut brown in winter (the owner cuts them back in spring as new foliage starts to emerge).

The silvery gray foliage of snow-in-summer (*Cerastium tomentosum*) and the white woolly leaves of *Helichrysum petiolatum* glow in the sun and brighten the slope at dusk. Lights along the steps and around the slope illuminate the garden at night.

When one plant starts to overtake another, or grows out of bounds, the owner simply snips it back. In mid-February and early April, a complete granular fertilizer (15-15-15) is scattered over the slope. An underground sprinkler system waters the slope in summer if the weather is hot and dry. ■

*By Steven R. Lorton*

RUSS A. WIDSTRAND

**WITH MORE THAN 7,000 PLANTS** *offered last year, you may need a pickup truck to shop at the Rancho Santa Ana Botanic Garden in Claremont. This year's sale promises a good selection of ceanothus, coral bells, and woolly blue curls.*

# Native plant sale season has arrived!

*Buy now for great values and variety*

**SOME SALES** *offer helpful information on each plant, as well as photos of natives in spring bloom.*

I T'S NOT BY CHANCE that the West's best native plant sales are held in fall. The sales, which are sponsored by nonprofit botanic gardens and native plant societies, run from mid-October through November. Some of the plants come from commercial nurseries, but many others are grown by knowledgeable hobbyists with a passion for natives. The bottom line? Unbeatable variety and prices.

That might explain why the sales are often such frenzied affairs. Even the most good-natured gardeners have been known to turn maniacal at the sight of, say, a coveted manzanita. But don't despair; with a bit of planning, you can get the *Arctostaphylos* of your dreams. Here's how:

• Make a list of the plants you want before you leave home. Once at the sale, proceed directly to your choices, then browse.

• Before the sale, learn all you can about the plants you want. Although well-informed staffers can answer questions at most sales, they are often swamped with customers.

• Shop early—plants go fast.

• Bring boxes to transport your plants home. Some sales offer carts to tote plants while shopping, but others don't, so arrive prepared.

Sales are going on throughout the West. Here are some to look for in Southern California. Dates and hours vary from year to year; call numbers listed to learn exact information.

## WHERE AND WHEN

**Claremont.** Early November. Mostly natives, including a good selection of woolly blue curls (*Trichostema*). Sponsor and location: Rancho Santa Ana Botanic Garden, 1500 N. College Avenue. (909) 625-8767.

**Encinitas.** Late October. Natives and other drought-resistant plants, subtropical fruit, and bamboo. Sponsor and location: Quail Botanical Gardens, 230 Quail Gardens Drive. (619) 436-3036.

**Malibu.** Mid-October. Native plants, gifts, books, and educational exhibits. Sponsor: Los Angeles–Santa Monica Mountains Chapter of the California Native Plant Society (CNPS). Location: Michael Landon Community Center, Malibu Bluffs Park, 24250 W. Pacific Coast Highway. (818) 345-6749.

Mid-November. Plants, gifts, books, and educational exhibits. Sponsor: Los Angeles–Santa Monica Mountains Chapter, CNPS. Location: Calamigos Ranch, 327 S. Latigo Canyon Road, which is 500 yards west of the intersection of Kanan Dume Road and Mulholland Highway. (818) 345-6749.

**Riverside.** Late October. Introduced plants and natives, including Verity hybrid monkey flower (*Mimulus*). Sponsor: Friends of the UC Riverside Botanic Gardens. Location: UC Riverside Botanic Gardens, at the eastern edge of the campus. (909) 787-4650.

**San Diego.** Mid-October. Native plants, bulbs, and seeds. Sponsor: San Diego Chapter, CNPS. Location: Casa del Prado in Balboa Park, across from the Natural History Museum. (619) 277-9485.

**San Luis Obispo.** Early November. Native plants and seeds, books, and posters. Sponsor: San Luis Obispo Chapter, CNPS. Location: Great Western Bank, Madonna Plaza, 297 Madonna Road. (805) 528-2658.

**Santa Barbara.** Mid-October. Mostly natives, plus hard-to-find Mediterranean plants. Sponsor and location: Santa Barbara Botanic Garden, 1212 Mission Canyon Road. (805) 682-4726.

**Sun Valley.** Late October. Native plants and seeds, books, and gifts. Sponsor and location: Theodore Payne Foundation for Wildflowers and Native Plants, 10459 Tuxford Street. (818) 768-1802.

**Ventura.** Mid-October. Natives, including Southern California coastals. Sponsor: Channel Islands Chapter, CNPS. Place: Ventura High School, corner of Poli Street and Seaward Avenue. (805) 650-9845. ∎

*By Lynn Ocone*

**FIERY FALL COLOR**
*surrounds these nursery
shoppers. For more on
the deciduous trees and
shrubs shown here, see
page 268.*

# NOVEMBER

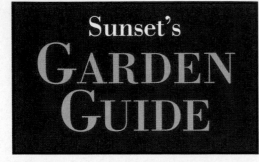

# More planting, a start on pruning, and high-gear garden cleanup

The inspired selection of perennials pictured at right has transformed what was once an over-planted coastal Southern California hillside—laden with aged *Euryops pectinatus* and Indian hawthorn—into a slope of nearly constant fragrance and color. Where others saw only utility, Kennedy Landscape Design Associates of Woodland Hills, California, saw plenty of possibilities. The resulting garden uses an assortment of low-growing, spilling perennials to create a natural, colorful transition from a meadow below up to the patio and house.

Not too surprisingly, the patio area overlooking the slope has become one of the most favored and enjoyable areas in the landscape. Massive hanging patio planters filled with long-blooming plants frame the hillside garden and views to the ocean. A palette of pink, lavender, blue, and purple—with some accents of silver—dominates the design.

The designers achieved year-round flowering with perennials such as pink breath of heaven (*Coleonema pulchrum*), a white variety of Mexican evening primrose (*Oenothera berlandieri*), Peruvian lily (*Alstroemeria*), *Gaura lindheimeri*, and Mexican sage (*Salvia leucantha*). Foliage filler is provided by *Artemisia* 'Powis Castle', bush morning glory (*Convolvulus cneorum*), fountain grass (*Pennisetum setaceum* 'Cupreum'), and rush (*Juncus patens*). Warm onshore breezes send currents of potpourri-scented fragrances from the garden onto the patio and into the house. Nutmeg-, lemon-, and rose-scented gerani-

**DIVERSE PERENNIALS** *in artful planting scheme make this coastal garden an eye-catching companion to a hillside patio. Ocean breezes traveling up the slope fill the patio with the aroma of scented geraniums and fragrant lavenders.*

ums, along with French and English lavender, produce heavenly aromas.

Although maintenance is required through most of the year, primary care is done in fall, when the perennials are substantially pruned back to develop a natural and well-proportioned appearance. In spring, bulbs such as daffodils, ranunculus, tulips, freesias, and Dutch irises bloom to fill spaces created by the pruning, ensuring an abundance of cut-flower material. Iceland poppies and other annuals provide dramatic seasonal color in late fall and winter.

## Mum's the word for color

Whether you display them indoors or outdoors on a porch or patio, few flowers brighten fall days like chrysanthemums in pots. Most potted mums are forced into bloom in greenhouses and sold in flower year-round. Late summer and fall, however, is the mums' natural flowering season.

The range of flower colors and forms available is suggested by the plants pictured at right. Flower forms include anemone shapes (as in the orange-flowered plants shown), quills, and pompons. Though these plants have names such as 'Mercury', 'Venus', and 'Sun', like most mums they are usually not sold with labels identifying the varieties.

Flowers can last up to six weeks, even indoors. Mums will bloom longest outdoors if placed in filtered shade and watered regularly. Indoors, they do best in bright but indirect light. As flowers fade, pinch them off.

Once the mums have finished blooming, you can either discard them or plant them outdoors. Most mums are hardy in all but the coldest climates and will bloom again next fall if grown in well-drained soil in a place that gets full sun.

## Bring home beneficial bugs with flowers

Several garden companies now offer flower seed blends that help attract beneficial insects such as syrphid flies, mud daubers, ground beetles, and ladybugs to your garden. In addition to providing habitat, pollen, and nectar for their guests, the flowers in the blends can provide a lovely color display as well.

The mixes usually include both annual and perennial flowers whose pollen and nectar are more easily accessible to bugs with short mouth parts than are those of tubular flowers. Common insect-friendly plants include yarrow (*Achillea*), native buckwheats (*Eriogonum*), candytuft (*Iberis umbellata*), and evening primrose (*Oenothera*). Some mixes are developed primarily for agriculture, so they contain plants such as radishes, clovers, and alfalfa that are usually not planted as ornamentals.

Now, during fall planting season, is the prime time to sow seeds. If you plant soon, flowers will start blooming in late winter and early spring, attracting and nurturing beneficial bugs that will eat or parasitize early-arriving baddies such as aphids. Plant in open areas, borders, or

NORMAN A. PLATE

**MUMS COME** *in shades of radiant orange, golden yellow, and elegant white.*

263

**GIANT FLOWER TRUSSES** *appear on 'Lem's Monarch' rhododendron in late May.*

NORMAN A. PLATE

large beds. Sow the seed as you would for wildflowers, and water regularly until autumn rains come. For continued bloom, supplement with irrigation during dry periods through the year, although some plants, including native buckwheat and yarrow, are drought resistant.

Peaceful Valley Farm Supply is one mail-order source that offers several seed blends of plants selected for nearly year-round bloom. A low-growing mix and a country-flower mix are among the choices. You can also buy seeds of specific plants and blend your own mixtures. To request a free catalog, call (916) 272-4769.

### A rhody fit for a monarch

Spectacular blooms like that of *Rhododendron* 'Lem's Monarch' (pictured above)

are still a half-year away; but in the Pacific Northwest and Northern California, this is the time to think about rhodies.

There's no better time to plant rhododendrons than early this month. Temperatures will be cooler, winter rains will begin soon, and rhodies planted now will be established by spring, when they'll burst into bloom with a good root system supplying plenty of water to sustain the spectacular flower show.

The blossoms, however dramatic, are just a part of this wonderful plant's value. Leaf, form, and size are also important considerations.

If you happen to become enamored of the big, 6- to 8-foot form of 'Lem's Monarch', you can look forward to an equally regal flower next spring. Considered one of the biggest flower trusses in the *Rhododendron* kingdom, it

measures almost a foot wide. The flowers are an intense pink that fades to "blush pink," according to official nomenclature, though most gardeners would call it white.

'Lem's Monarch' is not difficult to find. Prices vary, depending on the size of the plant.

### Put the kettle on for the birds or warm up their bath

When winter comes to cold areas, the birds that don't head south have a problem. Though water may be abundant, it doesn't do them any good if it's frozen. Here are two techniques to use to supply drinking water for birds.

The first method is useful when temperatures drop below 32° at night and rise above freezing during the day. Just pour one or two teakettles of boiling water into the bird-

bath first thing in the morning to melt away the skim of ice and replace cold water with warm. Keep birds away from it for a few minutes while it cools down.

The easier solution, which is also a better choice when you get several days of sub-freezing weather at a stretch, is an electric birdbath heater. It won't keep the whole bath thawed all the time, but it will keep at least a circle of ice-free water available for birds to drink.

You can buy a heater from a wild bird store, or by mail order from Stokes Seeds (716/695-6980), which sells a Nelson birdbath heater for about $40.

### A ground cover of many colors

Although the gardens at Casa Pacifica in San Clemente, California, are grand in scale, one of our favorite plants there is small. It's a thyme ground cover called 'Doone Valley'.

What's great about 'Doone Valley' thyme—aside, of course, from its toughness—is the way it changes color and shape with the seasons. In the spring, when we saw it, the leaves of this lightly lemon-scented plant were deep green and its small flowers were pink. In summer, the flower clusters elongate and the leaves become variegated with streaks of gold. In cold climates during the winter, the leaves will actually turn an orange-red before reverting to green again as the weather warms back up.

Like all thymes, 'Doone Valley' likes partial sun and fast-draining soil. In the fall, after the blooms are spent, you should shear or trim the plant to keep the stems from becoming woody and unsightly. Also, 'Doone Valley' is a creeper. Because it sends out new roots from the creeping stems, it doesn't do well with drip irrigation systems. We suggest you let it creep a bit, but the plant looks best in

CHAD SLATTERY

**PURPLE SEA LAVENDER** *here escaped to grow wild along the coast of Orange County, California. It can survive on rainfall alone, but regular watering will increase bloom.*

clumps and mounds.

A good source for 'Doone Valley' thyme is Mountain Valley Growers, 38325 Pepperweed Rd., Squaw Valley, Calif. 93675, (209) 338-2775; free catalog available. They sell dozens of varieties of thyme ground covers.

## Perennials for people on the coast

Plants on the seacoast, particularly those right in the sand, are subject to harsh and demanding conditions. Beach plants must tolerate salty sea spray, winds, overcast and foggy skies, and sandy, saline soil that dries out quickly.

Which is not to say that your selection is limited to masses of ice plant. Several colorful perennials have proven themselves rough-and-tumble enough to thrive next to the ocean.

Sea lavender (*Limonium perezii*) is the queen of coastal perennials. You can see it growing wild along the cliffs in Laguna Beach, California, with bright purple flowers blooming most of the year.

Another good-looking perennial is red valerian (*Centranthus ruber*). It is long blooming, with red, white, or rose-pink flowers suitable for cutting. It self-sows and grows like a weed, and is best used in informal plantings or combined with complementary plants such as daylilies. Both sea lavender and red valerian will survive on rainfall alone once they are established, but they bloom better and look more attractive if given supplemental irrigation.

Lavender (*Lavandula*) and rosemary (*Rosmarinus officinalis*) are Mediterranean plants that are perfect for seaside gardens. Dwarf rosemary (*R. o.* 'Prostratus') is the creeping form, spreading to 8 feet or more; it's often used in cascades over sea walls.

Ivy geraniums (*Pelargonium peltatum*) provide continuously colorful flowers all year long. They are the best choice for containers on decks or boat docks, as long as you are willing to give them regular attention. This means routine watering, about twice a week for average-size containers, and monthly feedings with a complete water-soluble fertilizer (15-30-15).

Other perennials that are proven performers in coastal gardens include lavender lantana (*Lantana montevidensis*), daylilies (*Hemerocallis*), and lily-of-the-Nile (*Agapanthus orientalis*). *Agapanthus* 'Peter Pan' is a dwarf variety, with smaller foliage and flowers.

Although these perennials are drought tolerant, they will need regular waterings until they are well established.

## Protect new trees from winter sun and wind

Fall-planted trees have an advantage in most areas: they get a full winter to settle in and send out roots before top growth starts in spring. But first-year trees face some real challenges.

*Sun.* On exceptionally cold, clear winter days, the sun sweeps across the sky at midday, its light hitting the south side of the trunk at a fairly shallow angle. The thin strip of bark that's most perpendicular to the sun's rays heats up while the rest remains cold. The bark splits and dies, killing the cambium beneath and injuring the tree. You can prevent this by wrapping the trunks of young trees loosely with cardboard, burlap, or rolls of commercial tree wrap. Some gardeners paint the bark with white latex to reflect winter sun; this offers less protection, but it's better than nothing.

After the tree becomes well established in your garden, its bark will thicken up enough to resist winter sun without protection.

*Wind.* Strong winter winds can blow down a tree whose roots haven't had time to take hold. To keep that from happening, drive two 5-foot stakes into the soil on opposite sides of the rootball (not through it). An imaginary line between the stakes should be perpendicular to the direction of prevailing winds. Now slide your hand up the trunk far enough to easily straighten out the tree's top: this is the right height for the support.

Tie a rope or hose between the two stakes, looping it loosely around the trunk. (If you tie it too tight, the growing tree will strangle in its noose). Make sure there's plenty of play so trees can sway: you're trying to keep the tree from blowing over, not pinion it to a mast. As the tree sways in winter winds, its roots grow stronger and its trunk thickens at ground level.

## Tip of the Month

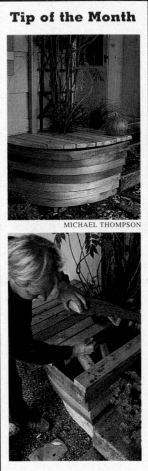

MICHAEL THOMPSON

*This simple structure hides plumbing outlets and stores a garden hose, but it also serves as a bench. John Nausieda of Portland built the frame from pressure-treated 2-by-4s, then wrapped ¼-by-4 cedar benderboard around the frame and screwed it in place so each board was overlapped slightly by the one above it. The lid of 2-by-4s lifts off in two parts. Nausieda left a notch in the rear of the lid to accommodate a wisteria vine that crawls up the side of the house.*

THE TINY 'ISIS' FUCHSIA *is a favorite of bonsai enthusiasts. Prune all fuchsias aggressively now for thick blooms in spring.*

JOEL ZWINK

## Fuchsia tips from pros in the know

Tired, leggy fuchsias will regain their lush green fullness and drip with dozens of blooms next spring if you prune heavily when plants are most dormant. Two people who ought to know are Jill and Bob Meyer, owners of Stubbs Fuchsia Nursery in Encinitas, California. In their benign coastal climate, pruning time is now; in colder regions, wait until late winter or early spring.

"May is our peak. The hanging baskets are so pretty I don't want to sell them," says Jill. "The secret," adds Bob, "is to prune aggressively in November—give or take a month—and then to pinch back the new growth through mid-March."

Pruning and pinching promote thick, compact growth inside the plant, Bob says. "This gives more support for later growth, encourages more flowers, and helps the plant handle summer heat later on."

Bob advises cutting a fuchsia back to the edge of its pot and shaping the plant like an inverted bowl (tall in the middle, short on the sides). "It'll look like sticks, but fuchsias are amazingly resilient. So go ahead and prune as you would

a rose—really go at it."

By the end of December in mildest-winter regions, your fuchsia will show new growth. Each tender shoot will have several pairs of leaves along its length; pinch the new growth back to one of these sets of leaves. "It doesn't matter which one," Bob says.

Growth will continue from this point, forming two new branches. When each has three or four sets of leaves— four to six weeks later—pinch again. "When you're happy with how it looks, when it's green and full and not sparse, stop pinching," Bob says. You can expect flowers six to eight weeks later.

You also need to examine your fuchsia for pests, protect it from frost, and fertilize regularly. The Meyers feed their fuchsias once a month with a complete fertilizer such as 18-18-6. Their preferred potting soil is a fast-draining mix of 50 percent redwood compost, 30 percent peat moss, and 20 percent perlite.

The most popular of the nursery's 200 fuchsia varieties are frothy double forms in pastel shades. Others worth considering include dainty magellanicas that resemble earrings; tiny 'Isis', favored by bonsai enthusiasts for its

¼-inch blooms; and 'Sunray', a heat-tolerant newcomer with variegated white-and-green leaves.

## Get garlic into the ground

Planting garlic at the right time of the year is essential to growing good crops, and in frosty but mild-winter areas such as California's Central Valley, this is the month to get those cloves into the

ground. Garlic grows best when planted in well-drained soil and given full sun. At planting time, divide the bulbs into individual cloves and plant them scar ends down, 1 to 2 inches deep and 3 to 4 inches apart. Water planting beds. Full-size bulbs should be ready for harvest next summer.

Besides regular white California garlic, you might want to plant some other types. If you can't find these varieties locally, try the two mail-order sources listed here. The initials after each variety are keyed to the sources that follow. Order soon; supplies of some varieties may be limited.

*Elephant* garlic (WAB), related to the leek, produces heads weighing as much as a pound each. The large cloves have a mild flavor.

*'Inchelium Red'* (FF) has yellowish bulbs marked with red. It has a spicy flavor.

*Purple stripe varieties* (FF) produce purplish heads, with large, fleshy cloves. These store well.

*Rocambole* (FF, WAB) produces a rich, mild garlic flavor. Purple skin is easy to peel. Flower stalk produces small bulblets for planting next season.

**FF** Filaree Farm, Route 2, Box 162, Okanogan, Wash. 98840; (509) 422-6940. Catalog costs $2.

**WAB** W. Atlee Burpee & Co., 300 Park Ave., Warminster, Pa. 18991; (800) 888-1447. Catalog is free.

## This manzanita takes dry shade in stride

It's not easy to find plants that can tolerate the dry soil and filtered sun or light shade found under native oaks and other drought-tolerant trees. One relatively new plant that thrives in these conditions is *Arctostaphylos* 'Pacific Mist'.

Introduced in Northern California by Saratoga Horticultural Research Foundation, in San Martin, 'Pacific Mist' is a prostrate grower, reaching 2 to 2½ feet tall and spreading to 5 feet or more. With its soft, gray green foliage, it looks a bit different from the common low-growing manzanitas with leathery-looking leaves. But its dark reddish brown bark and white urn-shaped flowers that appear in clusters in late winter are typical of other manzanitas.

'Pacific Mist' is adaptable to a wide range of climates, and it will tolerate heavy soil better than many manzanitas. Water 'Pacific Mist' regularly to get it established, then cut back irrigation to once a month in summer. If you plant it under oaks, use drip irrigation so water won't hit the trunks of the trees.

If your nursery doesn't stock 'Pacific Mist', ask the staff to special order it for you from either Monterey Bay Nursery or Rosendale Nursery in Watsonville, California (both are wholesale only)

## Instant big trees for Washingtonians

A treasured tree dies or blows down, or a new neighbor builds an eyesore next door. You need a big tree—fast. Who ya gonna call? Big Tree Transplants of

PETER O. WHITELEY

**PETITE SPECIES TULIP** *called Tulipa batalinii 'Yellow Jewel' pokes up through a layer of bark mulch.*

Washington.

This booming business sells more than 300 kinds of specimen-size trees, some up to 35 feet tall. Ashes, cherries, katsuras, pin and red oaks, plums, sycamores, and zelkovas are among the offerings. Trees cost from $150 to $2,000. Transplanting services are available for trees purchased from Big Tree Transplants and for homeowner-supplied trees. Installed trees supplied by Big Tree are guaranteed for one year.

Big Tree Transplants uses large tree spades to move plants with up to 11,000-pound rootballs and 12-inch trunk diameters. By means of their unique digging and boxing method, they can even handle 52,000 pounds of rootball and a 3½-foot trunk diameter. The nursery, located off Interstate 5 between Everett

and Marysville, is open by appointment only; call (206) 252-5900.

## New guide to pest management

Integrated pest management is a commonsense approach to pest control that seeks to use the least environmentally disruptive measures to control damaging insects.

This approach is detailed in a new 327-page guide that many western gardeners will find useful. *Pests of Landscape Trees and Shrubs: An Integrated Pest Management Guide* (publication 3359 of the University of California Agriculture and Natural Resources Publications) is illustrated with more than 1,000 color photographs and drawings to help identify plant pests. There is a 50-page problem-solving chapter orga-

nized by plant species, including oaks, roses, and many other common ornamentals.

The $32 guide is available from ANR Publications, 6701 San Pablo Ave., Oakland, Calif. 94608; to order by credit card, call (510) 642-2431.

## A jewel of a tulip

For adding dashes of spring color in ground covers or rock gardens, *Tulipa batalinii* is a real gem. Although these tulips are diminutive (5 to 8 inches tall), their flowers form handsome cups about 1½ inches across.

'Yellow Jewel' is shown at left in landscape designer Page Sanders's Palo Alto, California, garden, growing in a bed with 'Catlin's Giant' ajuga and Rocky Mountain columbine (*Aquilegia caerulea*). The tulips generally appear in late spring and last about a month. Unlike most hybrid tulips, these species tulips naturalize easily. This is their fourth year of bloom in Sanders's garden.

*T. batalinii* is available in four other colors: 'Apricot Jewel' (apricot with yellow interior), 'Bright Gem' (yellow orange; fragrant), 'Bronze Charm', and 'Red Jewel'.

Bulbs are available from these two mail-order sources:

*Daffodil Mart,* Route 3, Box 794, Gloucester, Va. 23061; (800) 255-2852 for orders only or (804) 693-6339 for information. Cost is $4 to $7 for 10 bulbs; $25 minimum order, plus shipping.

*McClure & Zimmerman,* Box 368, Friesland, Wis. 53935; (414) 326-4220. Cost is $3.65 to $4.65 for six bulbs, plus shipping.

## For the desktop, a compact dracaena

Bristling with long, thin, deep green leaves, *Dracaena deremensis* 'Janet Craig' is a popular house plant. It's a beauty, but because it can grow up to the ceiling, it's too large for many indoor situations.

**BRANCHES GLOW** *with lemon yellow spring flowers from hybrid flannel bush 'California Glory'.*

If space is limited, look for the desktop variety called *D. d.* 'Janet Craig Compacta'. Its leaves are medium green, just 6 inches long, and densely packed on much shorter stems. It looks like a wholly different plant, not a miniature of 'Janet Craig'.

Though the compact variety will grow to 6 feet tall in optimal conditions (compared with 9 to 15 feet for the standard), most plants remain much shorter. Buy a 12- to 14-inch-tall 'Janet Craig Compacta' in a 6-inch pot and you won't have any trouble keeping it in bounds. If it grows too tall, just prune it off at the height you want; the lower part will resprout.

## Bring home some autumn colors

This is the season when many deciduous plants at nurseries, like the one shown on page 260, will be wearing their fall colors. Shop now for the trees and shrubs whose autumn foliage color fits best in your garden, and plant immediately to give them all winter to send out roots.

You're likely to see many of the following plants at nurseries, depending on where you live. Barberry (*Berberis thunbergii*), with bright berries and flame-colored leaves, grows well everywhere. Sour gum (*Nyssa sylvatica*) won't take extreme cold, but performs well even in mild winters. American sweet gum (*Liquidambar styraciflua* 'Palo Alto') is hung with spiny fruits after its red-orange leaves drop. The leaves of the maidenhair tree (*Ginkgo biloba*) turn butter yellow before they drop. Crape myrtle (*Lagerstroemia indica* 'Zuni') needs hot summers and mild winters. Red Japanese maple (*Acer palmatum* 'Atropurpureum' ) has colored leaves all season. Scarlet maple (*Acer rubrum* 'October Glory') is well-named for its fast-growing frame of scarlet showing early every autumn.

## Flannel bush, an uncommonly showy California native

The common flannel bush (*Fremontodendron californicum*) is one of the most distinctive California native plants. The evergreen shrub reaches 10 to 20 feet high and produces big lemon yellow flowers.

Common flannel bush is native to the Sierra foothills, and it also grows well on the floor of the Central Valley. Plants must have excellent drainage or they'll quickly succumb.

November is an ideal month to plant flannel bush, since winter rains will help plants become established; they need little water in summer. They are best planted with other drought-tolerant natives, such as ceanothus. Plant flannel bush in a spot where passersby won't brush against its leathery green leaves, which have fuzzy hairs on their undersides that cause skin irritation.

Nurseries also carry hybrids between *F. californicum* and *F. mexicanum*, the southern flannel bush. These hybrid plants generally resemble common flannel bush but have larger flowers and bloom over a longer period. *Fremontodendron* 'California Glory' (see photo at left) bears cup-shaped yellow flowers up to 3 inches across on an upright plant. 'Pacific Sunset' has deep orange yellow flowers up to 4 inches across.

Nurseries sell plants in 5-gallon cans for about $22 to $30.

## A handy guide to garden literature

So much material is being published these days about the horticultural arts and sciences, it's nearly impossible to keep up with it all. Fortunately, author Sally Williams is keeping track in *Garden Literature: An Index to Periodical Articles and Book Reviews* (Garden Literature Press).

The index is published quarterly (the fourth-quarter issue is an annual accumulation). Articles are listed alphabetically by author and subject. Book reviews are listed alphabetically by author and book title. The annual subscription fee for the indexes is $50. To subscribe, send a check or money order to Garden Literature Press, 398 Columbus Ave., Suite 181, Boston 02116. Back issues (to 1992) and custom lists are available.

## Indoor/outdoor autumn color

We know a gardener who waits all year to prune the Japanese maple that grows just outside his front window. Finally, when the maple leaves explode with autumn color between October and November, he snips off a few branches and brings them indoors. He displays them in a container near the window (pictured below), where their colors echo the show outside.

*By Melanie Baer-Keeley, Debra Lee Baldwin, Sharon Cohoon, Steven R. Lorton, Jim McCausland, Ben Marks, Lynn Ocone, Kathleen Sommer, Lauren Bonar Swezey, Lance Walheim*

STEPHEN CRIDLAND

**A DOUBLE DOSE** *of fall color: prunings on display in entryway came from the Japanese maple outside the window.*

**ADD TO THE COMPOST.** As you snip off faded blooms, mow grass, and weed, add this garden waste to the compost pile. Cut long perennial stalks and branches into small pieces to speed up decomposition.

**BAIT FOR SLUGS.** You may weaken and slow down the army, but the war never ends. Slugs just keep coming, so you must keep baiting, even in winter. Put bait out in the garden wherever it will stay dry. A jar or can set on its side, secured with a stick, stone, or loop of stiff wire, and filled with a tablespoon of bait makes a good trap that extends the life of the bait. Be very careful if you have pets, especially dogs, who may sniff the bait and slug carcasses and be tempted to lick the toxic chemical; they could get a fatal dose.

**CARE FOR HOUSE PLANTS.** By now, all plants but cymbidiums (see item below) should be indoors. Plants that bloom indoors in winter will need fertilizer.

**CHILL AND PAMPER CYMBIDIUMS.** Leave cymbidiums outdoors this month until they've been through a couple of cold snaps, but bring them indoors before a hard freeze. The exposure to cold makes them set a good crop of buds on flower spikes. These sturdy orchids should remain indoors in the Pacific Northwest from mid- to late November through March. Place them in strong light, but away from direct afternoon sun. Through December, feed plants with a complete liquid fertilizer that is low in nitrogen and high in phosphorus and potash.

**CUT BACK CHRYSANTHEMUMS.** Cut plants back to within 6 inches of the ground after the last flowers fade. They'll send out new shoots in spring.

**DIVIDE LILIES.** Use a spade or fork to lift bulbs from lily beds. Separate them, then replant in soil enriched by mixing in a teaspoon of dry 10-10-10 fertilizer or a handful of well-rotted manure or compost.

**DIVIDE OR MULCH DAHLIAS.** In normal winters, dahlias can stay in the ground without trouble. But if you'd rather not risk losing a prized plant, protect tubers by laying on a 4-inch layer of mulch (leaves or straw work well). You can also dig and divide tubers now. If you haven't done so in the last three years, you'll be amazed at how dividing and replanting will stimulate next year's flower production.

**DIVIDE RHUBARB.** Dig and divide rhizomes now. Leave one bud per division. Replant divisions 3 to 4 feet apart just under the surface of well-amended, quick-draining soil.

**GROOM LAWNS.** Give lawns one last mowing and edging. Rake up leaves and other debris.

**GROOM MIXED BORDERS.** Cut back all but the perennials you want left standing for winter interest, such as *Sedum* flower heads, iris pods, and ornamental grasses and their flowers. But even these plants need to be cleaned around, snipped free of damaged or blackened foliage, and generally tidied up. Cut off evergreen foliage damaged by summer sun or drought, and rake beds; you'll be limiting the cover for slugs and insects. Spread a layer of compost over beds.

**PLANT BERRIES.** Bareroot plants of blueberries, cane berries, currants, and gooseberries should be set out as soon as you get them home.

**PLANT CAMELLIAS.** Sasanquas and other early-flowering kinds will be starting to flower this month. They are very good plants to keep underneath house eaves, where their flowers get protection from rain. Be certain to give these camellias ample water.

**PLANT PEONIES.** For spectacular bloom next spring and summer, plant herbaceous and tree peonies in rich, well-amended soil now.

**PRUNE SHRUBS AND TREES.** First remove dead, diseased, and injured wood. Then step back and eye the plant for shape. Prune out crossing branches and ones that are closely parallel, then take out more if you want to show off the plant's form.

**SOW HARDY ANNUALS.** Candytuft, clarkia, larkspur, linaria, and wildflower seed mixes can all be sown now.

**SPREAD LIME.** If you need to reduce the acidity of your soil, spread lime over lawns and planting beds and around trees and shrubs, following label instructions. Dig or till lime into fallow vegetable plots.

**WINTERIZE TOOLS.** Use fine sandpaper or steel wool to smooth steel parts of shovels, hoes, cultivators, and other tools. Then wipe the metal with machine oil to ward off rust. Sand wooden handles, then apply linseed oil or paint them. Store the tools you won't be using in a dry place for the winter.

# November Checklist

## NORTHERN CALIFORNIA

**CARE FOR HOUSE PLANTS.** As days get shorter and the sun changes position in the sky, house plants may not be getting enough light. Most need bright, indirect light. If a plant is sitting in a dark corner, move it to a brighter area. Plants may need less water as the days grow cooler (unless the house is kept warm), but they still need periodic feeding with a fertilizer applied at reduced strength.

**CLEAN UP DEBRIS.** Pull up what's left of summer annuals and vegetables that have stopped producing. Also, rake up leaves and pick up fallen fruit to help eliminate overwintering sites for insects and diseases. Add debris (except weeds that have gone to seed and diseased plants) to the compost pile.

**DIVIDE PERENNIALS.** Lift and separate overgrown clumps, add organic matter to the soil, and replant divisions. To divide acanthus, agapanthus, and fortnight lily, you may need to force clumps apart with a spading fork.

**FEED COOL-SEASON CROPS.** Your annuals and vegetables probably need feeding if you didn't mix in a controlled-release fertilizer at planting time. Use an organic fertilizer, such as fish emulsion, or apply a complete fertilizer in either liquid or dry form.

**FEED LAWNS.** If you haven't already done so this fall, or if the fertilizer you're using requires a second application (follow label directions), feed lawns now with a granular lawn food. Use one that's designed to release nutrients over a long period of time so the lawn will be supplied with small amounts of nutrients throughout the winter.

**FIGHT EROSION.** If you garden on a slope, make sure you have enough plant material there to keep the hillside from eroding if rains are heavy this winter. If the slope is bare or is covered with young plants whose roots haven't knitted the soil together yet, sow seeds of wildflowers and a perennial grass such as blue wild rye (*Elymus glaucus*).

**PLANT ANNUALS.** For instant color, you can still buy plants in 4-inch pots (it's probably too late to set out sixpack plants; they'll just sit in the cool weather until spring). Gently loosen the roots before planting.

**PLANT FOR PERMANENCE.** November is a good time to set out cold-hardy ground covers, shrubs, trees, and vines in *Sunset Western Garden Book* zones 14 through 17. Wait until spring to set out tender plants, such as bougainvillea, mandevilla, and princess flower. Bare-root roses and trees start appearing in nurseries next month; plan ahead and determine your garden needs and available space.

**PLANT GARLIC.** Choose a site in full sun with well-drained soil. Plant in raised bed, if your soil is heavy and poorly drained. Mix in plenty of compost. Plant cloves of common (artichoke-type), elephant, and rocambole garlic about 2 inches deep.

**PLANT PERENNIALS.** Nurseries have a wide assortment in sixpack, 4-inch, and 1-gallon containers. Look for artemisia, campanula, columbine, coral bells, coreopsis, dead nettle (*Lamium*), delphinium, gaillardia, Oriental poppy, penstemon, phlox, salvia, and species geraniums.

**PLANT SPRING-BLOOMING BULBS.** Before buying, carefully examine bulbs; choose only firm ones that aren't sprouting. Chill bulbs of crocus, hyacinths, and tulips for six weeks before planting. Place bulbs in paper bags, label, and store in refrigerator; keep them away from apples. Plant bulbs such as daffodils in the ground immediately.

**PULL MULCH BACK FROM CITRUS.** To help protect citrus from frost damage, pull mulch back from under the tree canopy. This allows the ground to absorb heat during the day and release it at night.

**SOW WILDFLOWERS.** For colorful spring bloom, choose a mix that's suited to your climate or buy individual kinds and develop your own color combinations. You can also buy mixes for specific purposes, such as attracting butterflies or beneficial insects.

**SPRAY FRUIT TREES.** After leaves have fallen, spray peach and nectarine trees with fixed copper or lime sulfur to control peach leaf curl. To control brown rot on apricot trees, apply a fixed-copper spray as label directs.

**WATER.** If rains are late or sporadic, water newly planted lawns, landscape plants, and vegetables often enough to keep the soil moist. Periodically check established plants, and water when necessary. Drought-tolerant plants can go longer between watering than azaleas and other thirsty plants.

San Rafael

Walnut Creek

Oakland

San Francisco

San Jose

Monterey

Coastal (zone 17)

Inland (zones 14–16)

**COMPOST.** Add garden debris and fruit and vegetable scraps to the compost pile. A simple composter can be made with a 12½-foot length of 12- to 14-gauge wire fencing; bend it into a cylinder about 4 feet in diameter, and hook the cut edges together. To fill, alternate 1- to 2-foot layers of garden debris with 2 to 3 inches of soil. Sprinkle nitrogen fertilizer every 2 feet. Keep the pile evenly moist, and aerate it by turning it every two weeks or so.

**DIG CORMS AND TUBERS.** If you haven't done so already, dig up dahlia and begonia tubers and gladiolus corms. Trim any dead stems or leaves, brush off the soil, and store in a cool, dry place for the winter.

**FERTILIZE.** If you planted cool-season flowers and vegetables last month, feed now with a high-nitrogen fertilizer.

If ground covers, shrubs, or trees didn't grow well last summer, or had yellowish foliage, feed them with a high-nitrogen fertilizer. Feed bluegrass, fescue, or ryegrass lawns if you haven't already done so this fall, or make a second application now if one is necessary (follow directions on the fertilizer package).

**FIGHT EROSION.** On bare or recently-planted slopes and hillsides, sow seed of annual and perennial ryegrass to prevent erosion during winter rains.

**PLANT FOR PERMANENCE.** It's not too late to plant most ground covers, shrubs, and trees. Wait until December to start planting bare-root roses, fruit trees, and vines. Wait until spring to plant cold-tender plants, such as bougainvillea and citrus.

**PLANT OR REPLACE LAWNS.** There is still time to sow or lay sod of cool-season grasses, but keep in mind that this winter's new lawn will be next summer's water guzzler. Consider reducing turf areas to conserve water. Or replace lawn with water-thrifty ground covers.

**PLANT PERENNIALS.** Nurseries have a wide assortment in sixpacks and pots. Choices include alyssum, basket-of-gold, campanula, columbine, coral bells, coreopsis, delphinium, dianthus, English daisy, gaillardia, gloriosa daisy, Oriental poppy, penstemon, phlox, and salvia.

**PLANT SPRING-FLOWERING BULBS.** Most nurseries continue to have a good supply of bulbs.

**PLANT VEGETABLES.** You can still sow seeds of peas and spinach. Plant onion and garlic (see item on page 266).

**PLANT WINTER COLOR.** This is the last month to set out cool-season annuals such as African daisy (*Dimorphotheca*), calendula, English and fairy primroses, Iceland poppy, pansy, snapdragon, stock, sweet alyssum, sweet William, viola, and wallflower.

**SOW HARDY ANNUALS.** For spring bloom, sow seeds of bachelor's button, clarkia, forget-me-not, Johnny-jump-up, linaria, pansy, and sweet alyssum.

**SOW WILDFLOWERS.** Sow wildflowers now and let winter rains germinate the seeds. For planting tips, see the item on page 230.

**SPRAY TO CONTROL PEACH LEAF CURL.** Rake fallen leaves and remove old fruits from peach and nectarine trees. Then spray trees thoroughly with fixed copper or lime sulfur.

Valley and foothills (zones 7–9, 14)

Mountain (zones 1, 2)

**TIDY UP.** A thorough cleanup will eliminate hiding places for earwigs, slugs, snails, and sowbugs. Rake fallen leaves, pull up spent summer annuals and vegetables, and except for weeds that have gone to seed, add all plant debris to the compost pile. Prune dead or broken branches from shrubs and trees. To reduce overwintering pests, remove fruit remaining on deciduous trees as well as any that has fallen on the ground.

Redding

Lake Tahoe

Sacramento

Fresno

Bakersfield

# November Checklist

■

## SOUTHERN CALIFORNIA

□ **CHOOSE CHRYSAN-THEMUMS FOR IN-DOOR COLOR.** Buy potted mums now for best selection. Pinch spent blooms to encourage unopened buds, water regularly, feed every other week, and provide bright, indirect light. When flowers fade, cut off blooms, leaving stems 6 to 8 inches long. Break apart the pot's individual plants and transplant them into the garden for color next fall.

□ **DIVIDE DAHLIAS.** Withhold water and fertilizer to encourage dormancy, then cut brown stalks to about 12 inches. Dig tubers before heavy rains begin. Divide, using a sharp knife, leaving 1 inch of stem and one or more buds at each base of each division. Apply soil sulphur to cut areas. Store divided tubers in sand or vermiculite in a cool location until spring.

□ **MANAGE PESTS AND DISEASES.** Spray a multipurpose fungicide on peach, nectarine, and apricot trees to prevent leaf curl. Control caterpillar damage to cabbages, geraniums, and petunias by spraying with *Bacillus thuringiensis* (BT). Watch for slug and snail activity; handpick in the early evening and morning, or use barriers, baits, or traps.

□ **PLANT BULBS.** While supplies last, buy anemones, daffodils (*Narcissus*), Dutch irises, freesia, lilies, ranunculus, sparaxis, and watsonia. In frost-prone regions, hurry to plant the last of the spring-blooming bulbs. In all but high mountain areas, prechill crocus, hyacinth, and tulip bulbs for at least six weeks in the crisper of your refrigerator; plant between Thanksgiving and New Year's.

□ **PLANT COOL-SEASON VEGETABLES.** Sow seeds of beets, carrots, kohlrabi, peas, radishes, rutabagas, and spinach; set out seedlings of broccoli, cabbage, cauliflower, celery, collards, endive, kale, leeks, lettuce, and parsley; divide and plant garlic bulbs. Plant sweet onions from seed by mid-November for harvest in June; short-day varieties suited to coastal and mild inland areas include 'Crystal Wax', 'Granex', and 'Grano'.

□ **PLANT FLOWERING GIFT BASKETS.** Plan ahead for the holiday festivities by creating flowering baskets that can be planted in the garden after the holidays. Line baskets with plastic, then layer with charcoal, perlite, and potting soil. Choose plants with similar needs for light and water, such as cyclamen and maidenhair ferns or poinsettias and variegated ivy. Water conservatively and place in sunny, cool locations.

□ **PLANT NATIVES.** In coastal and inland areas, plant bush poppies, California fuchsia, ceanothus (wild lilac), coral bells, fuchsia-flowering gooseberry, mahonia, manzanita, penstemon, and toyon (California holly).

□ **PLANT SPRING-FLOW-ERING PERENNIALS.** Plant in full sun: agapanthus, carnation, daylily, delphinium, gaillardia, gerbera, gloriosa daisy, penstemon, perennial candytuft, scabiosa, and society garlic.

□ **PLANT WINTER, EARLY-SPRING COLOR.** Along the coast, in sunny spots, plant annual phlox, calendula, Canterbury bells, larkspur, lobelia, pansies, stock, and violas. In areas with partial shade, plant cineraria, cyclamen, and primroses. In frost-free inland areas that get full sun, plant African daisies, gazanias, Iceland poppy, and sweet William. In areas of partial shade, try bergenia, columbine, and foxglove. In frost-prone zones, plant flowering kale; frost makes the colors more brilliant.

□ **PROTECT PLANTS FROM FROST.** In areas where temperatures occasionally drop below freezing, move the following under shelter, or cover on nights when frost is predicted: cactus, epiphyllums, ferns, fuchsias, hibiscus, ice plant, plumeria, and succulents. Keep plants on the dry side and don't fertilize (new growth is especially frost-tender). Also, protect young avocado, citrus, and macadamia trees by wrapping trunks with cardboard or old blankets.

□ **SELECT TREES FOR FALL COLOR.** In inland valleys and low foothills with hot, dry summers followed by an autumn chill, plant Chinese pistache, crape myrtle, Japanese

maple (red-leaf types turn brighter in the fall), and tulip tree. Best bets for coastal gardens are ginkgo, liquidambar, and nandina.

□ **SOW WILDFLOWER SEEDS.** In coastal and inland areas, use packages of mixed wildflowers, or sow alyssum, baby blue eyes, California poppy, clarkia, larkspur, linaria, lupine (soak or scarify seeds), and scarlet flax. Choose a sunny location, rake into weed-free soil, and water until rains take over; don't fertilize.

□ **SURVEY SASANQUAS.** Camellias are well suited to Southern California. Select and plant sasanquas now; they're beginning to bloom and are entering dormancy. Debud to encourage larger flowers, water regularly, and feed with a low-nitrogen fertilizer. Apply chelated iron with zinc to intensify color and prevent chlorosis.

□ **WATER TREES DEEPLY.** If rains are delayed, irrigate conifers and eucalyptus by letting a hose drip beneath the tree overnight. Increased sap flow protects against beetle larvae, which tunnel into the tree's cambium layer.

Santa Barbara

Pasadena

San Bernardino

Santa Monica

Los Angeles

San Diego

☐ Zones 18–21

▦ Zones 22–24

## ANYWHERE IN THE WEST, TACKLE THESE CHORES:

☐ **BUY SPRING-FLOWER-ING BULBS.** Nurseries and garden centers are stocked with all kinds of spring-flowering bulbs now. Buy before they're picked over. In cold-winter areas, plant all kinds immediately. In the low desert, chill bulbs of crocus, tulips, and hyacinths for six weeks in the refrigerator, away from apples (the crisper works well). Label bulbs clearly.

☐ **CONTROL WEEDS.** There are spring weeds, summer weeds, and fall weeds. Hoe the fall weed crop or throw them into the compost pile if they don't have seedheads or flowers.

☐ **MAKE COMPOST.** As the weather cools off, you can speed up the composting process by grinding plants before you throw them into the pile. If you have lots of fallen leaves, for example, go over them with your mower, then dump the bagful of shredded leaves into the compost pile.

☐ **PRUNE TREES AND SHRUBS.** After leaves fall from deciduous trees, you can prune. Remove dead, diseased, and injured branches, watersprouts, and crossing or closely parallel branches. Then shape by pruning.

☐ **SOW SPRING WILD-FLOWERS.** Broadcast seeds in cultivated beds and water well. When seedlings emerge, watch for weeds and remove them.

## IN THE INTERMOUNTAIN WEST, DO THESE CHORES:

☐ **BRING IN HOUSE PLANTS.** If you haven't done it yet, bring tender plants into the house for the winter. Rinse them off in the shower with lukewarm water, check for insect pests, and put them in a place that gets plenty of light.

☐ **DIG AND DIVIDE DAHLIAS.** Stop watering a few days before digging dahlias, then carefully unearth them with a spading fork. Discard tops, brush off dirt, and let tubers cure for a few days in a dry, frost-free place. Then store them in boxes of peat, vermiculite, or sand.

☐ **GROOM LAWNS.** Mow one last time, rake leaves before they mat up and smother the grass, and edge the lawn. Once frosts set in, growth slows or stops.

☐ **GROOM PERENNIAL BORDERS.** Be judicious as you cut back perennials, leaving the ones that, though they don't have their summer colors, do have seed heads or dried flowers for winter interest (and for bird food).

☐ **MAINTAIN TOOLS.** Put an edge on all your tools, from hoes and shovels to pruning shears, then wipe them down with oil (machine oil for metal parts, linseed oil for handles), and store them in a dry place for the winter.

☐ **MULCH EVERYTHING.** Put a 3- to 4-inch layer of organic mulch around semihardy plants, under trees and shrubs, and over bulb beds that might otherwise heave during hard winter frosts.

## IN THE SOUTHWEST'S LOW AND INTERMEDIATE DESERTS:

☐ **CONTROL APHIDS.** Blast them off new growth with a hose, then spray with insecticidal soap. Soap sprays work best when you dilute them first with distilled (rather than tap) water.

☐ **CONTROL SNAILS, SLUGS.** Put out bait, or handpick them during cloudy weather or in the morning after you've watered.

☐ **CULL SPLIT CITRUS.** Most kinds of citrus grow faster this month, so fast, in fact, that fruit can split. Pick off and discard split fruit, which attracts fungus and insects to otherwise healthy trees.

☐ **OVERSEED BERMUDA LAWN.** Mow your warm-season Bermuda grass at a height of about ½ inch, then overseed with 10 to 20 pounds of rye per 1,000 square feet. You can use annual or perennial rye; the coarse-leaf annual rye costs less, stains more, and needs more frequent mowing than its perennial cousin. A month after sowing, fertilize new lawn grass to help it fill in quickly.

☐ **PLANT COOL-SEASON ANNUALS.** In sunny places, set out ageratum, aster, bells-of-Ireland, calendula, candytuft, clarkia, cornflower, foxglove, larkspur, lobelia, painted daisy, petunia, phlox, snapdragon, stock, sweet alyssum, and sweet pea. In shady spots, set out dianthus, English daisy, pansy, primrose, and viola.

☐ **PLANT TREES AND SHRUBS.** This is the best time of year to plant hardy trees and shrubs, including acacia, cassia, *Cordia boissieri*, desert spoon, fairy duster, mesquite, oleander, palo verde, *Salvia greggii*, and Texas ranger. Water these plants in well, and they'll be able to handle next summer's heat better than spring-planted nursery stock. Stake tall trees to provide support while roots become established.

☐ **PLANT VEGETABLES.** Sow seeds or set out plants of asparagus, beets, broccoli, brussels sprouts, cabbage, carrots, cauliflower, celery, endive, garlic, kale, kohlrabi, leeks, lettuce, mustard, parsley, peas, radish, spinach, Swiss chard, and turnips.

☐ **PRUNE AND FEED ROSES.** Remove faded flowers, pruning lightly as you go. Take out dead, diseased, and crossing canes, and prune for shape. Then apply a complete fertilizer, watering it in well, to encourage a flush of winter blooms.

☐ **SOW WILDFLOWERS.** Sown now, these should come up fairly quickly. Try blackfoot daisy (*Melampodium leucanthum*), desert bluebells (*Phacelia campanularia*), desert globe mallow (*Sphaeralcea ambigua*), firewheel (*Gaillardia pulchella*), Mexican hat (*Ratibida columnifera*), and Mexican tulip poppy (*Hunnemannia fumariifolia*). If rains are infrequent, irrigate to keep seed plots moist until plants are at least 2 inches tall. ∎

WESTERN RED CEDAR
(Thuja plicata) and
vine maple (Acer
circinatum).

# Western natives...
# at home in your garden

Native plants bring a rich diversity of texture and color to home gardens. Today, they also make ecological sense: they've evolved to survive the climate of a particular region and to live on what nature provides. For busy gardeners, this translates to a bonus: most natives largely take care of themselves. The following pages identify some of the West's best natives for your home garden, grouped according to three broad geographical regions: The Pacific Northwest (pages 274–277); California (pages 278–281); and Mountain climates and the arid Southwest (pages 282–285).

When selecting a plant, keep in mind that though a plant is native, it may not be inherently unthirsty. In each region there are natives that come from moist habitats and will need plenty of garden water. And all native plants that have been growing in nursery containers need water while they are becoming established in a garden (for large trees, this can take several years). Only after plants are established can you cut back on water for those types that thrive naturally with little moisture.

In the following charts, we list appropriate climate zones (from 1 to 24) for each plant based on *Sunset*'s *Western Garden Book*. The symbols following a plant's zone adaptations highlight its sunlight and moisture needs and note whether conspicuous flowers are a feature.

*By Lauren Bonar Swezey*

## Pacific Northwest

Not all the Northwest is gray-skied and rain-drenched. In these lists you'll find not only moisture lovers like wild ginger *(Asarum caudatum)* but also tough customers like mountin hemlock *(Tsuga mertensiana)* and creeping mahonia *(Mahonia repens)* that hail from harsher, drier climates.

## Trees

| Plant | | | |
|---|---|---|---|
| **Alaska cedar** *(Chamaecyparis nootkatensis)* Z 4–6, 15–17 | ☼ ❂ | ● | |
| **Alpine fir** *(Abies lasiocarpa)* Z 1–9, 14–17 | ☼ ❂ | ●● | |
| **Douglas fir** *(Pseudotsuga menziesii)* Z 1–10, 14–17 | ☼ | ●● | |
| **Garry oak** *(Quercus garryana)* Z 4–6, 15–17 | ☼ | ◐ | |
| **Incense cedar** *(Calocedrus decurrens)* Z 1–12, 14–24 | ☼ | ◊ | |
| **Lodgepole pine** *(Pinus contorta latifolia)* Z 1–9, 14–19 | ☼ | ◊◊ | |
| **Madrone** *(Arbutus menziesii)* Z 3–7, 14–19 | ☼ | ● | ✿ |
| **Mountain hemlock** *(Tsuga mertensiana)* Z 1–7, 14–17 | ☼ | ◐ | |
| **Oregon ash** *(Fraxinus latifolia)* Z 4–24 | ☼ | ◊●● | |
| **Pacific dogwood** *(Cornus nuttallii)* Z 2–9, 14–20 | ☼ ❂ | ● | ✿ |
| **Vine maple** *(Acer circinatum)* Z 1–6, 14–17 | ☼ ❂ | ● | |
| **Western red cedar** *(Thuja plicata)* Z 1–9, 14–24 | ☼ ❂ | ●● | |
| **Western yew** *(Taxus brevifolia)* Z 1–6, 14–17 | ☼ ❂ ● | ◊● | |
| **White fir** *(Abies concolor)* Z 1–9, 14–24 | ☼ ❂ | ●● | |

**LODGEPOLE PINE**
*(Pinus contorta latifolia)*

Key to symbols
(gives range of conditions)

Z  = Zone

✿ = Flowers

☼ = Full sun

❂ = Partial shade

● = Full shade

◊ = No water once well established

◐ = Drought tolerant

● = Ordinary water

●● = Constant moisture

**RED FLOWERING CURRANT**
*(Ribes sanguineum)*

MICHAEL THOMPSON

**BUNCHBERRY**
*(Cornus canadensis)*

DAVID McDONALD

**SEDUM SPATHULIFOLIUM**
*'Cape Blanco'*

# Perennials, Ferns, Grasses

| Plant | |
|---|---|
| **Camass** (*Camassia quamash*) Z 1–9, 14–17 | ☀ 💧 ✿ |
| **Checker lily** (*Fritillaria lanceolata*) Z 1–7, 15–17 | ☀◐ 💧 ✿ |
| **Columbia lily** (*Lilium columbianum*) all zones | ◐ 💧 ✿ |
| **Deer fern** (*Blechnum spicant*) Z 1–9, 14–17 | ●💧💧 |
| **Dryas octopetala** Z 1–6 | ☀ 💧 ✿ |
| **Erythronium revolutum** Z 1–7, 15–17 | ☀● 💧💧 ✿ |
| **False Solomon's seal** (*Smilacina racemosa*) Z 1–7, 14–17 | ☀◐ 💧 ✿ |
| **Five-finger fern** (*Adiantum aleuticum*) Z 1–9, 14–21 | ◐● 💧💧 |
| **Iris, Pacific Coast and hybrids** Z 4–24 | ☀◐ 💧💧 ✿ |
| **Lewisia** Z 1–7 | ☀◐ 💧 ✿ |
| **Piggy-back plant** (*Tolmiea menziesii*) Z 5–9, 12–24 | ◐● 💧💧💧 |
| **Sedum spathulifolium** all zones | ☀◐ 💧💧 ✿ |
| **Shooting star** (*Dodecatheon*) all zones | ☀◐ 💧 ✿ |
| **Sword fern** (*Polystichum munitum*) Z 4–9, 14–24 | ●💧 |
| **Trillium ovatum** Z 1–6, 14–17 | ◐● 💧💧 |
| **Twinflower** (*Linnaea borealis*) Z 1–7, 14–17 | ☀◐● 💧💧 ✿ |
| **Vancouveria** zones vary | ◐ 💧💧 ✿ |
| **Western columbine** (*Aquilegia formosa*) all zones | ☀◐ 💧 ✿ |
| **Wood fern** (*Dryopteris expansa*) Z 4–9, 14–24 | ◐● 💧 |

# Ground Covers, Vines

| Plant | |
|---|---|
| **Bunchberry** (*Cornus canadensis*) Z 1–7 | ●💧 ✿ |
| **Creeping mahonia** (*Mahonia repens*) Z 1–21 | ☀◐ 💧💧💧 ✿ |
| **False lily-of-the-valley** (*Maianthemum dilatatum*) Z 1–9, 14–17 | ◐ 💧 ✿ |
| **Wild ginger** (*Asarum caudatum*) Z 4–6, 14–24 | ●💧💧💧 |
| **Wild strawberry** (*Fragaria chiloensis*) Z 4–24 | ☀◐ 💧 ✿ |

**REDTWIG DOGWOOD** (*Cornus stolonifera*)

**OREGON GRAPE** (*Mahonia aquifolium*)

**WESTERN COLUMBINE**
(*Aguilegia formosa*)

**FIVE-FINGER FERN**
(*Adiantum aleuticum*)

# Shrubs

**Arctostaphylos media** Z 4–9, 14–24

**Evergreen huckleberry** (*Vaccinium ovatum*) Z 4–7, 14–17

**Golden currant** (*Ribes aureum*) all zones

**Longleaf mahonia** (*Mahonia nervosa*) Z 2–9, 14–17

**Ocean spray** (*Holodiscus discolor*) Z 1–7, 14–17

**Oregon grape** (*Mahonia aquifolium*) Z 1–21

**Pacific wax myrtle** (*Myrica californica*) Z 4–6, 14–17, 20–24

**Red flowering currant** (*Ribes sanguineum*) Z 4–9, 14–24

**Redtwig dogwood** (*Cornus stolonifera*) Z 1–9, 14–21

**Rocky Mountain maple** (*Acer glabrum*) Z 1–3, 10

**Salal** (*Gaultheria shallon*) Z 3–7, 14–17, 21–24

**Saskatoon** (*Amelanchier alnifolia*) Z 1–6

**Sierra laurel** (*Leucothoe davisiae*) Z 1–7, 15–17

**Silktassel bush** (*Garrya issaquahensis*) Z 4–9

**Western azalea** (*Rhododendron occidentale*) Z 4–24

**Western hazelnut** (*Corylus cornuta californica*) Z 1–9, 14–20

# California

From rhododendrons on the cool north coast to Joshua trees in the incandescent southern deserts, California encompasses a plant diversity impossible to characterize. These plant lists reflect the varied climatic regions, proving that there not only are plants for all gardens but that many natives are widely adapted.

Key to symbols
(gives range of conditions)

Z = Zone

❀ = Flowers

☼ = Full sun

✷ = Partial shade

● = Full shade

◊ = No water once well established

◖ = Drought tolerant

◆ = Ordinary water

◆◆ = Constant moisture

CHARLES MANN

**WESTERN REDBUD**
*(Cercis occidentalis)*

CLAIRE CURRAN

**MONKEY FLOWER**
*(Mimulus aurantiacus)*

**PACIFIC COAST IRIS**

# Trees

| | | | |
|---|---|---|---|
| **Alaska cedar** (*Chamaecyparis nootkatensis*) Z 4–6, 15–17 | ☼ ✷ | ◆ | |
| **California bay** (*Umbellularia californica*) Z 4–10, 12–24 | ☼ ✷ | ◊ | |
| **California buckeye** (*Aesculus californica*) Z 4–10, 12, 14–24 | ☼ | ◖ | ❀ |
| **California sycamore** (*Platanus racemosa*) Z 4–24 | ☼ | ◖ | |
| **Fir** (*Abies*) several; zones vary | ☼ ✷ | ◖◆ | |
| **Incense cedar** (*Calocedrus decurrens*) Z 1–12, 14–24 | ☼ | ◊ | |
| *Lyonothamnus floribundus asplenifolius* Z 15–17, 19–24 | ☼ | ◖ | ❀ |
| **Madrone** (*Arbutus menziesii*) Z 3–7, 14–19 | ☼ | ◖ | ❀ |
| **Oak** (*Quercus*) many; zones vary | ☼ | ◖ | |
| **Pacific dogwood** (*Cornus nuttallii*) Z 2–9, 14–20 | ☼ ✷ | ◖ | ❀ |
| **Pine** (*Pinus*) several; zones vary | ☼ | ◊◆ | |
| **Port Orford cedar** (*Chamaecyparis lawsoniana*) Z 4–6, 15–17 | ☼ ✷ | ◆ | |
| **Quaking aspen** (*Populus tremuloides*) Z 1–7 | ☼ | ◆ | |
| **Tanbark oak** (*Lithocarpus densiflorus*) Z 4–7, 14–24 | ☼ ✷ | ◖ | ❀ |
| **Western cottonwood** (*Populus fremontii*) Z 7–24 | ☼ | ◆ | |
| **Western redbud** (*Cercis occidentalis*) Z 2–24 | ☼ | ◊◖ | ❀ |

**WILD MOCK ORANGE**
*(Philadelphus lewisii)*

**BLUE-EYED GRASS**
*(Sisyrinchium bellum)*

**BUSH ANEMONE**
*(Carpenteria californica)*

# Perennials, Ferns, Grasses

| Plant | | | |
|---|---|---|---|
| **Beach aster** (*Erigeron glaucus*) Z 4–6, 15–17, 22–24 | ☼ ❋ | ◌ | ✿ |
| **Blue-eyed grass** (*Sisyrinchium bellum*) many; Z 4–24 | ☼ ❋ | ◌◑ | ✿ |
| **California fuchsia** (*Zauschneria, Epilobium*) Z 2–10, 12–24 | ☼ | ◌ | ✿ |
| **California sagebrush** (*Artemisia californica*) all zones | ☼ | ◌ | |
| **Checkerbloom** (*Sidalcea*) Z 4–9, 14–24 | ☼ | ◑ | ✿ |
| **Common yarrow** (*Achillea millefolium*) all zones | ☼ | ◌◑ | ✿ |
| **Coral bells** (*Heuchera*) zones vary | ☼ ❋ | ◑ | ✿ |
| **Deergrass** (*Muhlenbergia rigens*) Z 8–24 | ☼ ❋ | ◌ | |
| **Inside-out flower** (*Vancouveria planipetala*) Z 4–6, 14–17 | ❋ | ◌◑ | ✿ |
| **Iris,** Pacific Coast and hybrids Z 4–24 | ☼ ❋ | ◌◑ | ✿ |
| **Lyme grass** (*Elymus*) Z 8, 9, 14–24 | ☼ ❋ | ◌ | |
| **Matilija poppy** (*Romneya coulteri*) all zones | ☼ | ◌◌ | ✿ |
| **Monkey flower** (*Mimulus*) water needs and zones vary | ☼ ❋ | | ✿ |
| *Penstemon heterophyllus purdyi* Z 6–24 | ☼ ❋ | ◌ | ✿ |
| **Purple needlegrass** (*Stipa pulchra*) Z 5, 7–9, 11, 14–24 | ☼ | ◌ | |
| **Royal beardtongue** (*Penstemon spectabilis*) Z 7, 14–23 | ☼ ❋ | ◌ | ✿ |
| **Scarlet bugler** (*Penstemon centranthifolius*) Z 7–23 | ☼ ❋ | ◌ | ✿ |
| *Vancouveria hexandra* Z 4–6, 14–17 | ❋ | ◑◑ | ✿ |
| **Western columbine** (*Aquilegia formosa*) all zones | ☼ ❋ | ◑ | ✿ |
| **Yellow-eyed grass** (*Sisyrinchium californicum*) Z 4–24 | ☼ ❋ | ●◑◑ | ✿ |

# Ground Covers, Vines

| Plant | | | |
|---|---|---|---|
| *Aristolochia californica* Z 7–9, 14–24 | ❋ | ●● | ✿ |
| *Clematis ligusticifolia* all zones (best in 1–6, 15–17) | ☼ | ◑ | ✿ |
| **Manzanita** (*Arctostaphylos*) many; zones vary | ☼ | ◌ | ✿ |
| **Wild ginger** (*Asarum caudatum*) Z 4–6, 14–24 | ● | ●● | |
| **Wild lilac** (*Ceanothus*) many; Z 1–9, 14–24 | ☼ | ◌◑ | ✿ |

# Shrubs

Blue elderberry (*Sambucus mexicana*) all zones

Bush anemone (*Carpenteria californica*) Z 5–9, 14–24

California storax (*Styrax officinalis californicus*) Z 8, 9, 14–24

Catalina cherry (*Prunus lyonii*) Z 7–9, 12–24

Coffeeberry (*Rhamnus californica*) several; Z 4–24

Coyote brush (*Baccharis pilularis*) Z 5–11, 14–24

Currant (*Ribes*) several; water needs and zones vary

Flannel bush (*Fremontodendron*) several; Z 7–24

Hollyleaf cherry (*Prunus ilicifolia*) Z 7–9, 12–24

Island bush poppy (*Dendromecon harfordii*) Z 5–8, 14–24

Island bush-snapdragon (*Galvezia speciosa*) Z 14–24

*Lavatera assurgentiflora* Z 14–24

Lemonade berry (*Rhus integrifolia*) Z 15–17, 20–24

Lupine (*Lupinus arboreus*) Z 14–17, 22–24

Mahonia several; zones vary

Manzanita (*Arctostaphylos*) many; zones vary

Pacific wax myrtle (*Myrica californica*) Z 4–6, 14–17, 20–24

Purple sage (*Salvia leucophylla*) Z 8, 9, 12–17, 19–24

Redtwig dogwood (*Cornus stolonifera*) Z 1–9, 14–21

*Salvia* 'Allen Chickering' Z 10–24

*Salvia clevelandii* several; Z 10–24

Silktassel (*Garrya*) several; water needs and zones vary

Spice bush (*Calycanthus occidentalis*) Z 4–9, 14–22

Sugar bush (*Rhus ovata*) Z 7–24

*Symphoricarpos albus* all zones

Toyon (*Heteromeles arbutifolia*) Z 5–24

Western azalea (*Rhododendron occidentale*) Z 4–24

Wild buckwheat (*Eriogonum*) many; zones vary

Wild lilac (*Ceanothus*) many; Z 1–9, 14–24

Wild mock orange (*Philadelphus lewisii*) Z 1–17

Woolly blue curls (*Trichostema lanatum*) Z 14–24

SPICE BUSH
(*Calycanthus occidentalis*)

ISLAND BUSH POPPY
(*Dendromecon harfordii*)

WOOLLY BLUE CURLS
(*Trichostema lanatum*)

# Mountain and Southwest

Dryness is a common climatic thread in these regions; most of these plants accept limited water rations. But altitude or lack of it dramatically affects regional climate as a whole: cold winters, relatively cool summers, and a short growing season in the mountains contrast sharply with the enervating heat, mild winters, and cooler-months growing season of the low deserts.

**MEXICAN EVENING PRIMROSE** (*Oenethera berlandieri*)

SCOTT ANGER

## Key to symbols
(gives range of conditions)

Z = Zone
❁ = Flowers
☼ = Full sun
☀ = Partial shade
● = Full shade
◊ = No water once well established
◖ = Drought tolerant
◆ = Ordinary water
◆◆ = Constant moisture

**MEXICAN HAT**
(*Ratibida columnifera*)

## Trees for Mountain regions

| | Sun | Water |
|---|---|---|
| *Betula Occidentalis* Z 1–3, 10 | ☼ | ◆◆◆ |
| Colorado spruce (*Picea pungens*) Z 1–10, 14–17 | ☼ ☀ | ◆ |
| *Juniperus monosperma* all zones | ☼ ☀ | ◖ |
| Lanceleaf cottonwood (*Populus acuminata*) all zones | ☼ | ◆ |
| Pine (*Pinus*) several; zones vary | ☼ | ◊◊ |
| Quaking aspen (*Populus tremuloides*) Z 1–7 | ☼ | ◆ |
| Rocky Mountain juniper (*Juniperus scopulorum*) all zones | ☼ ☀ | ◊◖ |
| White fir (*Abies concolor*) Z 1–9, 14–24 | ☼ ☀ | ◆◆ |
| Wild plum (*Prunus americana*) Z 1–3, 10 | ☼ | ◖ |

## Trees for the Southwest

| | Sun | Water | Flowers |
|---|---|---|---|
| *Acacia smallii* Z 8, 9, 12–24 | ☼ | ◖ | ❁ |
| Arizona sycamore (*Platanus wrightii*) Z 10–12 | ☼ | ◖ | |
| Blue palo verde (*Cercidium floridum*) Z 10–14, 18–20 | ☼ | ◖◆ | ❁ |
| Desert ironwood (*Olneya tesota*) Z 12, 13 | ☼ | ◊◊ | ❁ |
| Desert willow (*Chilopsis linearis*) Z 10–13, 18–21 | ☼ | ◖ | ❁ |
| Emory oak (*Quercus emoryi*) Z 10–13 | ☼ | ◖ | |
| Feather bush (*Lysiloma microphylla thornberi*) Z 10, 12–24 | ☼ | ◊◆ | ❁ |
| Foothills palo verde (*Cercidium microphyllum*) Z 10–14, 18–20 | ☼ | ◖◆ | ❁ |
| Mesquite (*Prosopis*) Z 10–13 | ☼ | ◊◖ | |
| Sonoran palo verde (*Cercidium praecox*) Z 12, 13, 18–20 | ☼ | ◊◖ | ❁ |
| Texas ebony (*Pithecellobium flexicaule*) Z 10–13 | ☼ | ◊◆ | ❁ |
| Whitethorn acacia (*Acacia constricta*) Z 10–24 | ☼ | ◊ | ❁ |

## Perennials, Ferns

Blackfoot daisy (*Melampodium leucanthum*) Z 1–3, 10–13

Bluebell of Scotland (*Campanula rotundifolia*) Z 1–9, 14–2

Firecracker penstemon (*Penstemon eatonii*) Z 1–3, 7–13, 18–21

Mexican evening primrose (*Oenothera berlandieri*) all zones

Mexican hat (*Ratibida columnifera*) all zones

*Monarda fistulosa* all zones

*Penstemon barbatus* all zones

*Penstemon pinifolius* all zones

Prairie or sand penstemon (*Penstemon ambiguus*) all zones

Prairie smoke (*Geum triflorum*) all zones

Rocky Mountain columbine (*Aquilegia caerulea*) all zones

Rocky Mountain penstemon (*Penstemon strictus*) Z 1–3, 10–13

Sulfur flower (*Eriogonum umbellatum*) all zones

White evening primrose (*Oenothera caespitosa*) Z 1–3, 10–13

ROCKY MOUNTAIN PENSTEMON
(*Penstemon strictus*)

CHARLES MANN

## Shrubs

Apache plume (*Fallugia paradoxa*) Z 2–23

Cliff rose (*Cowania mexicana stansburiana*) Z 1–3, 10–13

Coral berry (*Symphoricarpos orbiculatus*) all zones

Curl-leaf mountain mahogany (*Cercocarpus ledifolius*) all zones

Golden currant (*Ribes aureum*) all zones

New Mexican privet (*Forestiera neomexicana*) all zones

Rabbitbrush (*Chrysothamnus nauseosus*) Z 1–3, 10, 11

Redtwig dogwood (*Cornus stolonifera*) Z 1–9, 14–21

*Rhus glabra cismontana* Z 1–10, 14–17

Rocky Mountain maple (*Acer glabrum*) Z 1–3, 10

Rocky Mountain thimbleberry (*Rubus deliciosus*) Z 1–5, 10

Saskatoon (*Amelanchier alnifolia*) Z 1–6

Silver buffaloberry (*Shepherdia argentea*) Z 1–3, 7, 10, 14–24

Wild mock orange (*Philadelphus lewisii*) Z 1–17

BRISTLECONE PINE (*Pinus aristata*)

## Ground Covers, Vines

*Calylophus hartwegii* Z 1–3, 10–13

*Clematis ligusticifolia* Z 1–6, 15–17)

Creeping mahonia (*Mahonia repens*) Z 1–21

*Humulus lupulus neomexicanus* all zones

Kinnikinnick (*Arctostaphylos uva-ursi*) Z 1–9, 14–24

*Zinnia grandiflora* all zones

APACHE PLUME (*Fallugia paradoxa*)

## Perennials, Annuals

ZINNIA GRANDIFLORA

| Plant | Light | Water | Flower |
|---|---|---|---|
| **Blackfoot daisy** (*Melampodium leucanthum*) Z 1–3, 10–13 | ☀ | ◐ | ✿ |
| **Desert marigold** (*Baileya multiradiata*) all zones | ☀ | ◐ | ✿ |
| **Firecracker penstemon** (*Penstemon eatonii*) Z 1–3, 7–13, 18–21 | ☀◗ | ◐ | ✿ |
| **Mexican hat** (*Ratibida columnifera*) all zones | ☀ | ● | ✿ |
| **Parry's penstemon** (*Penstemon parryi*) Z 12, 13 | ☀◗ | ◐ | ✿ |
| *Penstemon barbatus* all zones | ☀◗ | ◐ | ✿ |
| *Penstemon superbus* Z 12, 13 | ☀◗ | ◐ | ✿ |
| **Prairie or sand penstemon** (*P. ambiguus*) Z 7–15, 18–21 | ☀◗ | ● | ✿ |
| **Rocky Mountain penstemon** (*Penstemon strictus*) Z 1–3, 10–13 | ☀◗ | ◐ | ✿ |
| *Verbena bipinnatifida* all zones | ☀ | ◐ | ✿ |
| *Verbena gooddingii* all zones | ☀ | ● | ✿ |
| **White evening primrose** (*Oenothera caespitosa*) Z 1–3, 10–13 | ☀ | ◐ | ✿ |

## Shrubs

| Plant | Light | Water | Flower |
|---|---|---|---|
| **Apache plume** (*Fallugia paradoxa*) Z 2–23 | ☀ | ◐● | ✿ |
| **Autumn sage** (*Salvia greggii*) Z 8–24 | ☀◗ | ◐● | ✿ |
| **Blue sage** (*Salvia chamaedryoides*) Z 8, 9, 14–24 | ☀ | ◐ | ✿ |
| **Brittlebush** (*Encelia farinosa*) Z 7–10, 14–24 | ☀ | ● | ✿ |
| **Chuparosa** (*Justicia californica*) Z 10–13 | ☀ | ● | ✿ |
| **Fairy duster** (*Calliandra eriophylla*) Z 10–24 | ☀ | ◐● | ✿ |
| **Hop bush** (*Dodonaea viscosa*) Z 7–9, 12–24 | ☀◗ | ◐ | |
| *Leucophyllum* many; Z 7–24 | ☀ | ◐ | ✿ |
| **Mealy-cup sage** (*Salvia farinacea*) all zones | ☀ | ◐ | ✿ |
| **Squawbush** (*Rhus trilobata*) Z 1–3, 10–13 | ☀ | ◐◐ | |
| *Tagetes lemmonii* Z 8–10, 12–24 | ☀ | ● | ✿ |
| *Tecoma stans angustata* Z 12, 13 | ☀ | ◐● | ✿ |
| **Texas olive** (*Cordia boissieri*) Z 8–24 | ☀◗ | ◐● | ✿ |

WHITE EVENING PRIMROSE
(*Oenothera caespitosa*)

## Ground Covers, Vines

| Plant | Light | Water | Flower |
|---|---|---|---|
| **Baja evening primrose** (*Oenothera stubbei*) all zones | ☀ | ◐● | ✿ |
| *Calylophus hartwegii* Z 1–3, 10–13 | ☀◗ | ◐ | ✿ |
| **Mexican evening primrose** (*Oenothera berlandieri*) all zones | ☀ | ◐● | ✿ |
| **Trailing indigo bush** (*Dalea greggii*) Z 12, 13 | ☀ | ◐ | |
| *Zinnia grandiflora* all zones | ☀ | ◐● | ✿ |

## Grasses, Accent Plants

AGAVE WEBERI

| Plant | Light | Water | Flower |
|---|---|---|---|
| *Agave* several; zones vary | ☀◗ | ◐● | ✿ |
| **Bamboo muhly** (*Muhlenbergia dumosa*) Z 8–24 | ☀◗ | ◐● | |
| *Hesperaloe parviflora* Z 10–16, 18–21 | ☀ | ◐● | ✿ |
| **Ocotillo** (*Fouquieria splendens*) Z 10–13, 18–20 | ☀ | ◐ | ✿ |
| *Yucca* many | ☀ | ◐ | ✿ |

CHARLES MANN

# The art of rock walls

*Garden walls built of dry-stacked stones transcend their humble origins*

**Small is beautiful**
*Barely more than a foot high, this low retaining wall abuts a set of garden stairs. Design and construction: Bill Gorgas, San Francisco.*

PETER O. WHITELEY

**Is it a wall or a sculpture?**
*Landscape designer Topher Delaney envisioned an abstracted stone wall on this hilltop site, and stonemason Edwin Hamilton of Sebastopol, California, created it with granite shapes that evoke Druid ruins or a Robert Motherwell painting.*

Long before there were bricks or concrete, there were rocks. They were free, plentiful, and virtually indestructible. Almost anyone could pick them up, pile them together, and make a wall that would separate property, define courtyards, hold steep hillsides in place, or form planters in gardens. Of course, the professional rock workers, or stonemasons, went on to grander things, such as castles and cathedrals.

In today's world there's not much call for monumental rockwork, but the timeless skills of the stonemason are resurfacing on a smaller scale in the residential garden wall. In the hands

## An intimate sunken garden with built-ins

*A wrought-iron snake slithers up the intricate wall of granite, basalt, and sandstone (left) in the backyard garden of Rob and Mary Morrow (above). Stonemason Edwin Hamilton ringed the flagstone patio with walls containing a built-in bench, stairway, barbecue, and wood storage bin (below) framed in granite shapes found at an abandoned quarry.*

DAVID DUNCAN LIVINGSTON

of a skilled stonemason, a rock wall goes beyond its utilitarian role and becomes a thing of striking, permanent beauty.

The purest forms of stonework are mortarless or "dry-stacked" walls, which rely only on friction, weight, and the shape of the rocks to hold them together. The best work is as thoughtfully composed as a painting. It has graceful lines and balanced proportions, and it elegantly integrates stones of differing sizes and shapes.

The examples shown here advance the traditional craft with subtle nudges or bold strokes. They vary in scale from a foot-high garden wall made of stones most of us could lift to a taller retaining wall made of several-ton boulders that were lifted by crane. Some incorporate built-in seating, storage, fountains, and cooking areas. One forgoes function almost altogether; it implies a wall, but is really more of a sculptural assemblage of massive forms.

Unlike the rocks in fieldstone walls that march across farm-lands, few of the ones in these walls retain their natural shape. Most have been sculpted and hewn with the same tools that stonemasons have been using for centuries: heavy hammers and broad-pointed chisels. Shims and wedges are also employed to split boulder-size rocks. Typically, the skills and

## Timeless tools, long-lasting walls

*Stonemason George Gonzalez (left) uses a maul, point-tipped chisel, and blunter pitching tools (below) to fit stones together with the precision of a giant jigsaw puzzle. His garden alcove (above) has a recirculating fountain centered in its back wall.*

trade secrets of stonemasonry are passed on from a master stonemason to apprentices.

Granite and basalt are popular choices for walls, but a competent mason can shape many of the other types of stone commonly found at rock yards. Masons will take rocks with irregular or rounded shapes and score, chip, or sometimes cut them to create straight edges and vertical faces. Stacked-rock retaining walls start with a broad, partially buried base and then angle, or "batter," back into the hill to resist the outward force of the earth behind. Freestanding walls are battered on both sides.

The cost of rocks and of transporting them, combined with the time and skill required to cut and fit them, makes dry-stacked walls more expensive than those made of wood or concrete. On average, a dry-stacked wall with some cut stone costs about $35 per square foot.

However, no other type of wall can match a well-crafted rock wall for rugged good looks, the ability to blend naturally with plantings, and durability. There's something fundamentally satisfying about adding a garden wall that will outlast a wood-framed house. As master stonemason George Gonzalez says, "I like to build a wall that will last 500 years." ■

*Peter O. Whiteley*

**THE SULLIVAN SAND POND** *is ringed by (clockwise, from left) blue sage, Mexican evening primrose, Helichrysum 'Limelight', Verbena bonariensis, and buffalo and mosquito grasses.*

# Garden design on a child's level

*A Fullerton sand pond and meadow is practical without sacrificing aesthetics*

MIKE SULLIVAN DIDN'T plan on converting his Fullerton, California, backyard into Jurassic Park. What he had in mind was a contemplation garden, Japanese in spirit, centered around a lily pond. Not his best idea, his wife, Elisa, delicately suggested. "Neither practical nor prudent with two toddlers underfoot," she says.

Sullivan rebounded quickly. By filling the planned pond with sand instead of water, he salvaged his basic landscaping design. In the process, he also created a 150-square-foot sandbox for son Matthew and daughter Halley that is now the envy of their playmates.

The sand-pond idea changed the purpose of the garden, as well as the rest of its design. Instead of the serene spot originally envisioned, the Sullivans now aimed for a miniature adventure park that would exercise their children's imaginations as well as their limbs.

"We wanted it to feel like a place you might stumble onto while hiking in the Sierra and decide to hang out in for an afternoon," Mike says. "We thought that the design would encourage playacting rather than just running around."

## FILLING A DRY POND

The Sullivans began by carving out an irregular oval depression at the rear of their flat, rectangular yard. On top of a gravel foundation, they filled in the space with sand and edged the pond with boulders to create the look of a small, dry wilderness creek bed in midsummer. The excavated dirt was piled into a small slope nearby and planted with buffalo and mosquito grasses. Left unshorn, this grassy patch simulates a mountain meadow.

The Sullivans then turned their attention to the perimeter of the sandbox. Here they planted native shrubs, including blue sage (*Salvia clevelandii*), Matilija poppy (*Romneya coulteri*), and California fuchsia (*Zauschneria*). Perennials such as daylilies, Mexican evening primrose, and statice were added for color, while grasses—including evergreen miscanthus—continued the meadow motif. All were selected for their informal effect, low water requirements, and (in a few cases) ability to withstand occasional youthful trampling.

As a play space, the sand pond has surpassed the Sullivans' expectations. "The kids spend 3 or 4 hours at a stretch out here," says Elisa. "They love molding and shaping the sand, and the setting is perfect for their action scenarios—their toy dinosaurs look right at home."

Water from garden hoses, used to create moats and waterfalls for these scenarios, drains into the 3- by 3- by 3-foot gravel bed underlying the 8 to 12 inches of sand. The sump not only keeps the sand dry but also acts as an aquifer. "Water recharges the ground rather than draining off into the ocean," says Mike.

Leaf litter and plant debris can be raked out of the sand, but the Sullivans often leave it in place, believing it makes the pond look more like a natural dry creek bed.

Neighborhood cats might have presented a less tasteful problem, but the Sullivans' cat, Freeway, largely solved the dilemma. She chases away intruders wishing to use the sand pond as a litter box and, thoughtfully, declines to use it as one herself.

The mountain meadow, on the other hand, hasn't been quite the unqualified success the sand pond has. Though the Sullivans love the romantic look of the tall grass billowing in the breeze, and think it makes a scenic setting for lawn picnics, Easter egg hunts, and other family parties, Matthew and Halley complain that it scratches their bare legs.

"Mowing it more often will eliminate the seed heads, which are what they object to," says Mike. "And leaving it tall around the edges will keep it from looking too much like turf."

Chances are it will remain wild enough for the children's toy dinosaurs. ■

*By Sharon Cohoon*

NORMAN A. PLATE

# An emblem for the season

*It's easy to make a harvest hang-up from fresh and dried ingredients*

**T**HERE'S SOMETHING about fall that makes us want to bring the natural beauty and bounty of the season inside. As we found out, gathering autumn's rich colors and deep textures can be as easy as a trip to the local grocery store.

When shopping for the ingredients to make this decorative hang-up, we chose whatever seemed appealing from among the ornamental foods stocked for the holidays: colorful dried corn and squash, pecans, walnuts, artichokes, sheaves of wheat. What resulted is one of many possible interpretations.

You, too, can bring the harvest indoors. Keep in mind that you are free to do what we did—select ingredients that appeal to you and arrange them however you like.

## HOW TO GET HUNG UP
## STEP-BY-STEP

*Gather tools and materials.* You'll need a hammer and a few nails, a wire cutter, a glue gun (or silicone glue), a screwdriver, and a few rolls of florist's wire, available at craft stores.

*Attach with wire.* To attach the ornamental corn and squash, start a hole in one end of each vegetable the quick way—with a hammer and nail. Pull out the nail, then screw in an eye hook or a flat wood screw (make sure the nail is thinner than either). Tie one end of a 10- to 12-inch length of wire to the eye hook, or circle the wire beneath the head of the screw and cinch it tight.

To attach the wire to a nut, make a tiny loop at one end of a 5- to 7-inch length of wire. Set the loop on top of the nut and place a dot of glue over the loop with the glue gun. Hot glue sets fast, but silicone does not—read the label carefully for drying time.

*Group the elements.* After each piece has been strung with wire, put like with like: corn in one group, squash in another, etc. Set aside the artichokes and wheat for now.

*Twist together.* First, place a nail in the door or wall where you want to hang the arrangement. Next, starting with the cluster of corn, twist all the wires together to create a single cable. Tie the top of this cable to the nail. Twist the squash wires together in the same manner and then attach to the nail in the wall. Adjust the length of the squash cable as needed for a more snug display.

To attach artichokes, loop wire underneath the leaves and then attach the wire to the nail. Use clumps of nuts and groups of miniature ornamental corn, their wires twisted together as described above, to fill in spaces around the artichokes, squash, and larger ears of corn. Attach to the nail in the same manner as the rest of the vegetables.

*Arrange the elements.* When all the nuts and vegetables have been securely fastened to the nail, you can shift individual pieces into more desirable positions. Use glue to hold clusters in place, or adjust wires at the nail.

*The finishing touch.* Top off the hang-up with two crisscrossed sheaves of wheat. You can tie them together using raffia and attach them to the nail with wire. If the hang-up is kept in a dry location, it can last from two to four weeks. Design: Dennis W. Leong. ◼

*By Rosalva Welsch*

**ATTACH WIRE** *to fresh fruit, dried corn, or whole nuts with an eye hook, wood screws, or glue gun.*

EACH DAY *Teresa Mullen (left) and Tanya Washington harvest organically grown lettuces for Fresh Start Farms's salad mix.*

ANDY FREEBERG

## COMMUNITY ACTION

# Back to the land for a fresh start

*A San Francisco lot produces salad greens for restaurants and helps the homeless*

 VACANT LOT IS familiar in the urban landscape. So the one at Divisadero and Ellis streets in San Francisco never seemed unusual. Unoccupied for 25 years, it was surrounded by a dilapidated chain-link fence, littered with garbage and broken glass, and invaded by weeds—not exactly eye-catching.

But now, behind a rebuilt fence, dozens of beds of rich brown soil produce gourmet lettuces, mustards, and spinach. In its new incarnation as an organic vegetable garden, the lot is receiving attention, and its new beginning extends well beyond the quarter-acre lot.

Seven homeless adults, each with children, are learning to plant, harvest, wash, and market the crops grown there. Fresh Start Farms is a year-old project that trains and employs homeless people to produce crops to sell to local restaurants.

Ruth Brinker, the project's founder, has been developing programs for people in need for more than a decade. One successful program, Project Open Hand, provides meals to people with AIDS in the San Francisco Bay Area. At Fresh Start, Brinker offers the participants wages and skills to help them make a smooth transition to permanent housing and employment.

The vacant lot turned microfarm is leased for $1 a month from the San Francisco Redevelopment Agency. Finding the lot and wading through city bureaucracy to get permits took Brinker a year and a half. But once she secured the property and word got out about the project, donations of topsoil and labor to clear and grade the lot came quickly.

The project is the first step in what Brinker hopes will be a proliferation of such farms. "It's part of our genetic memory to work in the soil," Brinker says. "Connect people with nature, and they are home again."

The farm grows and sells fresh organic produce year-round to city restaurants. Twenty-five salad ingredients are grown in a 44-bed garden; two beds are harvested each day to create a salad mix that may include 'Merveille de Quatre Saisons' and 'Rouge d'Hiver' lettuces, mizuna (a type of mustard), 'Tyee' spinach, and Joi Choi, an Asian cabbage.

Before one sprout had peeked through the soil, Brinker had secured orders for the salad mix from such well-known San Francisco restaurants as Aqua, Stars, Fleur de Lys, and Oritalia. Bruce Hill, executive chef at Oritalia, uses the mix in his appropriately titled Fresh Start Farms Garden Salad. Hill, one of the biggest fans of the project, says, "The quality is amazing. The mix is so fresh—it travels only seven or eight blocks to get to my restaurant." Freshness is key to the enthusiasm for the mix. Brinker is proud to make a delivery and be able to say, "This was harvested a half-hour ago."

The project has not been without challenges on gardening and staffing fronts. True to its microclimate, the site is windy and water evaporates quickly. And child-care problems caused three of the initial participants to drop out. But for the seven gardening pioneers who remain, the program is working.

Teresa Mullen heard about Fresh Start Farms through Homeward Bound, the agency that secured housing for all of the participants. Before she entered the program, Mullen was on welfare and looking for work to support herself and her children. "This seemed like a good spot to get into the work force," she says. Now she's putting her skills to work growing vegetables for her table at home, too.

For more information about this project, write to Fresh Start Farms, 1095 Market St., Suite 302, San Francisco, Calif. 94103, or call (415) 695-9670. ■

*By Christianne Selig*

FRESH START FARMS *founder Ruth Brinker delivers salad mix half an hour after harvest.*

**HOLIDAY TOPIARIES**
*give seasonal decorations a fresh, natural elegance. See page 304 for step-by-step instructions.*

# DECEMBER

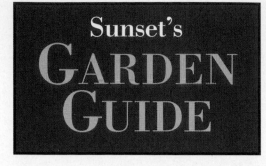

# Sunset's GARDEN GUIDE

# December in the West—from poinsettias and orchids to snow shovels

I t's that time of year when many merry gardeners spend more time indoors decorating the house than they do outdoors tending the garden. For most households, holiday decorating means displaying at least a few poinsettias.

What's hot in poinsettias this year? Look for the striking new Freedom series and 'Monet', introduced by Paul Ecke Ranch, a premier poinsettia grower in Encinitas, California.

Freedom poinsettias have dark green foliage, which is much richer-looking than that of other types of poinsettias. The leaves also tend not to drop prematurely if given suitable growing conditions. In fact, Ecke Ranch received reports from home growers that the Freedom poinsettias lasted well into spring. Colors in the Freedom series include Jingle Bells (red with pink flecks), Marble (pink and white), Red (deep burgundy), White (cream), and Pink.

'Monet' is a blue-ribbon winner in the Society of American Florists' new varieties competition. Its multicolored bracts (modified leaves) daubed with shades of red, deep rose, and cream remind some of Claude Monet's paintings.

Look for Freedom and 'Monet' poinsettias at nurseries and florist shops this month. Plants do best when daytime temperatures stay below 70° and nighttime temperatures are from 60° to 65° indoors or no lower than the low 50s outdoors. Set plants in bright, indirect light, and keep the soil around them moderately moist.

**NEW POINSETTIAS** *for the holidays include (clockwise from lower left) the Freedom series—Red, Jingle Bells, Marble, another Red, and White—and 'Monet'.*

## But aren't poinsettias poisonous?

The most widely sold potted plant in the United States, poinsettia has a commonly believed but poorly documented reputation for being poisonous. To determine whether the plant is truly dangerous, Ohio State University conducted extensive research. Their conclusion: though poinsettia leaves and flowers might give you a stomachache if you ate them, they wouldn't kill or seriously hurt you. With this in mind, you should still keep poinsettias out of the reach of small children.

## A freckle-faced viola from seed

*Viola sororia* 'Freckles', a newly cultivated viola found wild in Wisconsin, was first noticed for its white petals flecked with violet blue, as though somebody had passed over it with a spray gun. The flowers were sterile, so it was assumed that the plant produced no seeds.

Not so. This viola forms seeds in ground-level pods that aren't connected with the blossoms above.

You can plant the hardy

**Electric snow throwers** are the best solution for most people. The plug-in models are light and quiet, and they can throw snow 15 to 30 feet at the rate of 700 pounds per minute. If you have to tackle deeper snow, go over it twice. The cord limits this machine's range to about 100 feet—fine for most suburban uses. Cost is $200 to $300.

**Single-stage gas throwers** have one auger and can throw snow 25 to 30 feet at 1,700 pounds per minute. Most of these throwers are powered by low-maintenance, long-lasting 2-cycle gasoline engines. Look for models guaranteed to start in two pulls. Cost is $400 to $650.

**Two-stage gas throwers** have an auger and an impeller—the auger for crunching snow, the impeller for throwing it. With the ability to throw snow 30 to 40 feet at 2,200 pounds per minute, they work best in wet, heavy, deep snow, or drifts pushed onto your property by snowplows. These machines have 4-cycle gasoline engines and multi-speed transmissions (so you don't have to push them). Cost ranges from $900 to $2,500.

## Dust control for indoor plants

Like any object in your house that sits in one place month after month, house plants collect dust. Besides giving plants a dingy look, dust cuts down on the light they receive and serves as an ideal breeding ground for mites and other insect pests. Monthly cleaning helps solve these problems.

The classic small-plant solution is to cover the pot with a garbage bag, place it in the shower, then rinse the foliage with a shower of lukewarm water. Be sure you rinse both tops and bottoms of leaves.

For larger plants, you can sponge off the leaves with lukewarm water or use a commercial leaf-cleaning preparations sold at garden centers.

new viola this month in the desert or this coming spring in cold-winter climates for a profusion of flowers later. First blooms will appear in spring in the warm-winter areas and in summer where winters are cold.

Order 'Freckles' viola seed from Thompson & Morgan, Dept. 500-5, Jackson, N.J. 08527. Send $5.94 (includes postage and handling) for a

packet of seed (Item 8873) and a catalog.

## What you need to know about snow shovels and throwers

When snow falls thick and fast, you can deal with it in several ways.

**Snow shovels** are fine if you have the time and are in

good cardiovascular shape. But if you're not, you risk having a heart attack, according to exercise physiologist Barry Franklin of William Beaumont Hospital in Detroit. Franklin presented a study on the subject this year to the American College of Cardiology, stating that the combination of extreme cold and strenuous aerobic exercise is what puts you at risk.

## Common tool a cut above the rest

Is there any good way to cut leaves of tough, stringy plants like New Zealand flax or giant bird of paradise? Pruning shears don't work very well—they cut only partway through the leaves, often getting hung up on the wiry fibers. A sharp knife isn't any better and can be treacherous to work with. A saw is out of the question.

Horticulturist Randy Baldwin, manager of San Marcos Growers in Santa Barbara, California, has come up with a solution that he likes a lot. Noticing that the serrated blade on his folding multipurpose tool was effective on stringy plant tissue without being dangerously sharp, he went to a cutlery store looking for a larger version. He found a knife on sale that had the same distinctive serrations—two shallow followed by one deep—bought it, and had the perplexed store clerk grind off the sharp tip for safety. Baldwin reports that the knife easily cuts most of the troublesome strap-leafed plants, as well as ornamental grasses. In fact, he's so happy with it that he didn't give it to his field man as he had planned; he keeps it in his personal tool kit.

Baldwin says his knife cuts all the grasses and perennials he's tried it on, along with

WILLIAM B. DEWEY

**TO CUT** *the tough leaves of flax or bird of paradise, use a sharp knife whose blade has a pattern of one deep and two shallow serrations.*

even smaller varieties of running bamboo such as *Arundinaria*. It works well on the living leaves of New Zealand flax, but not as well on the dead ones or on the flower stalks. And it doesn't work at all on anything woody; it's not a saw. Baldwin recommends wearing heavy work gloves—the blade is meant for cutting fish and could easily slice through a finger.

Many manufacturers make knives similar to the one Baldwin found. His, called the Barramundi Filet Knife, is made by Kershaw and sells for $24.95 (model 1246ST). The blade is 6½ inches long; the foot-long knife comes with a sturdy plastic sheath. Gerber makes The SilverSerrater in two lengths (6- and 7½-inch blades); it also sells the same knife under the brand name Fiskars. Sog offers The Pentagon, with a 5-inch blade, and Spyderco sells The Catcherman, which has a 4½-inch blade. Whatever the brand, look for the distinctive, but nowadays common, serration described above. That's the key to the success of these knives as garden tools.

## Dreaming of a white Christmas? Create one with plants

A colorful display of plants on the front porch makes an inviting welcome to holiday visitors. Plants with red flowers or foliage are an obvious choice, but white plants can make an even more elegant show. Besides white-flowered poinsettias, here are some other plants with white flowers or foliage to look for in nurseries this month.

Plants with clear white flowers include potted chrysanthemums, cyclamen, fairy and English primroses, snapdragons, stock, and some violas. You might also look for early-blooming camellias such as 'Alba Plena' and 'Nuccio's Blend'. Evergreen plants with white variegation

or markings on the leaves can also add dramatically to the show. Some of the best include *Pittosporum tobira* 'Variegata', society garlic (*Tulbaghia violacea* 'Silver Lace'), and various euonymus, hollies, and ivies.

## A new book on growing roses the natural way

With so many books available on rose gardening, you might wonder why you would need another tome about roses. But *The Natural Rose Gardener,* by Lance Walheim (Ironwood Press, 1994; $17.95), is different from the rest. Sure, it has plenty of beautiful pictures of roses (170 glossy color photos), and like most books, it lists many kinds of roses: more than 300 are described in chapters covering old garden roses, shrub roses, hybrid teas, floribundas, grandifloras, miniatures, and climbing roses.

What makes this book different is the author's focus on landscaping with roses *naturally*. Walheim believes roses should be integrated into the landscape. Photos throughout the book show roses growing in mixed perennial borders and among shrubs.

The book's other important message is that you don't have to maintain an arsenal of toxic chemicals to grow roses. Walheim tells how using some pesticides can actually make matters worse: "Spraying with broad-spectrum insecticides—those that are effective on all insects—reduces many natural insect predators and parasites, and can eventually result in a buildup of insect pests…." At the back of the book are sections on preventive controls for pests and diseases and alternatives to toxic chemicals.

The book also includes a Rose Selection Guide to choosing roses for specific situations or preferences.

Look for this title at bookstores, or order from Iron-

wood Press, 2968 W. Ina Rd., Suite 285, Tucson 85741; cost of $21.45 includes shipping.

## Yes, you can grow artichokes in California's Central Valley

When you think of artichokes, you probably think of cool, foggy summers along the Northern California coast, where most of the commercial crop is grown. Although cool weather does prolong the harvest season of high-quality buds, you can also grow delicious artichokes in the Central Valley (crops are unreliable at higher elevations). This is a good month to set out plants. Most nurseries will be offering bare-root divisions or plants in 1-gallon cans. 'Green Globe' is the most common variety.

Artichoke plants get large, so choose a planting area with plenty of room (at least 4 square feet per plant) that receives afternoon or filtered shade. Amend the soil with organic matter, such as compost, and set the plants so the crowns are just above soil level. Don't let plants dry out. Water and fertilize regularly.

Artichoke plants will grow foliage all winter and spring, then send up buds in late spring or early summer. Harvest the buds before the "leaves" start to open. When plants start to yellow and wither, cuts stalks to the ground.

When grown in warmer weather, the outer leaves of an artichoke can be tough, so peel off the outer layer to get to the delicious interior.

## Top-rated roses

Every year, the American Rose Society (ARS) surveys more than 23,000 members to determine ratings for new roses. The results of the Roses in Review survey are published in the *Handbook for Selecting Roses,* a buying guide from the ARS (Box 30000, Shreveport,

La. 71130; $3).

The survey rates roses on a scale from 1 to 10, 10 being a perfect score, and lists the color and classification of each rose. Only 17 roses have rated 9.1 or higher.

If you're looking for a good garden rose that will perform well under a wide range of conditions, you might try one of these top-rated roses: 'Jean Kenneally' (apricot miniature, 9.7); 'Touch of Class' (orange-pink hybrid tea, 9.5); 'Sally Holmes' (white shrub, 9.5); 'Minnie Pearl' (pink-blend miniature, 9.4); 'Pierrine' (orange-pink miniature, 9.4); 'William Baffin' (deep pink Kordesii shrub, 9.4); and 'Snow Bride' (white miniature, 9.3).

Roses with 9.2 ratings are 'Pristine' (white hybrid tea); 'Jeanne Lajoie' (medium pink climbing miniature); 'Mme. Hardy' (white damask); and 'Pink Meillandina' (medium pink miniature).

Those receiving 9.1 ratings are 'Olympiad' (medium red hybrid tea); 'Dortmund' (medium red Kordesii shrub); 'Henry Hudson' (white hybrid rugosa shrub); 'MEIdomonac', usually sold as 'Bonica', (medium pink shrub); 'Rise 'n' Shine' (medium yellow miniature); and 'Lady Banks' (*Rosa banksiae*, a white species rose).

## Orchids in the oaks

Ten years ago, orchid aficionado Gary Gallup attached a clump of *Laelia anceps* pseudo-bulbs to a coast live oak in his Southern California garden. Today, the clump is a grand, thriving 3-foot mass of more than 100 bulbs. The magnificent flowers on 2-foot spikes bloom from late November into March.

"I've never done a thing but water them," says Gallup of these Mexican natives. He sprays the orchids with water twice a week during the summer, and that's it. "Don't fertilize," he says, "or they grow but don't flower."

WILLIAM B. DEWEY

**LAELIA ANCEPS ORCHIDS** *are well suited to the mild-climate areas of coastal and inland Southern California. The secrets to profuse winter blooms are to attach plants firmly to the host tree—in this case a coast live oak—and never to fertilize.*

Gallup says the key to success with these epiphytes is to secure them firmly to their perch: if the plant moves, the roots won't hold on. He attaches a single plant with a hot glue gun, or staples the rhizomes to the tree. As an alternative, you could wrap the plants with fishing line or plastic nursery tape. If you purchase a laelia on a bark slab, tack the slab to the tree. Trees with shedding bark, such as sycamores, are not reliable supports. Laelia clumps spread slowly, so you may want to group a few plants together for an impressive show early on.

Curiously, the plants are dormant when in bloom, which makes winter the ideal planting season. Look for laelia orchids at specialty nurseries, or order plants by mail. A good retail and mail-order source is the Santa Barbara Orchid Estate, 1250 Orchid Dr., Santa Barbara, Calif.

93111; (805) 967-1284. Prices range from $17.50 per plant for the species shown here to $35 for the rare variety *L. a.* 'Alba'. Stewart Orchids (Box 550, Carpinteria, Calif. 93014; 805/684-5448) is another good source.

## Nandina as a house plant?

Nandina, or heavenly bamboo, (*Nandina domestica*) in a host of varieties is proving to be as successful indoors as it is out. Nandina is not prone to diseases and is capable of standing more than its fair share of neglect. But to stay healthy and keep its color (green on mature growth; often red, pink, or bronze on new growth), this plant needs ample light. In cloudy or overcast areas like the Pacific Northwest and California's coastal regions, nandina does best next to a south- or west-facing window, where many other indoor plants would suffer burn. In fact, the more sun you give it—short of leaf burn— the greater the chance the plant will bloom and set its red fruit clusters.

Plant nandina in a generous pot filled with rich soil mix; water regularly. Feed it with a complete indoor plant food from April through October. Trim off dead leaves.

## Protect citrus from the cold

Historically, the coldest nights in California's Central Valley occur a week or two before or after Christmas. So be ready to protect citrus trees and fruit this month and next.

Citrus trees have varying degrees of hardiness, but it's important to remember that the fruit is often less hardy than the foliage.

The foliage of lemons (with the exception of 'Meyer', which is hardy) and Mexican limes should be protected if temperatures are expected to stay below 30° for more than an hour. Most other citrus need protection if tempera-

## Tool of the Month

*Snip, snip, snip...Anyone who spends time pruning knows how important it is for the shears to feel comfortable in the hand. The new Wilkinson Sword 900 Series Professional Horticultural Pruners have the most comfortable handles of any shears we've tried. They also have a coated blade for reduced friction, an alloy body for durability, and a notch for cutting garden wire. A ribbed thumb catch prevents accidental closure. The pruners sell for $34.95 plus $5 shipping; order from Kinsman Company, River Road, Point Pleasant, Pa. 18950; (800) 733-4146.*

tures are expected to drop below 27° to 28° for more than an hour. Temperatures colder than these will damage most fruit even if the foliage can withstand temperatures several degrees colder.

Watch for still, starry nights, which are often harbingers of freezing temperatures, and monitor weather forecasts. Coldest temperatures usually come just before dawn. In a valley, low spots generally get colder than sloping land.

Protect citrus by covering the trees with old sheets, burlap, plastic, or other material, propped up with stakes or poles so the cover doesn't touch the leaves. Remove the cover during the day. Some people string warm Christmas lights underneath the protective canopy for added heat at night. If covering trees isn't practical, try running sprinklers over the foliage or at the base of trees to raise temperatures a degree or two.

## Newsletter for heirloom gardeners

Gardening with heirloom plants has become increasingly popular during the past few years. Several seed catalogs are devoted exclusively to supplying heirloom seeds to home gardeners. Other suppliers are increasing the number of heirloom seeds they sell, in response to consumer demand. Books also have been published on the subject.

You can read all about heirloom plants in a quarterly newsletter called *The Historical Gardener: Plants and Garden Practices of the Past.* Currently in its third year, the 12-page publication provides sources for seeds and plants, guidance on how to create a historical garden, garden advice from historical publications, and stories on North American garden heritage. Subscribers who need individual assistance about where to find seeds, plants, and other resources can send their requests with self-addressed, stamped envelopes.

If you'd like a sample copy of the newsletter ($3) or a one-year subscription ($12), send a check to *The Historical Gardener,* 1910 N. 35th Place, Mount Vernon, Wash. 98273; (206) 424-3154.

## A catalog of historic apples

If you'd like to grow a bit of history, the Living Tree Catalog of Historical and Biblical Fruits offers 39 apple trees, as well as apricots, pears, plums, and other minor fruits, whose stories date back as far as 500 years.

One such antique is 'Yellow Bellflower', a sweet dessert apple, which was brought around Cape Horn by Captain Henry Morgan in 1857 and planted in an orchard at Stinson Beach. The story goes that Morgan sold his apples for $1 each to miners living in San Francisco.

'Skinner's Seedling' was last mentioned in an 1891 book on California pomology, whose author reports that this apple "originated with Judge H. C. Skinner on the bank of Coyote Creek, east of San Jose." The author describes the fruit as very large, with a rich lemon yellow color, and "very tender, juicy flesh . . . quality best." The tree was thought to be extinct, but in 1985, orchardist Harold Reep found one growing in Mendocino that still had its zinc label attached. The Living Tree Nursery propagated new trees from the old one and reintroduced 'Skinner's Seedling'.

All of the apple trees listed in the catalog are grown in Living Tree's orchard in Bolinas; they are chosen for their suitability to Northern California's climate. For a copy of the catalog, send $4 to the Living Tree Nursery, Box 10082, Berkeley, Calif. 94709; call (510) 420-1440. Now is the time to order bare-root trees for planting in January; 1-year-old whips cost $17 to $24.50, plus shipping.

## A book about natural enemies, natural friends

If you cultivate plants, you cultivate insects. Most bugs are beneficial, but the bothersome ones can wreak havoc in your garden. Here's a new book that can help you learn to control plant enemies and attract friends.

*Natural Enemies of Vegetable Insect Pests,* by M. Hoffmann and A. Frodsham (Cornell University, Ithaca, N.Y., 1994; $18.85), tells you everything you ever wanted to know about the enemies of garden-damaging insects. These are the good guys: soldier bugs that lance Colorado potato beetle larvae, wasp larvae that eat hornworms alive, ladybugs that gobble 200 to 300 aphids per day.

This book crawls with assassin bugs and robber flies, a whole world of creatures that can help or frustrate you. It tells which are worth buying or cultivating, how to keep the best of them around, and why most ladybugs fly away when you release them in the garden (it's instinct). To get a copy of the book, send $22.50 (includes shipping) to Resource Center, 7 Business/Technology Park, Cornell University, Ithaca, N.Y. 14850.

## Christmas trees from seedlings

If you've ever thought about growing Christmas trees in your garden, but didn't because the only plants available were pricey specimens in containers, Tiny Timber Company offers an inexpensive alternative—if you have the patience to wait a few years for trees to mature.

Nursery owners Dan and Carol Faber sell seedlings of Alberta spruce, arborvitae, noble and silver firs, incense cedar, and Western red cedar for 50 cents to $1.25 each; Fraser and grand firs, sequoia, and Western hemlock in pots cost $5 to $6 each. Garden clubs and neighborhood groups may want to buy in bulk, since discounts are available for volume purchases of seedlings.

The nursery, about 20 miles south of Olympia, is open by appointment, but the firm will ship seedlings. For a price list of plants, send $1 to Tiny Timber Company, 18144 Applegate St. S.W., Rochester, Wash. 98579. For more information, call (206) 273-9731. You can also buy trees directly from the Fabers at the Olympia Farmers' Market, 401 N. Capitol Way. Market hours are 10 to 3 Saturdays and Sundays, November through December 18.

*By Owen Dell, Steven R. Lorton, Jim McCausland, Lauren Bonar Swezey, Lance Walheim*

## December Checklist

**PACIFIC NORTHWEST**

☐ **ACCUMULATE COMPOST.** Debris downed by the wind, leaves left over from autumn cleanup, and seasonal greens that have gone over the hill should all go on the compost pile. Clip conifer branches into short lengths to speed decomposition.

☐ **BUY CAMELLIAS.** Winter-flowering plants are now in good supply. They make great Christmas gifts. Buy one for yourself and put it in an entry or outside a window for an especially festive holiday display. You may want to add bows that match or contrast with the flowers, or perhaps a string of white lights. In January or February, you can put the plant in the ground.

☐ **CARE FOR CHRISTMAS TREES.** Place cut trees in stands with reservoirs; make sure there's always enough water to cover the base of the trunk. Water living trees with ice cubes (cover the soil surface) to keep soil moist and to cool the roots; limit their indoor stay to two weeks or less.

☐ **CARE FOR HOLIDAY PLANTS.** They need plenty of light and an even supply of water. Keep them away from drafts and heater vents. Remove decorative foil from the pot, or perforate foil at the bottom and set the pot on a saucer.

☐ **CHECK STORED BULBS.** If any bulbs (except dahlias) show signs of rot, toss them out. Cut rotten spots out of dahlia tubers, dust them with sulfur, and store treated tubers apart from the others. Bulbs, corms, and tubers that look shriveled will usually plump up if you sprinkle a little water over them.

☐ **PREPARE CACTUS FOR BLOOM.** To encourage a good crop of buds, keep spring-flowering indoor cactus cool and on the dry side from mid-December to February. Begin feeding in February with a ¼-strength liquid fertilizer applied at every second watering. Keep cactus in a bright spot.

☐ **PRUNE FOR HOLIDAY GREENS.** We always tell readers that they may want to postpone pruning in the fall, leaving the greens for Christmas decorations. If that's what you did, now is the time to prune. But don't get carried away by pruning for indoor decorations. Prune to shape handsome plants, then use what comes off indoors. Remove (and dispose of) dead and diseased branches first. Next, go after branches that are crossed or that are parallel and too close. Thin plants to show their form. Cut where you won't leave ugly stubs, and angle cuts so you don't see them at eye level.

☐ **ROTATE INDOOR PLANTS.** Give indoor plants a quarter turn every week to ensure even growth. Marking the pot with chalk helps you keep track of turns.

☐ **SAND ICY WALKS.** Scatter sand freely over icy walkways. Unlike salt, it does not harm plants. But don't use sand on decks; it scars the wood.

☐ **TAKE HARDWOOD CUTTINGS.** If you'd like to try propagating new plants, take 6-inch tip cuttings of evergreens such as aucuba, some barberries, holly, and evergreen honeysuckles; and pencil-thick cuttings of deciduous plants like forsythia, hydrangea, rose, rose of Sharon, spiraea, and weigela. Dip cut ends in rooting hormone and plant in a potting mix (equal parts commercial loam and builders' sand work

well). Keep the rooting medium constantly moist. To make a mini-greenhouse for leafy evergreen cuttings, put three or four stakes in the pot so they are higher than the cuttings, then put a plastic bag over the stakes and secure it by placing a rubber band around the bottom of the pot. Keep cuttings in strong light but out of direct sun. When cuttings have rooted and are growing well, transplant them into larger containers.

☐ **TRY GROUND-LAYERING.** Low-growing branches of evergreen plants can be encouraged to form their own roots through a technique called ground-layering. Use a knife to scrape away about a ½-inch square of bark from the underside of the limb, then treat the cut with rooting hormone. Push it just into the soil (which you've cultivated a bit) and stake it down or lay a stone on top of it. By the end of next summer, the branch should have established a self-sustaining clump of roots, and you can cut the branch from the parent plant and transplant it.

☐ **WATER.** Check plants in pots and under eaves. Foundation plantings under a roof overhang may be bone-dry. Remember that well-watered plants are usually better able to survive a hard freeze than drought-stressed plants.

# December Checklist

## NORTHERN CALIFORNIA

**APPLY DORMANT SPRAY.** To smother overwintering insect eggs and pests, such as aphids, mites, and scales, spray deciduous flowering and fruit trees as well as roses with dormant oil after leaves have fallen. For complete coverage, spray branches, trunk crotches, and the ground beneath the tree's drip line. Spray on a calm, dry day.

**CHOOSE A LIVING CHRISTMAS TREE.** Most nurseries carry dwarf Alberta spruce, Aleppo pine, Colorado blue spruce, giant sequoia, and Monterey pine. Before bringing the tree indoors, hose it down and water it thoroughly. Inside, set the tree in a cool location with the pot on a waterproof plastic saucer. If the saucer is clay, set it on plastic or a waterproof cork mat. Check soil moisture daily.

**CHOOSE CAMELLIAS.** Select sasanquas and early-flowering japonicas while they're blooming. Sasanquas are good choices for espaliers, ground covers, informal hedges, and containers. Some are upright, others are spreading or vinelike. Plants tolerate a fair amount of sun. Among the sasanquas, choices include 'Egao', 'Rainbow', 'Shibori Egao', and 'Yuletide'. Japonicas make handsome specimen plants and espaliers; look for 'Alba Plena', 'Chandleri Elegans', 'Daikagura', 'Debutante', 'Magnoliaeflora', 'Nuccio's Carousel', 'Nuccio's Gem', and 'Wildfire'.

**CLEAN UP.** If you didn't do it earlier, remove dead foliage from dormant perennials now. Rake up fallen leaves. Chop garden refuse into small pieces with loppers or a shredder for compost. Toss diseased plants in the garbage.

**KEEP CUT CHRISTMAS TREES FRESH.** The best way to prolong the freshness of a cut tree is to saw an inch or so off the bottom of the trunk just before setting it in the stand. Use a stand that holds water and keep the reservoir full (check daily during the first week). Keep the tree away from heaters and use cool-burning lights.

**PLANT BERRIES AND VEGETABLES.** Late this month, bare-root artichokes, asparagus, berries, and grapes appear in nurseries. Buy and plant early while roots are still fresh. If soil is too wet to plant, temporarily cover roots with moistened mulch (roots must stay moist) or plant in containers.

**PRUNE FOR HOLIDAY GREENS.** Long-lasting choices include evergreen magnolia, juniper, pine, and redwood. Less desirable are deodar cedar, spruce, and Western hemlock, which drop needles sooner.

**SHOP FOR FLOWERS.** Most nurseries have a good supply of colorful flowers in 4-inch pots; you can cluster these in large containers or in the ground. Choices include azaleas, calendula, Christmas cactus, cineraria, cyclamen, English primrose, fairy primrose, kalanchoe, pansies, poinsettias, *Primula obconica*, and snapdragons.

**SPRAY FOR PEACH DISEASES.** To control peach blight and peach leaf curl, spray trees with fixed copper (in wettable powder form) or lime sulfur mixed with dormant oil, if you didn't do so last month; repeat in January or early February. Spray on a dry day and follow label directions carefully.

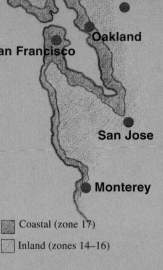

Coastal (zone 17)

Inland (zones 14–16)

**TEND GIFT PLANTS.** Place plants in a cool spot (away from drafts and furnace vents) where they will get bright, indirect light. Don't let plants sit in water; remove any decorative foil or cut a hole in the bottom of the foil and set the pot on a saucer. Feed every two weeks with high-nitrogen fertilizer.

## December Checklist

### ■ CENTRAL VALLEY

**BUY AND PLANT BARE-ROOT STOCK.** Bare-root planting season starts late this month. Nurseries offer berries, fruit and ornamental trees, roses, and perennial vegetables such as artichoke, asparagus, and rhubarb. If soil is too wet to plant, temporarily cover roots with moistened mulch (roots must stay moist) or plant in containers.

**CARE FOR CHRISTMAS TREES.** The best way to prolong the freshness of a cut tree is to saw an inch or so off the bottom of the trunk when you get it home. Hose off the foliage, then place the tree in a stand that holds water, and keep the reservoir full (check daily the first week). If you choose a living tree, hose it off before you bring it in and limit its indoor stay to two weeks at most. Keep all trees away from heaters and use cool-burning lights.

**CLEAN UP.** Remove dead foliage and stems from dormant perennials. Rake and remove leaves from the lawn. Chop refuse into tiny pieces, using loppers or a shredder. To reduce overwintering pests, dispose of leaves and fallen fruit gathered from around fruit trees.

**PROTECT PLANTS AGAINST FROST.** Killing frosts often hit this month. See the item on protecting citrus on page 298.

**PRUNE.** As you cut holiday greenery from conifers, holly laurels, magnolias, and pittosporum, you can do some light pruning as well. Also, start pruning dormant fruit trees, roses, and shrubs.

**SPRAY DORMANT TREES.** To control peach blight and peach leaf curl, spray trees with fixed copper (in wettable powder form) or lime sulfur mixed with dormant oil if you didn't do so last month; repeat in January or early February. To smother overwintering insects such as aphids, mites, and scales, apply horticultural oil to roses and deciduous flowering and fruit trees after leaves have fallen. Cover the tree completely with spray.

Valley and foothills (zones 7–9, 14)

Mountain (zones 1, 2)

**TEND GIFT PLANTS.** Place plants in a cool spot (away from drafts and furnace vents) where they will get bright, indirect light. Don't let plants sit in water; remove any decorative foil or cut a hole in the bottom of the foil and set the pot on a saucer. Feed every two weeks with high-nitrogen fertilizer.

Redding

Lake Tahoe

Sacramento

Fresno

Bakersfield

## December Checklist
### ■
### SOUTHERN CALIFORNIA

■ **CARE FOR INDOOR PLANTS.** Plants grown indoors are subjected to dry air from heating systems. Place potted plants on trays of moistened pebbles, group plants close together, and use a mister to keep humidity high.

■ **CONTROL WEEDS.** Mustard and grasses such as bromegrass, foxtail, and perennial ryegrass easily overtake young plants seeded or grown in your garden. Spot-spray with broad-spectrum herbicides or pick by hand before weeds get out of control.

■ **MAINTAIN FRUIT TREES.** Leafless fruit trees should be pruned and sprayed with dormant oil to protect trees from disease without harming beneficial insects or affecting fruit. If rains come within 48 hours of spraying, repeat treatment. Prune to open canopies to light and air circulation. Clean up and dispose of debris under canopies.

■ **MONITOR IRRIGATION.** Coastal Southern California is famous for sunny, dry December and January days with buffeting Santa Ana winds. Be on the lookout for stressed plants, especially ones recently planted. Deep-water as needed.

■ **PLANT AND PRUNE FOR FIRE SAFETY.** The native plants on hillside properties that burned in last year's fires should be thoroughly regenerating now. Retain but thin most of this vegetation, spacing large shrubs 15 feet apart. Trim off branches on the lowest third of each shrub. Remove dead wood. Woody ground covers should be kept low by cutting out wayward branches. Avoid the temptation to overseed and overplant seemingly bare areas; excessive fuel loads may result.

■ **PLANT WINTER BERRY PLANTS.** Brighten holiday decorations indoors and gardens outdoors with fruiting trees and shrubs such as California holly or toyon (*Heteromeles arbutifolia*), California pepper tree (*Schinus molle*), cotoneaster, holly (*Ilex*), and the strawberry tree (*Arbutus unedo*). Plants are in full berry now in gardens and at garden centers.

■ **PREPARE TROPICALS FOR FREEZING.** Inland gardens are endangered by freezing temperatures. Cover frost-sensitive citrus, succulents, and tropicals with cheesecloth or old sheets at night, removing each morning. Move potted plants under arbors or eaves. Water well; plants tolerate freezing temperatures better in damp soil.

■ **PROPAGATE HARDWOOD CUTTINGS.** Propagate deciduous plants such as birch, cottonwood, and willow, and small-leafed evergreens such as junipers and other conifers. Each cutting should be about ⅜ inch in diameter and about 5 inches long. Plants may either be dormant or have vegetative growth just beginning to show. Plant in a well-draining medium, but keep ambient humidity high. Rooting hormone is desirable, but the amount varies by species: willows require little or none, junipers need a lot.

■ **PROPAGATE ROOT CUTTINGS.** Propagate rhizomatous perennial plants as roots continue to get plump and vigorous in moist winter soils. Plants that may be grown by this technique are Japanese anemone (*Anemone hybrida*), Matilija poppy (*Romneya coulteri*), and Oriental poppy (*Papaver orientale*). Choose pencil-thick roots, and trim them to 3 inches in length. Lay two or three root cuttings on well-draining soil tamped into a pot. Cover cuttings with ½ inch of soil. Keep soil lightly moist, not soggy. Place in a sheltered location until weather warms.

■ **SELECT BARE-ROOT FRUIT TREES.** Deciduous fruit trees are now available bare-root. Southern California's inland areas are appropriate for some, but not all, varieties. Some consistent low-chill favorites are 'Beverly Hills', 'Golden Delicious', and 'Gravenstein' apples; 'Aprigold', 'Blenheim', and 'Royal' apricots; 'Babcock' and 'Tropi-berta' peaches; 'Flordahome' pears; and 'Santa Rosa' plums. Select trees with sturdy stems and well-healed grafts.

Santa Barbara
Pasadena
San Bernardino
Santa Monica
Los Angeles
San Diego

□ Zones 18–21
▨ Zones 22–24

## ANYWHERE IN THE WEST, TACKLE THESE CHORES:

**CARE FOR GIFT PLANTS.** If you plan to keep azalea, cyclamen, kalanchoe, ornamental pepper, and other small gift plants, give them plenty of light and water and feed them regularly (especially while they're blooming and setting fruit), and place them out of drafts.

**CARE FOR LIVING CHRISTMAS TREES.** While they're indoors, keep trees away from fireplaces and heater vents. Water regularly; for slow, cool, even irrigation, cover the soil surface with a layer of ice cubes. Take your tree to a sheltered place outside immediately after Christmas to let it acclimate. If the temperature is well below freezing where you live, put the tree in a cool place (like an unheated porch) out of direct sun until temperatures start rising above freezing every day, then take it outside.

**MAKE COMPOST.** Compost piles work year-round if they have oxygen, moisture, and something to eat (equal parts of green and brown garden waste). Keep adding garden and nonmeat kitchen waste to your pile, turn it weekly, and add water when needed. Too much rain can wash out nutrients. If steady rain is predicted, cover the pile with a tarp.

**PREPARE INDOOR CACTUS FOR BLOOM.** Allow spring-flowering indoor cactus to dry out from mid-December through February, then water and apply a weak solution of fertilizer every second watering. Keep it in a bright spot to promote blossoms.

## IN THE INTERMOUNTAIN WEST, DO THESE CHORES:

**CHECK STORED BULBS.** Look over stored summer bulbs (begonias and glads), and throw out any that show signs of rotting. You can save imperfect dahlia tubers by cutting out bad spots, dusting with sulfur, and storing away from the others.

**FEED THE BRUSH PILE.** Leaves can go into the compost pile, but larger debris (fallen branches and accumulated pine needles) should go in a brush pile. Think of it as long-term compost that breaks down in years rather than months. Small birds love such piles and often nest in them.

**MULCH.** It's not too late to put a 3- or 4-inch layer of mulch over bulb, perennial, and shrub beds that might be damaged by alternate cycles of freezing and thawing. Coarse compost, leaves, and straw work well.

**SAND ICY WALKS.** Sand is a better choice than salt for use around plants, since it's nontoxic and can be swept into the garden when ice is gone. Don't use sand on wood or tiled surfaces; it scars them.

**WATER.** When the weather is above freezing, water dry spots in the garden and in containers. Check plants under eaves: foundation plantings under roof overhangs may be bone dry.

## IN THE SOUTHWEST'S LOW AND INTERMEDIATE DESERTS:

**FERTILIZE DECIDUOUS FRUIT TREES.** They benefit greatly from winter fertilizing. For trees at least 4 years old, apply 9 pounds of 10-10-10 fertilizer now, then 3 more pounds right after harvest.

**PLANT ANNUALS AND PERENNIALS.** You can plant calendula, candytuft, cyclamen, dianthus, Iceland poppy, larkspur, pansy, petunia, primrose, snapdragon, stock, sweet alyssum, and viola. If you live in a frost-free area, set out bedding begonias and cineraria as well.

**PLANT BULBS.** As early as possible this month, plant daffodil, gladiolus, ranunculus, and prechilled tulip bulbs. (To chill tulips, store bulbs in the vegetable crisper of the refrigerator for at least six weeks before planting.)

**PLANT NATIVES.** Set out nursery stock, water in well, and mulch. Then watch the weather: if winter rain is scant, follow up with regular deep watering to help roots get established.

**PRUNE CHRISTMAS GREENS.** When you cut evergreens for swags and wreaths, you're pruning. Make each cut just above a side branch, thinning the tree or shrub evenly as you work. While you're at it, remove dead, diseased, and injured branches; to finish the job, prune for shape. You can spray cut greens with an antidessicant to prolong freshness.

**SHOP FOR BARE-ROOT PLANTS.** Berries and roses are usually the first to come in, followed by fruit trees and perennial vegetables such as asparagus, horseradish, and rhubarb. To keep plants from drying during the trip from the nursery to your garden, wrap roots in wet burlap or pack with damp sawdust, then plant as soon as you get home.

**SOW PEPPERS, TOMATOES.** Start seeds of peppers and tomatoes in a warm indoor spot now. Give them plenty of light, regular watering, and light fertilizing; transplants will be ready to go in the garden by late February or early March. A bottom heating cable speeds germination.

# SNIP-AND-STUFF
# TOPIARIES

## BY LAUREN BONAR SWEZEY

Seattle floral designer Martha E. Harris adds a touch of warmth and freshness to the season with natural, elegant, and simple holiday topiaries. Whether displayed on a mantel with garlands and candles or on the dining room table as a long-lasting center-piece, they'll span the holidays from Thanksgiving to New Year's.

"Topiaries aren't a new idea," says Harris. "It's the materials that give them a fresh look. Some plants can even be plucked right from the garden."

Her current favorite is 'Sunset' heath-er (*Calluna vulgaris*), at center in the large photo. "I love combining rich magenta flowers with greens and golds." For several years, Harris has decorated trees with small bouquets of heather. "One day when I needed an accessory to go with a garland, it occurred to me that heather would be lovely as a topiary."

Heather has another advantage: "It dries crisp without shattering for a few months," says Harris, "and you don't need to keep it moist." Other favorites include seeded eucalyptus (*Eucalyptus nicholii*), at left in photo, and Califor-nia pepper berries. Although Harris buys both at the flower market (heather can also be purchased at many flower markets across the West), they can be har-vested fresh in some gardens. You'll need one big bunch of fresh material (about six or

## START WITH GARDEN CLIPPINGS, FOAM, AND WIRE

**1** For a 12-inch-tall topiary, fold the 14- by 20-inch piece of 1-inch chicken wire into a cone shape, bending edges together to secure; trim bottom with wire-cutting shears to even. With a knife, carve a piece of floral foam to fit the pointed top. Carve a sec-ond piece to fit below the first inside the wire cone. (For larger trees, fill in with extra blocks of foam.) Harris says perfection is not nec-essary, but the more foam stuffed inside the cone, the easier it is to add plant material. If a corner of the foam juts out through the wire, just shave it off with a knife. Next, fill the bottom of the container—the tree base—with floral foam so it's level with the top of the container. Insert the two bamboo sticks 1 or 2 inches apart in the center of the foam in the con-tainer. Next, make holes in the cone (to eventually attach it to the container base) by stabbing the sticks through the foam cone from the bottom up; remove cone.

**2** Starting at the top of the cone, poke in 1½- to 2-inch-long pieces of seeded eucalyptus or other material (strip about 1 inch of foliage to create a stem), working down in a spiral.

**3** After stuffing cone, anchor it to the con-tainer base by reinserting dowels into cone. Finally, says Harris, "give the topiary a haircut with scissors to even out the shape." It takes approximately 1½ to 2 hours to make one tree. For a round topi-ary, cut a half-ball out of foam to fit the container.

REX RYSTEDT

seven branches) per 12-inch tree. Harris also suggests holly and *Skimmia japonica* because of their festive red berries, and boxwood, hydrangea, lavender, rosemary (at right in photo), and the leaves and berries of other kinds of eucalyptus. As with fresh flower arrangements, holly, skimmia, and boxwood need to be kept moist in the floral foam that's used as the base.

Harris creates different shapes to fit different home decor. Traditional tabletop topiaries are cone-shaped and round, but you can also have fun with architectural shapes, such as squares and rectangles. She recommends making different sizes if you plan to group them together on a mantel or end table.

Topiaries also make fine gifts. For a festive look, Harris ties a gold ribbon around the pot.

### CONTAINERS AND OTHER MATERIALS

First, find an attractive container that will enhance the arrangement. "You can use almost anything—a small, low silver vase, a brass dish, a small tin, or a clay pot," says Harris. "But don't use glass or the foam will show through."

You'll also need some supplies, available at craft stores, to make the topiary core. The amount of supplies you'll need depends on the size of the topiary. For a 12-inch-tall, cone-shaped tree, you'll need a 14- by 20-inch piece of 1-inch chicken wire for the frame, two thin (about ⅓-inch-thick) 7-inch-long bamboo stakes, and three blocks of floral foam.

If you use fresh material that needs moisture, soak the floral foam after stuffing, then keep it moist. If dry materials begin to look dull after a while, brighten them by spraying with clear acrylic or acrylic hair spray. ∎

KEVIN CANDLAND

**EDIE O'HAIR KNOWS WELL** *the virtues of shrub roses. She grows hundreds of them in her 5-acre garden.*

# The top 10 shrub roses for your garden

*These hardy plants with the casual appearance provide flowers and fragrance almost year-round*

LAST FALL, WHEN TOM Carruth declared that "shrub roses are exploding," we listened. Carruth, the research director for Weeks Roses in Upland, California, is among the rosarians we regularly check with for rose news and facts. Spurred by his enthusiasm, we called two other Southern California pros—Clair Martin, curator of the rose garden at the Huntington Botanical Gardens in San Marino, and Keith Zary, research director for Jackson & Perkins in Somis—to hear their thoughts on the subject. All agreed that shrub rose availability and popularity are burgeoning.

Precisely what makes a shrub rose a shrub rose, though, is less clear. "They are superior landscaping roses that don't fit neatly into traditional rose categories" was Martin's nontechnical definition. Carruth's criteria were just as casual: a shrub rose, he said, should have an attractive informal habit that requires little pruning, be highly disease resistant, and flower profusely much of the season. Given these definitions, a shrub rose could be anything from a diminutive 3-foot 'Gourmet Popcorn' to an assertive 10-foot 'Sally Holmes'.

To make the designation "shrub rose" a bit more helpful, we asked each rosarian to pick his or her favorite varieties. After tallying up their picks (factoring in overlapping choices and, in some cases, subjective criteria such as depth of passion for a particular variety), we came up with a list of the 10 best shrub roses currently available. To our delight, we found all 10 growing in Edie O'Hair's garden in Temecula, California.

The sizes given below are for roses grown in mild-climate areas of the West. Your plants will be smaller if you live in a colder region. All of our choices are hardy to at least -10°.

## SMALL SHRUBS FOR GROUND COVERS AND BORDERS

**'Baby Blanket'** is a new rose, introduced in 1993 by Jackson & Perkins. Not surprisingly, Zary is the only one of our experts experienced with the plant, but he says it's the best ground cover rose he's seen because both foliage and growth are dense, the light- to medium-pink flowers bloom constantly, and the plant is extremely disease resistant. It reaches 30 inches high and spreads to 5 feet.

**'The Fairy'**, introduced in 1932, is a time-tested rose. It forms a 3-foot spilling mound with large clusters of small, mildly fragrant pink flowers.

**'Gourmet Popcorn'** is a vigorous, bushy, and slightly cascading miniature that reaches 3 feet high and spreads as wide. Slightly fragrant semidouble flowers in massive clusters are bright white with showy yellow stamens. Leaves are glossy dark green. This is an excellent plant for containers.

## MEDIUM SHRUBS FOR BORDERS AND HEDGES

**'Abraham Darby'**, a David Austin English rose, reaches 5 feet or higher with long, arching canes. The large flowers, produced singly or in clusters, are deliciously fragrant and have a deeply cupped old-rose look. Petals are soft peachy pink on the inside and pale yellow on the reverse.

**'Bonica'** rates extremely high with all three pros. It is an upright arching shrub 4 to 5 feet high, spreading about equally wide. Large clusters of medium-pink double flowers bloom all season. Showy red hips ornament the plant in fall. It is excellent in a large container, used as a hedge, or planted en masse.

**'Carefree Wonder'** is a 4- to 6-foot rounded, bushy shrub. Flowers are large and bright pink with a soft pink reverse. The shrub's semiformal habit makes it suitable for a hedge.

**'Iceberg'** is top-ranked by all three of our experts. It blooms practically nonstop all season. Slightly fragrant pure white double blossoms open in large clusters. Vigorous and hardy, the upright bush with shiny deep green leaves reaches 5 to 6 feet tall and spreads to 5 feet wide.

**'Lavender Dream'** appears as a fountain of blooms with impressive clusters of semi-double pinkish lavender flowers coating long, arching canes that grow to 5 feet. Leaves are matte light green. It is the only lavender rose the experts gave a top rating.

## LARGE SPECIMEN SHRUBS THAT STAND ON THEIR OWN

**'Dortmund'** produces large clusters of fragrant, lacquer red single flowers with white centers; blooms are recurrent. Leaves are shiny green. The hardy shrub grows to about 6 feet tall.

**'Sally Holmes'** is a massive shrub reaching to around 10 feet and spreading slightly wider. Three-inch single flowers open buff peach and age to white in huge hydrangea-like clusters. Leaves are glossy dark green.

## PLANTING AND CARE

One of the virtues of shrub roses is that under the right conditions, they don't need intensive pruning and spraying to look good and stay healthy. For best growth, plant in full sun and fertile, well-drained soil with enough growing room so that at maturity air circulates freely between plants.

For vigorous growth and abundant blooms, water and fertilize regularly. Water deeply to moisten the entire root system. Apply a 2- to 3-inch layer of mulch at the base of each plant to save water and minimize weeds. Feed established roses every four to six weeks during the growing season, starting when the buds begin to swell in spring. Cut spent flowers throughout the season to encourage new blooms.

Since shrub roses are naturally shapely and free-blooming, they need no hard pruning. For a natural look, simply remove dead and diseased wood, and shape plants by cutting wayward branches.

For a more formal look, lightly shear bushy plants like 'Bonica' and 'Gourmet Popcorn' after a bloom flush. If you want to prune hard to alter a plant's shape or size, do so during winter dormancy.

Edie O'Hair opens her garden to the public each spring. If you want to plan a visit, you can call O'Hair during March at (909) 676-0938 for tour information. ■

*By Lynn Ocone*

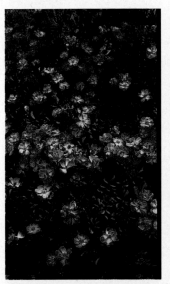

**A SHRUB ROSE BY ANY OTHER NAME:** *White 'Iceberg' and pink 'Bonica' (above) are probably the most popular shrub rose varieties; 'Lavender Dream' (top left) was the only purple flower chosen by our panel; at 10 feet tall, 'Sally Holmes' (left) can stand on its own; 'Dortmund' (bottom left), with its lacquer red blooms, is perhaps the most exotic-looking of the bunch; and 'Carefree Wonder' (below) gets naturally bushy, making it suitable for training as a hedge.*

# Miniature cymbidiums for the holidays

*Plants are in peak bloom this month, just in time for gift giving*

**MINIATURE CYMBIDIUM** *Golden Elf 'Sundust' is one of the new fragrant, heat-tolerant hybrids suitable for bright atriums. It can produce more than one crop of flowers per year.*

O VER THE YEARS, cymbidiums have become a favorite of gardeners in mild-winter areas of the West. They're easy to grow, particularly in coastal gardens, and bloom with very little care. Their exquisite-looking flowers appear during drab winter months when other plants are dormant.

Standard cymbidiums grow 3 to 4 feet tall, have long strappy leaves, and produce large flowers 3 to 5 inches across. Bloom time for standards usually runs from early winter to spring.

Less well known are the miniatures, which bloom earlier than the standards; peak season—November to January—is just in time for the holidays.

Flowers are smaller (1 to 3 inches across) and appear in greater numbers than the standards', with some varieties producing as many as 42 flowers per spike. Some miniatures also may produce two spikes per bulb.

Plants are generally restrained in size. They're usually 1½ to 2 feet tall, with flower spikes 1½ to 2½ feet long, although some plants from crosses between minis and standards (still referred to as minis because of the small flowers) are almost as large as standards.

In general, miniature cymbidiums are much more manageable than standard cymbidiums. Lauris Rose, of Cal-Orchid in Santa Barbara, likes minis because "you can display them without bringing in the great out-of-doors."

Carson Barnes, of the Rod McLellan Co. in South San Francisco, says, "They never turn into hogs. In a 16-inch container, standard cymbidiums weigh as much as 60 pounds, and you need a hand truck to move the

NORMAN A. PLATE

**COLORS HAVE BECOME** *clearer and range from reds, rusts, and yellows to pinks, greens, and white. Flower shapes also vary; orchid enthusiasts often prefer the more rounded petals like those of the green cymbidium at top right.*

containers around."

The Rod McLellan Co. prefers to grow their mini-cymbidiums in short 6-inch pots. When the plants outgrow the pots, the minis are divided and sections are replanted back into the same pots. Some gardeners opt for larger containers such as 2-gallon cans.

Many miniature cymbidums have another advantage over standard cymbidiums: they tolerate higher temperatures, allowing them to grow in a wider range of climates, such as those of inland areas.

## BIG NEWS IN FLOWER COLOR, FRAGRANCE, AND REPEAT BLOOM

"Just 10 years ago, we didn't have the variety of colors we have now in miniatures," explains Gary Gallup, of Gallup & Stribling Orchids in Carpinteria, California. "Colors were muddy. With the new hybrids, we now have clear pinks, greens, yellows, and reds. We're still not quite there on the whites, which have pinkish or greenish undertones."

In fact, miniature cymbidiums are available in nearly every color but blue and true black. New colors include oranges and apricots. Most miniature cymbidiums have darker, contrasting lips. But you'll also find a few albino flowers—with no contrasting lip color—such as Golden Elf 'Sundust', a clear yellow shown on the facing page, and Lovely Bunny 'Othello'.

Other developments in the improvement of miniature cymbidiums are fragrance, repeat bloom, and heat tolerance, derived from hybridizing plants with a species native to India and Southern China. All of these characteristics are found in Golden Elf 'Sundust' and Peter Pan 'Greensleeves' (which is green with a maroon lip), and in 'Nut' (light tan to chocolate brown).

This new group will bloom when nighttime temperatures are in the upper 50s, a characteristic that makes it possible for them to bloom in bright atriums. They also are small (about 14 inches tall).

## WHERE DO CYMBIDIUMS GROW?

If you live in *Sunset Western Garden Book* zones 15 to 24—from coastal Northern California to San Diego—cymbidiums are a cinch to grow, as long as they're protected from temperatures below 30° and given bright light, but not midday sun (healthy leaves should be light green, not dark). When temperatures drop below freezing, the best place for cymbidiums is under the eaves or beneath a patio cover.

In hot inland areas and colder climates, cymbidiums need extra care. Since miniature cymbidiums tolerate higher temperatures than standards, they do better in inland areas. But they'll need watering more often there than in cooler climates, or a more humid environment during hot spells.

In the Northwest or at elevations where winter temperatures are cold, you can leave cymbidiums outdoors until Thanksgiving (watch the thermometer) and then bring them indoors to a bright location. This should give them the chilling—a differential of at least 20°—they need to set flower spikes. Come March or April, the plants go outdoors again. The other option is a cool greenhouse, or choose one of the new heat-tolerant hybrids more suited to indoor culture.

A **TRIO** *of miniature cymbidiums growing on Weegie Caughlan's patio in Los Altos Hills, California, includes red Devon Lord 'Viceroy', white Showgirl 'Glamour Jane', and yellow-green Mini Mint 'Maxine'.*

NORMAN A. PLATE

## WATER AND FERTILIZE REGULARLY

Besides bright light, cymbidiums need regular water and fertilizer to produce a mass of blooms. Plants growing in 1- to 2-gallon cans in coastal areas usually need watering about once a week. In short 6-inch pots or in warmer areas, water two to three times a week. Each time you water, soak the potting mix thoroughly; avoid getting water on the leaves. Cut back on watering during the winter.

Most orchid growers recommend fertilizing with high nitrogen liquid fertilizer (30-10-10 or 25-9-9) from New Year's to the Fourth of July (winter to summer) and low nitrogen (6-30-30 or 6-25-25) from the Fourth of July to the holidays. Apply it weekly, diluting it by half the recommended rate (unless the label already lists a dilution for weekly feedings). If you don't want to bother with two fertilizers, you can use a 20-20-20 formulation all year. Make sure the potting medium is moist before fertilizing.

The major pest of cymbidiums is snails, which are especially fond of new flower spikes. Use bait or handpick. Also, control scale and spider mites when necessary.

## REPOT EVERY THREE YEARS

You may have heard that cymbidiums bloom best when plants are crowded, but a crowded clump will decline eventually, since there isn't enough room for new bulbs (actually pseudobulbs) to form and grow.

Repot plants when bulbs bulge against the side of the pot or when the medium has decomposed; do this after bloom has finished but before midsummer. Take the plant out of the pot and remove the old bark. Trim the roots to about 3 to 4 inches. You can repot into a larger container (allow 2 to 3 inches between the plant and edge of the pot),

or divide the plant and replant divisions in same-size containers.

To divide, allow three to five pseudobulbs (with leaves) per section. Cut off rotted bulbs and dead roots; leave on firm brown "back bulbs" if they connect green bulbs together.

Use a potting medium of cymbidium mix or six parts fine bark, six parts medium bark, and one part coarse (#3) agricultural perlite (soak bark in water first, then add perlite). In warmer areas, mix in a finer medium so it holds more water.

Mound bark mix in the bottom of the pot and position the roots on top of it. Fill in around the plant, tamping mix down firmly around the roots. Cover the bases of bulbs by *no more than ½* inch. Set plants in a shady area and water sparingly or mist them for four weeks.

## WHERE TO GET PLANTS

Most nurseries and garden centers sell miniature cymbidiums during the bloom season. Prices range from $17 to $25 for plants with one spike to $35 to $45 for three to four spikes. Orchid shows and sales also offer a great selection at good prices.

You can also buy minicymbidiums by mail, which is one of the best ways to find unusual varieties. The following suppliers offer good selections of varieties.

***Cal-Orchid, Inc.,*** 1251 Orchid Drive, Santa Barbara, Calif. 93111; (805) 967-1312.

***The Orchid Park, Inc.,*** 2929 Etting Rd., Oxnard, Calif. 93033; (805) 488-0055.

***The Rod McLellan Co.,*** 1450 El Camino Real, South San Francisco, Calif. 94080; (415) 737-2452.

***Santa Barbara Orchid Estate,*** 1250 Orchid Dr., Santa Barbara, Calif. 93111; (805) 967-1284.

***Stewart Orchids,*** Box 550, Carpinteria, Calif. 93014; (805) 684-5448. ∎

*By Lauren Bonar Swezey*

MICHAEL THOMPSON

**BLOOMING** *Gardenia jasminoides makes its first appearance in nurseries this month. Place it in a decorative pot and lavish it with plenty of sun.*

# Gardenias in your living room?

*Yes, these beauties will grow and bloom indoors in the Northwest, if you give them what they need*

IT'S EASY TO FALL IN love with a blooming gardenia. Those creamy blossoms have flawless complexions and smell like heaven. One whiff and you're back at your senior prom, sporting a corsage of two or three blooms. The leaves are as green and lush as the summers of your youth.

So you buy a plant, take it home, and adore it—for a while. Then you learn what every gardenia-smitten gardener in the Northwest knows: growing gardenias here can be a challenge.

Unless these lovelies get enough heat, they won't bloom. They dislike cold, wet soil. And sometimes, seemingly for no reason, the big, plump buds turn black at the stem and drop off.

But given the right conditions, gardenias can grow and bloom beautifully indoors in the Northwest. Next month the first blooming gardenias begin to appear on the market, followed by more in February, then a rush in March and April. Learn what the plants like, treat them well, and chances are you'll have a treasured gardenia for years to come.

## THE BIG MUSTS: SUN, WARMTH, AND WATER

Gardenias' waxy, dark evergreen leaves may suggest a plant that prefers low or partial light. But in fact, it needs sunlight. When you get one home, put it in a south-facing window or greenhouse where it will get as much sun as possible. Turn the pot a quarter turn each day to expose all sides to sunlight. A small mark with chalk will help you remember how far to turn the pot each day.

Plants need ample water. Keep soil moist, but don't let the pot stand in water. Mist foliage, daily if you can, adjusting the nozzle on a plastic spray bottle so that it pushes out a cloud of fine water drops. Mist until the leaves look dew-soaked.

Expect some leaf drop during these dark days of winter. And if you don't get some bud drop, you're lucky. If the ends of new shoots look limp, snip them off.

## ALSO NEEDED: FAST-DRAINING SOIL

In April, at the beginning of the growing season, repot the plant in a container one or two sizes larger than the nursery container. Gardenias demand perfect drainage; use packaged potting soil mixed with a little ground bark or peat moss. Plant them high (like rhododendrons or azaleas, with the top of the rootball slightly above soil level) and singly (they don't like to be crowded by other plants or competing roots).

After danger of frost is past, move the gardenia outdoors. Put it on the north side of the house for a week, then move it to the east side for another 10 days to two weeks, then finally move the plant into full south sun. Keep it well watered.

Gardenias are heavy feeders. In April, begin fertilizing monthly with a complete liquid plant food, or every two weeks with half-strength liquid plant food such as 10-30-15. When you add fertilizer to the soil, you may also want to mist the leaves with a solution of half-strength liquid plant food. You can expect a flush of bloom on the plants in summer and sporadic bloom on into autumn. Continue feeding through October.

About every three years, the plant will need repotting. Check the drain hole; if hairlike roots are growing out of it, it's definitely time to repot. If the plant has developed any leggy growth, April is the time to cut it back so that thick, new growth will emerge.

## PLUS A LITTLE T.L.C. IN THE WINTER

In October or as soon as frost threatens, move your gardenia back indoors to the sunniest location possible and continue the annual cycle you began in January. Stop fertilizing. Continue to water and mist the plant regularly, and turn it daily for even exposure to sunlight.

Buds left on the plant will probably open indoors. Expect some leaf drop; like ficus, gardenias pout if they are moved or their temperature changes much.

If the plant gets dusty, set it in the shower, hose it off with a hand-held sprayer, and let it drip dry. ■

*By Steven R. Lorton*

**ORNAMENTAL PEAR TREES** *and conifers, planted in pairs, flank a gravel path. Daylilies and liriope send fountains of foliage over the path, and spreading plants such as bergenia creep across it.*

# A Seattle landscape with a Provençal accent

IT'S NOT UNCOMMON to see English landscaping styles in Northwest gardens. But this Seattle garden has a different European accent. Cynthia and Ray Lute drew inspiration from the gardens of Provence in southeastern France. Cynthia designed the landscape, and she and Ray started planting in fall two years ago. Just two summers later, the garden was ready for a grand wedding party.

Because of the size of the property (¾ acre) and the plants the Lutes used (the smallest one was transplanted from a 5-gallon can), this was a costly project. However, the design ideas can be adapted for smaller gardens, and smaller budgets can be accommodated by starting with smaller plants and allowing them time to grow. November is a great planting month.

Cynthia began by laying out lines for paths, formally shaped beds, and large, symmetrical, and dense plantings, which would later become overgrown and softened by loose, spilling branches and foliage.

The paths were laid out on dirt, filled with a 2-inch base of crushed rock, and topped by a 1-inch layer of pea gravel. Most plants won't become deeply rooted in the gravel, and those that do can be easily removed or left to enhance the romantic look of the path.

## DESIGNING WITH PLANTS

To bring symmetry to the design, she used plants in pairs. Two large flowering pears (*Pyrus calleryana* 'Chanticleer') flank the main path near the street entry. Farther along this path is a pair of silvery-leafed ornamental pears (*Pyrus salicifolia*). Near the entrance to the house is a pair of Irish yews. In various spots along the paths, espaliered apples and pears form living fences.

Beds between the paths are filled with plants that grow fast and spread or self-sow freely. For fillers, Cynthia used lady's mantle (*Alchemilla mollis*), which was allowed to go to seed and naturalize; lamb's ears (*Stachys byzantina*); shrubby evergreen *Euphorbia characias wulfenii*; *Artemisia* (especially *A.* 'Powis Castle'); dozens of kinds of lavender; and antique shrub roses. For grassy textures, she chose numerous varieties of daylilies, liriope, and ornamental grasses.

Clematis, kiwi (*Actinidia deliciosa*), and roses scramble up walls. Plants in big terracotta pots dot the garden and outdoor stairways. The potted plants range from summer flowers, such as geraniums, to 'Meyer' lemon trees that spend winter in a greenhouse.

Once the plantings became established, this garden proved to be water thrifty. Most of the plants have vigorous, efficient root systems that enable them to get through dry summer weather with little attention from the hose. ■

*By Steven R. Lorton*

**FOUR JADE PLANTS,** *pruned to reveal branch and trunk pattern, form an instant grove in a bonsai dish. This can go indoors or out (as long as it's protected from frost).*

PETER CHRISTIANSEN

# Jade forest in a bonsai dish

*Plant a miniature grove for indoor display*

Taking inspiration from the art of bonsai, *Sunset* designer Dennis Leong made this miniature forest in a dish. For the "trees," he chose jade plant (*Crassula argentea*) because it is easy to find, inexpensive, grows well indoors, and doesn't mind having its roots crowded. The approach we show isn't true bonsai, but many of the techniques and materials are the same.

When you shop for jade plants, you'll find that some have bigger leaves than others. Choose plants with smaller leaves, since they'll be more in scale with the grovelike arrangement.

The materials you need are shown below. We used a 9- by 13- by 2¼-inch ceramic bonsai dish, which is in scale with the four small jade plants chosen for the project.

The most time-consuming step is preparing the dish for planting. Jade plants have to be wired in place initially because they tend to be top-heavy and have very small, fibrous root systems for support.

Once you've finished preparing the dish as shown in the steps below, decide how you're going to line up the plants and which direction each will face. Staggering the plants and varying the spaces between them creates a more natural look. You may need to do some preliminary pruning to make the jade plants fit together.

Take the tallest plant out of its pot first, spread its roots, and butterfly them over a mound of soil. Lay a 1- to 2-inch-wide strip of plastic mesh over the roots and tie it snugly in place with two ends of copper wire sticking up through the soil.

Repeat this process for each jade plant until all are securely in place. Then cover with more soil and another thin layer of gravel; water thoroughly.

Jade plants need bright light and occasional feeding; start by mixing some controlled-release fertilizer into the potting soil; repeat feeding every few months. ■

*By Jim McCausland*

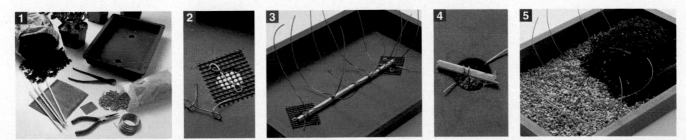

**STEP-BY-STEP FOREST:** **1** *You'll need potting soil (a cactus mix is good), four jade plants, a bonsai dish, gravel, 24-gauge copper wire, wire cutters, wooden chopsticks, plastic mesh, and pruners.* **2** *Put plastic mesh over each drainage hole and secure with double-looped wire (bent on underside).* **3** *Tie five 20-inch lengths of wire around the long chopstick in a spine-and-ribs pattern, as shown.* **4** *Long chopstick is secured to short piece of chopstick on the outside of the holes.* **5** *Cover the bottom of the dish with gravel, then add the potting soil.*

# Article Titles Index

# General Subject Index

*Bluebells*

NORMAN A. PLATE

*Freesia*

NORMAN A. PLATE

NORMAN A. PLATE

*Lily*

NORMAN A. PLATE

*Watsonia*